A RHETORIC FOR THE SOCIAL SCIENCES

A GUIDE TO ACADEMIC AND PROFESSIONAL COMMUNICATION

Kristine Hansen

Brigham Young University

Prentice Hall
Upper Saddle River, New Jersey 07458

Library of Congress Cataloging-in-Publication Data

Hansen, Kristine.
  A rehetoric for the social sciences: a guide to academic and
professional communication/Kristine Hansen.
    p. cm.
  Based on the author's dissertation (University of Texas, Austin,
1997).
  Includes bibliographical references and index.
  ISBN 0-13-440272-3
  1. Social sciences—Authorship. 2. Social sciences—Research.
3. Academic writing. 4. English language—Rhetoric. I. Title.
  H91.H36 1998
808".0663—dc21
                                            97-29505
                                           CIP

Editorial Director: *Charlyce Jones Owen*
Acquisitions Editor: *Maggie Barbieri*
Managing Editor: *Bonnie Biller*
Production Liaison: *Fran Russello*
Prepress and Manufacturing Buyer: *Mary Ann Gloriande*
Interior Design and Production Supervision: *Kerry Reardon*
Cover Design: *Rosemarie Votta*
Art Director: *Jayne Conte*
Marketing Manager: *Sheryl Adams*
Editorial Assistant: *Joan Polk*

This book was set in 10/12 Palatino by KR Publishing
Services and was printed and bound by Courier Companies, Inc.
The cover was printed by Phoenix Color Corp.

©1998 by Prentice-Hall, Inc.
Upper Saddle River, New Jersey 07458

Reprinted with corrections November, 2000.

Printed in the United States of America

10 9 8 7 6 5 4 3

ISBN   0-13-440272-3

Prentice-Hall International (UK) Limited, *London*
Prentice-Hall of Australia Pty. Limited, *Sydney*
Prentice-Hall Canada Inc., *Toronto*
Prentice-Hall Hispanoamericana, S.A., *Mexico*
Prentice-Hall of India Private Limited, *New Delhi*
Prentice-Hall of Japan, *Tokyo*
Prentice-Hall Asia Pte. Ltd., *Singapore*
Editora Prentice-Hall do Brasil, Ltda., *Rio de Janeiro*

*This book is affectionately dedicated
to my students*

CONTENTS

PART II: CREATING AND WRITING ABOUT NEW KNOWLEDGE

3   RESEARCH METHODS, WRITING, AND ETHICS   43

4   INTERPRETING DOCUMENTS   55

5   INTERVIEWING   93

6   OBSERVING   123

PART III: FINDING AND USING EXISTING KNOWLEDGE

9 LIBRARY RESEARCH AND WRITING   219

10 USING THE INTERNET AS A SCHOLARLY RESOURCE   257

PART IV: COMMON SOCIAL SCIENCE GENRES

11   PROPOSALS AND PROSPECTUSES   273

12   PUBLIC POSITION PAPERS AND OPINION PIECES   299

PREFACE

My purpose in this textbook is to offer guidelines for writing in genres that are typical of academic and professional communication in the social sciences. My intended audience is college juniors and seniors who are majoring in the traditional social sciences as well as related fields that study humans and their behavior, such as communications, education, family science, geography, international relations, linguistics, public health, and youth leadership. On my campus, students completing degree programs in these fields constitute the largest single group of graduates every year, and I presume they are numerous on other campuses as well. Yet, despite their numbers, there have been relatively few writing textbooks produced for this audience, particularly in comparison to the many professional writing texts for students in business or the equally numerous technical writing texts for students in engineering and the physical and natural sciences. Writing in the social sciences has seldom, if ever, been treated comprehensively in textbooks, even though writing is clearly an important part of the social sciences and is, in its own way, just as technical and demanding as writing in business, engineering, physics, or biology.

The very existence of business and technical writing texts is an acknowledgment that "good writing" depends to some extent on what a particular field values in writing. "Good writing" cannot be completely encompassed in the general prescriptions of the traditional freshman handbook. My first basic assumption is that good writing in the social sciences must be considered in relationship to the goals, the assumptions, and the knowledge making practices of these disciplines. All of these factors influence the genres and the styles that typify writing in the social sciences. My second assumption is that students majoring in the social sciences will need some instruction in how to think and research like a social scientist in order to write like one. With these assumptions in mind, I attempt to provide fairly comprehensive treatment of the kinds of writing students may have to do while majoring in various branches of the social sciences and later in their careers.

I approach writing in the social sciences as rhetorical. While this may be a new approach for a textbook on scientific writing, it is definitely not novel to consider social science discourse from this perspective. In 1953, Richard Weaver, a noted twentieth-century rhetorician, published an essay entitled "The Rhetoric of Social Science." More recently, social scientists such as Michael Billig, Richard Harvey Brown, Kenneth Gergen, John Lyne, John Nelson, Alan Megill, Donald McCloskey, and Herbert Simons, among many others, have all written about the rhetorical nature of social science discourse. Their work, as well as that of others cited in this book, has influenced my thinking a great deal.

To describe social science discourse as rhetorical is not to say that it is full of bombast, flowery phrases, or appeals to emotion, all aimed at deceiving. Rather, it is simply to acknowledge that social scientists attempt to persuade their peers by advocating their claims of knowledge in what Stephen Toulmin (1972) has called the "epistemic courts" of the various disciplines. Effective persuasion in these "courts" depends on the ability of social scientists to invent the substance of their arguments in accordance with the methodological assumptions and practices of their disciplines, to reason convincingly according to their field's particular logic, and to display their evidence and reasoning in the form and style of their genres. This book aims to teach students how to argue for a claim of knowledge in the epistemic courts where their interests will take them.

Chapters 1 and 2 explore the social dimensions of rhetoric and composing, thus helping students to understand that becoming a social scientist means trying on a field's ways of thinking and its ways with words. I argue that persuasion in the social sciences begins with conceiving and conducting research, not later in "writing it up," and I describe the social dimensions of the process of knowledge making, showing how social scientists review and criticize each other's methods, reasoning, and writing at every step in order to strengthen individual claims of knowledge and refine their collective bodies of knowledge. To capitalize on the book's emphasis on the social nature of producing and writing about knowledge, I propose that teachers arrange their classes so that students can collaborate and perform for each other the same kind of peer review that professionals do through all stages of research and writing.

The heart of the book is Chapters 3 through 8, which focus on the methods that social scientists use to create the evidence for new knowledge claims. In these chapters I present social science research methods as a species of rhetorical invention—the process of discovering or creating ideas, data, or information out of which a convincing argument may be created. To illustrate the rhetoric of the social sciences, I have included examples of professional writing to show how social scientists reason convincingly according to their field's particular logic and how they display their evidence and reasoning in various genres. These examples are annotated to point out various features of substance, arrangement, and style that make the writers' arguments persuasive. In addition, I have included examples of student writing that, while not parallel to the writing of the professionals in sophistication or persuasiveness, nevertheless show how students can be challenged to move beyond the typical essays and library research papers of first-year composition courses to have experiences with new kinds of research and genres. Particularly in Chapters 4 through 8 the student papers might be described in David Hamilton's (1980) words as "serious parodies of science"—writing that lets students try their hand at using their fields' methods of research and then displaying their evidence and reasoning in the genres that professional social scientists use.

Chapters 9 and 10 focus on the printed and electronic means the social sciences use to create and disseminate bodies of knowledge. Chapters 11 thorugh 13 discuss and illustrate related genres for proposing and evaluating research and for communicating to broader public audiences. Students' need to know about career-related genres is met in Chapters 14 and 15, which teach them how to write traditional and scannable resumes, letters of application for jobs, personal statements for graduate school, and memos. General principles of effective visual rhetoric are taught in Chapter 16, which gives a brief introduction to using computers to design easy-to-read documents, and Chapter 17, which provides a primer for creating effective graphics, an essential part of social science writing. The art of public speaking is treated in Chapter 18 because oral rhetoric is still an important means of publicizing new knowledge in the social sciences. Chapter 19 pays close attention to notable features of prose style in the social sciences, and Chapter 20 provides a guide to some common documentation styles.

ACKNOWLEDGMENTS

This book has been more than ten years in the making. It began with my dissertation on the rhetoric of the social sciences, completed in 1987 at the University of Texas at Austin. I owe a great debt to Lester Faigley, who guided me in that effort; Lester was then and continues to be a valued mentor and friend. I gratefully acknowledge the assistance of colleagues at Brigham Young University who have taught with various early versions of my attempts to create a text for students in our advanced composition course, Writing in the Social Sciences, and who have given me valuable feedback. They include Joyce Adams, John Beeson, John Bennion, Lynne Christy, Alison Craig, Paula Harline, Nancy Gunn, Nancy

Hawkins, Darwin Hayes, GaeLyn Henderson, Matt Jackson, Sherland Jackson, Melanie Jenkins, Pam Johstoneaux, Keith Lawrence, Lovisa Lyman, Michael Madsen, Dawn Meehan, Mary Pollington, Ana Preto-Bay, Sherilyn Ridenhour, Dean Rigby, and Tessa Santiago. I particularly acknowledge the help of my colleague Gladys Farmer, who has cheerfully encouraged me at every step and has gone the extra mile in offering advice and samples of student writing and in soliciting feedback from her students. I also acknowledge the assistance of my colleague Beverly Zimmerman, who read drafts of several chapters and saved me from more than one embarrassing error. Thanks to Julene Butler and Marvin Wiggins of BYU's Harold B. Lee Library for reading and evaluating Chapters 9 and 10.

The graduate students I have taught and worked with in teaching advanced writing have also shaped my thinking about pedagogy through their writing, their questions, and their teaching practices: Jane Brady, Marta Brantley, Kacy Faulconer, Brian Fuller, Craig Lawrence, Darin Merrill, and Jennifer Wiener. Without the help of two graduate students, Sheryl Cragun Dame and Neil Lindeman, this book would be much the poorer and might not exist at all. Neil served for over a year as my research assistant; he researched and drafted the early versions of most of Chapters 9, 10, 16, and 20. Drawing on her years of experience as a professional editor, Sheryl completely edited the first draft and offered much helpful advice for improving the substance, organization, and style of the entire book, particularly Chapters 14, 15, 16, and 20. I thank both Neil and Sheryl for their dependable and effective work and their good humor throughout the processes of drafting, revising, editing, and formatting the book for production.

I thank the students (many of whom have since moved on to graduate schools and careers) who have graciously consented to allow their undergraduate work to be published: David Barlow, Thad Barkdull, Geannina Segura Bartholomew, Kelli Boren, Janiel Cragun, David Dinger, Emily Gwilliam, Danielle Haglund, Trevor Hall, Tyler Lee, Melissa Lundmark, Kyle McLaughlin, Ashley McMaster, Rhett Neuenschwander, Greg Nielsen, Charmaine O'Donnal, Paul Rose, Victor Sipos, Susan Walley, Gabriel Waters, Kelly Welker, and Jemma Williamson. Both they and I are aware that their work is not perfect and that it will be the object of some criticism by students who use this book. But this criticism will only improve the chances that those students will produce even better work. I invite students who use this book to aim higher and to produce research and writing that will withstand the scrutiny and win the praise of their peers. I would welcome receiving copies of excellent student writing in all genres to consider using in future editions.

I express thanks to Jay Fox, Chair of the Brigham Young University English Department, and Randall Jones, Dean of the BYU College of Humanities, for supporting my research and writing with grants of time and money. Thanks to Nancy Perry at Prentice Hall, under whose encouragement and editorial supervision the project was begun, and to Margaret Barbieri, who took on the task of seeing it through to completion. Sharon Adams, computer support specialist at BYU, and Lori Clinton of the production staff at Prentice Hall, cheerfully helped with technical computer questions. I am also grateful for Kerry Reardon's helpfulness and professionalism in preparing the typeset copy. I thank the reviewers of the manuscript for careful reading and helpful criticisms that have improved the book: Jim Cullen, Harvard University; Joan Graham, University of Washington; Michael Hogan, Southeast Missouri State University; Kenneth M. Holland, University of Memphis; Jennie Nelson, University of Idaho; Jane Olmstead, Western Kentucky University; Thea Petchler, University of Minnesota; Elizabeth Renfro, California State University–Chico; John Ramage, Arizona State University; and Fred Schmidt, University of Vermont. Of course, I assume responsibility for any flaws that remain.

Finally, I thank my family for their interest and support, and I acknowledge a special debt to my friend Kathy Knaus for knowing when to prod and encourage me and when to comfort and calm. Most of all, I thank the more than 300 undergraduate students I have taught in English 315, "Writing in the Social Sciences." They have been among my finest teachers.

Kristine Hansen

REFERENCES

Hamilton, David. 1980. Interdisciplinary writing. *College English* 41 (March): 780–96.

Toulmin, Stephen. 1972. *Human understanding*. Princeton, NJ: Princeton University Press.

Weaver, Richard. 1985. *The ethics of rhetoric*. Davis, CA: Hermagoras Press. Original edition, Washington, DC: Regnery/Gateway, Inc., 1953.

I

RHETORIC
AND COMPOSING

The first two chapters of this book describe how the terms *rhetoric* and *composing* apply to writing in the social sciences. In Chapter 1 you will learn that writing about scientific knowledge is not a simple act of packaging facts in neutral words; instead, social scientists use the art of rhetoric to argue for their claims of knowledge. This does not mean that the documents social scientists write are attempts to manipulate their readers or bamboozle them with fancy words; rather, it simply means that social scientists often deal with probable and contingent truths. Through the social processes involved in producing new knowledge, social scientists refine their claims to make them as true to the evidence and as persuasive as possible for the audience of their peers. If their claims are to be accepted by the intellectual communities they belong to, social scientists must meet rigorous standards in their research and writing. They must understand their purpose and audience well and know how to use the language conventions that characterize the rhetoric of the social sciences.

In Chapter 2, you will find a brief review of the processes that take place when individuals compose documents, with particular attention given to the specialized kinds of prewriting that social scientists do. Beyond that, you will read about the social dimensions of composing to see how learning to think like a social scientist is connected with learning to write like one. Finally, since many social scientists research and write with their colleagues, you will find some guidelines for researching and writing collaboratively with your fellow students.

1

RHETORIC AND THE SOCIAL SCIENCES

The title of this book, *A Rhetoric for the Social Sciences*, yokes two terms—*rhetoric* and *science*—that are generally believed to name two things that are incompatible with each other. The word *rhetoric* is in many people's minds a name for "fancy talk," language that uses figures of speech or a flowery style to draw attention to itself. In other people's minds it might be a name for "empty talk" of the type politicians are frequently accused of using. In the view of still others, it is a synonym for "propaganda," deliberately slanted, misleading language that can result in various kinds of harm—from voting for scoundrels to participating in holocausts—when uncritical audiences believe what they're told. In all of these views, rhetoric is language that masks a lack of real substance in thinking or that distorts what is communicated, drawing attention away from the ideas by clothing them in beguiling dress. At best, rhetoric is language that attempts to persuade audiences by appealing more to their emotions than to their reasoning ability.

Science, on the other hand, is popularly believed to name a body of facts that have been produced by rigorously controlled methods. When properly carried out, these methods result in the discovery of objective truths—"objective" meaning that the truths are independent of the subjective perception of those who discovered them. These facts are considered to "speak for themselves"; they seem so obvious and logical that the language used to communicate them is also considered objective, neutral, transparent, and free from bias or emotion. Thus, scientific language has long been held to be the opposite of rhetoric. In popular thought, rhetoric is meant to persuade, sometimes in an underhanded way, while science merely explains the way things are, with no hidden agendas.

What, then, can rhetoric have to do with science, particularly the social sciences? What can it possibly mean to call this book a rhetoric *for* the social sciences? To answer these questions, it's necessary to provide a more complete understanding of both rhetoric and the social sciences. These fields of study both have long and fascinating histories, too long to cover in detail here, but a brief summary will help to show how the two are compatible, indeed why it is helpful to think of writing in the social sciences as rhetorical. As you read the following, you will see that language—even supposedly neutral scientific language—can't escape being rhetorical. And the consequences of that for you, as a student majoring in the social sciences, are important, because as you will see, studying what makes up rhetoric will help you to be both a more skillful analyst of the rhetoric you read and hear and a more effective practitioner of it yourself.

WHAT IS RHETORIC?

Rhetoric has been given many definitions in its 2,500-year-old history, most of them positive, unlike many contemporary understandings of the word. It comes from the Greek *rhetorike*, the name for the art of oratory, or public speaking. Not surprisingly, the great systematizer Aristotle, who attempted to catalog so many other fields of learning, also codified the art of rhetoric. Aristotle defined rhetoric as the art of finding "the available means of persuasion" in any situation where persuasion was required. His book *Rhetoric* explains how to find and arrange ideas for a speech, how to appeal to various audiences, and how to choose the right style—in short, how to use language skillfully to express one's thoughts so as to win the confidence and assent of others. He recognized that such a powerful art could be used for unethical purposes, but he believed that in itself, the art of rhetoric is neither moral nor immoral. He thought that rhetoric used by a moral person to argue for good purposes would be inherently more persuasive and therefore superior to the rhetoric of an immoral person with evil ends in mind.

Another ancient Greek teacher, Isocrates, also believed that rhetoric should be used for virtuous aims, but that in itself rhetorical skill could not make people virtuous. Isocrates held a school in Athens for many years in which he taught his students to be effective leaders in public affairs; he also attempted to teach them to be ethical by example and by challenging them to choose good and noble ways of making their arguments effective. Since ancient Athens was a true democracy in which each citizen was expected to participate personally, instead of by electing representatives, a knowledge of rhetoric was paramount for each citizen, since making effective speeches was the way to influence the debates of the legislature and the judgments of the courts. (It should be noted here that participation in public life was limited to male citizens; women, slaves, and other noncitizens did not have this opportunity.) All other facets of education were intended to give young men a store of knowledge to draw on in their oratory.

The Roman rhetorician Quintilian extended Isocrates' ideas, declaring that the rhetorician should be a "good man, skilled in speaking." Quintilian laid a foundation for schooling the young in rhetoric and other fields of knowledge that lasted through the Renaissance in Western Europe. Although theories of rhetoric underwent some important changes during and after the Renaissance, the art and practice of rhetoric remained central to education in Europe and America until well into the nineteenth century, when the ideal of the citizen orator began to falter. Skill in oratory began to take a back seat then, as correctness in writing became the new goal in language arts instruction at the university.

If rhetoric was so respectable for centuries, how did it get the bad reputation that it now so often has? Actually, suspicions about rhetoric were voiced almost from the start, most prominently by Aristotle's teacher, Plato. He thought that the art of rhetoric in the hands of an unscrupulous person had the power to make bad ideas seem like good ones; he was also troubled that rhetoric could make merely probable ideas seem like true ones (see *Gorgias*). Plato believed that one must know absolute truths before learning to use rhetoric so that one might never use the art to deceive, either intentionally or unintentionally (see *Phaedrus*). Plato's fears about rhetoric have been justified over the centuries by people such as Hitler, Stalin, Mao Tse Tung, or Senator Joseph McCarthy, who have deceived others through their cunning use of language. As a result, the reputation of rhetoric has always had its shady side. On the other hand, Aristotle's, Isocrates's, and Quintilian's faith in rhetoric as a potentially positive force has also been justified by people such as Abraham Lincoln, Sojourner Truth, Susan B. Anthony, Winston Churchill, Martin Luther King, Jr., and Pope John Paul II, who have used artfully composed language to inspire their followers in times of crisis and change to achieve goals they believed would make their worlds better.

Although most people would agree that rhetoric based on absolute truth is preferable to rhetoric based on probabilities, they would also have to admit that knowing the truth about everything before advocating a course of action seems, if not impossible, then hopelessly idealistic, an unaffordable luxury, especially in the face of urgent decisions that we must make collectively all the time. In our shared public life, we have to decide such things as how to vote, spend tax revenues, create and sustain schools and colleges, plan cities and transportation systems, interact with our environment, encourage and maintain healthy families, help the poor, choose between arguments in a jury trial, and deal with criminals. We all respond to rhetoric as citizens of neighborhoods, cities, states, and nations, and we must often do so by the light of what we believe is probably true, rather than what we know for sure. Many of us also use rhetoric in the public sphere as we write letters to the editor, speak out at city council meetings, or simply urge others to vote for a candidate or an initiative. As a result, it is important to study rhetoric, both to understand how to analyze the rhetoric of others and how to practice the art ourselves.

Rhetoric will be defined in this book as *using words or other symbols skillfully to articulate and advocate your beliefs about something you assume to be true by addressing an audience whom you want to persuade to consider your beliefs, by choice and not coercion, and possibly to cooperate with you in achieving a shared goal.* Let's break that long, complex definition down.

Rhetoric is using language skillfully to articulate... The key words here are "skillfully," which means using communally accepted conventions of correctness, effective form, and a pleasing style; and "to articulate,"which means to state what you believe in precise words and clear sentences, arranged in a logical and compelling sequence.

...and to advocate your beliefs... The word "advocate" means that you actively argue for your beliefs, as an attorney argues for a client, using the kinds of logic, reasoning, examples, facts, evidence, statistics, or other data that you and your audience consider valid and trustworthy. But because human beings also have emotions which can be very powerful factors in how we make up our minds about an issue, an effective rhetorician will often advocate a case by appealing to emotions as well as reason, although an ethical rhetorician will avoid doing so in a cheap, manipulative way. Ancient rhetoricians recognized that rhetoric included both appeals to reason (the Greeks called it *logos*) and to emotion (*pathos*).

...about something you assume to be true... This part of the definition allows for either certain or probable knowledge. The key point is that you are convinced it is true or so probable that you are willing to urge that others consider and possibly share your view. In order for that to happen, your own conviction must ring true to your audience; they must perceive you as a credible and knowledgeable person with their best interests in mind, one who would not willfully mislead them. Your character, as conveyed in your rhetoric, becomes another type of appeal to the audience, in addition to reason and emotion. Presenting yourself as knowledgeable, credible, trustworthy, and well intentioned is called the ethical appeal, from the Greek *ethos*.

...by addressing an audience whom you want to persuade... Rhetoric by its very nature is communal; its aim is to construct the broadest possible consensus, encompassing as many members of the addressed audience as possible. Consensus comes by persuasion, which comes through understanding and successfully appealing to the needs, values, beliefs, and assumptions of individual members of the audience.

...to consider your beliefs, by choice and not coercion... By using threats, extortion, torture, or some other unethical means of exercising power, you might get others to say they agree with you and to cooperate with you, but you would-n't be using rhetoric. Rhetoric is language or other symbols used to put forward a point of view to an audience that is free to choose whether or not to agree with you. The audience has an important role to play in any rhetorical situation: They have to judge not only the soundness and logic of the argument offered them but also the character of the speaker or writer. If their emotions have been appealed to, they must decide if such appeals are fair and well intended.

...and possibly to cooperate with you in achieving a shared goal. Often, the purpose of rhetoric is simply to gain the audience's fair consideration of ideas, and, if possible, their intellectual assent. But it may also be used to go beyond assent, to persuade others to *act* upon their conviction—to vote a certain way, to join a movement, to volunteer for a cause, to make a change in their lives. The stronger and more persuasive your appeals, the more likely it is that people will act to join you in whatever efforts must be made to achieve a goal.

This book is based on the assumption that the above definition of rhetoric applies not just to public discourse but to university disciplines as well, the social sciences in particular. Like cities, states, and nations, academic disciplines are communities too—but they are highly specialized ones that people enter by choice rather than by birth or naturalization. As teachers and students, as current and future professionals engaged in understanding the world and creating bodies of knowledge, we use various types of rhetoric all the time to present our claims of knowledge to one another and to urge their acceptance.

Just as the founders of the United States agreed long ago to construct their society on the beliefs that "all men are created equal" and that power is located ultimately in the people, so academic disciplines are based on assumptions that the members of each discipline accept as valid. Although the rhetoric used in American political life is often scorned, we must not forget that using the power of language to act on each other is our principal way of bringing about change in our society. The goal of well-intended political rhetoric is to help us as citizens work toward building and maintaining a society that furthers the nation's founding principles—although it's clear that there is often disagreement about how to do that. Similarly, the rhetoric used in academic disciplines allows members of those disciplines to create and maintain—but also to question, criticize, and revise—the bodies of knowledge erected on their basic assumptions. No university discipline claims to be based on indisputable, absolute truths; in fact, the history of each field of academic study is replete with examples of how the field has changed its basic principles from time to time. Even though they are provisional, the assumptions of a discipline provide a basis for the research, writing, and talk that characterize each discipline. They enable something like a broad communal conversation to be carried on.

The specialized conversation of academic disciplines brings up another sense in which the word *rhetoric* is used. For centuries, the word has been used as the name for the book in which the art of rhetoric is laid out as an object of study and a guide for practice. Since this book will present practical advice for writing persuasively in the social sciences, it is in that sense a "rhetoric." It will instruct you how to write like a social scientist by teaching you about the genres and styles regularly used in the social sciences; more importantly, it will show you how these genres and styles reflect how social scientists reason and carry out research.

WHAT ARE THE SOCIAL SCIENCES?

The social sciences are the fields of learning and research that concern themselves with human behavior, human relationships, and the social, cultural, economic, and political institutions that human beings have created. Considering their broad scope, the social sciences encompass many university disciplines and subdisciplines. Although they might be named and grouped differently on various campuses, generally they include at least the following six disciplines: anthropology, economics, history, political science, psychology, and sociology. Yet other fields of study are commonly grouped with the social sciences because they also deal with human behavior and institutions. These include communications, linguistics, education, family science, organizational behavior, demography, geography, international relations, psychiatry, counseling, social work, and criminology.

Another way to identify the social sciences is to say what they are *not*. They are not the physical sciences, such as math, physics, or geology; they are not the biological sciences such as agronomy, botany, or zoology; and they are not the humanities and fine arts, such as literature, music, and theater. Yet even this negative definition is in some ways inadequate, as various social sciences might draw on one or more of these areas of learning. Most of the social sciences, for example, make use of mathematical and statistical procedures. Geographers must know something of geology, climatology, and cultural studies. Historians and archaeologists must often understand agronomy or botany to interpret practices or evidence from the past. Cultural anthropologists and sociologists are interested in the role that the humanities play in people's lives. Furthermore, there are cross-disciplinary fields, such as political geography, created when two social sciences intersect, or psychobiology, created when a social science field overlaps with a natural science. Perhaps it is best to focus on what all the social sciences have in common: They all aim to understand humans as individuals and as social beings, using empirical methods, in order to point the way toward solutions for personal and social problems, small and large, that confront us.

The social sciences are all relatively young as university disciplines, most of them having been established as separate fields of study and academic departments in the late nineteenth or early twentieth century. This is not to say that prior to that time no one thought about human behavior, relationships, and institutions. But many of the questions that now preoccupy the social sciences were generally treated within the single discipline of philosophy (and they still are, though differently from how they are treated in the social sciences). Then in the seventeenth, eighteenth, and nineteenth centuries the physical and natural sciences rose as powerful fields of study that investigated and explained the natural world with increasingly greater precision, yielding beneficial applications in such fields as medicine and industry. These achievements led some to think that a "science of man" or a "science of society" could also be established. They reasoned that, just as physicists and biologists could explain the laws of nature, and therefore predict and attempt to control the effects of natural processes, so the sciences of humans and society might uncover laws of individual and social behavior that would lead to developing better human beings and more just societies.

Some social scientists now believe that finding social and behavioral laws as consistent and reliable as the laws of nature is a utopian goal, since human beings and their interactions are often unpredictable, being influenced by more variables than one could possibly control. Nevertheless, all social scientists aim to develop the best tools and methods for understanding how individuals and groups think and behave so that they can state or predict with some accuracy the *probable* truth about whatever they might study—the causes of eating disorders, the reasons for voting behavior, the significance of headhunting among the Ilongot people, the possible outcomes of a trade alliance, why the sixteenth century was an age of exploration in Europe, why the Bay of Pigs invasion failed, or how to stem the tide of domestic abuse.

This emphasis on the probable, you will note, is consistent with the definition of rhetoric established earlier. If absolute certainty eludes social scientists—and most of them would admit that it does—they find themselves in the predicament that the philosopher Plato most feared in people's learning to use rhetoric. Social scientists have to make the case for what they have discovered based on what is probably true rather than what they know to be absolutely, objectively true. Is this situation as dangerous as Plato feared? If social scientists can't base their claims on absolute truth, will their writing be deceptive and therefore harmful?

The answer is, "It depends." It depends to a great extent on the assumptions the social scientists begin with. In the nineteenth century, there was a group of people who called themselves "scientists" and called their science "phrenology." They believed that they could determine intelligence and character traits from the shape of people's skulls. They developed instruments for measuring the parts of the skull, and they created elaborate, scientific-looking drawings of various skull types, with parts and attributes of each neatly labeled. For a time many people accepted the conclusions the phrenologists came to, which included that some races are inferior because their skulls tended to be formed differently from those of supposedly superior races. Most people today would consider phrenology a pseudo-science because when one examines its tenets and applications carefully, it becomes clear that one of its main purposes was to justify racial segregation and discrimination. This example shows that the assumptions of a group who call themselves scientists may be heavily imbued with political and ideological agendas that are masked because science presents itself as impartial and neutral.

The phrenology example shows there is some danger in proceeding from merely probable assumptions. Nevertheless, current theories of how knowledge is created and disseminated suggest that arguments based on probabilities may not pose a long-term danger, provided a scientific community's conversation is open, welcoming any responsible participant. These theories describe how the intellectual communities which develop and ratify new claims of knowledge function to examine, moderate, and even censor excessive or potentially dangerous claims. These theories contend that knowledge is not so much discovered as it is socially constructed.

THE SOCIAL PRODUCTION OF KNOWLEDGE

We often say that knowledge is "discovered," as if it were like an uncharted island where a ship lands one day. After that, the fact of the island's existence and location is known, and the captain of the ship usually gets the credit for discovering it. But if we stop to think about it, the captain must credit the shipbuilders who provided a seaworthy ship, and he owes a debt to the map makers and inventors of the navigational instruments that allowed him to chart a course across the ocean. Nor would he likely have succeeded in getting there alone, so he must credit the crew of the ship whose coordinated work kept the ship sailing on course in all kinds of weather. Perhaps he even owes some thanks to unpredictable and seemingly random events, such as a storm that blew the ship off-course for a day or an argument with the ship's mate about what to do in a certain situation; perhaps one of these seemingly unrelated events actually contributed to the island's discovery.

The point of this analogy is that no one acts completely alone in establishing a new fact or idea. Knowledge has a powerful social dimension, both in its origin and in its dissemination. Even if the ship captain had sailed alone, he would have been dependent on knowledge created earlier by others. More important, he wouldn't be able to establish his discovery of the island as a fact if all he had to offer as proof was his own word. Before the island's existence would be widely accepted as a fact, some kind of evidence would be required that others would find plausible. The captain's private knowledge would likely not count as a fact for anyone else until he could offer descriptions, pictures, artifacts, corroborating testimony, or other convincing evidence that he had made a discovery. The standards by which his claim of new knowledge would be judged are not his alone to set; he must be willing to submit his claim to judgment by standards that the community finds acceptable. The ship captain's claims must be persuasive to the audience to whom he makes them.

The analogy brings up other issues as well. First, despite the help that enables the captain to make his claim, in a society that believes in intellectual property, he will generally get all or most of the credit for the discovery. Second, the discovery of an island is important only in a larger political system that values adventurous voyages into the unknown and finds it important to know the location of islands. In some political systems this discovery might be unimportant, particularly if there were no resources or inhabitants on the island to exploit. And third, if there were inhabitants on the island, what about their perspective? What seems a discovery from the captain's point of view might seem like an invasion to the inhabitants. The words "uncharted island" take on a different meaning when you ask, "Uncharted to whom?" Perhaps the island was included on other people's maps long before our captain happened on it. These points remind us that credit and rewards for knowledge often accrue to those who already have power and status; that what counts as the discovery of an important fact is also socially determined; and that there are ethical problems to be considered in the production of knowledge.

In the social sciences it is in some ways harder to establish convincing claims of knowledge than it is to prove the existence of islands. Islands have a concrete, physical reality that can be empirically demonstrated. Although social scientists also claim an empirical basis for their knowledge, the concepts they deal in are nevertheless usually abstract. The facts that social scientists discuss do not lie about in the physical world, like stones waiting to be stumbled over. They are not discovered in the sense that islands might be; instead, they are created, constructed, or made. None of these words is meant to imply that there is a basic dishonesty in the facts, ideas, and theories of the social sciences—that they are somehow just fabricated out of thin air. There is a basis for social science concepts, but that basis often lies more in the social organization of the disciplines than in the physical reality of the surrounding world.

Saying this may make it sound like the social sciences are unconcerned with reality. On the contrary, they are very much concerned with reality, but these realities generally take the form of something like an economic trend, a cultural practice, an event in the past, a behavior, or an attitude. Because these realities are abstract, the social sciences must collectively negotiate their under-standing and ways of perceiving and describing them—in effect, their ways of making knowledge. This collective negotiation results in the social production of knowledge. It will become clear how knowledge is socially produced as we consider the steps that all social sciences follow in creating and establishing claims of knowledge.

THE PROCESS OF KNOWLEDGE MAKING STARTS WITH QUESTIONS

The social sciences, like the physical and natural sciences, were organized to answer questions that are of general interest to practitioners of those sciences. Questions are the starting point for all of the social sciences' knowledge-making practices. As the social sciences have grown and developed, questions that were asked initially have produced answers and theories that in turn have spawned new, often increasingly specialized, questions and refinement of the original the-ories. Thus, previous research affects present research, so much in fact, that a sci-entist planning to extend an established line of questioning, say on the relation-ship between parenting and personality, is expected to read all the previous lit-erature related to that question and to determine how the new questions relate to already established answers.

The boundaries of disciplines also direct the line of questioning. Most of the social sciences are concerned in some way with the institution of the fami-ly, but the questions a sociologist asks about the family might be very different from those an economist asks, which in turn are different from those a histori-an asks. As Ziman (1968) has noted, each field of science is like a corporate enterprise in which there are general overall goals and purposes, yet much spe-cialization throughout the ranks and divisions of the enterprise, each person spending his or her time and talents working with colleagues to create and maintain some part of the overall field. Although there may be some friction and disagreement—or sometimes even competition—within a particular field, there is usually general agreement about the overall goals because the research agendas of each social science are largely shared by their members. In each field some questions will be considered not worth asking because they seem unin-teresting, they appear to already have definitive answers, or because it's believed there is no good way of answering them.

Because there is some social pressure to conform to established research agendas, it is possible that some originality is stifled or some potentially interest-ing avenues are left unexplored. However, the social influences on the defining of research questions do not necessarily mean that an individual must cease to think critically and independently or give up the freedom to choose *how* to think. There are still ways for independent thinkers to inquire into issues that others consider uninteresting, and these mavericks often ask unusual questions and make surprising claims that persuade others to join them in changing the direction of a field. At such a time, rhetoric becomes an important tool for them to use.

ANSWERS COME FROM OBSERVATION

To answer the questions each social science deems important, individuals must somehow observe the reality that will produce an answer, whether that reality is a past event, a person's behavior, or a political trend. Here the word "observation" will be used in the broadest possible sense to include everything from examining documents to interviewing people to using scales to measure attitudes. But observation itself is also socially influenced in several ways. The reality that the social scientist observes must first be selected or defined as an object for investigation. Some part of reality must be focused on and marked off from other, related phenomena that surround it. Social scientists focus on a reality in the ways their disciplines have taught them to.

Yet even focusing carefully on something does not make it accessible to direct investigation. It is not possible to just "read off" the meaning of any particular object or event simply by looking at it, like reading the label on a can. The phenomenon must be interpreted. This interpretation is socially conditioned because observers view reality from the perspective created by their education, their cultural conditioning, and their personal backgrounds. In addition, observation always takes place from a particular standpoint because an observer can't stand outside of a particular time or space and observe something "as it really is." The act of observing is already the act of interpreting. Also, the interpretation one arrives at will depend on the questions one asks to begin with and on the methods and instruments that one uses to observe with. Since these often come from the intellectual community one belongs to, observation is in this way also socially influenced.

OBSERVATION RELIES ON METHODS AND INSTRUMENTS

Using methods and instruments with which to observe reality is the third common characteristic of all the social sciences' knowledge-making practices. Methods are discipline-sanctioned procedures for answering the questions of interest in that particular discipline. But no method ever just dropped from the sky. All methods are human creations; each method has a history, with a definite beginning and many changes and refinements along the way. So important is method that when social scientists write papers, articles, and books about their findings, they include detailed descriptions of the methods they used. They know that their claims of knowledge will be judged in part by how carefully they followed the procedures and met the standards their field currently considers acceptable. (You will read a great deal more about methods in Part II.)

INTERPRETATIONS OF DATA BECOME CLAIMS OF KNOWLEDGE

Social scientists use methods to create data, find evidence, or otherwise come up with results that can be interpreted and related to existing knowledge. Although findings are sometimes ambiguous and don't point to any larger conclusions, usually interpretations of new evidence either support or contradict existing claims. In either case, the social scientist's goal is to make valid and reliable statements. The validity of an interpretation is established by adequate evidence and sound reasoning about the evidence. Reliability is generally established through separate studies of the same phenomenon that reach similar conclusions, suggesting that the results will hold up over time. In order to make valid and reliable statements, social scientists go through the steps previously described, but they also subject their initial interpretations to careful scrutiny and criticism before disseminating them more widely. Social scientists working to answer a particular question often converse with their colleagues about their research throughout the whole investigation; in this way, they benefit from the advice and criticism of others even before they have written anything for others to read. They also write letters and e-mail, send faxes, and make telephone calls to communicate with others who are working on related problems and whose insights may help them in interpreting data and creating valid and reliable claims.

CLAIMS ARE DISSEMINATED FOR PEER REVIEW

When investigators have finished their research and have written a paper, an article, or other document, they do not print and disseminate their findings immediately. Most informally seek peer review by asking colleagues to read and criticize early drafts of the document they have written. Besides this informal peer review, each field has more formal ways of conducting peer review of new claims so that they will be as strong as possible before being submitted to the discipline at large. This formal kind of peer review generally takes place in at least two forums that are a part of every social science. In the first, a scientist might read a near-final draft of a paper at a professional conference or symposium, and the questions and comments the audience poses might cause the scientist to rethink and revise some parts of his or her paper. In the second, the scientist sends a draft of a paper to a journal or publisher. The editor then sends the paper to two or more reviewers who read it carefully and recommend publication, revision, or rejection. Very few articles or books are published without some additional revision recommended by the reviewers. Because the reviewers have different backgrounds than the writer, they may have different perceptions of what the writer has observed. By taking the reviewers' positions and perceptions into account, the writer can revise to make the final draft stronger and more acceptable to other members of the field to whom the research is finally disseminated.

What does all of this mean for you? It means that learning to think like a social scientist is a process of socialization into your field's assumptions about what knowledge is and about how to ask the right questions. It is learning to follow methodological procedures and techniques, often using instruments that yield precise results. It is learning to interpret results and make claims that your scientific peers can examine and criticize. Your goal in this process is to do your work so well and present it so persuasively that peers will ratify your claims as valid and reliable. Claims so ratified attain the status of facts. Knowledge making is a long process, and as you've seen, at every step it is a highly social one.

Because the processes for producing knowledge are social, the objectivity so often claimed by the social sciences is really a kind of *intersubjectivity*. That is, different persons, each with a different subjective consciousness, agree on the interpretation of particular observations. The facts social scientists agree on usually don't have the same kind of physical status as islands, but they are nonetheless true for the discipline that created them. The goal of any science is to achieve the widest possible intersubjective agreement about the facts. This social process of producing knowledge protects a discipline—and society at large—from whatever dangers might come from the idiosyncratic claims of individuals who want to claim they have discovered some new fact, when in reality they may have some other agenda in mind, such as self-aggrandizement, an early claim to a patent, or spreading a bias.

HOW PERSUASION CREATES CHANGE IN SOCIAL SCIENCES

Because knowledge is socially constructed in the way just described, it is fairly "safe" from the claims of cranks and crackpots who might have a pseudo-scientific ax to grind. The social nature of scientific investigation and the peer review system are actually rather conservative elements in the process of knowledge creation, acting to censor unconventional interpretations and claims. On the one hand, this kind of conservatism is probably good, because it prevents the scientific journals from being clogged with just anything somebody might want to write. On the other hand, this conservatism makes science somewhat resistant and slow to change, even when legitimate scientists make worthwhile claims. This resistance happens particularly when social scientists challenge existing facts. Because many established scientists have invested their careers in building up a body of knowledge, they may sometimes let personal feelings get in the way of dispassionate review of new claims, especially when they can exercise power as a reviewer or editor. Change does occur, but it takes time and convincing new evidence, presented persuasively with great rhetorical skill, to change previous perceptions and interpretations.

An example of what happens when new and old perceptions clash occurred in 1985 when members of the American Psychological Association (APA) met to review the second edition of the *Diagnostic and Statistical Manual of Mental Disorders (DSM-II)* in preparation for issuing the third edition (Leo 1985). This manual is an important one since it lists the names and definitions of all recognized mental disorders, thus ensuring that psychiatrists and clinical psychologists will have a common reference point by which to make similar diagnoses of similar ailments. It is also the authoritative book that hospitals and courts rely on when it is necessary to determine the mental state of an individual; and it is the standard that insurance companies use to determine whether or not a patient will be covered for the cost of having a mental illness treated. For legal, medical, and insurance decisions, a psychological disorder exists, in a sense, only if the manual says it does.

At the 1984 meeting of the APA, two factions of the field argued about whether or not a diagnosis called "masochistic personality disorder" should remain in the manual. Until that point it had been common for psychiatrists and psychologists to diagnose people (mainly women) who remained with abusive spouses as suffering from this disorder. One group of practitioners at the conference, influenced by new feminist theories in psychology and not convinced of Freud's belief that all women are naturally masochistic, challenged the accuracy of the name for this disorder. Although they agreed that many women do remain with abusive spouses, they argued that it was not necessarily because the abused women were masochistic—that they liked the abuse. They sought a name change for the diagnosis, from "masochistic personality disorder" to "self-defeating personality disorder." They reasoned that the new name better reflected what they believed were the real reasons an abused spouse does not leave: She may be so demoralized and terrorized by the abuse that she believes she has no other options than to remain in an abusive relationship.

Another group of practitioners at the conference, one that might be called traditionalists, were willing to add the new diagnostic label to the manual but were not ready to give up the concept of masochism. They believed that because some abused people might really be masochistic, the old diagnosis should also be retained in the manual. A dispute ensued and finally the feminist faction succeeded in persuading the traditionalists that the old diagnosis and its name should be removed from the manual completely.

This story illustrates that rhetoric can have important consequences in the "real world," influencing such matters as health care coverage. But it is not just about that; it is also about the strength of socialization and how it colors our perceptions. Psychiatrists from either group no doubt would perceive the fact of abuse in the same way: Seeing Mr. Jones beat Mrs. Jones would be, in effect, the same perceptual event for them. That Mrs. Jones remains with Mr. Jones despite the beating would also be a fact they could agree on. But they would interpret her reasons for remaining differently. The traditionalists, whose perceptions would be imbued with Freudian assumptions about women, would interpret Mrs. Jones' remaining as evidence of a masochistic personality, one that actually enjoys pain and violence. The feminists, whose perceptions would be colored by their socialization in feminist theories, would interpret Mrs. Jones as so disabled by a combination of low self-esteem, confused thinking, and lack of options that she would feel powerless to escape her situation. A difference in interpretation such as this cannot be reconciled by discovering the "real" reason for the behavior because that is actually impossible to ascertain with certainty. The difference can only be reconciled through a rhetorical process. That's what happened in this case: One party succeeded in persuading the other party that its interpretation of the event was the better one.

It remains to be seen how the greater presence of women in the social sciences and resulting new focuses of research will ultimately alter these fields. Just as the *DSM-III* illustration depicts how psychiatric diagnoses change, we can expect that more situations similar to that one will arise, in which a new interpretation might replace an old one, or two interpretations might be negotiated to come up with a third one, perceived as more accurate. Changing social relationships, disagreements about perceptual frameworks, and new interpretations can be negotiated through a rhetorical process that, if successful, enables the discipline to rethink some of its basic positions and then to proceed from more acceptable, more valid assumptions. If this process is not successful, however, frequently there is schism and division of a discipline into various theoretical camps and sometimes into new subdisciplines. The members of these camps may coexist peacefully enough in the same buildings on university campuses, but often they have less and less to say to each other. That is unfortunate because increased human understanding is thus slowed. Rhetorical transactions in academic life, as in public life, require good will, good faith, and patience in order to avoid the crippling outcomes of acrimony, fragmentation, and silence.

THE RHETORICAL SITUATION

This chapter opened with the claim that the words *rhetoric* and *social science* are compatible. It has focused mainly on demonstrating that social scientists, because of the interpretive nature of their research, need rhetorical skill to make their knowledge claims convincing to their audiences. The premise of this book is that writing in the social sciences is not simply a matter of packaging "objective" truths in "neutral" language. Because social scientists construct their claims from the methods of observation used in their fields, and because we perceive reality to some extent through socially constructed lenses, writing in the social sciences always has a persuasive dimension; hence, it is rhetorical. But the rhetorical skill social scientists need should never be confused with the magician's sleight of hand, which can seemingly produce five-dollar bills from behind someone's ear. As a social scientist, you must be sure your rhetoric is true to the highest standards of honesty and respect for others and to the most rigorous standards of inquiry your discipline has formulated.

Your rhetoric should result from a considered balance among the various elements that together define any *rhetorical situation*. The rhetorical situation is any situation in which rhetoric is called for—and that includes a great many! An abstract way of thinking about the elements of any rhetorical situation is shown in the diagram of Figure 1-1 (adapted from Kinneavy 1971). This diagram shows that in any situation in which you use rhetoric, you must consider four elements. First, rhetoric comes from a writer (or speaker) who has a purpose in speaking or writing. The purpose might be to inform, instruct, persuade, convince, entertain, delight, or otherwise express oneself. Second, rhetoric is directed toward an audience of readers or listeners (or both). The audience might be large or small; it might be close by or remote in time or space. Third, rhetoric is about some facet of reality (remembering that reality is to some extent socially constructed). Fourth, it is encoded in language—as well as in related ways of symbolizing meanings, such as pictures, graphs, or statistics.

Note that language, in the middle of the diagram, is the element that ties the other three elements together. This is significant because language, next to emotional bonds, is perhaps the strongest strand in the cord that connects us to others. To a great extent we know each other through the words we share. The way you use language as a writer is a way of conveying something about yourself to an audience who may never have met you. That is, you construct a *per-*

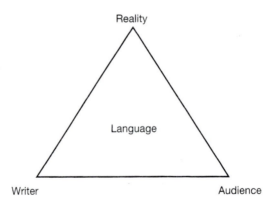

FIGURE 1-1   The Rhetorical Situation

sona or *ethos* through your writing that may reveal you to be educated, witty, friendly, aloof, or any one of many other possible descriptors. The language of much social science writing doesn't allow for a lot of variation in the persona you can convey. Some of the conventions of social science writing often convey the persona of the detached, thoughtful observer who doesn't let emotions get in the way. (More will be said about the writing style of the social sciences and its contribution to persona, or ethos, in Chapter 19.)

The reality that writers aim to share with an audience is also mediated to us in great part by language. What you have learned already about your major discipline has come to you mainly through words that you have read or listened to. These words have shaped your understanding of the realities your discipline examines. As someone now learning to write in your discipline, you must express what you know about reality to your audience through language. You must choose language that is as true to your experiences and observations of reality as you can make it, and as clear to your audience as you can make it. (More will be said in Chapter 2 about how to analyze your audience and judge the best way to construct a message for them.)

Since social scientists deal with issues that affect us all intimately, it is important that you consider carefully who your audience is and how to communicate with not only your peers in the social sciences but with laypersons as well. As citizens we face serious problems in our families, neighborhoods, cities, and nation, and in a world community that is becoming ever more tightly knit through political and trade alliances and through advances in communication and transportation. Therefore, we need whatever expertise social scientists can offer to solve these problems that loom so large. Clear communication is an indispensable part of whatever solutions are offered. Because the members of different social science communities often speak mostly to each other in their own discipline-specific language, there is a need for all of them to learn to use a more general rhetoric adapted to the ordinary citizen so they can translate their specialized knowledge for the general public. This book aims to help you acquire the rhetorical skill you will need to make a difference in the world, not only as a professional writing for your peers, but also as a citizen who cares about the community you live in and who can apply your expertise to make it better. The centuries-old ideal of the citizen rhetor, espoused by Isocrates and Quintilian, might perhaps be revived if you and fellow social scientists learn to be skilled writers, capable of using the rhetoric not only of professional discourse but of public discourse as well.

SUGGESTIONS FOR DISCUSSION OR WRITING

1. Before you read this chapter, how would you have defined rhetoric? How would you have defined social science? In what ways, if any, has reading this chapter changed your thinking?

2. What is the history of the discipline you are majoring in? When did it become a recognized division of the university? What changes has it undergone in its history? How would you characterize its aims when it first began? Are they the same now? If not, how have they changed?

3. How have your discipline's methods changed over time? Why have they changed? Why would today's researchers find the methods used by the first practitioners of your discipline inadequate?

4. Has there been a time when members of your discipline were divided about some issue, theory, or method? What was the conflict about? How was it resolved?

5. How would you characterize writing in your field? Do you believe it has a persuasive dimension to it? What sorts of evidence, data, and reasoning count as convincing and logical in your field's writing?

6. How do writers in your field construct an *ethos* (credible persona) in their writing? What kinds of appeal to *pathos* (emotion) are evident in their writing?

References

Aristotle. 1926. *"Art" of rhetoric*. Translated by J. H. Freese. Cambridge, MA: Harvard University Press.

Isocrates. 1929. *Antidosis*. Translated by George Norlin. Cambridge, MA: Harvard University Press.

Kinneavy, James L. 1971. *A theory of discourse*. New York: W. W. Norton.

Leo, John. 1985. Battling over masochism. *Time*, 2 December, 76.

Plato. 1925. *Gorgias*. Translated by W. R. M. Lamb. Cambridge, MA: Harvard University Press.

Plato. 1914. *Phaedrus*. Translated by H. N. Fowler. Cambridge, MA: Harvard University Press.

Quintilian. 1921. *The* Institutio Oratoria *of Quintilian*. Translated by H. E. Butler. Cambridge, MA: Harvard University Press.

Ziman, John. 1968. *Public knowledge: An essay concerning the social dimension of science*. London: Cambridge University Press.

2

THE INDIVIDUAL AND SOCIAL DIMENSIONS OF COMPOSING

Rhetoric of any kind seldom springs fully formed from anyone's mind. It has to be composed, often laboriously, in order to be effective. In ancient times, students often composed their orations mentally because they lacked convenient and inexpensive ways to compose in writing. In modern times, however, most composing is done in writing. So *composing* is the name we will use for the process of writing something—a term paper, a report, a letter, a review, or anything else—from start to finish. Actually, the "process" is really a set of subprocesses that interact and recur in various ways depending on what you are writing about, whom you are writing for, what kind of text you are writing, and your own unique history and preferences as a writer. As you no doubt know by now, composing does not usually begin when you first set pen to paper or turn on the computer. Before that point there is often a process of thinking, discussing, listing, outlining, researching, data gathering, or otherwise generating ideas and facts to write about. Composing thus begins with finding something to say, or what the ancient rhetoricians called *invention*.

Composing continues as you actually write a draft of your paper—as you decide how best to organize the matter of your paper, how to structure paragraphs and sentences, and which words will best express your intentions. (The ancients called dealing with these matters *arrangement* and *style*.) Nor does composing end when you finish a draft. At that point, you often ask others to respond to your ideas and criticize how you've presented them. Then you revise to improve the content and organization of your paper. Finally you edit to make your paper stylistically correct and effective. Even after all of that, you may begin a new process of composing as you attempt to improve your first composition.

Some of these subprocesses of composing can run simultaneously; for example, you can still be generating ideas and gathering information at the same time as you are drafting paragraphs and sentences. One subprocess can be interrupted for another to take place; you might pause in drafting, for instance, to revise and edit sentences and paragraphs already in place. Sometimes you may eliminate one of these composing subprocesses completely, out of choice or necessity, as for example when you write essay exams under time constraints and must do without outside criticism, revision, and editing.

Because of the various combinations and sequences of all the subprocesses that make up composing, it's safe to say that no two acts of composing are the same for two different individuals or even for the same individual writing two different documents. Because each act of composing and each person is unique, textbooks like this can offer only some observations that may help you reflect on how *you* write and decide whether your individual processes serve you well for all rhetorical situations. Despite the differences between individuals, this chapter offers some generalizations and advice that may help you in your writing. You'll find here a brief discussion of the subprocesses of composing, followed by an analysis of both the individual and the social nature of composing. Because collaborative writing is an important feature of writing in many of the social sciences, the chapter ends with advice for working successfully with others to produce jointly composed papers.

THE SUBPROCESSES OF COMPOSING

COMMON WAYS OF PREWRITING

If you took a writing class in your first year at college, your teacher may have used the term *prewriting* to describe a number of activities that you can do to get your mind working on what to write about in a paper and how to organize it. You may have learned of some or all of these common prewriting techniques: incubating, brainstorming, freewriting, questioning, discussing, clustering, and outlining. Each of these prewriting techniques can help you overcome writer's block because each helps you see that you *do* have something to write about by getting down on paper some of the thoughts that may be swarming through your mind. Simply getting your mind and your pen or computer cursor moving often helps decrease the anxiety you may feel when you are assigned to write a paper. You relax as you start thinking about the connections you can make between the ideas you've generated and captured in your prewriting. You start to see a main point you can argue for and the stance you can take in the paper.

SPECIALIZED KINDS OF PREWRITING

The above prewriting techniques are generally applicable to all forms and fields of writing. Other kinds of prewriting, however, are peculiar to academic writing, especially in the sciences. Though these are not always thought of as belonging to writing, they certainly belong to rhetorical invention—the process of finding something to write about. One such invention technique is keeping an *observation journal, log,* or *research notebook.* Another is using the *research methods* of the social sciences to create data to write about.

Observation Journals, Logs, and Notebooks. The social sciences all depend on observation of one kind or another and on careful recording of the data observed. For example, the historian must observe the previously unnoticed facts or the recurring patterns in the documents he reads in archives and libraries; he can't rely on only his memory to store all the information he discovers, so he keeps a research notebook or perhaps an organized card file; he might store either of these on paper or electronically as computer files. The anthropologist pauses often to take careful field notes of customs and behaviors she observes in the people she lives among; not only does she note their actions but she also speculates on what they may mean. The psychologist doing repeated laboratory experiments with rats must keep accurate records of the behaviors he observes. The sociologist who tape-records interviews with members of a particular social group supplements the tapes with notes about the context of each interview and facts about each respondent that she couldn't capture on the tape.

Though these methods of record keeping may seem to be more removed from composing than the prewriting techniques described earlier, they are no less important to successful composing. The social scientist may begin keeping a research journal or log with only a vague idea of what kind of text it will eventually grow into, but without the data recorded there, no paper of great value to other social scientists could be written. In most cases other social scientists expect that professional writing will be based on more than the thoughts in a writer's mind. This audience wants evidence that the observer was systematic and thorough in gathering, analyzing, and interpreting data that will support a claim. Without a research log or notebook to reread, the social scientist would be less likely to find the patterns that can often be discovered in the daily entries. In that sense, some method of regularly recording observations is a kind of prewriting, for without it, no findings could be established in a more formal document.

Research Methods. In addition to keeping notebooks, logs, or journals, social scientists carry out systematic research using the specialized methods of their disciplines. In the sense that all of these methods yield findings, evidence, or data that the scientist can then write about, these methods are also a highly structured form of prewriting. Certain methods have come to be associated with certain kinds of texts: participant observation with the genre called ethnography, experimentation with the experimental research report, observation of selected individuals with the case study. Chapters 3 through 8 discuss particular research methods in detail and illustrate the kinds of texts that result from several of these methods.

DRAFTING

Whether it comes from a technique such as brainstorming, rereading a research log, or creating data with a method such as the experiment or survey, prewriting is usually followed by drafting. Drafting is the composing subprocess in which you take the ideas or data you have invented through prewriting and determine what interpretation you can support or what claim you can make. Often you state this interpretation or claim directly at the beginning of the draft, and this statement becomes the main point or thesis of your paper. In some kinds of writing, however, the interpretation comes last, as in the discussion section of an experimental research report.

Besides interpreting your data as you draft, you also organize it in a particular sequence, according to the needs of your audience and the type of text you are writing. You organize on both a macro level, deciding what large "chunks" of information should come before other chunks, and on a micro level, deciding what sentences should precede other sentences within paragraphs. You also write the transitional phrases and sentences that will help your readers see how the parts connect. If you experience anxiety about writing, it helps when drafting to remind yourself that nothing has to be perfect the first time. A paper can go through several drafts—and usually should.

REVISING

Once you have a complete draft, the next step is usually to revise. To *revise* means to *re-see*. It means to pay attention to the overall structure of a text, considering again your sequencing of ideas, the proportions of space and emphasis you have given to particular points, and the amount of detail you have given in any particular part. When you revise, you do any or all of these three activities: **rearrange**, **add**, and **delete**.

One way you can decide which of these activities will improve your draft is to set it aside for a day. Reading it again after you have rested and gained some emotional distance from your paper will help you to view it critically. Another way to evaluate your draft for revision is to let others read it. As they tell you how they viewed your draft, you may see its strong and weak points more clearly so that you can rearrange, add, or delete to capitalize on the strengths and eliminate the weaknesses.

EDITING

Theoretically, there is no limit to the number of times you could revise a single paper. Practically, however, there are limits, and the greatest of these is time. Few students have the time to revise a paper more than two or three times, as the term rolls on and other assignments must take precedence. Eventually a deadline comes and you must submit a final paper. But everyone should take the time to edit a paper before handing it in. Editing differs from revising in that it is local, rather than global. In fact, it is best to wait until you have made large-scale, global revisions to your paper before you begin to edit. Otherwise, you might end up deleting something you've already spent time editing. After you get the structure the way you want it, you edit to polish the surface of your writing—making sure the sentences are clear and effective, choosing precise words, using appropriate grammar, and spelling and punctuating correctly.

COMPOSING WITH A COMPUTER

The computer has already been mentioned several times as a tool for composing. Computers have undoubtedly revolutionized most aspects of the writing process. Although some may argue that computers haven't necessarily made drafting any easier (especially if you don't type well), it's easy to see that a paper once drafted on a computer is easier to revise because you don't have to retype every new draft. The blinking cursor of a word processing program allows you to add text at any point; the delete function lets you get rid of useless words and sentences with a keystroke; and the cut-and-paste functions permit you to rearrange sentences or whole sections of a paper without the scissors and tape of yesteryear. Spell-checkers make it easier to submit correct copy, and printer programs allow you to use typographical features that can improve the readability of your writing (see Chapter 16).

Computers have done more than simplify drafting, revision, and editing. In some ways they have made prewriting easier as well. Via the Internet or specialized computers in libraries you can tap into huge databases, searching for and retrieving information more efficiently than in the past (see Chapters 9–10). You can also use your computer's memory, or a disk, like a research notebook, log, or journal to store bits of information that you can later retrieve and insert into a paper you are writing.

THE INDIVIDUAL NATURE OF COMPOSING

COMPOSING AS AN IDIOSYNCRATIC ACT

So far we have discussed the subprocesses of composing as if they were the same for everyone. But in fact they are not. In every act of composing, you will be able to exercise some of your unique preferences and habits. For example, some people like to begin composing by sitting alone in the library or another quiet place with their favorite pen and a pad on which to list their thoughts. Others prefer the background noise of a cafeteria and perhaps a conversation to test their ideas, using a napkin or scrap of paper for jotting down good ideas. Still others have become so used to writing with a computer that they can hardly write with pen and paper anymore.

When some people start drafting, they like to work at a neat desk in the early morning, wearing a robe or comfortable sweats, with a row of freshly sharpened pencils and a favorite beverage beside them. They are likely to be people who have to get other important tasks, like cleaning the apartment, out of the way first so they can concentrate on writing. Others write best late at night, with music in the background, oblivious to clutter in the room, dishes in the sink, and laundry piling up. Some people need three to four hours of uninterrupted writing time; others can write in 20-minute snatches.

Some revise as they go, shaping sentences and paragraphs to their satisfaction, even correcting spelling and grammar before proceeding to the next part. Others pour out words as they come, waiting until later to add, delete, rearrange, and edit. And all of us have our own prose style—a preference for certain words, a typical sentence length or construction, short or long paragraphs, few or many transitional elements. It's important to determine for yourself what times and places, what moods and physical states, which habits and rituals contribute to your productivity as a writer. It's also important to become conscious of style—both your own and others'—because the more aware you are of the stylistic options you have as a writer, the more control you have over shaping your meaning.

COMPOSING AS A PRIVATE ACT

Another sense in which composing is a highly individual act is that some writing is private. It isn't meant for others; it's just for you. You may keep a journal or a diary in which you record your thoughts about your life's experiences and your innermost thoughts and feelings. You may have the vague intention of someday letting family members or close friends read what you've written, but mostly the writing is for your own benefit. Even if you don't keep a journal, you may occasionally write as a way of helping you sort out complex matters—the pros and cons related to a particular decision you must make, for example, or as a way to blow off steam, such as a letter to someone with whom you've just had a heated argument (but which you probably wouldn't mail). Perhaps you make lists that are just for you—of things to do, resolutions for improving your life, books you want to read. Maybe you are a closet poet, someone who loves to write poems but wouldn't dream of showing them to others. And maybe you consider private the early writing you do for things that will eventually be read by others. Whatever your reasons for not sharing your writing with others, it's obvious that some pieces of writing are mainly for an audience of one—yourself—and the way you write them is nobody's business but yours.

But most writing is meant to "go public" eventually, and since it will then be read by others, there is automatically a social dimension to it. We will explore this social dimension at length since it affects how you compose, particularly how you compose in the social sciences. The more you understand writing as a social transaction, the more successful you will be in participating in the intellectual communities of the social sciences.

THE SOCIAL NATURE OF COMPOSING

LANGUAGE AS A SOCIAL MEDIUM

Just as creating knowledge is a social endeavor, so the act of composing is permeated with the influence and the awareness of others. Writing exists mainly for the purpose of communicating with others, after all, and it would be odd if it were not shaped by communal expectations and norms. Written language would not accomplish its purpose nearly so well if everyone could write in whatever way they chose. Imagine how much more difficult writing and reading would be if there were no standardized spelling, no common agreements about how punctuation marks should be used, no grammar rules, or even conventional forms such as the business letter. In times past there was more variation in spelling, punctuation, grammar, and form than there is now. The high degree of standardization in written English today is a result of increased literacy and increased numbers of books, newspapers, magazines, and other printed materials in the last two centuries. Both of these developments led to an increasing need for standardization so that schooling, reading, writing, editing, and printing could be more efficient and economical. Readers can understand writers more quickly and easily, writers can compose with greater confidence, editors can improve writing more surely, and typesetters can work more rapidly if there are norms and conventions that everyone understands and agrees on. So composing is social in the sense that the written language we use, with all its detailed conventions, is one that we share with others. Composing is social in other senses as well.

THE INFLUENCE OF AUDIENCES

The audience you write for exerts a powerful influence on what and how you write. For our purposes in this text, audiences can be divided into two general classes: professional and lay audiences. If you have written for one of your professors about their area of expertise (and what student hasn't?), you have written for a professional audience. You know the pressure you feel to include accurate and complete information as well as to write about it in the way you think your professor expects you to—using the right terminology and the form of presentation that will most likely convince the professor that, even though you are a novice, you are beginning to understand the discipline and its norms for communication.

On the other hand, sometimes you are the expert in what you are writing about, and your audience is relatively uninformed about the subject—a lay audience. If you think carefully about how to succeed in communicating with them, you will realize that specialized jargon will not be appropriate, that you may have to use comparisons to familiar things to help them understand difficult concepts, and that the organization of your writing must be appealing and accessible to them. This is not to say that writing for a professional audience should not also be appealing and accessible; rather, it means that the level of language and the organizational conventions you might use would differ if you were planning to publish your research in, say, both *Journal of Marriage and the Family* and *Parents' Magazine*.

Audiences can vary widely. Depending on your subject matter and your purpose in writing, you will likely have to consider many of the following audience characteristics that may affect how you address them:

relationship to you	age
purposes for reading your writing	social class
familiarity with the subject	education
opinions and attitudes	religion
political affiliations	disability
geographic location	prejudices
race or ethnicity	gender

The level of complexity of your subject matter, the words you choose, the examples you use, and even how you organize what you write should all be affected by your audience. The better you understand your audience, the more likely it is that you will make successful choices in writing documents that both inform and persuade your readers.

THE SOCIAL EVOLUTION AND INFLUENCE OF GENRES

The form of many documents is particularly determined by social norms. The social sciences, as noted in Chapter 1, function like highly selective and organized communities. As such they develop *genres*, forms of communication that provide socially constructed ways of dealing with rhetorical situations that occur again and again (see Miller 1984). For example, in the community of experimental psychologists, there is a recurring need for psychologists to inform their peers about research they've conducted and to persuade their colleagues that these experiments add something important to the group's existing knowledge. Over the years, the genre of the experimental research report has evolved to the point that it now has seven very predictable features:

1. A title that explains directly and unambiguously what the article is about.
2. An abstract summarizing the basic aim, methods, and findings of the experiment.
3. An introduction that contextualizes the experiment in a review of related literature and states the research focus.
4. A description of the methods used to conduct the experiment.
5. A presentation of the results of the experiment, often including tables and figures.
6. A discussion of the significance of the results.
7. A list of references to articles and books cited in the report.

These various parts of the report are indicated by headings or typographical features (such as italics or boldface print) that help readers identify the parts quickly and accurately.

Beyond these standard parts, there is a typical style of writing in experimental reports characterized not only by specialized vocabulary and preferred sentence structures but also by the stance the writer takes toward the subject and the audience as well. Any psychologist writing an article to publicize experimental findings would be wise to follow all of these genre conventions, not only because they help readers rapidly locate the information most important to them, but also because they show that the writer has internalized a way of thinking, researching, and writing that marks him or her as a member of the scientific community. All of these features of the genre subtly influence the persuasiveness of the claim the writer is making.

Other social science fields have developed their own genres: case studies, position papers, narratives, ethnographies, and so on. In every discipline, each genre represents the end result of an ongoing historical process of standardizing forms of discourse that enable the members of the discipline to establish and debate claims through books and journals. In a way, the members of every discipline carry on a conversation through their writing, and genre conventions simply make that conversation more understandable to all. All genres are dynamic, however, and the genres of every discipline are likely to change more rapidly than ever as electronic forums such as E-mail, listservs, and electronic journals become more important as mediums for exchanging ideas in professional communities.

The genres of each discipline reflect its assumptions about what knowledge is and how it is created: The methods of inquiry used, the kinds of evidence offered, and the presentation of the evidence show how the discipline's claims of truth are created and supported. But just as methods of inquiry shape genres, genres also shape methods. For example, as the discipline of anthropology began to establish itself, its main rhetorical genre, the ethnography, was shaped by the assumption that an outside observer, the anthropologist, could discover the important cultural practices of a given group of people (usually a "primitive tribe") through a process of neutral observation and then could report these practices in an authoritative manner, using "transparent" language (see Clifford 1986). A sort of imperialist assumption underlay this rhetorical practice: That the culturally superior anthropologist was able to determine and name the significance of the other culture's practices, in a sense intellectually "colonizing" the natives' culture for consumption by interested readers, usually those back home in the anthropologist's native culture. This kind of genre had a powerful effect on new anthropologists entering the field, because as they read previous ethnographies of this sort, they took these as proper models for their own writing. In just this way, once it is established, a genre shapes future inquiry—until someone begins to question the values and assumptions the genre embodies.

That kind of questioning in the last two or three decades has led some anthropologists to write very different ethnographies from those that were written in the early twentieth century. Many recent ethnographies are characterized by their concern with the ethnographer's subjectivity, with the unavoidably interpretive nature of observation, with what can't be observed and therefore can't be interpreted and recounted, with the constructed nature of the stories the ethnographer tells, and with the role of metaphor, style, and other rhetorical devices used in writing the ethnography. In short, as anthropologists have become more aware of the rhetorical nature of their writing, their writing has become more self-aware and, many would say, more honest. Anthropologists have always tried to make true claims; now they seem to be more conscious that their claims to truth can be only partial and contingent. These changes in the genre of ethnography will now inevitably shape how the next generation of anthropologists will approach their own inquiry.

This complex interaction between methods of inquiry and rhetorical genres means that for you, as a student majoring in a social science discipline, learning to read and especially to write in your field's genres is a way of becoming a full-fledged member of that field. But while reading widely in professional journals and imitating what you read may be an important first step, there is more to learning to compose in social science genres than just reading and imitating. Learning to compose in these genres successfully is actually a matter of being socialized into the field, of internalizing its assumptions about knowledge and how it is created. Some of this socialization happens without your thinking about it; it takes many years and gradually prepares you to become an active participant in the professional conversation that the genres were developed to carry on.

In this sense, learning to write for a *particular* social science discipline is a process that runs beyond the boundaries of this book or the time you may consciously devote to it in one course. All this book can do is teach you to examine how genres shape and are shaped by the kinds of inquiry your discipline is engaged in, so that you can be more conscious of how to compose its rhetoric successfully, and so that you can become more aware of the assumptions embodied in that rhetoric. These assumptions are not neutral; they reflect the values of the disciplines that created them. Sometimes these values and assumptions are (or, perhaps should be) challenged and changed. Anyone who wants to change them, however, must first know the discipline's rhetoric well enough to mount an effective challenge.

THE INFLUENCE OF GENRES ON WRITERS

As you learn to write as a professional in your discipline, the particular subjects you write about and the genres you write in also construct you as a person. In other words, the genres of your field offer you a role to play, a persona to inhabit as you write, and a stance to take toward your audience and the material you are writing about. Even though you are an individual with a unique past and personality, your individuality has been constructed by the various social forces you have encountered in your life—your family, your peer group, your community, schools, church, clubs, teams, the mass media, and many other influences. In each of these networks of relationships with others and with the objects they are interested in, you have occupied a certain position that teaches you how the network uses language, prompting you to use it in certain ways, too. In joining a professional discipline, you enter into yet another network of relationships sustained in large part by its rhetorical practices. You learn to occupy a position in that network and to use its language yourself to join in the conversation that maintains and furthers the discipline's projects. By becoming aware of how the rhetoric of your field constructs your thinking and your professional persona, you are more likely to control the rhetoric, speaking the language consciously and by choice, that is, rather than letting it "speak you."

COMPOSING COLLABORATIVELY

Another important sense in which composing is a social act is that composing may be done by more than one person. It is fairly common in some of the social sciences for researchers to work in teams—to collaborate. Perhaps some of your professors have assigned collaborative projects in courses you have taken. It is even more common for professionals outside the academy to collaborate on writing tasks, so it is worth understanding how to do it well, as there is a high possibility you will work on teams in your career.

Collaboration can lead to some important advantages: the division of labor, a high degree of individual specialization, collective reasoning and decision making that may be superior to individual thinking, and increased efficiency, resulting in time and money savings. Collaboration also has the potential disadvantages of friction and disagreement among team members, some people not doing their share of the work, incompatibility in writing styles, and—especially for students—difficulty finding time to get together. But these disadvantages need not be part of collaboration if you enter into it understanding the different ways groups can function and if you plan ahead so that you can counteract possible problems.

Researchers (e.g., Ede and Lunsford 1990) who have studied various collaborative groups conclude there is a continuum of possible models with two extremes. At one extreme, the team divides all tasks completely; at the other, the team works together through all phases of the work. As an example of the first, imagine that four students majoring in psychology are assigned to conduct an experiment to determine which of two kinds of peanut butter—one expensive and the other inexpensive—students prefer in a blind taste test. They might divide the labor of running and "writing up" the experiment as follows: Anne goes to the library to find related literature that provides a context for the experiment, and she recruits participants for the experiment. Ben purchases the peanut butter and other materials, prepares the laboratory for the taste tests, and administers the samples to the participants. David is at the lab to record the results and then later analyzes the data. Carla leads the team and coordinates the whole process. After that, Anne writes the introduction to the paper and creates the list of references. Ben writes the methods section. David writes the results section, including the tables, and the discussion section. And Carla takes all the parts, blends them into one finished and edited report, then adds the abstract and title.

This example might be an efficient division of labor and use of time, particularly if each team member is doing the tasks for which he or she has a talent, and if Carla successfully provides the leadership to ensure that the others carry out their roles well. But notice that the final paper might actually be stronger if the whole group, rather than just Carla, got together to join the parts and discuss the best ways of organizing paragraphs or phrasing sentences. Perhaps David, for all his skill in creating tables, has overlooked something important that Ben could help him remember; perhaps Anne will remember something from reading the previous literature that will strengthen the discussion. In other words, a complete division of labor throughout the whole process may not always result in the best product.

In the other extreme model of collaboration, all of the team members work together through all or nearly all phases of conducting the research and writing the report. This is roughly the model that was used by the four psychologists who wrote the influential book *Women's Ways of Knowing*—Mary Field Belenky, Blythe McVicker Clinchy, Nancy Rule Goldberger, and Jill Mattuck Tarule (an excerpt from their book appears at the end of Chapter 6). For their research, they interviewed 135 women at length, using a set of questions that they had previously constructed together. Usually only one researcher was present at each interview, as the interviews lasted from two to five hours, and they took place in different geographical locations (so in this phase there was some division of labor). Each interview was tape-recorded so that the whole team could listen to it; and all of the interviews were transcribed, producing five thousand pages of text that they all read.

To analyze all of these data, the researchers together developed some categories for coding the respondents' statements along certain dimensions; then they read and reread the transcripts, copying out quotations that illustrated various positions along these dimensions. The authors wrote independently but gathered as often as possible to discuss, to question, to rethink, and to rework each other's drafts. Over a period of five years, they shaped their study into a book. Their kind of collaboration is obviously time-consuming, and it can be emotionally draining. But it can also be very satisfying, especially if the group members enjoy working together and find a creative synergy in the give-and-take of lively discussion about ideas they have all become deeply involved in. And the results of such a dialogic form of collaboration are often far superior to what one person working alone could create.

Obviously, there are many ways to combine the two extremes of collaborating: A team can divide some phases of the work of creating and writing a paper but work as a group on other phases. Regardless of how the process is managed, here are some important guidelines for student groups to follow in order to make the experience of collaborating more successful.[1]

---

[1] Adapted from Chapter 2 of *Learning Together: An Introduction to Collaborative Learning* by Tori Haring-Smith. Copyright © 1993 HarperCollins College Publishers. Used by permission of Addison-Wesley Educational Publishers, Inc.

GUIDELINES FOR WORKING IN GROUPS

1. **Keep the group small enough to succeed.** Since academic group projects usually require some meetings outside of class, your chances of coordinating individual schedules are greater if the group is small. Having more than three or four people in a group usually increases the difficulty in finding a time when all the group members are free to meet.

2. **Get acquainted as individuals and determine each other's strengths.** Whether you choose your team members or your teacher assigns you to work together, you need to assess what talents you possess individually and collectively. Don't be shy about stating the special skills you possess: if you're a whiz in statistics, say so; if you can edit and proofread skillfully, everyone will be relieved to hear it. Each member should be equally forthright about any limitations that will affect his or her performance. For example, if you have a heavy course load and a part-time job, you should say so, as this will affect when the group can meet and the number or kinds of tasks you can be responsible for. It is almost always helpful to choose a leader, someone who will accept the responsibility of keeping the group on task and who can also monitor each person's performance and help motivate everyone. Exchange phone numbers at this stage, too, so that you can call each other if necessary.

3. **Lay the ground rules your group will abide by.** One such rule ought to concern how group meetings will be conducted so that each member will have relatively equal opportunities to speak. Another rule should address what you will do as a group if someone fails to do their assignments on time, or adequately, or even fails to do them at all. If your instructor will have you evaluate each other at the end of the collaborative process, he or she will probably provide evaluation criteria. But as a group you can also determine fair standards that you will all apply equally in judging each other's contributions as high or low quality. Having these rules and standards should help everyone proceed from the same assumptions and, later, make judgments about each member's performance. The rules can also state actions you will take, if necessary, if someone doesn't do their share. Having rules means that these actions are less likely to be construed as personal attacks and more as simple compliance with decisions the group made at the outset. For example, you might decide ahead of time that if all group members do their assigned part completely and well by the deadline that you will tell your teacher you all deserve the same grade. However, if someone's part is late, incomplete, or poorly done, the rest of the group will report to the teacher that the person should receive fewer points or a lower grade for their work (the severity of the penalty would have to be determined by agreement among the group members).

4. **Analyze the task you have designed or been assigned to do.** To analyze the task, ask questions such as these: Will you be conducting interviews, an experiment, or a survey? Will you be reading and analyzing documents? Will you be carrying out observations in natural settings? Will you be doing library research? How long will the eventual paper be? Has the teacher specified parts that it must have, or will you determine its organization completely? If you will determine the organization, spend some time thinking about what the eventual document might contain. Break the task into subtasks and discuss whether each should be accomplished by an individual, a pair of people, or more. Determine together a fair division of the labor, assigning tasks according to each person's particular abilities and limitations.

5. **Create a schedule for completing the subtasks.** Sometimes your teacher may impose a schedule for completing sub-tasks; other times, only a final deadline is given. If there is only a final deadline, set realistic intermediate deadlines that will help you monitor your progress and keep the work moving along at a steady rate. Remember that some delays are inevitable—a book you need will be checked out of the library, a group member may become sick and unable to finish an assignment, or the computer printer won't work. To help compensate for these setbacks, you can "pad" the schedule with a little extra time to allow you to meet the final deadline without too much stress.

6. **Hold regular meetings during the entire process to evaluate progress.** Your teacher may allow some class time for your group to work on its project, but even so you will probably need to meet at other times to keep the work moving along successfully. The group leader will need to be especially responsible to schedule meetings when all members can attend and to determine whether each person has completed their assignments. At these meetings you can share problems you have encountered and seek the advice of the others. You can also discuss what you have learned so far and begin developing the actual contents and form of the eventual paper.

7. **Draft, revise, and edit the paper as collaboratively as possible.** Once you have collected the data, found the evidence, or otherwise created what you will use in your paper, spend some time discussing as a group what it all means, and what the central arguments will be in your paper. Discuss and agree on how the paper should be organized. Then decide how you will create the first draft. Will you all get together around the computer at someone's apartment with plenty of pizza and soft drinks to keep you going? Will you work individually, each one taking responsibility for a different section? Will some of you work individually, while others work in pairs? Or will you find another solution?

If you choose to work individually on different sections, try to arrange for everyone to prepare their part on a computer, using a common word processing program, as this will make it easier to merge the parts later. After putting together a draft, either by group composing or by merging individual parts, print each member a copy and allow a day or two for everyone to review it and think about it. Then meet again to discuss how to revise it—what to cut, what to add, how to rearrange—and to focus on the details of editing—sentence structure, word choice, and punctuation. After agreeing on what the final draft should be like, assign one or more members to produce it, making sure that the best proofreader and editor in the group will be available to okay the final draft. Everyone should chip in to cover whatever costs are incurred—for high quality paper, laser printing, color graphics, and binding, for example.

8. **Evaluate the performance of your group and of individual members.** Your teacher may assign each of you to evaluate your group as a whole and each individual in it. In fact, if your teacher will grade your work, his or her evaluation will probably be affected by the way you grade each other. Even if no evaluation has been assigned, you may want to meet as a group one final time and consider how the process and the project might have been improved. This would be particularly important in a course in which your group will do more than one collaborative project. At the very least you should make some mental notes of what was successful and what was not so helpful. You can likely count on collaborating again in the future either in college or in your career.

GUIDELINES FOR INDIVIDUALS

In addition to the preceding advice for the entire group, here are some guidelines for you to follow as an individual so that you can contribute to the progress of any collaborative project you may be part of.

1. **Communicate with group members openly, honestly, and tactfully.** Your ideas are as important as anyone else's, so don't be shy about sharing them. Openly request the opportunity to be part of the group's conversation. If your other courses demand a lot of your time at the start of the project, you could offer to do more work at the end of the project to compensate. But don't promise to do what you can't possibly accomplish just to make a favorable impression. Tactfully express your concerns rather than attacking a team member's ideas or personality. Don't say bluntly, "That's a bad idea," but explain *why* you are concerned about the idea; for example, say, "That sounds like it will take more time than we have," or phrase your concern as a question: "Do you think we have time to do all that?"

2. **Listen carefully to other group members.** Listening is more than just being quiet when others are talking. It is also important to concentrate on what they are saying, watching their faces and body movements for clues to their meanings, their attitudes, and their feelings. Paraphrase what someone else has just said by asking, "Do you mean that…?" Paraphrasing is especially important when you are not sure of the other's idea or when you think you may disagree.

3. **Learn and practice the art of negotiation.** Don't automatically shy away from conflicts. Conflicts can be productive if they are followed by negotiation rather than a stalemate or a victory for one side and a defeat for the other side. Negotiation resolves conflict by first finding the areas of agreement and disagreement and then by working toward a "win-win" solution acceptable to all. Negotiation requires patience, tact, and skill, as well as a willingness to compromise sometimes in order to help the group reach a consensus. Avoid being so attached to your own ideas that you won't even consider the other person's point of view. In fact, you could even try advocating another person's position for a few minutes. This kind of empathetic role-playing can sometimes help you see the value of or at least the reasons for another person's point of view. By negotiating your way through conflicts, you and the other members of your group can all feel as if you "own" the solutions and the final product your group creates.

4. **Be a person whom others can count on.** Everyone's worst fear of collaboration (or worst experience with it) involves someone who is uncooperative or uncommunicative, someone unwilling to do their fair share, someone who agrees and then fails to do their assigned part, or someone who does such a poor job that the other group members feel penalized. Analyze yourself and your past performance in groups and determine if you have a tendency to be that kind of person. If you are the type of person who strongly prefers to work alone or who has had disastrous experiences working with others, you might ask your teacher if you can do the assignment alone or with people you already know and with whom you are likely to work well. But consider, too, that it may be time to change some of your habits and make a more determined effort to be a team player. Remember that the ability to work well with others is highly valued in the workplace and in graduate and professional schools, so to achieve your educational and career goals, now may be the right time for you to learn how to be an effective collaborator.

AVOIDING PLAGIARISM AND GIVING CREDIT

In addition to full-scale collaborations, composing may have partially collaborative dimensions at any point. Even when you are not working on a jointly authored paper, for example, you would be wise to seek responses from others about your writing. One helpful strategy in prewriting is simply to discuss your ideas with others, like a friend, a roommate, a mentor, or a tutor in your campus writing center. You can invite these same people to intervene in your composing process at the drafting, revising, and editing stages as well. It is particularly helpful to get a classmate's or tutor's response after you have a complete draft and before you begin to revise. Often, after you have spent hours on your writing, your paper seems so clear to you that you can't see its flaws. Or you know a part of your paper has problems, but you can't think how to fix them. A careful peer critic or tutor can offer you a reading that reveals where your paper doesn't communicate as well as you might think it does. Your teacher may even make this kind of review a mandatory part of composing your papers before you submit them for a grade.

In seeking feedback from others about your work, you are participating in a practice that is widespread in all professions. Virtually no professional in the social sciences or other fields publishes writing that hasn't been thoroughly reviewed by peers and then revised for improvement. There is a line to be observed, however, between acceptable and unethical use of others' help in your writing. You should ask others only for advice and instruction, not to do your work for you. As you probably know by now, using someone else's ideas or words without giving them credit is plagiarism. Buying an already written paper or hiring someone to write your papers is a serious breach of honesty that, if discovered, will result not only in academic and professional penalties but also, more significantly, in your failure to learn and develop your abilities.

You may certainly seek the help of others, however, as long as you accept the final responsibility for each phase of composing any paper you are assigned to write alone. If the form of the paper permits, you should graciously acknowledge the assistance others have given you—for example, in a preface, footnote, or letter of transmittal. If someone's contribution to your work turns out, in the end, to be more significant than simply offering advice and instruction, if they provide you with data to use in your paper or actually write some parts of your paper, for example, it may be more appropriate to consider listing them as a co-author. In all facets of collaborating with others—whether the collaboration is limited or full-scale—respecting others and attending to professional and ethical standards should be uppermost in your thoughts and actions.

SUGGESTIONS FOR DISCUSSION OR WRITING

1. What times and places, habits, or rituals seem to contribute to your being able to write well? What happens if you try to write at other times or in other places than the ones you are most comfortable with?

2. What kind of prewriting, if any, do you typically do for a writing assignment? Does it vary with the nature of the assignment? If so, how? What

kinds of prewriting described in this chapter were new for you? Which of them would you like to try and why?

3. Have you ever kept a research log or journal? What sorts of things did you write in it? Did any kind of larger paper result from it? If so, describe how you synthesized your entries into a coherent piece of writing.

4. How many drafts of a paper do you typically write? How much and what kind of revising do you do? How confident are you about editing a paper? Do you seek the advice of others before revising and editing?

5. Do you compose with a computer? What advantages do you find to using it? What disadvantages?

6. This chapter stresses that composing has a powerful social dimension to it. Which of the ideas presented here were new for you? Which were most interesting? Reflecting upon past writing experiences, can you see how social factors influenced how you composed? How, if at all, have this chapter and your own reflections changed how you think about writing?

7. This chapter discusses genre as a socially constructed way of responding to a recurring rhetorical need. What is an important genre in your discipline? What are its characteristics, for example, what are the typical parts, the usual style, and what sorts of arguments are made in this genre? What seems to be the recurring rhetorical need that prompted the evolution of the genre?

8. Have you ever been assigned to collaborate with classmates on a paper or project? If so, what were the advantages? What were the disadvantages? What ways can you see to prevent some of the problems often associated with collaboration?

REFERENCES

Belenky, Mary Field, Blythe McVicker Clinchy, Nancy Rule Goldberger, and Jill Mattuck Tarule. *Women's ways of knowing: The development of self, voice, and mind*. New York: Basic Books, 1986.

Clifford, James. 1986. Introduction: Partial truths. In *Writing culture: The poetics and politics of ethnography*, ed. James Clifford and George E. Marcus, 1–26. Berkeley: University of California Press.

Ede, Lisa, and Andrea Lunsford. 1990. *Singular texts/plural authors: Perspectives on collaborative writing*. Carbondale and Edwardsville, IL: Southern Illinois University Press.

Haring-Smith, Tori. 1993. *Learning together: An introduction to collaborative learning*. New York: HarperCollins.

Miller, Carolyn. 1984. Genre as social action. *Quarterly Journal of Speech* 70: 151–167.

II

CREATING AND WRITING ABOUT NEW KNOWLEDGE

In the next six chapters you will learn about methods of creating new knowledge in the social sciences. Chapter 3 provides an overview of quantitative and qualitative research methods and a discussion of the ethical obligations of the social scientist. Chapters 4 through 8 describe several different methods commonly used in the social sciences and illustrate the kinds of documents that usually result from each method. As you read these chapters, you will learn about methods of interpreting documents, interviewing, observing, surveying, and experimenting. It is not possible in a book this size to give more than a brief introduction to each method; it is particularly not feasible to discuss the statistical tests and procedures that are important components of some of these methods. Other courses, both undergraduate and graduate, will provide you with the detailed knowledge about methods and statistics that will enable you to become a full-fledged researcher in the social sciences.

But such courses may often skimp on teaching you how to write about the knowledge you create with methods; they often assume that "writing up" what you know is a simple process of packaging facts in words. In contrast, this book is based on the assumption that "writing up" begins the moment you decide what question you want to answer or what hypothesis you want to test. So this part of the book focuses on analyzing methods as a kind of rhetorical invention and on helping you understand how to create documents in the genres social scientists typically use to present persuasive arguments about the data or evidence these methods produce. You will find in this section both professional and student examples of documents that were created from the application of the various research methods.

3

RESEARCH METHODS, WRITING, AND ETHICS

RESEARCHING IS PART OF WRITING

If the goal of social science writing, as asserted in Chapter 1, is to achieve the widest possible agreement about some facet of whatever reality was investigated, then the documents that social scientists write are more likely to be persuasive when the social scientists have used a method their readers find acceptable. If scientists do not follow the procedures and meet the standards that their colleagues find persuasive, it really won't matter how eloquently they write the final document about their research. Their rhetoric will not be persuasive if the evidence it is based on has been gathered sloppily or interpreted carelessly. Since good writing in the social sciences begins with finding or creating the evidence that will eventually be used in the document, using a research method is a kind of prewriting—yet a highly structured kind, much more rigorous and time-consuming than, say, freewriting or brainstorming.

If you think of methods in this way, you should be more conscious throughout the research process of the paper you will write. You should begin thinking about the rhetorical situation for this paper even as you plan your research. For example, you should consider your audience from the first. What evidence will be sufficient to persuade them that your conclusions are reasonable and acceptable? What kinds of data will they expect in order to be convinced that your hypothesis was correct? The more you know about what your audience will require as sufficient proof, the more careful you will be as you plan your research, collect evidence or data, and consider the most plausible ways of interpreting it.

You should also be thinking about the genre of the paper you will be writing. What things are usually a part of such a paper—a review of literature? Quotations from primary sources? Vivid descriptions? Detailed narratives? Tables and graphs? The results of statistical tests? A bibliography? The better you understand the genre conventions of the paper you will be writing, the more likely it is that you will gather all the information you will need to write it. Instead of thinking of research as something you do first and then "write up" later, you should think of writing as something you are doing all along as you research—from the time you first formulate your question and choose a method to the time that you proofread your paper.

METHODS AS DISCIPLINED INQUIRY

A good definition of method would be simply "disciplined inquiry." This definition implies not only that the inquiry is focused and rigorous, but also that it is sanctioned by a discipline because it meets the discipline's assumptions about what knowledge is and its standards for judging claims of knowledge. The formalization of methods of inquiry is largely responsible for making the sciences what they are today. Although humans have probably always carried out intuitive or informal sorts of experiments that helped them learn how to preserve foods, dye fabrics, or make bricks, for example, it was only in the nineteenth century that the experimental method began to be considered a special form of inquiry that produces a special kind of knowledge called *science*. Before then, the word *science* could be applied to any field of study, including the arts, humanities, and theology; it simply meant *knowledge*. Now, however, we generally consider science a special kind of knowledge that has been created in an especially rigorous way so that its claims will have widespread and long-lasting validity.

When we realize that methods are human inventions and, as such, are not necessarily perfect at revealing all that we would like to know, we start to see that the claims of science also may not be perfect. This does not stop the quest for rigor, however. Methods are constantly refined by repeated use and by the criticism of peers in the scientific community so that the methods will yield ever more reliable results. Experimental scientists have refined their method, for example, to remove as much doubt as possible from claims of knowledge by focusing on certain variables in the complex flux of events surrounding them. By controlling other variables and their own biases, experimental scientists attempt to manipulate the selected variables to establish cause-and-effect relationships and then state laws that can then be used to predict future behavior. As a result of this remarkable endeavor to make experimental inquiry rigorous, the popular view of science is that it is knowledge produced by the experimental method.

However, the experimental method is not the only method of science, especially not the only one used by social scientists. Some social scientists long ago rejected the experiment as the one and only way of establishing valid claims of knowledge. For one thing, they point out, the experiment is simply not appropriate to answer some kinds of questions. Also, because experiments focus on selected variables to study while controlling others, they create artificial situations unlike those that exist naturally. If the object of the social sciences is to describe human behavior, they claim, then experiments may not be appropriate because, by their design, they may alter the very behavior that is of interest.

Some critics of the experimental method favor studying human behavior in natural, not controlled, settings; they reject the premise of control in favor of observing the multiplicity of factors that influence behavior. Like the experimentalists, their goal is also to question and to observe, to describe, and to generalize. But they have created other methods that will permit them to seek knowledge in the ways they consider most likely to produce meaningful findings. Each of the methods that social scientists have used in the twentieth century is rigorous in its own way, and each produces knowledge that may bear the label of *science* in the honorific sense. Each method has its strengths and its limitations; each is suited to answering some kinds of questions about reality and not others. To the extent that a method represents a discipline's consensus about the most rigorous way to investigate the questions that the discipline pursues—to that extent the method is considered reliable. And if a method is followed carefully, the knowledge it produces will be considered valid.

QUANTITATIVE AND QUALITATIVE METHODS

Methods are usually divided into two categories: quantitative and qualitative. As their names imply, quantitative methods yield data that can be expressed numerically, and qualitative methods produce data that must be described by their qualities or distinguishing characteristics. Two methods that are often quantitative are experiments and surveys; two that are generally qualitative are interviews and observations.

But there may be some overlap between these two categories of methods. For example, a questionnaire might ask both multiple-choice and open-ended questions. The answers to the multiple-choice questions can be counted and expressed as numbers; then other numerical operations can be performed on those numbers, yielding quantitative data. The answers to the open-ended questions, on the other hand, are qualitative data; they might have to be read several times to see what general patterns or themes emerge. Similarly, observation in natural settings is generally qualitative, with the observer attempting to record and describe what he or she observes. But the observer might also count certain repeated behaviors and then perform additional statistical operations on these data. So a written report of research might contain both quantitative and qualitative results.

Proponents of quantitative methods sometimes assume that these methods are superior because numbers are generally thought to be "hard" and factual, to have a solid and unambiguous meaning. It is often said that numerical data "speak for themselves" and require little or no interpretation the way that the "soft" and more "messy" qualitative methods do. Adherents of qualitative methods, on the other hand, often think these methods are superior because of the rich data they produce. For them, the details and the subtle differences in the data are precisely what is most interesting, and they relish examining the data and using their interpretive powers to make sense of them. They might view quantitative methods as too superficial, arguing that, in fact, numbers tell us very little about *why* people act or think as they do; like qualitative data, numbers have to be interpreted, too, in order to be meaningful. Despite these differences of opinion, both kinds of methods are valuable, and social scientists should be aware of the strengths and limitations of each in order to choose methods that are appropriate to answer the kinds of questions they want to ask.

A strength of quantitative methods is that they can be used with a large number of participants. If the participants in an experiment or the respondents to a survey are numerous enough and if they were randomly selected, therefore representative of the larger population from which they are drawn, then the results of the experiment or survey are said to be *generalizable*. That is, even without surveying or experimenting on the whole population, the results will presumably hold true for the whole population the sample represents. Another characteristic of quantitative methods that might be considered a strength or a limitation, depending on your viewpoint, is that experiments and surveys are usually designed and then pilot tested or repeated until all the "bugs" are worked out. With this kind of careful advance planning, surveys and experiments can yield very precise answers to highly focused questions. The data collected can often be quickly analyzed using computer software that will test relationships between any of the variables the researchers are investigating. The significant investment of time to plan and refine the study at the beginning is usually compensated for by speed in obtaining results.

Yet because they often require special equipment, computer time and expertise, or printing and mailing, experiments and surveys may cost more to conduct than many qualitative studies. Another limitation of quantitative methods stems from the way they transform data into numbers, particularly into means (numerical averages). The emphasis on the mean performance of a group effaces the individuality of the participants. Depth of description may thus be sacrificed to the desire to make broad generalizations.

In contrast, a notable strength of qualitative methods, such as interviews, observations, case studies, and analyses of documents, is that they allow researchers to describe in depth the individuals and circumstances they study. Although qualitative research is also carefully planned, it is not so precisely scripted that the researcher has no chance to pursue interesting questions that may arise during the investigation; qualitative methods offer much opportunity to branch, probe, and question. Rather than attempt to remove or minimize the researcher's subjectivity through rigorous control, qualitative methods actually foreground the subjectivity of the researcher as someone with an active, questioning mind, someone who makes informed decisions throughout the whole process of gathering and interpreting data.

Perhaps a drawback to qualitative research is that it is generally time-consuming to carry out well, so it usually includes fewer participants than surveys and experiments do. Although the texts that result from qualitative methods may contain many interesting observations and valid inferences, because they are typically based on observations of only a few participants, they are usually not considered generalizable to a larger population. Nevertheless, even with few participants, qualitative methods yield much data that must be laboriously recorded and transcribed, read and pondered, coded and categorized. Although qualitative research can often be done locally at little cost, it can also be expensive if it involves travel or special equipment.

It is good to be able to appreciate both qualitative and quantitative methods, for even though you may be inclined in your field to prefer certain methods over others, you will no doubt be influenced all your life by knowledge that is created by other methods. Understanding all methods, with their strengths and limitations, will help you to be a more critical reader of all kinds of research that you will encounter as a professional or as a citizen. Table 3–1 sums up the differences between quantitative and qualitative methods.

TABLE 3-1 A Comparison of Quantitative and Qualitative Methods

	Types	Advantages	Limitations
Quantitative Methods	Experiments Surveys	Possibility of large sample size Generalizability and breadth High degree of control	Loss of particularity Possibly high costs
Qualitative Methods	Interviews Observations Documents	Rich data Particularity and depth Large scope for interpretation	Low generalizability Overwhelming data Time consumption

ETHICAL CONSIDERATIONS IN DOING RESEARCH

Using Human Participants

Since social scientists are interested in human behavior and human institutions, they must naturally study other human beings when they conduct their experiments, surveys, interviews, or observations. Yet human beings are not like the rocks, plants, or animals that a physical or natural scientist might study. A geologist can climb around on a pile of rocks pretty much at will, chipping off pieces to take back to the laboratory. An agronomist needn't obtain consent from two strains of corn before cross-breeding them. And a zoologist doesn't worry much about rats' right to privacy (although the zoologist is expected to treat the rats humanely).

Obviously, humans are capable of much more complex kinds of behavior than rocks, corn, and rats. They also have rights and needs that social scientists must respect in their research. In fact, to prevent abuses of human participants in research, laws have been enacted in the United States to prevent physical, social, emotional, mental, or financial damage to any participant in a study and to protect their privacy. In addition, other laws restrict the use of certain vulnerable groups in social science research. University-related research conducted with human participants, including research conducted by students, must comply with these laws, whether it is conducted on campus or off. These laws ensure that social scientists will meet high professional and ethical standards in conducting their research.

Institutional Review Boards

In the 1970s the U.S. government issued regulations requiring all institutions that receive federal research funds to create and maintain committees that would oversee all research involving human participants. These committees are called Institutional Review Boards for the Protection of Human Participants, or *IRBs* for short. By now, on virtually all college campuses there is an IRB that is charged with reviewing and approving research involving human participants to make sure that it complies with the laws. You should find out what office or persons on your campus have been designated to review research, so that if you decide to conduct research involving human participants, you can comply with applicable policies and procedures. Typically, the IRB will require that you submit a formal proposal to conduct research with human participants. The IRB's focus in reviewing your proposal will be on the ethical and legal issues that may arise from it, rather than on its technical merits. You are under an ethical obligation to disclose everything you plan to do in your research and, once your proposal is approved, not to vary from your plan without seeking additional approval for the changes.

The laws mandate four conditions that must be met in social science research: confidentiality, informed consent, minimal risk, and protection of vulnerable groups.

Confidentiality.   First, researchers must ensure the *confidentiality of human participants*. On questionnaires, respondents generally are not asked to give their names, so their anonymity is easily preserved. However, researchers frequently ask respondents to give demographic information about themselves. Sometimes the researchers may know who gave certain answers, but they must ensure that others can't trace any answers to a specific person. Experiments and observations can also be conducted with little or no need to learn participants' names. If names seem necessary when investigators are writing the report of their research, they may use pseudonyms. Reports of interviews are more likely to require names, so the interviewer must determine whether the informants want the interviewer to use their real names or pseudonyms. If at all possible, a report of an interview for an oral history should include the informant's real name. Interviews with public figures—elected officials or other people who hold a public trust—would also include real names. Interviews conducted for the purpose of identifying attitudes and behavior would more likely use pseudonyms, since *who* said something is not as important as *what* they said.

Informed consent.   Second, human participants involved in research must know enough about the purposes of the study to give their *informed consent* before they participate. If you conduct an experiment, you must obtain written informed consent. If you conduct surveys and interviews, the participants can imply their consent by completing the survey or the interview, but you must still inform them of the purposes of the research so that they can choose whether or not to proceed. If you conduct unobtrusive observations of people going about their daily lives (e.g., counting how many people come to a complete stop at a stop sign), you are not required to obtain informed consent. However, if your observation somehow obtrudes in a participant's life so that they are aware of it, you must obtain informed consent.

Minimal risk.   Third, researchers must be able to show that participants will face *no risks of physical or emotional harm greater than those encountered in daily life*. Surveys might pose some risk if they ask a sensitive personal question, but this risk is usually neutralized because respondents may choose not to answer that question, and their responses are kept anonymous anyway. Experiments are the most likely to pose some emotional risk because they sometimes temporarily deceive participants. If the participants knew exactly what the investigators were trying to discover, then they might behave in a way that would alter the findings. By creating a ruse, the experimenters are better able to control how the participants act.

While some social scientists have argued that there should be no deception in research, others have maintained that temporary deception may be justified if the knowledge sought is important enough to justify the deception. The general consensus is that researchers should not tell participants something that is untrue, but they may temporarily withhold some information regarding the aim of the study. If the participants in an experiment are given general, yet still accurate, information, and if participation in the study does not pose a risk of significant emotional or physical harm, an IRB would likely approve it as meeting ethical standards *provided* the researchers debrief the participants afterward to inform them fully of the purposes of the experiment.

Protection of vulnerable groups. Fourth, the laws also carefully regulate and insist on strict monitoring of research conducted with the following *vulnerable groups*:

- People who are ill or physically disabled
- People who are institutionalized, in hospitals, jails, and prisons
- People who are mentally incompetent
- Those under 18 years of age (minors)
- Those over 65 years of age
- Pregnant women

RESEARCH THAT QUALIFIES FOR EXEMPT REVIEW

Research proposals submitted to an IRB usually fall into one of three categories: (1) exempt review; (2) expedited review; and (3) full board review. Since this textbook is introductory, it will focus on the least sensitive kind of human participants research, that which qualifies for exempt review and approval. Exempt status means that the full Institutional Review Board does not need to convene to review a research proposal. Instead, approval may be granted by someone whom the IRB designates to act for them or by a subcommittee of people who understand the ethical and legal standards that must be met. If you wish to do more sensitive kinds of research than that which will be described in this book, you should consult with your campus IRB to learn about research restrictions, the time required for approval, and other requirements you must comply with. You should also discuss your plans with a professor in your major field, because you will probably be required to have a faculty sponsor.

In order for research with human participants to qualify for exempt status, it must meet the following criteria:

- It must be nontherapeutic. That is, it must not be designed to produce a diagnostic, preventive, or therapeutic benefit to the participants.

- The data must be recorded in such a way as to **protect the identities of the participants.**
- There must be **no risk of criminal or civil liability** to the investigator or to his or her institution, if a participant's responses became known outside the boundaries of the research project itself.
- The research must **not deal with private aspects of the participants' behavior,** such as sexual practices or illegal drug use.

After meeting the above criteria, exempt research proposals are further defined as those in which the study of human participants is limited to one or more of the following:

- Research conducted in an educational setting, such as research on classroom management, pedagogy, or curriculum.
- Research involving the use of educational tests, so long as the participants can't be identified.
- Research involving the use of experiments, surveys, interviews, observations, or publicly available data, so long as the data do not lead to identification of any participants.

Although all of the preceding may seem like a formidable list of restrictions on research, there is still opportunity for you to use methods to answer interesting questions and thereby gain valuable practice in researching and writing. As you read the next five chapters, you will begin to think of questions that you can answer using social science methods. You will learn how to plan a research project. If you plan one that includes human participants, you will also need to prepare a proposal and seek approval before proceeding. Your campus IRB probably has a set of instructions and forms for you to fill out as part of a proposal. Chapter 11 presents an example of a complete proposal for research with human participants; by studying it, you will gain a sense of how a researcher must demonstrate compliance with the regulations that govern this kind of research. (Be aware, however, that the kind of proposal required on your campus may differ from the model presented in Chapter 11.)

PLAGIARISM AND FRAUD

In addition to meeting legal and ethical standards that prevent abuse of human participants, researchers in the social sciences must meet other ethical standards common to all professions. Two of the most important are not plagiarizing and not reporting fraudulent research results.

Plagiarism. Social science research usually builds on previous research; in fact, most social science documents review previous studies that attempted to answer questions related to those of the present investigation. Usually, the previous research is presented in summary fashion. Occasionally, however, some studies are reviewed at more length, and it becomes necessary to paraphrase or quote parts of the original research. In such situations, you must be careful to observe all the accepted conventions of paraphrasing, quoting, and documenting the previous research (see Chapters 9 and 20). You are not free to borrow someone's ideas or language without citing the author; if you do so, you are implying that you thought of those ideas and created those words yourself. While it may seem a trivial thing to borrow a few ideas or words without acknowledgment, it is a serious breach of professional integrity; and if it is discovered that you have plagiarized, there are serious consequences, similar to those following from the discovery of fraud.

Fraud. Fraud in social science research is reporting data that are fabricated (not actually obtained through the application of a method) or data that have been altered somewhat in order to provide more clear-cut conclusions. Data might be altered by conveniently leaving out findings that are inconsistent with the hypothesis or by altering numbers a bit in order to obtain a particular level of statistical significance. Some researchers may feel strong pressure to report data that is somewhat or even completely fraudulent, particularly if they have a lot at stake. For example, young researchers just beginning their careers may feel the need to publish as much as possible quickly, so they may cut corners to get results that are publishable; their promotion or grant funding may depend on successful research that finds its way to print quickly. Similarly, students wanting a good grade in a course or trying to complete a thesis for graduation may be tempted to "cook" the data a little to have a more impressive study.

THE CONSEQUENCES OF ETHICAL LAPSES

You should scrupulously avoid plagiarism and fraud in any degree. You may get away with either for a time, but if you plan to make your career as a researcher, you are foolish if you think you will never get caught. As Chapter 1 explained, the social sciences are communal and collaborative enterprises. As members of these fields work to create knowledge that will advance human understanding, each person depends on work that others have done. Each person owes a debt to earlier researchers who have established reliable knowledge and pointed the way to new research; this debt is acknowledged through proper citation of earlier work. Others in your field will have read much of the same research as you, and sooner or later they will realize when you have borrowed information without proper acknowledgment. Your failure to give credit where it is due will result in a weakening of the trust that makes a social enterprise like science possible.

Like plagiarism, fraudulent research weakens trust. Your peers will trust that whatever knowledge they borrow from you or others meets the highest professional standards of using methods and interpreting data. If your peers ignorantly attempt to base new research on earlier fraudulent work, it is like building a house on sand. Far from being small or one-time breaches of honesty, fraudulent studies can have a ripple effect throughout the whole research community. Perhaps this is why the social penalties are so severe when plagiarism and fraud are uncovered: These ethical lapses waste other people's time and often their money, thereby consuming their good will and slowing the progress of the whole community of researchers.

Social scientists whose plagiarism and fraud are discovered face not only the tarnishing of their reputations and the loss of their peers' respect, but also the loss of grant funding and sometimes their jobs as well. Students who plagiarize or commit fraud indicate to their professors that they are not ready to be trusted to enter into the community of professionals. Whatever your status, there is too much at stake to cut corners. It is far better to take the time to meet the ethical standards your field has established because they are there to protect everyone's best interests.

4

INTERPRETING DOCUMENTS

Reading and interpreting documents is the primary method of the historian, who could hardly write history without diaries, journals, letters, newspapers, magazines, immigration data, military records, parish registers, ships' passenger lists, and other documents from the past from which to cull facts and piece together an argument. But other social scientists may interpret documents as well. For example, political scientists concerned with theories of government, public policy, and social practices also read and interpret documents—constitutions, manifestos, court rulings, laws, census data, or the writings of Machiavelli, John Locke, Alexis de Tocqueville, and James Madison, among others. Some psychiatrists or psychologists may collect and interpret the writings of clients in therapy.

Sociologists may also interpret documents that relate to social behavior; this kind of research is often called *content analysis*. Archaeologists attempt to decipher ancient writings and drawings on papyrus, clay tablets, or canyon walls. Economists may interpret documents composed primarily of numbers, such as gains and losses on the stock exchange, budgets, or reports of the national debt and gross national product. Some historians have also become more interested in statistical data, as they attempt to write about common people and their daily lives rather than only about presidents, kings, and generals and the events they participated in.

INTERPRETATIONS DEPEND ON PRIOR KNOWLEDGE AND ASSUMPTIONS

In interpreting documents according to the methodological standards of their disciplines, social scientists are practicing a highly specialized kind of reading. Although reading may seem to be a very straightforward activity, one that you have probably been doing since you were about five or six years old, when you examine what goes into reading like a historian, a political scientist, a psychologist, a sociologist, an economist, or an archaeologist, you start to see what a complex practice reading is. An ordinary citizen simply reading the daily newspaper draws (often unconsciously) on complex cultural knowledge in order to make sense of a story about strife in Eastern Europe, a description of famine in Africa, or a report of the latest medical findings.

When social scientists read the documents of interest to them, they also draw on the assumptions, the accumulated knowledge, and the interpretive practices they have learned in their disciplines, not to mention their own personal backgrounds and experiences. They are able to discern relationships in and draw conclusions from documents that might mean little to the untrained reader. But even training in a particular discipline is no guarantee that all practitioners will see eye to eye on the meaning or relevance of a particular document. Within a discipline, two readers with different theoretical orientations may interpret the same text differently. For example, a historian with a Marxist orientation will read differently than a feminist historian.

Reading is not simply a process of decoding what a text says. If it were, there would be only one meaning for a given document. Yet, as we know, all kinds of documents, from poems and novels to wills and contracts to the U.S. Constitution, have been interpreted differently. Sometimes disputes about interpretation are settled in court, as in the case of wills and contracts. The meaning of various parts of the U.S. Constitution is also often disputed; frequently, the combined interpretation of just a handful of people determines the course of the nation, as in disputes that are resolved by a 5–4 vote of the Supreme Court. Occasionally, justices of that court have also reversed the decisions of earlier justices, as in the 1954 *Brown* v. *Board of Education* ruling that overturned an 1896 decision permitting racially segregated schools, thus demonstrating that interpretations may change with the times and the attitudes of the people. Sometimes competing readings of a document never are reconciled, as in the case of literary works. Several interpretations of *Huckleberry Finn* are possible, and one cannot be declared absolutely "right," although some interpretations will be more plausible and persuasive than others.

Different interpretations arise because we bring to our reading, just as we do to our observations of the world, our particular personal history, prior knowledge, theoretical positions,. assumptions, biases, and expectations. This is not to say that we can make a document mean anything we want it to—for example, we can't pretend that Lewis Carroll's poem "Jabberwocky" is a recipe for spaghetti sauce. (Well, we could, but we would not succeed in making anything edible from using it as such, and others might question our sanity.) Despite differences in readers, words do have relatively stable meanings and documents do bear a relationship to the worlds in which they were created and which they represent. Thus, part of reading sensitively involves understanding the context of a document and, if possible, the rhetorical situation that produced it. It helps to know who created the document, who the intended audience was, the purpose of the document, what it has reference to, and the words or other symbols used in it. The more we know about all these factors, the more our interpretation will be shaped by them—pushed in a certain direction. And the more that reasonable readers possess a similar understanding of a document's context, rhetorical situation, and the language it is written in, the more likely it is they will interpret it similarly.

STATISTICS MUST ALSO BE INTERPRETED

We often believe that numbers and statistics, unlike documents composed mainly of words, are easier to interpret because numbers are less ambiguous than words. It is true that numbers refer to the size or amount of something; therefore, given precise scales or procedures to follow, two different people asked to weigh, measure, or count the same thing should come up with the same number. Yet the resulting number in itself is often trivial; what the measurement signifies in relationship to other concerns still has to be established.

For example, Richard Herrnstein and Charles Murray, the authors of a book called *The Bell Curve* (1994), examined many years of data collected from administering IQ tests to Americans of all races. One of their findings was that, as a group, African-Americans have scored an average of 15 points lower on these tests than other groups. They interpreted this difference as principally due to the genetic inheritance of this racial group rather than to environmental factors. They then concluded that there is little point in spending tax revenues for social programs that attempt to improve education and job preparation for this group of Americans, because no matter how much is spent, it would not raise intelligence because, as they assert, it is largely inherited.

Other scholars agree that the 15-point difference in average IQ scores exists, but they interpret its significance very differently. They point out that a single factor—intelligence—cannot be the sole reason for the differences in test scores and therefore for differences in social and economic matters. The other factors that can influence a person's success in life are not only environment but also things such as character, personality, motivation, social skills, and common sense. Critics of Herrnstein and Murray note that IQ tests are often culturally biased and fail to measure various forms of intelligence. They conclude that what the average difference shows, if it shows anything, is that our society should create better ways of educating all its members and preparing them for the labor market (see, for example, Gould 1994; Heckman 1995; Brace 1996). As this example shows, numbers and measurements may be very precise, but they are mute about their meaning in relationship to larger issues and questions. Statistical facts don't necessarily speak for themselves; someone must speak for them, interpreting their significance. Because of their beliefs, assumptions, experience, and training, different people often interpret the same statistic differently.

Although reading and interpreting statistics and words is a fundamental practice in all of the social sciences, it is difficult to generalize about how to do it. Much of what you should do when you interpret documents or other artifacts will depend on the questions you are trying to answer and the quickness of your own mind in identifying a bit of evidence as significant or in perceiving a pattern in whatever you examine. A few guidelines for reading and interpreting historical documents are discussed below. Then two examples of interpreting documents follow—one from a professional historian interpreting a diary and one from two students who interpreted statistics they found about the criminal justice system. Both of these examples illustrate how an argument may be constructed out of the evidence found in documents.

WHAT HISTORIES ARE MADE OF

A German historian of the nineteenth century declared that the historian's goal is to write about the past *wie es eigentlich gewesen ist*—as it actually was. Contemporary historians have pretty much agreed that it is impossible to do that, for the past is not recoverable in its entirety. A historical document is a *trace* of the past, evidence that something happened, as a vapor trail in the sky is evidence that a jet plane just flew over. The trace is not the past itself, but it allows you to infer some things about the past. Obviously, the more traces of the past you can find, and the more they say similar things, the more secure you may feel about inferring a conclusion.

But it's also important to keep in mind that each document you examine was itself constructed by someone who was able to record only a fraction of what actually transpired, someone who selected from the multiplicity of events transpiring around them the ones they found important. Not only were particular events selected; they were also interpreted by the person who recorded them according to that person's interests, attitudes, and biases. There is no way to get outside of the accounts you read to check their accuracy to see if they correspond to the reality of the past. You can't check those records' accuracy against the past itself, only against other documents from the same era and other histories of that era.

These two kinds of corroborating sources are usually called primary and secondary. *Primary sources* are those that are closest to the time and the topic under investigation; they include such documents as letters, diaries, journals, memoirs, notes, and statistical data (but they may also include nondocuments such as eyewitnesses, photographs, audiotapes, videotapes, and artifacts). *Secondary sources* interpret primary sources. They are books and articles that scholars have written about the traces of the past they have found. Scholars not only create secondary texts; they also use each other's books and articles to interpret primary sources.

In the excerpt from *A Midwife's Tale* that follows, the main primary source used by the historian Laurel Thatcher Ulrich is Martha Ballard's diary, written in eighteenth-century Maine. Although previous historians looking at Martha Ballard's diary dismissed it for its triviality—its references to mundane tasks such as cooking, cleaning, weaving, and gardening—Ulrich was intrigued, as she says, by its "very dailiness" (9). To help her understand this primary source about domestic life and midwifery in early New England, Ulrich turned to other primary sources, such as court records, letters, newspapers, deeds, and maps. But Ulrich also used many secondary sources, works by other historians that focused on such matters as medical practices in the eighteenth century, the economy of early New England, and marriage and family life in that era. All of the writers of her sources constructed their documents for particular purposes and audiences. Ulrich constructed out of them a new document to serve a different purpose and the needs of other readers. She was awarded a Pulitzer Prize for her skill in interpreting what had seemed to be an insignificant diary and fitting together evidence from it and other sources to shed greater light on our understanding of life in colonial New England.

Ulrich's method illustrates another characteristic of history: It is *intertextual*. It makes connections between many texts—between two primary sources, between a primary and a secondary source, between two secondary sources—connections that have never been made before, creating a new text, one that is based on the sources that informed it but is also a result of the writer's new interpretive angle, selections, and rhetorical choices. A history, far from being like a transparent window revealing the past as it actually was, is more like a web, consisting of strands from other texts, woven together in ways their originators could not have foreseen.

To be persuasive, the writer of a new history must use the sources in ways his or her peers find acceptable. One reason for the extensive footnotes or endnotes and bibliographies in histories is to allow other readers to read the sources themselves and decide if the inferences the writer has made are justifiable. In that sense, documentation is one of the chief rhetorical devices that historians use to make their texts persuasive. By citing other reliable sources, historians show that they have considered all the available evidence and created their interpretations of the past out of real data, not their imaginations. However, like good fiction writers, historians must also be skilled in writing the narrative and descriptive elements of their histories so that they are realistic and convincing. So they do use their imaginations to envision the past and to create believable scenes of people acting in other times and places, though without going beyond what their sources permit them to say. In other words, they are writing stories—but not fiction.

READING HISTORICAL DOCUMENTS

In interpreting documents so that you can create your own new document, here are some steps to follow.

Define the question you are trying to answer about the past and limit it to something you can investigate, given constraints of time, budget, location, and availability of sources. As a student you probably don't have the time and resources to spend on a major project such as reading and explicating an entire diary, but you can still conduct interesting historical research in a limited time using resources available in local libraries, archives, and even your own home. For example, say you want to understand some very recent history: How the image of the computer has changed in mass media from a futuristic, science fiction type of invention to a tool that has today become a standard fixture in education, business, industry and many people's homes. Suppose you have only about four weeks to research this topic, and you have no funding for travel, long distance calls, or acquiring documents, so your main source of materials to answer this question is your campus and local libraries. In this case, you would probably decide to limit your study to just a few magazines that span a time period you could identify as important for investigating this issue. You might phrase your research questions like this: "How have the covers and full-page ads of *PC Computing* and *BYTE* magazines changed in the period from 1977 to 1992? What do the images on covers and in ads reveal about the changing conception and role of the computer in American culture?"

Locate suitable materials that preserve traces of the past (primary documents) or that interpret the past you are interested in (secondary sources). To begin to answer the above questions, you would check campus and local libraries to see if they have complete collections of the two magazines from the time period you want to review. You could also search library holdings to see what previous work, if any, has already been done on this or related topics. By reading any previous research on the general topic, you could avoid simply repeating an earlier study (though you may want to repeat it if you believe the method of the earlier study had flaws that you can avoid in your research). You could also connect what you learn to what other scholars have already established. This might help you to begin your research with some plausible guesses about what you'd find.

Connecting your findings to earlier ones would also shape your paper in such a way that it would contribute to building a body of integrated knowledge on this topic.

Determine the authenticity and reliability of the sources you locate. For historical topics, it's important to determine that the primary documents you are working with are authentic. Some historians have been embarrassed after basing their claims on documents that turned out to be forgeries. You must also determine that the secondary sources you've chosen are reliable, ones that meet high standards for scholarship. (See Chapter 9 for a discussion of how to determine the reliability of sources.) For the example used here, you would want to ask whether the magazines you have chosen to examine represent conceptions of the computer that are typical of the time period you are interested in. If you plan eventually to claim that these two magazines have documented an important shift in society's thinking about the computer, they shouldn't be obscure magazines but mainstream ones that contributed to the shaping of cultural images of the computer. You could check subscription records for the magazines to see how widely read they were, and you could compare them with one another and other computing magazines to see if they all have similar images in them.

Ask the journalist's questions as you read. These questions are *Who?*, *What?*, *Where?*, *When?*, *Why?*, and *How?* With reference to our example of images of the computer, you might ask these questions about the images you are looking at: What images are depicted? How are the images created—mostly by words? Or by a combination of words and pictures? Are the pictures drawings, black and white photos, or color photos? What is emphasized? How much text is there in comparison to photos and drawings? What does the text focus on? Who seems to be the audience the covers and ads aim at? Computer hobbyists? Business people? Families? Can you discern a shift in audience from 1977 to 1992? When in the time period you're studying did the mass-produced personal computer appear? How did its appearance affect the images recorded? By asking and answering questions such as these, you will start to see patterns in the evidence and begin to draw inferences that will become a claim to argue for in your paper.

Analyze systematically. Even limiting your examination to a 15-year period, you may not be able to look at all issues of the two magazines. But you could decide to look at every other issue, every fourth issue, or every tenth issue, so that you would be systematically sampling the available data. You should have some defensible method of selecting and reading the data so that you won't later be accused of simply looking for what you hoped to find while ignoring possible contrary evidence. Full-page ads might appear in several places throughout a magazine, for example, but they are often in the first few pages. To guard against the charge of selecting full-page ads that support your emerging thesis, you might decide to study only the first full-page ad in each issue you examine.

Take notes about what you find and how you interpret it. You should write notes describing what you see, including specific issues and page numbers in your notes so that you can eventually construct the bibliography for your paper. You should also photocopy several representative images to illustrate the trends that you identify. You might even want to construct a table or another way of counting the prevalence of certain repeated images. You would also do well to begin stating tentative interpretations of what these changes in images imply about society's conception of the computer.

WRITING ABOUT HISTORICAL DOCUMENTS

When you have gathered sufficient evidence to begin writing, follow these steps.

1. Outline a Plausible Argument by Asking the Following Questions:

Who is your audience? Ask yourself questions such as these: Who will read your paper? What do they already know about this topic? How hard to persuade will they be? What kind of evidence will be most convincing to them?

What claim will the evidence support? Which of the possible ways of interpreting the evidence seems most likely, most believable? State a tentative thesis, keeping in mind that you can alter it later if you feel your claim is too narrow, too broad, or skewed.

What evidence will best illustrate your claim? For the example used here, you will certainly want to describe the overall impression of the many images you looked at and probably include some photocopies that most strikingly illustrate those impressions. If you have come up with some categories of images that change over time, you might consider using a table or a graph to depict the changes. (See Chapter 17 for a discussion of how to place and refer to illustrations in your writing.) If you have used secondary sources, you must also decide what information you will quote, summarize or paraphrase from them. Remember to document any borrowed information.

What is the best way to organize the evidence to support the claim? A common way of organizing historical accounts is chronologically. But you could also organize by categories of images you've discovered, using some chronological organization within categories. You might also discern themes in the material you amass and organize your paper around them.

What documentation will you need? If you have used only primary sources, you would need at least a bibliography of the magazines and the particular issues that you used. If you have used quotations or reproduced images from your sources, you need to indicate with a footnote, endnote, or in-text reference where each borrowed item appeared originally. Any secondary sources used should also be cited in the bibliography. (See Chapter 20 for details of how to document sources.)

2. DRAFT YOUR PAPER

Actually, you will probably be drafting as you answer the questions given above. Expect to change your mind several times about what to claim, what to include, and how to organize it. Draft and redraft the paper or parts of it as necessary until you have shaped it to reflect the most plausible claims you can make, given the evidence you have.

3. SEEK FEEDBACK

Once you have a complete draft that you are fairly satisfied with, ask someone whose judgment you trust to read it and give you a response as to its overall effectiveness. Better yet, ask more than one person. Listen carefully to their comments, but don't feel compelled to follow everyone's advice. Let your draft sit a few days and reread it yourself, critically. You will no doubt see ways to revise it.

4. REVISE AND EDIT YOUR PAPER

Using the responses of others and your own sense of what the paper still needs, rearrange elements of your paper, delete unnecessary or confusing parts, and add details, transitions, and documentation to make your paper effective and correct.

A PROFESSIONAL EXAMPLE

In 1785, Martha Ballard of Hallowell, Maine, began to keep a diary of her daily life, including a great deal about her work as a midwife and healer among the townspeople. When she died in 1812, Martha Ballard had kept her record for 9,965 days and had attended 816 births over a span of 27 years. The diary includes entries from the seemingly trivial (details about the weather) to the sensational (references to a rape and a multiple murder). As mentioned, previous historians were inclined to dismiss the diary as too concerned with mundane matters to bother looking at it more closely. But Laurel Thatcher Ulrich was intrigued that there even *was* a diary written by a woman in that period, a time when few girls were taught to read and even fewer to write. By ferreting out and connecting many tiny details of the diary, then by relating these connected details to other primary documents and to knowledge already established in secondary sources, Ulrich was able to throw light on much that was previously little understood.

For example, Ulrich showed how much women's weaving of cloth in their homes contributed to the economy of early New England, how changing attitudes and practices in eighteenth- and nineteenth-century medicine led to midwives being replaced by doctors, and how marriage and domestic life were organized in that time and place. The following excerpt from Chapter 4 of *A Midwife's Tale: The Life of Martha Ballard, Based on Her Diary, 1785–1812*,[1] concerns common courtship and marriage practices that we might now find strange. In the margins are annotations to help you see how Ulrich used her sources to construct a convincing interpretation and argument.

[1] From *A Midwife's Tale* by Laurel Thatcher Ulrich. Copyright © 1990 by Laurel Thatcher Ulrich. Reprinted by permission of Alfred A. Knopf, Inc.

CHAPTER FOUR
NOVEMBER 1792
"Matrimonial writes"

OCTOBER

28   G   At home. A Marriag in my Family.
Cloudy fornoon, a little rain & Thunder, Clear before night. Cyrus
was not at home. Thee Matrimonial writes were cellibrated between
Mr Moses Pollard off this Town and my daughter Hannah this
Evening. Esquire Cony performed the ceremony. My son & his wife
& son tarry here.

29   2   At home. We killd three young Turkeys.
Cloudy. Dolly went to Mr Densmores, Mr Ballard to the hook. I have
been at home. Sally here helping the girls. Mr Pollard & Savage supt
here.

30   3   At home. Roasted a Turkey.
Clear & pleasant. Mr Ballard been to Colonel Sewalls & the Hook. I
have been at home. Sally & the girls put a Bed quilt in to the fraim
for Parthenia. Sarah Densmore & Dolly here the Evng.

31   4   At home.
Clear. Mr Ballard went to Pittston. Polly Pollard, Mrs Damrin, I &
my daughter Dolly quilted all day. Mrs Livermore afternoon. I have
been at home. Mr Town sleeps here.

NOVEMBER

1   5   At Mr Hodges Birth 38th. Son Town went home.
Cloudy & some rain. Mr Town left here after breakfast. The girls had
the Ladies to help them quillt. I was Calld to see Mrs Hodges at 4 h
pm. Shee was safe delivered at 11 h Evening off a very fine son her
sixth child. Mr Ballard came home.
Birth Ezra Hodges Son X X

*2   6   At dittoes & Mr Burtuns & Magr Stickneys. Birth 39. Bizer
Benjamins wife delivered of 2 sons Both dead.*[1]
Clear forenoon, Cloudy afternoon, rain at Evening. I receivd 6/ of
Mr Hodges & returnd home at noon. Left my patient cleverly. Calld
at Mr Burtuns. His Lady is cleverly. I Bot off him 2 iron kettles which
cost 7/, 1 spider at 3/6, 2 pepper boxes & 2 dippirs at /6 each, 2/, 1

This chapter title is a quotation from Martha Ballard's diary, preserving Ballard's 18th-century spelling. In this part of her diary, Ballard relates details about her daughter Hannah's wedding.

To open this and other chapters, Ulrich quotes extensively from Ballard's diary. This quoting helps the reader see the primary source the argument is based on.

The first number in each diary entry is the day of the month; the second number is the day of the week. Sundays were given a "dominical letter" rather than a number.

Ulrich reproduces the capitalization, spelling, and punctuation of the original to show how people wrote English in the 18th century.

Ballard recorded each baby that she delivered, and when she was paid for her services, she recorded "XX" by the name.

[1]Here Martha is reporting a delivery she did not attend.

yd binding /1, ginn 2/6, total 15/1.[2] I went to Magr Stickneys at 9 h
Evn. His wife delivered at 11 h 5 m off a daughter. I tarried all night.
Birth Benjamin Stickneys daughter X X

3   7   At Mr Stickneys & Mr Devenports.
Rainy forenoon. I tarried at the Magrs till after dineing. Recevd 6/ as
a reward. Mrs Conry came with me to Mr Devenports where we
spent the remainder of the afternoon. Returned home at dusk. I left
my patients Cleverly.

4   G   At home
Clear. I have been at home. Dolly here. Dolly not [sentence incom-
plete]

5   2   At home. J Jones here.
Clear. Mr Ballard at Pittston. Mr John Jones & a Mr Dutten here. My
girls washt. I at home.

6   3   At Mr Burtuns.
Clear. I went to see Mrs Burtun who has had an ill turn & is Better.
Dolly sleeps here.

7   4   At home. Ephraim was Banking the house.
Clear. Cyrus Came here. I have been at home. Helpt quillt on
Hannahs Bed quilt. We got it out late in the Evening.

Ballard notes that her new
son-in-law Moses Pollard
spent the night at her
home. Ulrich will find this
detail significant later in
this chapter.

8   5   At home. Mr Jones here, Son Cyrus also.
Foggy morn. Sun shone at 10 h. Cyrus went to his Brothers. Mr J
Jones here. I have been at home. Mrs Edson here to warp a web of
Mrs Densmores. Mr Pollard & Pitt here the night.

9   6   At home. Cyrus went to Pitston. Mrs Parker returned home.
Cloudy morn. Cyrus went to Pittston afternoon. It raind before night.
A sever N E Storm in the night. I have been at home. Mrs Bradbury
& Betsy Champny here.

10   7   At home
Cloudy & some rain. I have been at home. Stript Turkey feathers.

[2]In eighteenth-century accounting, a virgule (/) divided shillings and pence.
"7/" therefore means 7 shillings, "/6" means 6 pence.

11   G At home. Mr Pages & Jones here.
Clear part the day. Mr Ballard returnd from Pitston. Mr J Jones & Mr Page & son Jonathan dind here. Mr Pollard & Pitt supt. I have been at home. Mr Ballard paid John Jones 21 dollars in part of a note he had against him.

Ballard records that her new son-in-law ate supper at her home.

12   2 At home. Cyrus came up here.
Clear part of the day. Mr Ballard at the hook & to Joness mill. Cyrus came here at 6 hour pm. I have been at home.

13   3 At home. Cyrus sleeps here.
The sun rose clear. Cloudy some part the day. Mr Ballard is gone to Varsalboro. Cyrus up to Mr Savages 2 hour pm Clearing a wood road.

14   4 At Savage Boltons & others
Cloudy & a very Chilly air. I went up as far as Savage Boltons. He paid me 8/ at Mr Burtuns for attending his wife the 19th of January last. I Bot 2 purer dishes weight 5 lb at 2/, 1 coffee pot 3/6, six table spoons 1/8, total 15/2. I paid 7/2 cash. Mr Bolton answers 8/ of it.

15   5 At home. Cyrus & Dolly returned home.
Clear. Mr Ballard workt at the Bridg over the gully. I have been at home. Mrs Densmore dind & took Tea. Mr Seth Williams & his wife here. Cyrus came home. Has quit thee grist mill he has tended. Dolly returnd from her apprentiship with Mr Densmore. Cyrus tended Mr Hollowells mill 14 months. Capt Nichols has hired it now.

16   6 At home. Finisht a pair of hos for Dolly.
Snowd the most off the day. I have been at home. We killd 2 Turkeys. Mr Ballard went to Mr Pollards. Bot 5 1/2 lb flax at /9, 5 lb Butter at /10.

17   7 At home
Clear. Mr Ballard been up to Jonathans & to the hook. Cyrus went to Pittston and brot his chest & things home. I have been at home. Have not been so well as I could wish.

18   G At home. Mr Shubal Pitt and Parthenia Barton joind in Mariage.
Rainy. Mr Pollard & Pitt dind here. Thee latter was joind in the Bands of wedlock with Parthenia Barton. The ceremony performd by Samuel Duttun Esq. I have been at home. We had no Company Except our famely attend. Thee Justice gave the fee to the Bride.

Moses Pollard again ate at the Ballard home, when Parthenia Barton, Martha Ballard's niece, married Mr. Pitts.

After showing the reader some of the primary evidence her argument will be based on, Ulrich begins her analysis of 18th-century marriage customs here.

Ulrich notes that historians disagree on whether marriage was an economic or a romantic arrangement in the 18th century.

Endnote 1 refers the reader to a number of secondary sources that make claims about the nature of marriage in the period from 1300 to the early 1800s. This documentation bolsters the credibility of Ulrich's argument.

Ulrich claims that Ballard's diary supports the argument that marriage was still an economic arrangement in the late 18th century.

Ulrich comments on the very formal way Ballard referred to her son-in-law in her diary. The adjective "starched" shows that Ulrich perhaps finds the 18th-century formality excessive.

There were three marriages in the Ballard family in 1792, two of them described in the diary segment that opens this chapter. The other occurred in February, when Jonathan reluctantly married Sally Pierce, who had initiated a paternity suit against him. Martha's descriptions of the three weddings and the events surrounding them—one so dramatic, the others so placidly domestic—illuminate little-known marriage customs in rural New England.

Some historians see the mid-eighteenth century as a transitional time in the history of the family, an era when young people began to exercise greater freedom in choosing marriage partners, when romantic and sexual attraction between couples became more important than economic negotiations between parents. Others argue that romantic love and economic calculation had long coexisted in the English-speaking world, that well before the eighteenth century, marriages were primarily contracts between individuals rather than alliances of families.[1] Martha's diary supports the notion that children chose their own spouses; there is no evidence of parental negotiation, and little hint of parental supervision in any of the courtships she describes. The diary also confirms the prevalence of premarital sex. Yet there is little evidence of romance and much to suggest that economic concerns remained central. The weddings in the Ballard family were distinctly unglamorous affairs, almost non-events. For the women, they were surrounded by an intense productivity, a gathering of resources that defined their meaning and purpose.

"Thee Matrimonial writes were cellibrated between Mr Moses Pollard off this Town and my daughter Hannah this Evening," Martha wrote on October 28. The misspelling of "writes" for "rites" is a charming accident. Most of what we know about patterns of marriage in eighteenth-century New England comes from official records, the scanty "writes," of men like Henry Sewall, who was serving as town clerk in 1792 and who entered marriage intentions and sometimes marriage dates in the town book. Martha imitated the starched formality of such records in describing the groom as "Mr Moses Pollard off this town," as if he were some newly arrived gentleman rather than the grown-up son of her old friends Amos and Merriam Pollard.

Marriages were regulated under Massachusetts law according to "An Act for the Orderly Solemnization of Marriages" passed on June 22, 1786. This new legislation reflected the old colonial faith in community surveillance. A justice of the peace or minister could perform marriages only when the bride or the groom or both belonged to his town. Furthermore, the couple had to present a certificate signed by the town clerk indicating that their intent of marriage had been appropriately "published" either at three "publick religious meetings, on different days, at three days distance exclusively" or by posting for "the space of fourteen days, in some publick place."[2]

In 1792 Henry Sewall entered twenty-one intentions of marriage in the town book, noting that one engagement "fell through" before a certificate was issued and that another "broke off." In the case of John Chamberlain and Mary Brown, he wrote, the certificate was "barred by a written objection filed by his Father." That was in May. In December Sewall added: "Certificate issued by consent of the Father who filed the objections aforesaid." Martha's entry on December 16 fills in the details in this domestic drama: "John Chamberlain was marid the 10 instant, removed his wife to Sidney the 11th; Shee was delivered of a daughter the 12th and it Expired before night."[3] As we shall see, John Chamberlain's story was not unique.

Conscientious town clerks, and Henry Sewall was one, not only kept orderly lists of intentions filed and certificates issued but also tried to compile and enter into the official record lists of marriages actually performed. In April of 1793 three Hallowell justices "returned" their marriage lists to Henry Sewall. Samuel Dutton officiated at his only ceremony of the year when he joined Parthenia Barton and Shubael Pitts "in the bands of wedlock." Daniel Cony married only one other couple in 1792 in addition to Hannah and Moses Pollard. Parthenia and Hannah seem to have gone out of their way to avoid the most popular (or available) of Hallowell's justices, Joseph North.[4]

"Thee Matrimonial writes were *cellibrated* between Mr Moses Pollard off this Town and my daughter Hannah." Despite the verb there is little evidence of celebration in Martha's scanty description. Here was no gathering of far-flung (or even immediate) family and friends. Cyrus wasn't there, though it was a Sunday, his usual day at home, nor did Lucy and Ezra Towne ride down from Winslow. Except for Jonathan and his family, there seem to have been no other guests, not even the groom's parents, who were, after all, good friends of the Ballards. If anyone baked pies or cakes, Martha Ballard didn't say so, nor did the roast turkey appear until Tuesday, two days *after* the wedding. There is no more sign of special festivity in the entry for November 18: "Mr Pollard & Pitt dind here. Thee latter was joind in the Bands off wedlock with Parthenia Barton." In Martha's description, the wedding appears almost as an afterthought to the young men's presence at dinner.[5]

What is even more puzzling is the apparent failure of the brides to leave home. Through the month of November, Hannah and

Ulrich cites a primary source to show what laws newlyweds would have had to comply with.

Endnote 2 gives information about weddings for people who had no minister or justice of the peace to marry them.

By describing an incident when a marriage took place shortly before the birth of a baby, Ulrich foreshadows a similar incident she will relate later in this chapter.

Ulrich implicitly contrasts the quiet marriage customs of the 18th century with contemporary wedding celebrations.

By noting details from several different diary entries, Ulrich points out that 18th-century brides and grooms did not begin living together immediately after their weddings.

Parthenia continued to act like Martha's "girls," quilting, washing, and helping with the housework. Moses and Shubael came and went. "Mr Pollard & Pitt here the night." "Mr Pollard & Pitt supt." "Mr Pollard and Pitt waited on their wives & Dolly to Mr Pollards."[6] The entry for the day of Parthenia's wedding, "Mr Pollard & Pitt dind here," was part, then, of a larger pattern. What is especially striking is Martha's pairing of the two names. On November 8, when Martha noted that the two were "here the night," Moses was a husband, Shubael still a husband-to-be. Again on November 30 both men "took breakfast," apparently having spent the night. If they had been sleeping and taking meals there consistently, it would not have been necessary to note their presence.

Twentieth-century readers puzzle over such behavior because we think of a wedding as a discrete event, a brief and festive occurrence. The guests gather, the music plays, the proper words are said, and the celebration begins. It is difficult to imagine a "wedding" that meanders through six weeks of housework and family suppers, to comprehend a world in which brides sleep at home (with or without their grooms) for more than a month after they have been "joind in the Bands of wedlock." But that, in fact, is what happened at the Ballards' and in many New England households in the late eighteenth century. The rituals of marriage began with "publication" (in Hannah's and Parthenia's case six weeks before the ceremony) and ended when the young couples finally "went to housekeeping" at about the same interval after.

From putting together bits of evidence in the diary, Ulrich concludes that weddings in the 18th century were long, drawn-out affairs, not a discrete event lasting a day.

The phrase "went to housekeeping" had perhaps an even greater resonance than the words "joind in Mariage." Until Hannah and Parthenia actually left the house, they remained "the girls." Once they had gone, they were forever after "Daughter Pollard" and "Mrs Pitts." Martha later recalled that she had gone to housekeeping the same day as she was married, but in Hallowell that practice was unusual. All the marriages recorded in the diary followed the same leisurely pattern. Hannah, Parthenia, and Jonathan all went to housekeeping more than a month after marriage, as did Dolly and her cousin Betsy Barton three years later, and Ephraim, Jr., in 1804. (During the interval between Betsy Barton's marriage and her departure from the house, Martha noted that she and the other "girls" had "Closd an opperation for the itch and washt hoping they are Cured.")[7]

Ulrich uses the evidence she has found in the diary to claim that, in the 18th century, the most significant fact about a marriage was setting up a new household, not the wedding ceremony itself.

Henry Sewall's diary confirms the pattern. He was married in Georgetown on February 9, 1786, spent a few weeks with his wife's family, then returned to Hallowell, leaving Tabitha behind. Not until July 7, when Tabby arrived from Georgetown with "Miss Esther," presumably a cousin or sister, did the young couple "go to housekeeping." What is similar about all these cases is the coming and going of the groom—almost as in courtship—the bride remaining in her parents' house. When "Mr Pollard and Pitt waited on their wives & Dolly to Mr Pollards" (while the Ballards roasted a turkey at home), Hannah was making her first formal visit to her husband's family. Significantly, she and Moses were accompanied by other people, just as Tabby Sewall had been when she finally came from Georgetown to Hallowell.

According to Ellen Rothman, even in the early nineteenth century wedding rituals affirmed ties of community. A week of neighborly visiting following the wedding was more common than a journey, and when couples did take a trip, other people often went along. This practice began to change in the second half of the nineteenth century. "Beginning in the 1870s, etiquette books advocated that the couple leave the church—where middle-class weddings increasingly took place—together and alone, and that instead of the 'harassing bridal tour,' they enjoy 'a honeymoon of repose, exempted from claims of society,'" By the 1880s, "honeymoon trips to 'romantic' locations were expected to follow weddings."[8]

In the late eighteenth century, romance was still subordinate to the larger process of establishing a new economic relationship. The issue for Hannah and Moses was not where they would spend their wedding night but when and how they would begin housekeeping. Providing household goods seems to have been a joint responsibility of mother, father, and daughter. On October, eight days before Hannah's wedding, Martha bought a case of knives and forks, some small spoons, sewing silk, and 28 3/4 yards of a fabric she called "Camblesteen" from one store at the Hook and a dozen plates from another. Three days later, Ephraim returned to the second store to purchase six bowls (whether on his own credit or Martha's we do not know). For both of them the coming wedding was an excuse for collecting debts. On October 17 he brought home "9 1/2 yd. Camblet teen, 5 yds Linning, & 3 lb Tea and a handkf which he had off Mr Bridg for our attendance at Supreme Cort." A month later, Martha used a note of credit she had collected from Savage Bolton to help buy pewter dishes, a coffee pot, and six tablespoons at Burton's.

Information Ulrich found in another primary source corroborates her interpretation of Ballard's diary. Such corroboration makes her claim more persuasive.

Ulrich cites a secondary source to show that the custom of newlyweds having a honeymoon was established in the late 19th century. This fact also suggests that marriages before the late 19th century had less to do with romantic love and more to do with economic matters.

Ulrich reiterates her claim that marriage was mainly an economic arrangement. To further support this claim, Ulrich cites much evidence from the diary to show that Martha and Ephraim Ballard helped their daughter acquire the goods she would need to set up her own household.

Some of the text has been omitted here. The omitted part describes the pots, pans, and quilts the Ballards' daughter Hannah acquired before her wedding. It also describes the courting customs of young people in 18th century New England. (The omitted part contains notes 9–13.)

In Martha's diary the passionate intensity we associate with romantic love appears only as an aberration. "Enformed that Mr Smith was

Ulrich claims that Martha Ballard did not associate marriage with romantic love; in fact, she viewed romantic love as an aberration, as several diary entries attest.

gone away & is feared he Desirs to Deprive himself of Life on acount of Polly Hamlin's refuseing to wed with him," she wrote on February 27, 1786. For a time the woes of the abandoned suitor created anxiety—and entertainment—in Hallowell. "Smith & Polly Hamlin are in all Conversation at present," Martha wrote after taking tea at a neighbor's. By March 5 she could report a rumor that Smith had hanged himself, though ten days later he was back in town, apparently resigned to his fate.[14] In contrast, Martha described her own children's courtships as casually as she noted the black turkey sitting on its nest.

Even though romantic love was not a significant part of marriage, Ulrich cautions the reader against believing that sexual attraction played no role in choosing a mate.

Ulrich refers to evidence to support her contention that sexual attraction played a role in courtship. She shows that such attraction developed in the context of "frolics"—work parties that gave young people the chance to make the goods they would need for domestic life as well as the chance to interact socially. Various entries from Ballard's diary support this claim.

If Hannah or Dolly had been keeping the diary, there might have been more evidence of romance. It is a mistake, however, to draw too sharp a distinction between traditional notions of marriage as an economic (and sometimes spiritual) partnership and supposedly newer ideas that emphasized sexual attraction and romance. There is plenty of evidence from northern New England to suggest that sexual attraction played a central role in courtship, but there was no inherent conflict between that motive and the need to find a hardworking and productive spouse capable of bearing his or her full share of the work of a farm or business. Group work parties, often referred to in New England as "frolics," reinforced the connection.

In each of the two autumns before Hannah's marriage, there were quiltings at the Ballard house, each involving several days of individual and group work before the men arrived for a dance. On November 8, 1790, "The girls quilted a Bed quillt & went to Mr Craggs spent Evng." The next day, "The girls quilted two quilts. Hannah Rockwood & Mrs Benjamin helpt the Evening. We Bakt mins and pumpkin pies. Mrs Porter here." Then on November 10, "My girls had some neighbours to help them quilt a bed quilt, 15 ladies. They began to quilt at 3 hour pm. Finisht and took it out at 7 evening. There were 12 gentlemen took tea. They danced a little while after supper. Behaved exceeding cleverly.... Were all returned home before the 11th hour."

The next year, on September 19, Martha wrote that her girls had spent part of the day "peecing Bed quillts." This can hardly have been the intricate patchwork common to the next century, however, for they also managed to do the family wash that day and then to go to a neighbor's house with Moses Pollard at night. The next day they "put a Bed quillt into the fraim" and "Bakt cakes & pies." On September 21, they "had a quilting, got out one & partly quilted another," before the gentlemen arrived for refreshments and a dance.

Young men helped to celebrate the completion of quilts just as young women celebrated a house- or barn-raising by gathering for a dance. Huskings, too, brought young folks together for labor and fun—and sometimes, too, for abandoned drinking and sexual liaisons.[15] Martha was clearly relieved when at the raising of the sawmill there were only a few persons among the "vast concorse of men and children" who were "disguised with Licquor." Her comment after a quilting that the young folks "were all returned home before the 11th hour" contrasts with her report of a later husking and quilting at the Densmores', "my young folks there came home late," or of a winter frolic, "Jonathan and girls go sleigh riding, get home at half past 12 at night."[16]

> Ulrich uses entries from Ballard's diary to claim that there were clear limits on appropriate interaction with the opposite sex.

On one of her rare visits to church, Martha heard a visiting pastor (a "good old Gentleman" give a discourse "adapted to the youth." "His Exortations were Excelent," she wrote. "May they be deeply impresst on their minds for their future good."[17] As a parent—and a midwife—she knew too well the dangers facing the youth of her town. Yet the freedom and abandon of group "frolics" was limited. Barn-raisings and husking bees encouraged hard work and responsibility to the group even as they gave opportunities for sexual experimentation and carousing. Taverns, too, were never purely recreational, since they were the sites of political meetings, patriotic celebrations, and in some years town meetings and courts, as well as dances and drinking parties. The courting patterns and matrimonial customs of eighteenth-century Hallowell wove couples into the larger community, reinforcing gender roles, celebrating group identity, and, though it may not be so obvious, maintaining the boundaries within which sexuality might be expressed.

> Here, Ulrich prepares the reader for a new theme related to 18th-century marriage customs: What happened when couples had babies out of wedlock?

It snowed on October 23, 1791, the day Martha was summoned to Sally Pierce. Because this was going to be an illegitimate birth, she knew what she had to ask. She also knew what Sally would say.

> Ulrich dramatizes an important moment in Martha Ballard's work as a midwife—the day when she delivered her own illegitimate grandson.

Shee was safe delivered at 1 hour pm of a fine son, her illness very severe but I left her cleverly & returnd…about sun sett.

Sally declard that my son Jonathan was the father of her child. In the margin Martha wrote simply, "Sally Pierce's son. Birth 27th."

Before we can understand the full import of that entry, we need to know something about the legal position of unwed mothers in eighteenth-century New England. Massachusetts law had always defined sexual intercourse between unmarried persons as a crime. In the seventeenth and early eighteenth centuries, courts had punished men who fathered children out of wedlock as rigorously as the women concerned, often relying on testimony taken from mothers during delivery to establish the fathers' identity, but by the middle of the eighteenth century, most historians argue, fornication had become a woman's crime.

> Ulrich summarizes the laws concerning fornication in the 17th and early 18th centuries.

Ulrich cites a secondary source to show that in Massachusetts, the courts stopped prosecuting men for fathering illegitimate children about 1790.

Ulrich found that Lincoln County, Maine, also stopped prosecuting men for fornication during the same period of time.

Using details gathered from primary sources (court records), Ulrich created this table to show how the courts at the time gradually stopped charging and convicting men and women for fornication.

William Nelson has shown that while fornication prosecutions still accounted for more than a third of criminal actions in Massachusetts between 1760 and 1774, in only one case was the *father* of an illegitimate child prosecuted—a black man suspected of cohabiting with a white woman. By the end of the century, actions against women had also disappeared from court dockets. Prosecutions dropped from seventy-two per year in the years 1760 and 1774 to fifty-eight during the revolutionary years and finally to fewer than five after 1786. Nelson found only four prosecutions after 1790 in the entire Commonwealth. Lincoln County records show the same decline. Between 1761 and 1785, seventy-three women but only ten men were presented for fornication or related crimes. No women were presented after 1785.[18]

Table 1. Lincoln County Court of General Sessions, Fornication and Paternity Actions, 1761–1799

Date	Women	Men: "Unknown"	Presented	Convicted
1761–1765	9	2	1	1
1766–1770	20	3	3	2
1771–1775	11	2	0	0
1776–1780	12	1	2	1
1781–1785	21	0	4	4
1786–1790	0	0	3	2
1791–1795	0	0	6	6
1796–1799	0	0	0	0

NOTE: Kennebec County was separated from Lincoln in 1799. There are no fornication or maintenance cases in the first General Sessions Record Books for the new county. Unfortunately, court papers for the early nineteenth century have not survived.

Historians are still debating the significance of such changes. Some stress liberalization, arguing that as courts became more concerned with mediating property disputes than enforcing Puritan standards of moral behavior, sex became a private affair. Others perceive the decline in fornication prosecutions as reflecting generational tensions in a society that had given up the legalism of the Puritans but had not yet developed the repressive individualism of the Victorians. More recent studies have emphasized gender issues, arguing that changes in fornication proceedings reflected a larger argument over female sexuality, an argument vividly displayed in eighteenth-century novels of seduction, some of which openly challenged the prevailing double standard.[19]

Ulrich alludes to secondary sources that attempt to explain why the courts no longer prosecuted people for illicit sexual behavior.

Against such evidence, Sally Pierce's declaration appears a quaint and inexplicable throwback to an earlier era. It was not. Evidence from Martha's diary and from supporting legal documents casts doubt on the notion that sexual behavior had in fact become a private concern. The diary suggests that even in a newly settled lumbering town like Hallowell, sexual norms (though neither Puritan nor Victorian) were clearly defined and communally enforced, that courts seldom prosecuted sexual deviance because informal mechanisms of control were so powerful. It also casts doubt on the use of General Sessions records or elite literature to define the double standard. There were certainly inequities in the way male and female culpability was defined in this period, yet there is no evidence that in rural communities women who bore children out of wedlock were either ruined or abandoned as early novels would suggest.

Ulrich claims that Sally Pierce's paternity action against Jonathan Ballard, Martha's son, was not unusual or out of date. Ulrich claims that even though the courts no longer enforced proper sexual behavior, the communities still had ways of ensuring that women were not penalized while men escaped all responsibility.

The prosecutorial double standard originated in a 1668 Massachusetts law that introduced the English practice of asking unwed mothers to name the father of their child during delivery. At first glance, questioning a woman in labor seems a form of harassment. In practice, it was a formality allowing the woman, her relatives, or in some cases the selectmen of her town to claim child support. The man she accused could not be convicted of fornication (confession or witnesses were needed for that), but unless there was overwhelming evidence to the contrary, he would be judged the "reputed father" of her child and required to pay for its support. The assumption was that a woman asked to testify at the height of travail would not lie.

Ulrich explains the reasoning behind the custom of asking an unwed mother to name the father of her baby during labor.

NOTES FOR CHAPTER FOUR

1. For England, Lawrence Stone, *The Family, Sex and Marriage in England, 1500–1800* (New York: Harper & Row, 1977), describes the rise of what he calls the "affectionate nuclear family." Alan MacMarlane, *Marriage and Love in England 1300–1840* (Oxford, Eng.: Basil Blackwell, 1986), emphasizes the existence of a "Malthusian Marriage System" from the fourteenth century onward. Mary Beth Norton, following Lawrence Stone, emphasizes the restraints on young women in the mid-eighteenth century and the common recognition of a need for parental involvement in the formation of marriages, but believes women were granted greater freedom in the post-Revolutionary period, in Norton, *Liberty's Daughters*, pp. 51–60, 229–231. For New England, the most influential argument for a shift toward affective individualism is Daniel Scott Smith, "Parental Power and Marriage Patterns: An Analysis of Historical Trends in

Ulrich's dense endnotes for the excerpt given here show that she is a careful, thorough scholar. The credibility of her argument is enhanced through this meticulous documentation, and readers are more likely to trust her account of marriage customs. Skeptical readers can use the endnotes to check Ulrich's sources and then judge for themselves if her claims are justified. Endnotes are thus an important part of the historian's rhetoric.

Hingham, Massachusetts," *Journal of Marriage and the Family* 35 (1973): In family law there seems to have been a shift in the early nineteenth century from a notion of marriage as a property contract between father and son-in-law to a romantic personal contract between a man and a woman: Michael Grossberg, *Governing the Hearth: Law and Family in Nineteenth-Century America* (Chapel Hill: University of North Carolina Press, 1985), pp. 35–38.

2. Persons residing in a town that had neither a minister nor a justice of the peace could go to the nearest neighboring town: *The Perpetual Laws of the Commonwealth of Massachusetts, from the Establishment of its Constitution to the First Session of the General Court, A.D. 1788* (Worcester, 1788), pp. 253–256.

3. MMB, December 16, 1792. Actually Martha's dates fail to match Sewall's. He said the certificate was issued December 12 and that Joseph North married the couple on December 16. The marriage may have followed rather than preceded the delivery.

4. Based on marriage lists extracted from HTR, I. Also, see Nash, p. 582.

5. Except for the mention of a psalm, Henry Sewall's description of his own wedding is almost identical: "Was married to Miss Tabby Sewall about two o'clock," he wrote. "Mr. Ezekiel Emerson performed the ceremony. Her sisters with their husbands & Thomas were the only guests besides the family. Sang the 48 hymn of the 2 book": HS, February 9, 1786.

6. MMB, November 8, 11, 19, 1792.

7. MMB, March 14, 1795. Charles Gill and Betsy Barton had been married March 1, had made a brief trip to Winslow apparently in the company of "son and daughter Pollard," and had returned on March 7. The new bride lived at the Ballards until April 12, Mr. Gill coming and going just as in the other cases: MMB, March 15, 16, 18, 22, 1795, April 8, 11, 12, 1795. Sarah Parsons of Newburyport, Massachusetts, noted that after her marriage to Charles Porter Phelps of Hadley on January 1, 1800, she remained in Newbury while he went to Hadley. He came for her "the last of March," they visited in various places for the rest of the spring and summer, sometimes together, sometimes apart, "and went to housekeeping the first day of September": Sarah Parson Phelps Journal, Phelps Papers, Amherst College Library, Amherst, Mass.

8. Ellen Bothman, *Hands & Hearts: A History of Courtship in America* (New York: Basic Books, 1980), pp. 175–176.

9. MMB, October 26, 1792.

10. This statement is based on my own analysis of ten detailed household inventories from Hallowell, 1790–1796, using transcriptions of Lincoln County probate records at the Maine State Museum in

Augusta. Six of the inventories listed frying pans or skillets, nine of them had kettles or pots. Only two households had more than four pieces of cooking equipment; most had from one to three. On the broader question of household amenities, see Gloria L. Main and Jackson T. Main, "Economic Growth and the Standard Living in Southern New England, 1640–1774," *The Journal of Economic History* 48 (1988): 27–46. Living standards are, of course, relative. While the Mains found a sharp rise in household consumption in the third quarter of the eighteenth century, household possessions were still very limited. Less than 60 percent of households in the richest third of the population had forks, for example, less than a quarter had fine earthenware.

11. In describing a quilting held at Lucy Towne's house in Winslow just before the birth of a baby, Martha mentioned that she "helpt break the wool" that was used to fill the quilt and that a neighbor came to "Chalk" or mark the design to be stitched: MMB, September 23, 24, 25, 26, 1795. In the Ballard diary, quilting entries seem to cluster in the autumn. For other examples, see September 5, 9, 13, 23, 1791; and November 17, 1790.

12. Anna Tuels Coverlet, Maine, c. 1785 Wadsworth Athenaeum, Hartford Conn. The quilt is illustrated or described in Patsy and Myron Orlofsky, *Quilts in America* (New York: McGraw-Hill, 1974), Pl. 76, p. 216; Carleton L. Safford and Robert Bishop, *America's Quilts and Coverlets* (New York: Dutton 1972), Fig. 148, p. 112. The Wadsworth Athenaeum now lists this as a "Coverlet" rather than a "Manage Quilt" because there is no documentation for the former title.

13. MMB, May 8, 1795, December 23, 1794.

14. MMB, February 27, 1786, March 1, 5, 6, 14, 24, 1786, October 6, 17, 1786, March 26, 1790.

15. MMB, July 23, 1792, October 3, 15, 1788.

16. MMB, October 7, 1794, February 25, 1788.

17. MMB, August 25, 1793

18. William E. Nelson, *Americanization of the Common Law: The Impact of Legal Change on Massachusetts Society, 1760–1830* (Cambridge, Mass.: Harvard University Press, 1975), pp. 110–111; LCCGSP, Books 1–2.

19. The three points of view are exemplified by Nelson, *Americanization of the Common Law*, pp. 110, 251–253; Daniel Scott Smith and Michael Hindus, "Premarital Pregnancy in America, 1640–1971: An Overview and an Intepretation," *Journal of Interdisciplinary History* 5 (1975): 537–570; and Davidson, *Revolution and the Word*, pp. 106–109. For an excellent summary of the literature on eighteenth-century sexuality, see John D'Emilio and Estelle B. Freedman, *Intimate Matters: A History of Sexuality in America* (New York: Harper & Row, 1988), pp. 42–52.

A STUDENT EXAMPLE

Two college undergraduates, Victor Sipos and Trevor Hall, received an assignment in their advanced writing class to collaborate on an original research project. Because of their interest in legal matters and because of stories in the news about possible biases in the way the judicial system treats different groups, they chose to examine statistics to see if, in fact, justice is as blind as our society believes it to be. They decided to limit their investigation to the question of how impartial the justice system is in its treatment of men and women. Their research question was this: "Are men and women who have committed similar crimes treated differently by the courts and other elements of the criminal justice system?" Using their knowledge of how to locate appropriate sources in the library, they found much raw data in primary sources that could be used to answer their question. They decided to further limit their research by comparing the treatment of men and women in four different phases of the criminal justice system: pretrial treatment, convictions and sentencing, prison environment, and parole.

As Sipos and Hall began to compare the statistics for men and women, a clear pattern of preferential treatment for women emerged. They knew they could make this pattern quite clear in their paper, especially by using graphs that would show the extent of the unequal treatment in all four phases of the criminal justice system. But they didn't believe they could really explain the differences in the numbers without more research. That is, while the statistics were unambiguous, they still told the two investigators little about *why* the numbers are what they are. While Sipos and Hall might have made some plausible guesses to explain the numbers, they didn't want their paper merely to speculate on the reasons.

So they did a second study, conducting an informal survey of 12 professionals involved with the criminal justice system, including a corrections officer, a police officer, attorneys, probation officers, a superior court judge, and a justice of a state supreme court. (Their survey was not scientific because it was not random and the number of respondents was too small to draw statistically reliable generalizations from. See Chapter 7 for more specific instruction on how to conduct reliable surveys.) In a way, these 12 professionals might be considered secondary sources because they helped the researchers interpret the statistical data of the primary sources. Seeking the opinion of professionals involved with the judicial system gave Sipos and Hall some authoritative support for explaining the data they had collected. They were able to go beyond mere speculation about the significance of the numbers and confidently create a more solid argument, as the paper that follows will show.

Sipos and Hall's paper represents essentially the same kind of inquiry as Ulrich's: reading documents carefully to seek patterns and draw conclusions, and using other sources to enhance and confirm their own interpretations. Their investigation shows the kind of research undergraduates can do, even given limited time and resources. There are many interesting primary documents to be read and interpreted in your own college library—perhaps even in your family's attic. Let your curiosity and imagination guide you as you seek an interesting project for conducting this kind of inquiry.

Partial Justice Within the U.S. Judicial System:
Differing Treatment of Males and Females

by
Victor Sipos
and
Trevor Hall

In front of the U.S. Supreme Court building, a massive marble
statue called "Contemplation of Justice" depicts the Greek mytholog-
ical figure of justice, Themis. Symbolizing equality and fairness, she
wears a blindfold to show her impartiality in meting out justice
according to the law. American legal doctrine is based in this principle of blind justice which treats all citizens equally, without regard to
class, race, or gender. American history, however, has failed to live
up to this standard. Recent outcomes of judicial cases involving
Congressional abuses and corporate scandals have reinforced an
impression that the powerful and very wealthy receive preferential
treatment. Cries from civil rights activists protest the treatment of
minorities in the legal system. Yet little is heard of the differing treatment of males and females within the U.S. judicial system. Protests of
gender discrimination from women's groups make the examination
of gender equality within the judicial system important.

No one can contest the fact that males commit more crimes than
females: In 1991 over seven times as many males were processed
through the criminal justice system (*Correctional Populations in the
United States 1991*, 6). Yet, it remains questionable whether males and
females receive different treatment for the same offense. Before
beginning this research, we had no statistically founded idea whether
judicial treatment varied along gender lines or not. Speaking with
similarly uninformed people, we found widely differing ideas. Some
strongly felt that females get discriminatory treatment from a male-
structured system, while others thought females receive far lighter
punishment due to societal stereotyping of females as kinder and
gentler. To answer this question, we researched four areas of the judicial system: pre-trial treatment, convictions, prison environment, and
parole. We hypothesized that females receive lighter treatment due to
societal stereotyping.

Methods

On such a volatile issue as gender discrimination, we recognized the need to find unbiased sources, so we used only primary
data from government documents and statistical yearbooks, and we

looked only for data that were separated by gender. We converted some data to percentages to show proportional instead of numeric differences.

Believing that our lack of judicial knowledge might lead us to misinterpret the data, we also sent questionnaires to twelve legal professionals: two legal secretaries, a corrections officer, two supervising level probation officers, a major in the New Mexico state police, an associate legal defense counsel, three attorneys, an Arizona Superior Court judge, and a New Mexico Supreme Court justice. The questionnaire, consisting of statistical tables with primary data and five open-ended questions, asked the professionals to explain the general statistical patterns we found (see Appendix). The survey was conducted confidentially, so as excerpts from respondents' answers appear throughout this text, none of their names are cited, only their titles.

Results and Discussion
Pre-trial Releases

Within 72 hours of arrest, all suspected criminals receive a pre-trial hearing. During the hearing a judge determines whether to release the suspect or keep them in custody. Judges can grant two types of pre-trial release: bail bond or personal recognizance. Bond requires a suspect to deposit a stipulated amount of money, which is returned when the suspect appears for trial. Personal recognizance releases the suspect without bond. Following the pre-trial hearing the suspect appears at an arraignment hearing where the trial judge assumes jurisdiction and sets a "speedy" trial date, within 180 days of arraignment (Hall 1994). Therefore, if a suspect does not receive a pre-trial release—either bond or personal recognizance—that person could spend over six months in jail before going to trial.

In 1990, judges granted proportionally more pre-trial releases to female defendants than male defendants (Figure 1). Over 81% of female defendants received a pre-trial release, compared to less than 59% of males. While over 24% of females received personal recognizance releases, only 13% of males received such. Furthermore, while females received detention for an average of 49.2 days before their "speedy" trial, their male counterparts were detained, on average, over 61 days (*Compendium of Federal Justice Statistics 1990*, 26).

These statistics indicate a preferential bias toward females. Not only do females receive a far higher proportion of pre-trial releases than males, but among those releases twice as many are under personal recognizance. Not requiring monetary insurance that the suspect will appear at the arraignment (personal recognizance) implies

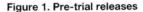

Figure 1. Pre-trial releases

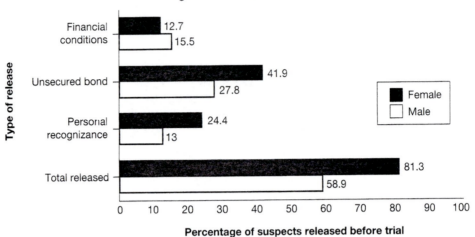

greater trust than if insurance is required (bond). According to the finding, then, females are viewed with far more trust. This finding did not surprise any of the twelve professionals we surveyed. They all mentioned that a bias exists and cited various reasons for it. Half of the respondents claimed that males commit more "violent" or "serious" crimes. Half claimed the courts wanted to return mothers to children as soon as possible. Several claimed that personal recognizance releases are more appropriate for females since they are more likely to conform to authority and meet the conditions of their pre-trial release.

Convictions

It is during the trial that the long-standing American adage "innocent until proven guilty" should manifest itself. As the prosecution and defense prepare arguments, the defendant's fate rests in the balance, and in the end "blind justice" should mete out equal punishment for equal offenses. If the defendant is found not guilty, they obviously receive no sentence. If the defendant is found guilty, however, the judges often have leeway in sentencing. Judges may imprison defendants or release them on probation, in effect placing them on warning. If convicts break parole stipulations, judges can sentence them to serve prison time.

Again, in conviction and sentencing, females receive lighter treatment in the judicial system than males. It is important to note that not all crimes are the same; violent crimes such as murder and rape traditionally receive stricter punishment than tax or immigration fraud. As Figure 2 shows, however, the *Compendium of Federal Justice Statistics* reports that a higher proportion of males are incarcerated (1990, 42) even when similar crimes are compared. Furthermore, as Figure 3 indicates, for the same type of crime, convicted males receive longer sentences than convicted females (1990, 43).

The range of the discrepancy between the figures varies from state to state (Figure 4). Taking the average of all convictions in the U.S., we find that in 1990 over 81% of male offenders received sentences, while only 54% of females received a sentence. Utah shows the largest discrepancy with over 75% of male offenders but less than 23% of female offenders receiving sentences (1990, 90). These findings surprised us the most. While we expected some discrepancy, we did not expect such a wide one. One respondent to our survey, an attorney with twenty years experience in two thousand cases, pointed out that male judges tend to be older and find sentencing males easy, but feel uncomfortable sentencing females. He claimed female judges are

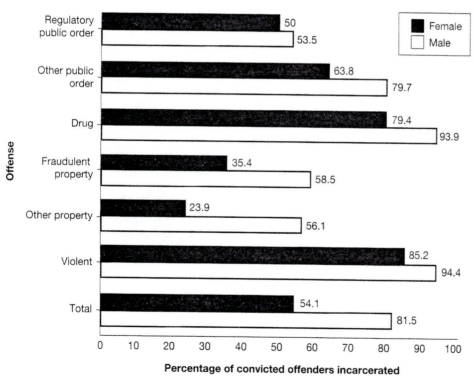

Figure 2. Convicted offenders incarcerated, 1990

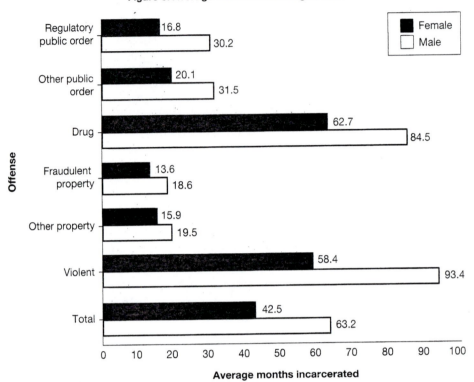

Figure 3. Average incarceration length, 1990

typically younger and favor female defendants, believing they have been oppressed by a male-dominant society. Another attorney claimed that male judges feel emotional and physical attraction for female defendants. A New Mexico Supreme Court justice agreed that judges view females differently than males. He explained the discrepancy by claiming that older male judges have more traditional views and see females as more gentle. If these claims are true, they expose a clear bias in the system. A subjective element obviously exists within the U.S. judicial system. One attorney with seventeen years experience summed it up with a pragmatic justification: "Males look meaner and nastier during sentencing, while females cry."

Prison environment

The prison environment determines an inmate's quality of life. This environment includes several factors such as health conditions, work requirements, and protection from other inmates. Males and females are seldom housed in the same facilities. Though U.S. pris-

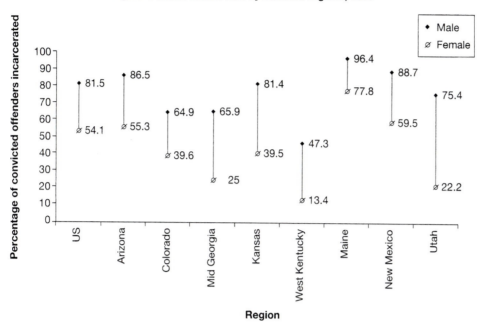

Figure 4. Incarceration rate by selected regions, 1990

ons hold over seventeen times more males than females (*Sourcebook of Criminal Justice Statistics 1992*, 590), the U.S. Department of Justice reports that over 33 times more males than females die while in prison (*Prisoners in State and Federal Institutions 1987*, 32). While much of this discrepancy may be explained by higher aggressiveness in males, Figure 5 displays how the higher death trend results also from causes such as suicide, illness, and accident (*Prisoners in State and Federal Prisons 1987*, 32). While overcrowding currently plagues facilities for both men and women, the problem is increasing at a faster rate in men's than in women's facilities (*Correctional Populations in the United States 1991*, 605).

We believed one reason for the discrepancy in prison deaths could be that females, in general, receive kinder and better treatment. Initially, we suspected a higher death rate for males resulted from their more violent nature. Three-fourths of our respondents agreed, mentioning that males act more aggressively, resulting in a higher mortality rate. The respondents also claimed that males have greater physical strength, territorial instincts, and access to dangerous tools. And while their comments may be true, statistics show that violence is not the major cause of prison deaths. Death by illness far outnumbers other causes of death (*Prisoners in State and Federal*

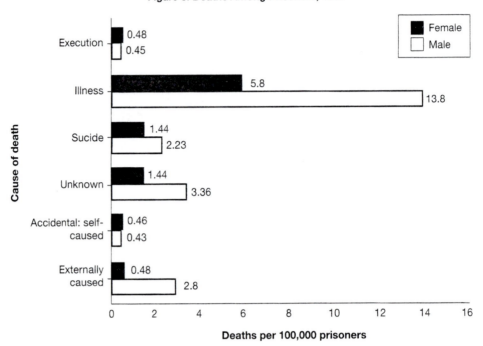

Figure 5. Deaths Among Prisoners, 1984

Prisons 1987, 32). We conclude that the prison environment is less healthy for males than females. One-third of the respondents proposed a supporting theory: the longer prison terms served by males lead to poorer health. After females have been released, males continue serving sentences in unhealthy prison environments, where they suffer higher susceptibility to health problems and death.

Parole

During a prison term, inmates receive merits and demerits based on behavior. If the inmate receives enough merits, a parole board may review his or her case. Parole boards hold the authority to alter an inmate's sentence by granting the prisoner parole, allowing them to leave prison and serve out the remainder of the sentence in public, under supervision of a parole officer.

The U.S. Department of Justice reports that of all prisoners paroled in 1990, 39% of males and 35% of females violated parole, very similar percentages. Further, as Figure 6 shows, even the ways parolees violated their parole were essentially the same (*Compendium of Federal Justice Statistics 1990*, 52). Yet, while over seventeen times as many males were in prison, only three times as many were paroled.

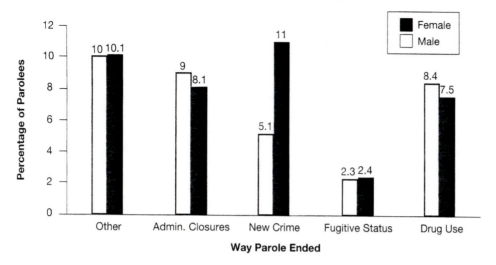

Figure 6. Results of Federal Prison Parole, 1990

As these statistics show, the pattern of preferential treatment for women continues. Professionals pointed to the same general reasons for bias in this phase of the judicial system as they did for other phases. They viewed females as more gentle and willing to comply with parole stipulations. A mother's place, they say, is with her children, and therefore she should leave the prison setting sooner than males. A New Mexico Supreme Court justice stated that "women are still a protected class and get disparate treatment."

Conclusion

Although we hypothesized that women would get preferential treatment in the justice system, we did not expect such conclusive results. The statistics, however, clearly showed a discrepancy in the treatment of males and females in four phases of the U.S. judicial system. Professionals in the field readily admitted that the numbers do not lie—a bias does exist. Every respondent alluded to a stereotype of females being the gentler, more obedient sex, a stereotype which they all felt justified lighter treatment.

The sheer size of the discrepancy—and the lack of public concern regarding it—allows us to draw some interesting conclusions. Regardless of marble monuments and high-minded philosophies, American justice is not blind; instead she views the world through the same lenses as the public which she serves. In this time of rising awareness of gender inequality, the American public must decide if biased justice is acceptable. If our society's inner sense of justice considers the discrepancy unacceptable, then we must somehow amputate the biases. However, if our sense of justice accepts—as we feel it does—the preferential treatment of females, then the current trend in the U.S. judicial system will continue. We believe that as the American public honestly considers the assumptions underlying this discrepancy, they will likely reach the same conclusion as one of our respondents, an Arizona Superior Court judge. He said that, while seeking equal application of the law may be philosophically correct, it contradicts a fundamental premise in our society: the genders *are* different, and gender differences connote different societal responsibilities. Therefore, equal treatment under the law may not be in harmony with our inner sense of justice.

<u>Works Cited</u>

Federal Bureau of Investigation. 1993. *Uniform crime reports.* Washington, D.C.: Government Printing Office.

Hall, Robert M. 1994. Attorney in Albuquerque, New Mexico. Interview by authors. 4 February, Provo, Utah.

U.S. Department of Justice. 1993. *Sourcebook of criminal justice statistics, 1992.* Washington, D.C.: Government Printing Office.

——. 1991. *Correctional populations in the United States, 1990.* Washington, D.C.: Government Printing Office.

——. 1990. *Compendium of federal justice statistics, 1990.* Washington, D.C.: Government Printing Office.

——. 1990. *Federal criminal case processing, 1980–89.* Washington, D.C.: Government Printing Office.

——. 1990. *National corrections reporting program, 1990.* Washington, D.C.: Government Printing Office.

——. 1987. *Prisoners in state and federal institutions on December 31.* Washington, D.C.: Government Printing Office.

——. 1985. *Compendium of federal justice statistics, 1984.* Washington, D.C.: Government Printing Office.

Appendix: Survey Instrument

We are conducting an empirical study for a college research paper. Your answers to the following questions will remain confidential. By filling out this questionnaire, you imply your consent to let us use your answers in our study.

1. Your field of experience in criminal law (job title):

2. The *Compendium of Federal Justice Statistics 1990* lists the following statistics:

Average sentences

Type of Crime	Male Sentence	Female Sentence
Violent Crime	93.4 months	58.4 months
Fraudulent Property Offense	18.6 months	13.6 months
Drug Offense	84.5 months	62.7 months
Public Order Offense	30.2 months	16.8 months

Why do males receive longer average sentences?

Percentage of convicted offenders sentenced to incarceration

Type of Crime	Male	Female
Violent Crime	94.4	85.2
Property Offense	56.1	23.9
Drug Offenses	93.9	79.4
Public Order Offense	79.7	63.8

Why is a higher percentage of males incarcerated for each type of crime?

3. According to the *Compendium of Federal Justice Statistics 1990*, 59% of men and 81% of women received a pretrial release. Why does such a discrepancy exist?

4. According to the *Compendium of Federal Justice 1990*, 39% of men and 35% of women break parole. According to US Bureau of Justice statistics, 23% of men and 35% of women are paroled. Why is a larger percentage of women paroled when they show roughly the same behavior on parole?

5. According to the *Sourcebook of Criminal Justice Statistics 1992*, a 17:1 ratio of men to women existed among federal prison inmates. During the same year there was a 33:1 ratio of male to female deaths within federal prisons. Why do you think twice as many men as women died within the prison system?

SUGGESTIONS FOR RESEARCH AND WRITING

1. If your parents or some other family members have saved letters, perhaps from a courtship or a period of military service, obtain and read the letters, looking for one or more themes that you could develop in a paper. Use the letters as primary sources, quoting from them to support your interpretations. If appropriate, locate and use secondary sources that will help illuminate the time period in which the letters were written. Use appropriate citations and provide a bibliography for all your sources.

2. Often when states, communities, or colleges approach an important anniversary (the bicentennial of their founding, for example), they write a history of the time period just ended. If you live in a place where an important anniversary is about to be commemorated, see if you can contribute to writing its history. If someone is coordinating the history, you may be assigned to read and interpret documents that contribute to one part of the total history. On the other hand, if no one is in charge of writing a history, you might volunteer to pore over documents that have been saved and write a brief history of some part of your city, state, or college.

3. How has student life changed on your campus in the past 60 years? There is likely to be an archive of student newspapers and yearbooks on campus that you can explore to answer questions that are interesting to you about your parents' and grandparents' college days. Here are some possibilities: What were the important campus issues in the 1950s? How important were sports or the Greek system or queen contests in the 1960s? Have students become more politically aware over the last 20 years? Have students become more career-oriented since 1980?

4. Study magazine ads for a particular kind of product (e.g., alcohol, cigarettes, cars, or headache remedies) over a period of 20–30 years. Note how the ads change, if they do, to appeal to different needs or desires of the consumer. What can you infer about how the ad makers viewed consumers in a particular time period?

5. Some scientists have suggested that men and women look for different characteristics in their potential mates. Test that hypothesis by getting several different editions of a local newspaper that carries personal ads from single people looking for a relationship with a member of the opposite sex. Compare the ads from women and from men and try to determine if they are seeking different qualities. What things, if any, appear to be repeated? How important are physical characteristics in the ads? Age? Personality traits? Particular interests or hobbies? Write a paper summarizing and illustrating your findings.

6. Television programs are a type of text. They begin as written documents, but the viewer watches a script enacted, rather than reading it. Watch reruns of a particular TV program over a period of several weeks, say

"Leave it to Beaver" or "Happy Days" and study how one character is developed. From that character's words and actions, try to infer what viewers valued in the era when the program was current and popular. Another possibility would be to compare two programs that featured African-Americans as the main characters, for example, "Sanford and Son" and "The Cosby Show." How do the characters, the plots, and the values differ between these two shows?

7. Identify one of the oldest of the major journals in your field. Check your library to see if it has the earliest volumes of the journal; skim several early volumes to identify a main research topic then. Read carefully two or three articles that report investigations of that topic. What are the research questions or hypotheses? What methods are used? What are the findings and how are they interpreted? How does the state of knowledge at that time compare to the present understanding of that topic? What can you infer about how your discipline has changed?

REFERENCES

Brace, C. Loring. 1996. Review of *The bell curve: Intelligence and class structure in American life*, by Richard J. Herrnstein and Charles Murray. *Current Anthropology* 37 (February Supplement): S156–S161.

Gould, Stephen J. 1994. Curveball. *New Yorker*. 28 November, 139–149.

Heckman, James J. 1995. Lessons from the bell curve. *Journal of Political Economy* 103 (October): 1091–1120.

Herrnstein, Richard J., and Charles Murray. 1994. *The bell curve: Intelligence and class structure in American life*. New York: Free Press.

5

INTERVIEWING

Interviewing is a widely used method of data gathering in the social sciences. This method is the primary one of anthropologists, folklorists, and some sociologists; it is also commonly used by political scientists, psychologists, and linguists. Both print and broadcast journalists rely on interviewing as their main way of gathering information for news stories. Interviews can be highly structured, following carefully predetermined questions aimed at gathering precise bits of information; or they can be very open ended, guided only by a general purpose. Skilled interviewers in most fields learn how to conduct both kinds.

Interviewing is commonly also used to supplement other methods of data gathering. For example, observational research and experimental research might be followed by an interview in which participants are questioned about the behavior they exhibited. Surveys may be conducted orally, in which case they are a type of interview. The study of documents may also be supplemented with interviews. A researcher can compensate for the gaps in documents by interviewing people who are knowledgeable about whatever time, people, or customs are described in the documents. Since some individuals and groups tend not to create many documents that would tell future generations about them, and since it is impossible to interview the dead, some oral historians work to preserve the history of individuals and groups before they die. For example, many of the Allied soldiers who liberated the Nazi extermination camps in the 1940s have either already died or are now advanced in age. Historians have interviewed many of these former soldiers to create a record of their impressions when they first found the survivors, the bodies, and the ovens at such places as Auschwitz and Buchenwald.

Usually, we think of interviewing only one person—at most two or three people—at a time, but a new type of group interview is emerging as an important research tool. This group interview, called focus group research, is used frequently in marketing, opinion polling, education, social psychology, and law. Focus group research could well be an important method for you to learn about. However, it is fairly difficult for undergraduates to conduct focus group research, given the difficulty of getting several people in one place at the same time and given the typically limited resources students have for funding research projects. Therefore, this chapter will provide basic instructions for conducting interviews only with individuals.

Interviewing is one of the easiest and least expensive methods of research that students can try. But it is not a trivial method by any means, for as this chapter will show, there are a number of things you will need to consider as you plan and conduct an interview in order to have something worth writing about at the end. First, you prepare for the interview and for recording information. Then you conduct the interview itself. Finally, you use the data collected to construct a written record of the interview or contextualize the information from the interview to support the thesis of a broader argument.

PREPARING FOR THE INTERVIEW

An interview will be only as successful as the preparation that precedes it. Begin with the end in mind. Think about your reasons for conducting the interview. What do you want to find out? How will you eventually use the information you obtain? What kind of document will you be writing? Will it be simply a transcript of the interview? Will it be part of a larger research project that includes information from other sources as well? Once you have answered questions like these, you are ready to follow the steps below to prepare for a successful interview.

FIND INFORMANTS

How you find people to interview depends on what you're looking for. Sometimes you may want to know what a particular person thinks—a famous writer, a government official, a successful business executive, a noted scholar. In that case, you simply ask the person for an interview. Other times, you may want to know about a particular topic—events in the past, how to do something, or how people south of the Alleghenies pronounce the word *greasy*. In that case, you must find people who possess the kind of information you want.

Suppose you want to collect information about woodcarving, an art that some of the older men in your community, including your grandfather, practice. Your grandfather would be an obvious person to interview; he might also refer you to others. There are other possible ways to locate woodcarvers whom you could interview: Local museums that display carvings, specialty shops that market them, and newspaper ads are all possible ways of getting leads for interviews. Simply asking around is another way to find informants. For example, if you wanted to interview old-timers about the history of a small town, you might stop at the local cafe and ask the regular customers who some likely informants are.

CONTACT THE INFORMANTS

If time permits, you can send a letter stating your aims and why you want to interview the person you've contacted. The letter gives the person time to think over the invitation and decide whether they can be helpful to you. Follow the letter with a phone call, a visit, or both. If time is more pressing, a telephone call or personal visit may be the first contact. Be prepared to state clearly what you want and why you think that person will be a good informant. Ask a few questions to get acquainted with your informant and find out if he or she really has the kind of information you are looking for and is willing to share the information. If both of you are willing to continue, arrange for a mutually agreeable time and location for the interview. It may be possible to conduct the interview over the telephone if time, distances, or scheduling conflicts prohibit a face-to-face meeting.

DO NECESSARY BACKGROUND RESEARCH

You should come to the interview knowing as much as you can about the informant and the subject you will discuss. If the informant is well known, you may be able to read about him or her in the library by finding biographical information, previous interviews, or articles or books they've published. Whenever you can, learn about your informant's background. Learn also the terminology you will need. You should know the basic vocabulary and issues related to the topic of the interview so that you can ask intelligent questions and understand the answers. The interview time will not be as profitably spent as it might be if your informant must give you an introduction to the basic assumptions, ideas, and terms involved.

PLAN YOUR QUESTIONS

Either write your questions out completely or list the topics you want to cover in the interview. But study them long enough so you have them well in mind when you go because you shouldn't let your questions get in the way of having a real conversation. For example, don't plan to simply read from your list mechanically, checking off items on it, as if you can't wait to be finished. Plan to be flexible because in some cases you may want the interview to follow the course suggested by whatever the informant brings up. You will not be able to anticipate all the questions you should ask; therefore, a critical skill to develop as an interviewer is the ability to listen attentively to your informant and follow up interesting or provocative information with questions that draw out a little more information or pursue the implications of what has been said. It can be helpful to conduct a mock interview first, asking a friend to play the role of the informant. By rehearsing your questions in this way, you will feel better prepared when you conduct the real interview.

PREPARE THE MATERIALS YOU WILL NEED

At a minimum, you will need a notebook and pens or pencils to take notes. If it is possible, however, you should plan to record the interview, using audiotape or, in some cases, videotape. You will need to get the consent of your informants to use mechanical recording devices; you may also need the approval of an Institutional Review Board (see Chapter 3) and you may need to have your informant sign a consent form (see Chapter 11). There are potential advantages and drawbacks to all three means of recording the proceedings of the interview, as explained next.

RECORDING THE INTERVIEW

NOTE TAKING

Taking notes has the advantage of costing little and perhaps of making informants feel more at ease than they often do in the presence of a tape recorder. But writing while you attempt to be an attentive listener and at the same time think about your next question is difficult at best, and it slows the interview down. There is the possibility that you may not write down as much as you should or that you will write something inaccurately. Oversights and errors such as these obviously will impair the quality of what you eventually write about the interview. However, some interviewers, such as journalists, often cannot use recorders so they practice to become adept at taking notes efficiently. They sometimes check the accuracy of what they have written by later telephoning their informants to be sure that their written representations of the interview, particularly quotations, are accurate.

AUDIOTAPING

You must decide if it is necessary to make an audiotape by evaluating your purpose in the interview and the necessity of having a complete record of what was said. If your goal is simply to ask someone a few questions to fill a class assignment and if nothing further will be done with the interview data, making an audiotape may be an elaborate and unnecessary step. On the other hand, if your purpose requires that you be more thorough and careful in recording, consider taping the interview.

Because tapes provide a more complete and permanent record of an interview than notes, they are indispensable for data collection in fields such as folklore, oral history, anthropology, sociology, and linguistic mapping of regional dialects. If you conduct research in one of these fields, and particularly if you plan to become a professional, purchasing a good tape recorder could be a wise investment in your future. If you are not ready to make that investment, you can often borrow or rent the recorder; purchasing the tape itself is not a big expense. There are also devices you can attach to a telephone to tape record an interview—which you must only use with the informant's permission, of course.

Once you have the equipment, however, you must familiarize yourself with how to use it and be prepared for the kinds of mechanical failures that can disrupt an otherwise well-planned interview. Edward Ives (1995) suggests you practice using the equipment in mock interviews before the real thing. If possible, Ives advises, you should have an external microphone for your recorder because you will be able to position it better to pick up both your informant's and your own voice. Ives also reminds you to check the batteries, microphone, and electrical cord before you go, and to pack an extension cord in case you will need it. When you start the interview, record a few words; then stop and play them back to be sure the recorder is working before you proceed.

Ives (1995) also suggests you let your informants know at the time you arrange for the interview that you would like to tape it. If they are reluctant, try to reassure and gently persuade them of the value of a taped interview. If they still object, you could pack the recorder along anyway; they may decide to permit you to turn it on once they see how slow the note taking process makes the interview. But if they do still decline to be recorded, you must respect their wishes. Never secretly record an interview.

VIDEOTAPING

What is true of audiotaping is often doubly true of videotaping. A good video-cassette recorder can be expensive, and learning to use a video recorder skillfully takes time. The location of the interview also must be conducive to good recording, with adequate lighting and background motion and noise kept to a minimum. You must weigh these considerations against what you gain by having a visual as well as auditory record of the interview. Is it important to capture such things as the informant's facial expressions, gestures, and movements? Will you be trying to interpret these visual cues as well as to analyze the spoken words of the informant?

For many social scientists, the words spoken in the interview are all they want to record. For others, however, videotapes permit them to analyze the participants' nonverbal behavior as well as their words. With videotapes they can view the behavior more than once, and different observers can view the same event. Using categories they have previously agreed on, these observers can code the behaviors they see and calculate a statistic, called interrater reliability, to determine the consistency of the observational analysis (see Chapter 6). More detail about videotaped interviews is beyond the scope of this chapter, so the next section focuses mainly on using audiotape to preserve an accurate record of the interview.

CONDUCTING THE INTERVIEW

Whatever method you choose to record the interview, when you finally come face to face with your informant, you must first set him or her at ease. Some informants may think that their lives are so "ordinary" that no one could possibly be interested in what they have to say. As a result, at first they may not say very much; they may have to warm up to you and the topic first, so be patient if the beginning seems slow and difficult. Others may be a little suspicious of your motives; if so, reassure them of what you said in the initial contact about your aims and about what will eventually be done with the information they give you. Some informants may be nervous about talking into a tape recorder and will "clam up." However, most will probably relax after a few minutes. It may help to let them know you are a little nervous, too.

If you are taping the interview, and if the tape will become part of an archive (as is common in folklore and oral history research), Ives (1995) suggests you let the informant listen to you record your opening statement. Speaking directly into the microphone, state the date and your name. Then state the name of the person you are interviewing and the topic of the interview. Then casually tell the informant what the purpose of the interview is and ask if the person grants permission for you to record the interview. In this way you can record the verbal acknowledgment of the person.

After stating the preliminaries, begin by asking a few easy or general questions. Then you should direct the interview intelligently, using good on-the-spot judgment about where to go next. For example, you could vary the order of questions from what you initially planned. If the informant wants to talk about something that obviously interests him or her, you should probably permit the digression and bring it back to your topic when you can. Shifts and tangents can often be revealing, making you aware of dimensions of the topic that you hadn't considered. Don't be afraid to probe your informant's answers more deeply to get more and better information. Use follow-up questions to get more detail, such as "Where?" "When?" or "Who else was there?" Don't fire these questions too rapidly at the informant, however. Remember that silence can also be probing, so don't rush to fill every silence with more words; give your informant time to think and to answer at length.

Because notes and audiotape have no visual dimension, Ives (1995) notes that you may have to put into words what your informant is showing through gesture. If the informant says, "It was about this big," judge the distance displayed and say something like, "About four feet tall and two feet wide?" Record accurate information that will help explain a gestured "this" and "that" or "here" and "there." The record you make of the interview is for all the people who will later be interested in it, so try to preserve information they would get if they were present at the interview.

The length of interviews will vary. One hour is a good rule of thumb, but good information can be collected in less time, depending on your purposes. If you spend longer than an hour or two, you may wear out your welcome and overtax the informant. You may need more than one interview session to get all the information that you want. For example, if you are doing an oral history and your informant turns out to have a wealth of good information to offer, ask if you can come back another time to continue interviewing. Even if you think you have gleaned all you can in one interview, you may realize later that you need a brief follow-up interview, either in person or by telephone, to fill in gaps or answer questions that have arisen since your interview. Your informant may also remember more in the meantime, and you may be pleasantly surprised by what else you will gain from an additional interview.

When you finish interviewing, you may need to have the informant sign a consent form allowing you to use the information in a public way (see Chapter 11 for more information on consent forms). When you are sure that no more interviews will be necessary, write a thank you note to your informant to express your gratitude for the time they gave you. Let your informant know where the interview data will be archived, if it will be. If the interview will be published, let them know where and when. If it won't be published, you can at least offer to send a copy of the report you will write.

MOVING FROM NOTES OR TAPE TO TEXT

Immediately after an interview, write complete and careful notes about the circumstances of the interview. Consider what contextual information is important for future readers of the interview to know. For example, you may want to note the surroundings in which the interview took place, what the informant looked like, or who else was present. If you audiotape the interview, include in your notes any information that will help explain any background noises or other voices. If you will be depositing the tape in an archive, you will need to know what requirements the archive has for the notes to accompany the tape. Think of future listeners to the tapes and include in your notes whatever would help them to make better use of it.

After writing notes about the context of the interview, you must consider how to "write up" the interview in a paper that will allow readers to know what went on without actually listening to the tape or trying to reconstruct the interview from your notes. There are basically four ways to make a text out of an interview.

TRANSCRIPTS

The first type of text is a *transcript*—a literal word-by-word rendering of the entire interview, including the "ums" and "ahs," the pauses, the laughter, and the incomplete or convoluted sentences that are a part of any conversation. Transcription of an interview is a time-consuming process but often a necessary one to be sure that no possibly relevant detail is omitted. Transcriptions are seldom published unedited, but they are sometimes considered primary documents, and if they are worthy of preservation, they are often stored in archives along with tapes. Most oral history archives require complete transcripts.

The completeness of the transcription and the extra features it might include depend on how it is to be used. Linguists might want you to use a special phonetic alphabet or diacritical marks on words to indicate how they were pronounced; psychologists might want you to include pauses, laughs, "ums," and "ers." Other nonverbal features can be noted in brackets. Decide how closely the transcript must follow the tape. You may decide to leave out the false starts and "ums," simply noting that you have done so; but generally you would not correct grammar, usage, or sentence structure because these may reveal important things about the informant. Use your judgment as to how to punctuate the transcript. When you are finished transcribing, listen to the tape again and compare it to the transcript. Oral historians sometimes send the informant a copy of the transcript and ask for it to be returned with corrections noted. For oral history, the corrected transcript becomes the primary document. But folklorists consider the tape the primary document and the transcript is merely supplemental.

DIALOGUE OR EDITED TRANSCRIPT

The second type of text is the *dialogue* or *edited transcript*. On paper, a dialogue looks like the script for a play, with the speaker's name given in boldface or capital letters right before their words. The words following the speakers' names represent essentially what they said in the sequence in which they said it, but the words have been edited to omit the verbal tics such as "uh" and to improve syntax and clarity. If you edit a transcript, you should include a note at the beginning or end indicating what kinds of editorial changes have been made; you should also note in the text when you have inserted a word or phrase for clarity by including it in brackets.

The following excerpt is from an interview with Mary Field Belenky, one of the authors of *Women's Ways of Knowing*, a part of which is reproduced later in this chapter. This excerpt shows the dialogue method of presenting an interview (it also presents interesting information about how interviewers and informants can become collaborators). The words of the interviewers (Ashton and Thomas 1990) and the informant (Belenky) in this dialogue are represented by "Q" (for question) and "A" (for answer).

Q. Are you positing a much larger group of collaborators than the four of you who coauthored *Women's Ways?*

A. Absolutely. The women we interviewed were themselves drawn in. A word that seems better than *collaboration* is *dialogue* because it suggests that our so-called research subjects were real participants in the project. In a very real sense they were also, much of the time when we were writing, the audience. Let me tell you about Lillian Rubin's *Worlds of Pain*, a study of lower middle-class marriages—a study that is, like ours, based on interviews. Rubin had a pact with the people that she interviewed: they would review and approve any writing she did before it went to publication. She notes that none of those people had much criticism of her writing, so she didn't change or reedit the work in light of it; but I believe, because she had this pact to give them the work before publishing it, that she wrote *to them* in a way—and it's a beautiful book. Rubin's book was a model for us, even though our sample was too large to promise everybody we would get their permission. But as our book was written, we very much had in mind that it would be read by the people we had interviewed.

Q. So the audience you had in mind as you were writing was a friendly audience, women who could benefit from the information as you organized it?

A. Absolutely. But the information wasn't just what *we* were thinking or organizing; it was also *their* words because we worked from transcripts of the interviews. In fact, when the book first came out many women said that we had given words to things they'd always thought. It seemed funny at first, a backhanded kind of compliment. Here we'd done this extraordinary thing. But giving words to these ideas was exactly what we tried to do, and that's a lot to do. Moreover, I think we ought to teach ourselves and our students that we can have real choices about audience. We all need to understand how writing the same material for different audiences changes the voice. That is very empowering knowledge to have.

Q. How did you coordinate the actual writing of *Women's Ways*?

A. We had a month-long pajama party at a cottage on the shore, a big rambling mansion on the ocean. We spent the month trying to frame the book and talking through the process of writing it; by the end of the month, we had a reasonably firm view of its shape, so we sketched out a table of contents. Then when we looked at the plan, it made sense that one person or another would write certain chapters. Certainly, some decisions were arbitrary, but for the most part we saw a clear and rational division of labor that made deep sense. We also made a decision which in retrospect I think was very smart: that we would not put our names on different pieces. I don't know why we made that decision, and I'm still not sure why that was so smart. But I think it was, and it's probably one of the reasons the book ultimately developed the one-voice quality that it has.[1]

INTERVIEW SUMMARY

The third type of text is one that presents mainly a *summary of the interview* with occasional quoting of the informant's words as they were spoken. This kind of text is commonly found in newspapers and magazines. This way of writing up an interview gives the writer more control of how to sequence the information obtained in the interview. The writer can select from the entire contents of the interview those parts that help him or her to support a particular interpretation or overall claim about the interview. Of course, an ethical interviewer will not deliberately select some kinds of information or distort what was said to present a biased claim that would not be supported by a reading of the entire transcript of the interview.

However, the writer's ability to select and determine the order of presentation does mean that the final "write-up" of an interview can be quite different from the interview itself. The student paper at the end of this chapter illustrates this kind of text. The students who wrote this paper conducted four interviews with people who have disabilities. The investigators wanted to learn what labels people with disabilities prefer for describing themselves and their

---

[1] From Evelyn Ashton-Jones and Dene Kay Thomas, "Composition, Collaboration, and Women's Ways of Knowing: A Conversation with Mary Belenky," *Journal of Advanced Composition* 10 (Fall 1990), pp. 278–279. Reprinted by permission of *JAC*. Copyright © 1990 by the Association of Teachers of Advanced Composition.

particular disabilities. Their paper is organized to compare the answers given by the four informants and to summarize the significance of all the data.

SYNTHESIS AND ELABORATION

The fourth kind of text is a *synthesis and elaboration* of interview data, used mainly when the text is based on many interviews, each one with a different informant, but each one aimed at gathering information to answer a particular research question. The writer analyzes the transcripts of all the interviews, looking for points of similarity and difference and for ways of categorizing the information revealed in all the interviews. The writer then presents the findings in a way that generalizes about all the interviews, occasionally interspersing quotations from different informants to illustrate a point. The professional example presented next illustrates this way of writing about interview data.

A PROFESSIONAL EXAMPLE

The excerpt reproduced below comes from *Women's Ways of Knowing* by Mary Field Belenky, Blythe McVicker Clinchy, Nancy Rule Goldberger, and Jill Mattuck Tarule.[2] These authors interviewed 135 women of all ages and from many walks of life. Some were college students; others the authors met through social service agencies. On the basis of all the data collected, the authors concluded that women use five ways of knowing. The following excerpt discusses the second way, received knowing. You will note as you read that the authors define what received knowing is by integrating quotations from their informants and references to secondary sources, other scholarly works about similar topics. The authors use the secondary sources to interpret their informants' words and experiences. By the end of the chapter, you will see there are far fewer illustrations from the interviews and more references to secondary sources and more interpretations of the significance of this category of knowing. In this way, the authors create a persuasive argument for the existence of the received knower category by grounding their conclusions not only in quotations from the interviews but in other well-established literature. The annotations in the margins will help you see how the authors construct an argument from the two kinds of data they integrate.

---

[2] Mary Field Belenky, Blythe McVicker Clinchy, Nancy Rule Goldberger, and Jill Mattuck Tarule, *Women's Ways of Knowing: The Development of Self, Voice, and Mind* (New York: Basic Books, 1986), pp. 35–43. Copyright © 1986 by Basic Books, Inc. Reprinted by permission of Basic Books, a division of HarperCollins Publishers, Inc.

Received Knowledge:
Listening to the Voices
of Others

> She never did and never could put words
> together, out of her own head.
> —George Eliot
> *Middlemarch*

The chapter opens with an illustration of Ann, who first began to think of herself as a "knower" when she had a baby. The authors point out that Ann is typical of many women, who seek knowledge from those they consider authorities.

FOR ANN, becoming a mother—rather than having had a mother—provided the first profound experience of human connection. She said, "My life was really, really dull. The only thing that really stands out is the birth of my children. That's the only important thing that has happened to me ever. So that is about it."

Many women, like Ann, experience giving birth to their children as a major turning point in their lives. Often, parenthood initiates an epistemological revolution. In response to our question, "What was the most important learning experience you have ever had?" many mothers selected childbirth. It is as if this act of creation ushers in a whole new view of one's creative capacities.

Ann had to reassess herself as a knower when she anxiously assumed the responsibilities of parenthood. Being responsible for a dependent infant can easily bring into question a world view that assumes that one is "deaf and dumb" and dependent on others for care. Although such a view might have been highly adaptive for surviving a demeaning childhood, it is inadequate as a basis for mothering. Needing help, Ann turned to the experts at a children's health center and found with relief that they knew everything. They were easily available and highly responsive.

The reference to "deaf and dumb" is to silent knowers, the category discussed in the previous chapter.

> They were wonderful. It just seems that they know all the answers to everything that has to do with children. They have been just everything to me. They've been like a security blanket. You know, I can call anytime something happens—even at night time. They are always friendly and cheerful. You don't have to be afraid.

The authors note that the authorities Ann listened to were unusual because they encouraged Ann to think of herself as knowledgeable.

The authorities were very supportive of Ann. Responding to her in her own terms, they drew out her questions, concerns, and ideas and refrained from dictating theirs. Unlike many professionals, they continually emphasized *her* competence, not theirs. "Their confidence in me really spurred me on. I'd walk in there and they would say, You're wonderful. You're a great mother, you're great. I'd walk out of there feeling so good. I'd feel like I could tame the world." The authorities also used language that she could understand. "When you need them, they take the time to explain things. You know, they are all very patient; they spell it all out—'cause I'm not too smart."

Finding that she could hear, understand, and remember the things they taught her, she began to think of herself as a learner for the first time. "They teach you everything there is to know about babies. If it has anything to do with health problems, a nutritional problem—there's nothing I could learn anywhere that they haven't already taught me." Ann became a storehouse of information. Not only could she receive knowledge from others but she could also pass that knowledge on to others. "I now feel very knowledgeable as far as kids go. I advise all my friends with kids, you know. I say, 'This is what I've learned at the center.' I've learned a lot. I feel like I could go in there and they could hire me—you know—that's how much knowledge they have given me."

The authors quote again from Ann to show that she did increase her confidence that she could know things herself and teach others.

Listening as a Way of Knowing

This heading indicates the authors will next discuss a major component of received knowing—listening.

Unlike the silent, who think of themselves as "deaf and dumb" and are unaware of the power of words for transmitting knowledge, women who rely on received knowledge think of words as *central* to the knowing process. They learn by listening. As Rachel, a college freshman, said, "I enjoy listening to discussions. I find I am doing okay just through listening."

A young student who had moved from jail to a community college was exhilarated to hear from other students—"those who know."

The authors quote two other informants to show how important listening is for received knowers.

The women who are students here know so much and I know nothing. I like to sit back and just listen to what they have to say. A lot of times I feel that way. When I started college I knew nothing and it was for me to get from both the students as well as the professor. Because when I walked into the classroom, I was twenty-one years old and these grown people sitting in the room—they had to know something.

This woman experiences listening as a very active and demanding process. "You get a real taste, putting your mind to work—sitting in class concentrating—listening and really getting something from it. Unless you're taking something *in*, it's not worth it."

The ideas and ideals that these women hear in the words of others are concrete and dualistic. Things are right or wrong, true or false, good or bad, black or white. They assume that there is only one right answer to each question, and that all other answers and all con-

The authors refer to a secondary source, William Perry, to explain that they find received knowers think in dualistic terms, something that Perry noted in his research.

Quoting their informants again, the authors show that received knowers think it is more important to listen to words than to speak them. They claim that received knowers usually doubt their ability to speak intelligently.

This subheading indicates the authors found friends were very important to received knowers. The authors develop this topic at length.

The authors quote more informants to show that women in the category of received knowers find it important to have friends who think just like they do.

But the authors point out that received knowers are usually not aware of the extent to which they allow others to influence their thinking. The authors allude to the fairy tale "The Emperor's New Clothes" and to research that supports this interpretation.

---

trary views are automatically wrong. These characteristics were so salient in William Perry's (1970) description of this perspective that he named this outlook *dualism*.

While received knowers can be very open to take in what others have to offer, they have little confidence in their own ability to speak. Believing that truth comes from others, they still their own voices to hear the voices of others. Rachel described the voicelessness she experienced her first year at college: "I don't talk in class very much myself. I am not a participator. Everybody at college is sort of outgoing. Everybody I've met has a vocabulary a mile long. My problem is—is that I have trouble communicating. Even if I have it straight in my head, it's very difficult for me to talk." Another woman recalled a similar experience. "Before I used to talk and the wrong words would come out and people would say, 'What, what?' They would never understand me."

LISTENING TO FRIENDS

The received knowers are frequently surprised and relieved to hear others saying the very same things that they would say. One of the adolescent mothers felt nervous talking with most people, but not with her aunt who had both a baby and a husband exactly like hers.

> My aunt is special. She acts more like my best friend. I could tell her what I could tell nobody else. Anything and everything. We don't get nervous talking to each other. We think alike. Like you can talk to somebody about how you feel and they feel the same way you do. The same thing. It's really strange—like, see, her husband and my husband are just about the same—they don't talk at all. They're alike. We're alike. We think the same things.

Ginny, upon entering an early college and depending on receiving knowledge from others, was delighted to find that her ideas were identical to those held by her new friends. "Everyone in my dorm gets along. We do about the same thing. Usually if one person doesn't like it, everybody else is not going to like it because we have the same thoughts about it."

The young received knowers have a literal faith that they and their friends share exactly the same thoughts and experiences. They relish having so much in common and are unaware of their tendency to shape their perceptions and thoughts to match those of others. Looking to others for knowledge they are likely to be among those who could see the emperor in full regalia. (See, for example, Asch

1952; Costanzo and Shaw 1966; Saltzstein, Diamond, and Belenky 1972.) The young women who hold this perspective celebrate and magnify the experiences of similarities and intimacies with others. To us these relationships have a symbiotic quality that was not observed among the other women we interviewed when they described their friendships. But as we will see, it is exactly these kinds of relationships that provide women with experiences of mutuality, equality, and reciprocity that are most helpful in eventually enabling them to disentangle their own voice from the voices of others. It is from just such relationships that women seem to emerge with a powerful sense of their own capacities for knowing.

The authors imply that it may be important to women to go through a stage of received knowing so that they can find their own voices and gain an enhanced view of themselves as knowers.

Ginny provided an example of how transformative relationships with peers could be. As she said, during her freshman year she and her friends had "the same thoughts," but by the time they were sophomores, each spoke with a distinctive voice. In her second interview she said,

The authors illustrate how one woman, Ginny, moved through the stage of received knowing.

> Before, you know—you do just what everyone else does. You don't show what you really feel. You don't just stand out and say something. You didn't even know what your friends were thinking half the time—they'd just agree with everyone else. Now we tell each other just about everything. If you get really mad—you just go yell at them! They'll sit there and listen to you. They don't get really upset. They usually try to stop [doing whatever it was]. You are really open. It really helps. You know, they'll listen and that's helped a lot, I think.

Ginny and her friends had learned to speak with one another in a way that they could cultivate most easily in relationships imbued with care, trust, and endless discussions.

The authors conclude that caring relationships with friends permit the development of an individual voice and mind.

LISTENING TO AUTHORITIES

Although most women find the powers of their voice and mind most readily in relationships with friends, those who think that they *receive* all knowledge are more apt to think of authorities, not friends, as sources of truth. They equate receiving, retaining, and returning the words of authorities with learning—at least with the kind of learning they associate with school.

The next subheading indicates that listening to authorities was as prominent in the interviews as listening to friends. The authors note that most of their informants think of authorities, not friends, as the source of truth. They illustrate their point with Ann.

Ann, we saw, could learn verbatim what was right and wrong from the experts at the children's health center. Although Ann gained considerable confidence in her ability to receive, retain, and even pass on knowledge that others gave her, she still feels that she could not generate facts and ideas through reflection on her own experience. "I have to rely on the experts. I've never been one to make decisions. Whenever I need to know about something, I have to go to someone who knows. I have to rely on them because I don't know anywhere else."

Before, feeling "deaf and dumb," Ann depended on authorities to actually *do* things for her. Later, she heard "right answers" coming from authorities in words that she could understand. She depended on authorities to *tell* her what was right and wrong. Before, she wanted to be shown.

Angela entered a prestigious college as a received knower. When Angela sought "truth" she looked to authorities and imagined it being passed on from one person to another. "I tend to trust more what a professor says than what a student says. I have more faith in the teacher, that what he says is correct and concise. Whereas the student might be giving her opinion; it might not be the right one. The teachers are always more or less right." And why are professors always more or less right? Angela says, "They have books to look at. Things that you look up in a book, you normally get the right answer." As typical of received knowers, Angela did not realize that authorities have the capacity for constructing knowledge. In their view authorities must receive "truths" from the words of even higher authorities. They assume that all authorities are infinitely capable of receiving and retaining "the right answer" with impeccable precision.

Wanting to do the right thing but having no opinions and no voice of their own to guide them, women in this position listen to others for directions as well as for information. A young woman from the community college found guidance in her brother. "My brother—he is a person who will talk and reason with you. He's calm. He's calm and he will talk things out. I listen to him—whatever he tells me. Whatever my brother tells me, I do. I do it because I know that he has thought it out and he's not going to tell me nothing but the best that's for me. I trust him." It was not her own but her brother's voice that this young woman heard and followed as she searched for the ideas that would give shape to her life.

Maria, too, had always looked to her elders for the "right answer." As a foreign student entering a progressive early college, she was faced with many changes, most prominent of which was the lack of adults willing to guide her every move. She was accustomed to being told everything. "In my old school, they give the courses they want to give. You don't choose your courses. And my parents—you know, they told me that it is wrong when whatever I was doing was wrong. Then if something was right, they would tell me." In her new school Maria had to make her own choices and be responsible

The authors use the case of Angela to show how received knowers view authorities, such as professors, and how they believe these authorities receive their knowledge from even higher authorities. Received knowers do not yet realize that "authorities" construct knowledge.

The authors conclude that received knowers want to receive directions as well as information from authorities. They illustrate this point with two examples.

The authors show how difficult it was for Maria to "boss" herself when she had no authorities to tell her what to do. She couldn't determine right and wrong for herself.

for those choices. She worried how she would do that. "At the beginning, I wasn't so sure that I was gonna be bossing myself, doing whatever I wanted, and [still be able] to choose what was right and wrong. Still—you know—I still have a long way to go. [Laughs.] I don't know." "Bossing" herself without the guidance of adults' dictates, while facing cultural diversity, made the task seem overwhelming: "I really don't know. I really don't know—[long pause]—what's right and what's wrong yet. I mean, anything can be wrong or anything can be right. [Little laugh.] Anything!" No matter how contradictory, "truth" is still absolute to Maria. She has no way to determine "truth" without the aid of an authority.

Being recipients but not sources of knowledge, the students feel confused and incapable when the teacher requires that they do original work. Angela had a professor who burdened her with just such expectations. She said he was wrong—"wrong in his method of teaching," not, of course, "wrong because of what he said." Knowing all the "right answers" himself, the professor refused to pass them on. "He would make you feel stupid. He would make you find the answers on your own. And he wouldn't even give you any hints on what the right answers were." How could she learn if the teacher refused to pass along his knowledge?

The authors point out that received knowers have trouble with assignments that ask them to do original work. Received knowers blame the teacher for not telling them how to think and what to do.

Those who think of knowledge as received rather than constructed assume that the authorities can dispense only one right answer for each problem. As Rachel said, "In most cases, there is a right or a wrong answer. No matter how you say it, it is right or it is wrong."

Ann, who had learned so much from the agency staff she consulted, considered our question "What would you think if two of your advisers from the children's center gave you the opposite advice?" The possibility that her advisers might give her contradictory information filled her with amazement. Her teachers, who knew everything, could not possibly disagree. She exclaimed, "Oh, that's never happened!! I don't know what I would do…maybe I'd go eeny, meeny, miny, mo. I don't know really." If faced with this dilemma, Ann would have to choose between her advisors' views on the most arbitrary basis.

The authors illustrate the dualistic thinking of some of their informants, showing how they used arbitrary criteria to make decisions in the absence of authoritative directions. These knowers seem incapable of imagining that authorities might disagree.

We posed a similar question to another woman, working out of the same perspective, about her child's teachers. She, too, seemed astonished at the idea that the authorities might disagree with one another. Equating status with truth, she would "go with the head teacher," the one who had authority over the other.

In response to the same question, Rachel said she would gather her facts by going "right to the studies." But then we asked her, "What if the studies disagreed with one another?" "I don't know," she responded. "They'd make two studies—and one is—?" Her voice trailed off in bewilderment. Her resolution to the unimaginable dilemma was: "I'd just have to go with what most people believe in." Bigger is better. The bigger in status or in number, the greater in truth.

For those who adhere to the perspective of received knowledge, there are no gradations of the truth—no gray areas. Paradox is inconceivable because received knowers believe several contradictory ideas are never simultaneously in accordance with fact. Because they see only blacks and whites, but never shades of gray, these women shun the qualitative and welcome the quantitative.

The authors restate the problem of dualistic thinking and illustrate its consequences.

The women holding this outlook are never consciously ambivalent, never attracted and repelled by the same object. It is all or nothing with them. If a thing is partly wrong, it is worthless. The remarks of one young mother illustrate the point.

> I only like to read the books that LaLeche League [an organization supporting breastfeeding of infants] recommends. Because the other books—I know that there will be things in them that I might not agree with. And then it kind of ruins the whole book for me, even if it's just *one* thing in there that the doctor or author recommends that I don't agree with. Suddenly, the whole book is—you know, not as interesting.

The authors point out that received knowers can't tolerate ambiguity; they are very literal minded.

The received knowers are intolerant of ambiguity. They believe that for every poem there is only one correct interpretation. They have trouble with poetry. It is not clear to them why poets do not just say right out what they mean. Literature is full of equivocation, and they do not see why this is so. They are *literal*. They read the lines and follow the plot; they cannot read between the lines. There isn't anything between the lines. People who see things there are making them up. They add up the facts, the numbers, and the items marked "correct." They like predictability. They want to know what is going to happen when. They like clarity. They want to know exactly what they are expected to do—what they are "responsible for." As a young college student said, "I think my mind is really structured. I have to have things all clearly laid out in front of me."

Received knowers want learning to be like a job where the requirements are laid out, one works hard, and then one is rewarded for knowing facts. Opinions do not matter.

In deciding whether to take a course, students in this position want to know how many tests and papers there will be and how long the papers. How many pages of how many books will they have to read? Exactly how will their grade be computed? They think that grades should take the form of hourly wages: The longer you work, the higher the grade.

These women either "get" an idea right away or they do not get it at all. They don't really try to *understand* the idea. They have no notion, really, of understanding as a process taking place over time and demanding the exercise of reason. They do not evaluate the idea. They collect facts but do not develop opinions. Facts are true; opinions don't count. As a college student says,

> There are absolutes in math and sciences. You feel that you can accomplish something by—by getting something down pat. Work in other courses seems to accomplish nothing, just seems so worthless. It doesn't really matter whether you are right or wrong, 'cause there really isn't a right or wrong. Um-hm. [Laughs.] You can't say. It's all guesswork.

She "learns" the material; that is, she stores a copy of it, first in her notes and then in her head. She does not transform the material; she files it "as is." She willingly reproduces the material on demand, as on an exam; but she feels betrayed if the teacher asks her to "apply" it or to produce materials on her own. Unlike the silent women, who do not see themselves as learners at all, these women feel confident about their ability to absorb and to store the truths received from others. As such, they perceive themselves as having the capacity to become richly endowed repositories of information. They may be quite successful in schools that do not demand a reflective, relativistic stance.

Received knowers expect to show they have learned by simply reproducing the facts they have been given.

Received knowers succeed in schools that stress rote learning.

Most of the women we interviewed who still held this perspective came into our study through the social service agencies or were very young students just beginning their college careers. In the highly selective colleges, where we were able to talk with the same students several times over a span of one to four years, it was exceedingly rare for a student to continue looking outside the self for the source of knowledge. In pluralistic and intellectually challenging environments, this way of thinking quickly disappears. If it is not rapidly dislodged, the student is likely either to drop out or to be pushed out early in the game (Clinchy and Zimmerman 1982; Goldberger 1981).

The received knowers in the study tended to be very young college students or women from social service agencies.

Many colleges, as well as some high schools, are becoming increasingly dedicated to dislodging this perspective and stimulating the development of more adequate conceptions of knowing. (See also Parker 1978; Perry, 1970, 1981.) Reliance on authority for a single view of the truth is clearly maladaptive for meeting the requirements of a complex, rapidly changing, pluralistic, egalitarian society and for meeting the requirements of educational institutions, which prepare students for such a world.

Secondary sources show that received knowing disappears in schools that don't reward it.

The authors conclude that received knowing is not functional in today's world.

A STUDENT EXAMPLE

Four students wrote the following paper using information they gathered from four interviews. One of the students, Ashley McMaster, was majoring in sociology and the other three, Melissa Lundmark, Charmaine O'Donnal, and Jemma Williamson, were majoring in therapeutic recreation. They decided to work as a team because of their common interest in working with people who have disabilities and because they each knew people whom they could interview. At the time they were planning their research, there had been many recent proposals to change the terminology used to describe people with disabilities. Some derided these proposals as mere "political correctness" while others thought they were necessary changes. The students decided to ask people who have disabilities what they thought about these new labels and other labels used to describe various disabilities.

Because of time constraints, the students were not able to interview more than four people, so the generalizability of their findings is limited. However, they were able to provide quite detailed accounts of the four interviews and to draw some useful conclusions for their readers. Their questions could be used by other student investigators to interview other people with disabilities and learn whether these research results are valid elsewhere.

Labels: What Individuals with Disabilities Prefer

by
Melissa Lundmark
Ashley McMaster
Charmaine O'Donnal
Jemma Williamson

Introduction

As students in therapeutic recreation and sociology we are very familiar with the issue of labeling individuals with disabilities. We believe in order to fully comprehend this issue it is important to first understand the feelings of those who are most affected. We wanted to determine how individuals with disabilities prefer to be labeled and how they feel labeling affects them.

Methods

In order to determine the feelings of individuals with disabilities, we chose to conduct in-depth interviews (see Appendix). We selected four individuals who have physical disabilities. Two of the informants have spinal cord injuries; one has extensive use of the upper extremities, but the other does not. The third informant is deaf, and the fourth is blind. All of the individuals that we interviewed are students between the ages of 22 and 26. We focused on this age group because we assume that young people with disabilities are more affected by the contemporary arguments about "politically correct" language. We conducted the interviews in pairs so that one of us could write while the other asked questions.

Participants

We interviewed four participants (all names have been changed):

- Tim (26) has a spinal cord injury and has been in a wheelchair for four years. He has use of his upper extremities.
- Brett (22) has a spinal cord injury and has been in a wheelchair for six years. He injured his spinal cord at the 5th cervical vertebrae, meaning that he has impairment in both extremities.
- Andrew (24) has a congenital hearing impairment. His parents discovered that he was deaf when he was 2 years old, and he began wearing hearing aids which help him to hear general

sounds. He went to a hearing school, and learned to speak by watching his mother, who would say whole sentences to him.

- Shannon (25) has a genetic eye disease that began to affect her eyesight at age 12; it has gradually deteriorated to the point that she now has only peripheral vision.

<u>Results</u>

<u>Tim</u>

Tim explained that the label he would like people to use in reference to his disability is an *individual with a disability*. He feels that this label focuses more on him as an individual, rather than on his disability. This is also the term he uses when referring to others with disabilities.

He has noticed that people who do not know him well are sometimes uncertain of how to refer to his disability. However, those who know him well are not bothered by the issue. He gave an example of how a person once called him with news and started the conversation by saying, "Are you sitting for this?" Overall, he is not too concerned about how most people actually refer to his disability because he does not pay much attention. When he has to describe his disability to others, such as in a phone call, he asks, "Is the place accessible for wheelchairs?" or "accessible for an individual in a wheelchair?"

When discussing specific terms that can refer to disabilities, Tim feels they mostly are "just terminology." He prefers the term *disabled*, but does not mind the term *handicapped*. However, he feels *handicapped* has gained negative connotations in the general community. Although it does not offend him personally, he is sensitive and respectful to others, and therefore adopted the term *disabled*. He commented on a few other terms, one being *wheelchair bound*, saying that it "makes it sound like I am tied to my wheelchair." He also feels *spinal cord injury* is an easier term for those who do not know the difference between *quadriplegic* and *paraplegic*. Although he does not care about most terminology, he is offended by the term *cripple*. "*Cripple* implies that I am fully dependent."

In general, Tim is not too concerned about commonly used terms. He stated "As long as terminology doesn't misinterpret my potential, it's fine. People are offended because terms tend to misinterpret them, which damages the contribution they could make by imposing limitations."

<u>Brett</u>

When we asked Brett what label he prefers others to use in reference to his disability, he said, "the best thing to say is that I'm in a wheelchair." Brett explained that most people refer to him in this way simply because they aren't aware of the actual nature of his injury. He feels that using this type of label is just easier for everyone. He also said that he doesn't mind being called *disabled*. Rather lightheartedly, Brett explained that he frequently notices the uncertainty of others. He said, "People don't know how to phrase their conversations. For example, one friend of mine gets really embarrassed when he says 'let's walk over there.'" In spite of the fact that he obviously can't walk, Brett assured us that he isn't offended by such natural language.

When we asked Brett how he describes his disability to others he said, "it entirely depends on the situation." If he is talking with any type of medical professional or highly educated person, he says that he has a "C5 injury." Most of the time, however, he says, "I'm in a wheelchair" or "I use a wheelchair" because he has learned that most people don't know what C5 means. Interestingly, Brett admitted using this phrase "in a wheelchair" with others who have disabilities similar to his own. As a side note, Brett explained that sometimes he and friends who are disabled jokingly refer to one another as "handicappers."

We asked Brett which word he preferred: *handicapped* or *disabled*. Without hesitation, he explained that he prefers the label *disabled* much more. Brett said that even though he's not sure why, the word *handicapped* holds a negative connotation in his mind. He explained that for some reason, this label makes him think of "Jerry's kids." He also said that he really doesn't care if people use the term *person with a disability*. In addition, Brett explained that he doesn't mind the phrases *wheelchair bound* or *confined to a wheelchair*. However, he said that the label *physically challenged* sounds "corny." He also strongly dislikes the terms *quadriplegic* and *paraplegic*. During his years of rehabilitation, he was frequently referred to as a "quad." He explained that this word seems to place him in a category that allows for little improvement. He feels that this label gives him a generic identity as someone who has no movement below the neck, even though he actually does have some use of his upper extremities.

Overall, Brett said that he feels people get too caught up in terminology. Even though he has certain preferences, he realizes that it is often difficult for people to know what to say. In fact, he wishes that people felt comfortable enough to just ask him how he was injured. Brett did admit, however, that sometimes he feels a little "strange" when people who are highly educated use out-dated labels. Furthermore, Brett explained that labels only become really significant if they limit the potential of the disabled individual.

Shannon

In our interview with Shannon, she indicated that she generally does not care what labels people use in reference to her visual impairment. However, she stated that if people want to be more accurate, *partially blind* would be the term to use since she does have partial vision. When asked if she notices the uncertainty that people have concerning her disability, Shannon answered that people will ask her questions, but they do not know how to word them appropriately. Shannon has discussed the labeling concern with others who have more severe visual impairments and blindness, and she reported that they agree that labels are not important.

When asked what labels most people actually call her, Shannon responded that professionals usually will say *visually impaired*, but the general public will say a variety of things such as she is "kind of blind" and "she can't see." When describing her situation to others, Shannon simply says, "I have an eye disease." We asked how she refers to others with the same disability, and she stated that the terms that she uses depends on the severity of the visual disability. Terms that she uses are *totally blind*, *partially sighted*, and *visually impaired*. The latter of the three does not mean that an individual is completely blind, according to Shannon. Her opinion on *visually impaired* is that the term means that there is still some vision.

We next asked Shannon which label, *disabled* or *handicapped*, she prefers. She had no preference, but she mentioned that she is sad when people get too caught up in terminology and worry about which label to use. The terms *person with a disability* and *person with a handicap* do not mean much to her. Of the three specific labels related to her disability, *blind* is acceptable only if it accurately describes the condition. She prefers the second term, *visually impaired*. However, the third term, *visually challenged*, she does not like, because it is a "stupid" label and it tends to glorify the condition.

Asked if there were any other labels we did not mention that particularly offend her, she said that the verbal labels do not bother her much. It is the way people treat her that offends her. To our final question she replied that labels do not affect her if they are part of the contemporary phraseology.

Andrew

Andrew does not have any strong feelings about the labels people use in reference to his disability. When asked what he preferred, he said we could call him whatever we wanted, because he doesn't really care what people call him. As for other people, he said that their feelings about labels depend on how they were raised in their family. Because of his upbringing, Andrew did not grow up thinking he was different from his other friends until he went to a deaf camp when he was 12 years old. When he was 17, he attended a program called "Especially for Deaf Youth" and then decided that he would learn sign language so that he could communicate with other deaf people.

It doesn't bother Andrew to have people call him *handicapped*. He said he knows he has a handicap—his hearing. But, he also feels that everyone has some type of handicap, whether they smoke, wear glasses, etc. Andrew does not mind either of the terms *handicapped* or *disabled*. During the interview, he did not understand how the terms *individual with a handicap* or *individual with a disability* were any different from the previous words. One possible reason for this could be that the interviewer was using American Sign Language (ASL) to ask his preference on these labels. In ASL, the way a person signs "handicapped person," and "person with a handicap" is the same. It is signed "H-C PERSON," or "PERSON H-C." Since they were both signed the same in ASL, Andrew most likely did not differentiate between the two in his mind.

When asked if specific labels offend him, such as *deaf* and *hard-of-hearing*, Andrew said he does not mind either of them, but that different people will usually use different terms. For example, he said that deaf people who see that he can speak call him "hard-of-hearing." Hearing people who see him sign call him "deaf." And physicians have their own vocabulary regarding hearing losses. Since Andrew cannot hear anything without his hearing aids, doctors usually call him "profoundly deaf." None of these terms offend him, and he accepts any of them because they come from different perspectives.

Although Andrew does not mind what he is labeled, he said that it can affect other deaf people, depending on their self-esteem and social skills. And more importantly, it may have a greater impact on the people who are using the labels—those who do not have the disability.

Conclusions

When asked what term they prefer people to use in reference to their disability, Tim and Brett, who are both in wheelchairs, prefer terms that focus on them as individuals, rather than their disabilities. Neither Shannon nor Andrew expressed concern over the ways they are labeled. All of them mentioned that acquaintances feel uncomfortable with what terminology to use, but their close friends and family do not express uncertainty. Tim, Brett, and Shannon said that people are sometimes concerned about phrases like "Let's *walk* over there," or "*Look* over here." However, once their friends get to know them better, the disability no longer matters as much.

Andrew, Brett, and Shannon said that the way a person refers to their disability depends on that person's education or profession. Brett said that he expects professionals to use more accurate terms. When describing their disability to others, both Brett and Andrew adjust their terminology depending on the person or situation. They use whatever terms best facilitate communication. When describing others with their same disability, all of the participants use terms similar to the ones they prefer to be called and similar to how they describe themselves.

Tim and Brett, both in wheelchairs, prefer *disabled* over *handicapped* because they feel that *handicapped* has negative connotations. Shannon and Andrew do not prefer one term over the other. However, they all agree that the terms *person with a disability* or *person with a handicap* are just a matter of semantics. Both Brett and Shannon strongly dislike phrases that use the word "challenged." They both feel that these labels are patronizing. Brett and Tim both feel offended by older terms, such as *cripple*.

All of the participants feel that labels can negatively affect individuals with disabilities if used improperly. Tim and Brett both said that labels can place limitations on individuals' opportunities. Shannon feels that anything outside of "normal phraseology" can be offensive. Andrew mentioned that labels do affect individuals, depending on their self-esteem and social skills. He also feels that labeling may affect the people using the labels more than it affects those with the disability.

Although most of our participants expressed label preferences, our overall feeling was that individuals with disabilities are not overly concerned with what people call them. They are more concerned with treatment than terminology. We need to remember that a person who is blind, deaf, or in a wheelchair is *first* an individual, and *second* an individual with a disability. From these interviews we conclude that people can overcome the barriers of terminology by getting to know the person as a human being and not focusing on the disability.

Appendix

We are students conducting these interviews for a class research assignment. In general, we are interested in how individuals with disabilities prefer to be labeled. By going ahead with this interview you are giving us permission to use your answers in our research paper. Your name will be kept anonymous.

Demographic Information
Age:
Gender:
Have you had this disability since birth? Yes or No
If not, how long?

Questions
1. What label would you like people to use in reference to your disability? Why?
2. Have you noticed people who are uncertain about how to refer to your disability?
3. How do most people refer to your disability?
4. How do you refer to yourself when you need to describe your disability to others?
5. What kind of labels do you use to refer to others with disabilities?
6. We are now going to read a list of words. We want to find out how these terms make you feel.

	Prefer	Offend	Don't Care
handicapped			
disabled			
(Why do you prefer, feel offended, or do not care?)			
Person with handicap			
Person with disability			
Physically challenged			
If applicable:			
wheel chair bound			
confined to wheel chair			
uses a wheel chair			
paraplegic			
quadriplegic			
spinal cord			
blind			
visually impaired			
visually challenged			
deaf			
hearing impaired			
hard of hearing			
hearing loss			

7. Are there any that particularly offend you or you prefer?
8. Is it important to you what labels people use? Why?
9. How do you think labels affect you in general?

SUGGESTIONS FOR RESEARCH AND WRITING

1. Interview a notable person on your campus or in your community. Do some background research on the person and the contributions for which he or she is noted. Plan some questions that will further illuminate that person's life or achievements and arrange for an interview. After conducting it and writing a report, try to interest your campus or local newspaper in publishing all or part of your interview.

2. Interview one of the professors in your major field to learn more about the field. Ask the professor to describe his or her own education and research in the field. Get the professor's perspective on the major developments in the field during his or her career span. Consider how what you learn from this interview corroborates or contradicts your understanding of the field from the courses you've taken or books you've read. Another possibility in this interview would be to focus on the kinds of writing this professor does: What genres does he or she most often write in? What sort of process does he or she follow? What is hardest about writing? What has become easier? What advice does the professor have for you to help you learn to write in your field?

3. What was happening on your campus 50 years ago? In your community? In the United States? Identify some important events or social, cultural, educational, or industrial developments that occurred at that time. Locate a person in your community who can tell about those events or developments from firsthand experience. Identify some likely informants by asking around, by advertising, or by visiting a senior citizens' center. Then arrange for interviews to collect an oral history concerning the event or development you are interested in.

4. Collect some of your family's history by interviewing your grandparents, aunts, uncles, and parents. Where did your ancestors come from? Where did they first settle? What was life like when your grandparents were growing up? Your aunts, uncles, and parents? What can your grandparents and aunts and uncles tell you about your parents that your parents haven't told you? What are some of the memorable events in your family's history that ought to be recorded for future generations?

5. Identify a local expert on a social problem you are interested in and interview that person to learn how the problem is understood or dealt with locally. For example, if you are interested in the problem of domestic violence, interview the director of a shelter where victims of domestic violence may seek refuge. If you are interested in your community's response to the problem of homelessness, interview the person who directs your city's homeless shelter. As a way of learning about career or volunteer experiences you could have, interview the person in your city or county govern-

ment who is responsible for low-income housing, the director of a rape crisis center, a worker at a suicide prevention center, or a social worker.

References

Ashton-Jones, Evelyn, and Dene Kay Thomas. 1990. Composition, collaboration, and women's ways of knowing: A conversation with Mary Belenky. *Journal of Advanced Composition* 10 (Fall): 275–292.

Ives, Edward D. 1995. *The tape-recorded interview: A manual for field workers in folklore and oral history.* 2d ed. Knoxville: University of Tennessee Press.

6

OBSERVING

Observing is such a fundamental activity in daily life it may be difficult to think of it as a scientific method. You observe the weather and decide how to dress for the day. You observe your family members' or co-workers' moods and decide whether to treat them with kid gloves or joke, argue, or have a heart-to-heart talk with them. These kinds of daily observations are valuable on a personal level, but observation becomes a scientific method only when it is purposeful and systematic, when it attempts to analyze and explain phenomena in a way that other scientists find plausible, and when it draws reliable and lasting conclusions.

Imagine you were a personnel manager who observed that your employees seemed to work less enthusiastically on Monday mornings right after the weekly staff meeting. This observation would give you a significant objective for making further observations. You could start to keep systematic notes of what behaviors the employees exhibited and what was happening in the staff meetings. If you realized that frequently the meetings centered on how the employees were falling short in their work, and then you also observed that these meetings were followed by a lot of time wasting and grumbling around the office water cooler, you might infer that negative motivational strategies were not successful with your employees. You then would have some good reasons, based on observational data, for trying different incentives to get your employees to work harder.

Observing is really the basis of all methods. In reading documents, you must be observant to notice the details and the connections that reveal something new about your subject. In interviewing, you should observe the person you are interviewing—their face, their gestures, their dress, and their surroundings—for what these tell you that the person's words don't. Surveying and experimenting, the methods discussed in Chapters 7 and 8, are controlled but indirect methods of observation; both use instruments and measurements to make selected observations rigorous and precise. Direct observation of human behavior, even though it is more difficult to control and make precise, is often the best method to use to answer certain kinds of research questions because it occurs in natural settings, unlike experiments. Also, unlike surveys or questionnaires, direct observation does not depend on the observed people's willingness to report their behavior honestly or their ability to remember it accurately.

But direct observation is not without flaws. One obvious flaw is that the observer might be selective in what he or she observes, failing to see or hear something that is critical for understanding the observed phenomenon completely. Our personal background and biases may make us sensitive to perceiving some kinds of data and not others. Another flaw is that our sensory organs—the basic tools of observation—can become tired, overstimulated, or so accustomed to the environment that we fail to notice something important. Even when we augment our senses with instruments such as audio or video recorders, we still have to use our senses to interpret the data recorded. Still another problem is that the act of observing often influences the very behavior that is under investigation. Social scientists have long noted that changes in people's behavior often result simply from the fact that they know they are being observed. Users of observational methods have devised some ways to compensate for these flaws, ways that will be explained later in this chapter.

KINDS OF OBSERVATION

There are many different ways of using observation as a method, but they can be lumped into four categories: unobtrusive observation, structured observation, case studies, and participant observation.

UNOBTRUSIVE OBSERVATION

Unobtrusive observation occurs when the persons being observed don't realize it. The observers simply carry out their observations in natural settings without drawing attention to the fact that they are doing research. For example, researchers who want to learn how children develop the ability to interact with other children could go to a nursery school and observe toddlers at play through a one-way mirror. Because the children don't know they are being observed, they should behave normally, and the researchers should be able to gather data on which to base generalizations helpful for parents, teachers, psychologists, and others who work with children. Unobtrusive observation is ethical as long as there are no physical or emotional risks to the observed persons and no benefits they would be entitled to share in.

STRUCTURED OBSERVATION

Structured observation occurs when participants realize that they are part of an observational study, and the study has been devised to answer questions determined ahead of time. An example of structured observation is the excerpt from Deborah Tannen's study of differences between males and females in two-person, same-sex conversations, which you will read later in this chapter. This research was structured in the sense that the sixteen participants—pairs of friends at four different age levels—were taken to an office in which a video camera was set up. They were then instructed to have a serious or intimate conversation while the camera recorded it and the investigator went away. The setting and the instructions no doubt made it a bit difficult for the participants to perform on demand for the video camera. However, they did not know how the investigator would analyze the videotape. In fact, Tannen did not analyze the tapes in the way she initially she expected to, so the observation was unstructured in this important way. Still, the initial structuring of the observations permitted Tannen to draw her unexpected and interesting conclusions.

CASE STUDIES

Case studies can be considered a special kind of structured observation. Typically, a case study involves intense observation of one individual—at most very few people—over a long period of time, usually as a part of the individual's clinical treatment for a physical, psychological, or social problem. The observer—who might be a medical doctor, a therapist, or social worker—establishes a high degree of rapport with the observed person, while still remaining detached enough to make objective descriptions of what is observed. The observations may include much more than simply watching a person; interviews, tests, and mental and physical examinations may all be additional means of collecting data that lead to conclusions about the case. Although it may seem that conclusions from individual case studies are not generalizable, many similar cases are often compared to draw inferences that have significance for a broader population. (Because case studies are generally conducted by licensed professionals and require a great deal of time to complete, they are usually not a feasible kind of research for undergraduate students, so little more will be said about them.)

PARTICIPANT OBSERVATION

Participant observation is the favored method of cultural anthropologists and sometimes of sociologists and social psychologists. As the name implies, the observer becomes a participant in the phenomena he or she is observing. Anthropologists call this method "ethnographic research" because the end result is a text in the genre called ethnography (from *ethno* meaning "people" and *graphy* meaning "writing"). An anthropologist may not become a complete participant in the culture he or she observes (learning to shrink heads, for example, may be going too far!), but sociologists and social psychologists usually try to because they are more likely to study people in their own culture. For example, to learn what it means to be homeless in America, some sociologists have assumed the role of a homeless person, living on the streets without access to the comforts of a bed or bathroom, wearing cast-off clothing, and begging for money for food.

One assumption underlying participant observation is that a researcher cannot adequately understand the reality and significance of others' lives without becoming an insider in their daily experiences. Participant observers do not believe, as experimenters do, that researchers must be detached from whatever they study. Another assumption is that the researcher should bring to the study as few preconceived theories as possible. The goal of participant observation is to let understanding emerge from deep involvement in the experience. To gain this understanding, the researcher collects as much data as possible to sort out later, not by using predetermined analytical categories but by finding themes in the material that the researcher believes explain the most about the observed phenomena. Participant observers readily admit the role their subjective perception plays in the construction of the knowledge they finally write about. They do not pretend that knowledge is objective and self-existent because they realize that a different observer would have a different experience and therefore create a somewhat different text.

Clearly, there are limits to what participant observation can reveal. One of these limits might come from *ethnocentrism*—the tendency of observers to understand and judge what they observe in terms of their own culture and experience. Assuming that ethnocentrism can be overcome, though, it is still questionable whether a researcher really can "go native," for example in becoming a homeless person, when all the time they know they have a home to return to and a way of earning an income. On the other hand, there is also a danger that the researcher might begin to identify so completely with the group studied that he or she will lose the ability to think objectively and critically about the experience. Some police undercover agents who have infiltrated the criminal world in order to gather evidence to convict lawbreakers, for example, have been seduced by the lifestyle they have pretended to live and become corrupt themselves.

Another problem is logistical: To provide the deep understanding that it aims for, participant observation usually requires a long period of time, and the massive data that accumulates in such a study can be formidable when the time for analysis arrives. A final problem stems from the ethical questions that may arise: Is it right for someone to beg if they really have the means to provide for themselves? Should participant observers gain entrance into the groups they study by means of a false story about themselves? If they are candid about their true identity, can they really become a part of the group enough to understand it?

Questions such as these show that observation is not as straightforward or easy as it might seem. But social scientists have developed ways of dealing with many of the concerns that threaten the reliability of the information gained with this method. As you read the following steps for using this method, think about how you can plan observational research to eliminate or compensate for some of its drawbacks.

MAKING OBSERVATIONS

DEFINE YOUR PURPOSE

The first step in any kind of observation is to define your purpose. For some kinds of research you can state a very definite, limited purpose. Suppose you wanted to know, for example, whether male or female students speak out more often in class without first raising their hands. You could state your research question very specifically and answer it with fairly uncomplicated observations. For other kinds of research, such as participant observation, a very general, broadly stated purpose is more typical because the researcher wants to be open to the experience rather than bringing preconceived notions to it. So a very general question such as, "What is the daily life of a homeless man like?" is more appropriate as a starting point. In participant observation, the focus of the research can and often does change, becoming more specific as the observer spends more time conducting the research.

SELECT PEOPLE, SETTING, AND BEHAVIOR FOR OBSERVATION

After defining your purpose, you need to decide what person or persons you will observe, where you will observe them, and what behavior you will look for—but not necessarily in that order. As noted already, with participant observation you will know whom you want to study and often where, but usually not the particular behaviors you'll watch for. You define your focus more gradually as you become acquainted with the people and surroundings you are in. With unobtrusive observation, it may be best to choose the setting first and then observe the people who happen to be in it. Say you wanted to observe how people react when strangers sit in a vacant seat right next to them rather than choosing one farther away. A public place where there are many people who are not familiar with one another would be the ideal setting for conducting this research—perhaps a library, an airport, or the lobby of a busy public building.

Sometimes it's best to decide first what specific behaviors you will look for. For example, if you wanted to do a structured observation of how a seven-year-old explains a procedure, such as putting together a toy, to a three-year-old, you would have to create a setting that would be conducive to this kind of observation. Then, of course, you would have to find children who could participate in the study. Using children in a study would require clearance from an IRB (see Chapter 3) as well as the people who are entrusted with the children's care. Often the observational research you can do depends on the availability of and access to the kind of people you want to study, as well as access to special settings and equipment that make the observations feasible.

RECORD DATA

After defining your purpose and choosing a setting with people and behaviors to observe, the next step is to devise a way of recording data about your observations. There are several different ways to record data. One thing not to do is simply trust your memory to retain very complex information for very long. Preferably, you should record what you observe as it happens, or very soon afterwards, before proceeding with more observations. Here are some ways to make a record that you can refer to repeatedly as you later analyze your data.

Keep a notebook or log. Writing extensive notes in a log or diary is the preferred recording system of participant observers. Often they can't take notes very well while mingling with the people they are studying, so they find ways to do this privately. Nonparticipant-observers, watching students in a classroom, say, or children at play could usually write while they are observing without significantly disturbing either the process of observation or the behavior of interest. The notes you take can be of two kinds—descriptive and evaluative. Descriptive notes aim simply to capture the observed behavior as precisely as possible without making judgments about it. Evaluative notes are your first, rough attempts to interpret the meaning of the other notes—to make sense of the data as it grows. Upon reflection, you may change your first interpretations, but capturing your thoughts while observing should stimulate better analytical thinking about the data.

Work with one or more collaborators. Because observing and recording at the same time can prove difficult when complex behaviors are under study, sometimes observers work with collaborators. Usually the collaborators determine ahead of time what the salient items or activities are that they will observe. Suppose you wanted to conduct a study of strangers' reactions when someone takes a vacant seat right next to them rather than choosing one farther away. This study should include at least two researchers—one to sit by strangers and the other to unobtrusively watch and record the observed person's behavior. For even more control of the accuracy of the observations, still another collaborator could watch and record each interaction from a different vantage point. Then all three of you could compare your observations and determine the most accurate way of describing what happened.

Devise a coding system. If you have determined ahead of time exactly what behaviors you intend to watch for, you can make a simple grid for checking off the behaviors each time they occur. For example, if you wanted to observe whether male or female fourth graders interrupted class discussion more frequently by talking out of turn, you could devise a coding system with two columns, one labeled "Boys" and one labeled "Girls." Each time you observed a boy or girl make a comment without raising a hand first, you would simply make a check in the appropriate column. To track individual boys and girls who talk out of turn, you could make a seating chart and simply make check marks under the students' names each time they exhibited the behavior.

Coding systems for more complex behavior are more difficult to devise. The categories for these coding systems might be based on a review of literature, your hypotheses, or preliminary observations. For example, to devise a coding system for the study of sitting by strangers, you could do some preliminary observations in order to come up with the categories that describe all possible behaviors. Your preliminary observations might show that those whose personal space was invaded by a stranger sitting next to them usually reacted in one or more of several ways. Using this information you could come up with categories for your coding system—for example, "shifts in seat away from intruder," "moves chair," "walks away," "stares at intruder," "makes a comment to intruder," and so on. You might make a grid for recording observations, as the students did whose research is presented at the end of this chapter.

Use mechanical recording devices. A final way of recording observations is to use mechanical recording devices such as audiotapes or videotapes. Rather than writing field notes, some participant-observers record their observations by speaking into a tape recorder. Anthropologists make extensive use of audio recorders to capture the language and music of the cultures they study. Social psychologists studying crowd behavior have worn hidden microphones and tape recorders to capture comments from people in the crowd. Audiotapes allow the researcher to listen again and again to what was recorded so they can discern patterns in the data and draw conclusions.

Videotaping observations allows the same opportunity to view the behaviors repeatedly, watching for things that the observer might miss without a permanent record of the event. Both video and audio recordings also allow for multiple trained observers to check the data to see if they discern the same things and draw the same conclusions.

MAKE CONCLUSIONS RELIABLE

Reliability is an important concept in social science research. It means that the findings of a particular study are consistent and stable—likely to be the same if the study were repeated. Some threats to the reliability of observational research have already been noted, such as the tendency of observers to be selective about what they observe or to interpret and judge the behaviors they observe by ethnocentric standards. Social scientists acknowledge that it isn't possible to completely eliminate human frailty and error from observational research, but to ensure that results are as reliable as possible, people who do this kind of research can take the following steps.

Get an adequate sample or provide a thick description. There are human and material limits to how much time you can spend in research, how many people you can observe, and how many different behaviors you can attend to. But readers of your research will not be persuaded that your conclusions are reliable unless the conclusions are based on evidence that appears sufficient and representative. In other words, readers will expect most observational research to be based on an adequate sampling of the entire population you could have observed; or, if sampling is not feasible, readers will expect that conclusions are based on a sustained, in-depth study of the phenomena.

Getting an adequate sample means including enough people in your observation (this depends on the kind of observation you are doing), spending enough time observing, and focusing on a sufficient number of the different kinds of behaviors you are interested in. For example, if you were to do the sitting-by-a-stranger study in 30 minutes one afternoon at a bar and only include five different observations, readers could rightly protest that your conclusions aren't based on enough data to be reliable. They might also point out that the results are probably not representative since a bar is a place where it is perhaps more common for strangers to sit next to each other and a place where you aren't likely to encounter people from all walks of life.

Adequate sampling isn't a critical issue for case studies and participant-observation, however. The length of time spent accumulating data and the depth and insight of the researcher's observations are what count in persuading readers the conclusions are reliable. Ethnographers speak of providing a "thick description," one that may be based on only a few individuals but is nevertheless rich, detailed, and penetrating.

Use multiple observers. Another way of assuring readers that your observations have produced reliable conclusions is to use multiple observers. If at least two people have been trained to observe for the same things and they tend to agree on what happened in the observations, there is less chance that the observations are simply the result of the observer's experience and biases, or that the observations have been tainted by the observer's fatigue or boredom. The technique of using multiple observers is often combined with recording systems such as coding devices and audio- and videotaping so that all observers can independently listen to or watch and code the same observations. If two or more observers independently code behavior the same way, it is more likely that the observations are reliable. There is even a way of calculating what is called "inter-rater reliability" to get a statistic that shows how often the observers agreed with each other.

However, for case studies and participant observation, multiple observers are usually not considered necessary for reliability. Readers tend to believe the conclusions from these kinds of research in proportion to the writer's skill in providing evidence that he or she has been thorough in gathering data over a long period of time, interpreting it, relating it to other knowledge, and supporting the conclusions drawn.

Triangulate observations with other methods of research. A final way that researchers can increase the reliability of their conclusions is to *triangulate* observation with other methods of answering their questions. The word *triangulation* comes from navigation; it is a method of locating an unknown point by using two known points to create a triangle intersecting all three points. In research, then, triangulation is a way of determining if your conclusions are reliable by comparing them to conclusions from other research methods that you have confidence in. So observational data could be compared to survey and interview data, for example, that sought to answer the same or similar questions. If there is a high degree of correspondence in the results from all three kinds of research, you may feel more confident that the observational data is reliable.

ANALYZING AND WRITING ABOUT OBSERVATIONS

After collecting data through your observations, your next step is to analyze and interpret them carefully so that you can write about your findings. The simpler and the more quantitative your observations were, the more straightforward your analysis will be. For example, if you hypothesized ahead of time that boys in a fourth-grade classroom would speak out more often than girls without raising their hands, then you simply counted and compared the number of times both groups exhibited the behavior, you would be able to confirm or reject your hypothesis quickly and report your findings without spending much time on analysis.

On the other hand, if you did a qualitative study of events in a college sorority during Rush Week, acting as a participant-observer, you would usually not have a hypothesis nor would you have data already neatly coded into predetermined categories. Instead, you would need to sift through all your notes and begin seeking a general focus that would allow you to organize your findings and draw useful conclusions. In either a quantitative or a qualitative study, however, your goal is to make your analysis illuminate the questions that led you to do observations and then to draw conclusions that provide greater understanding of the people and phenomena you have studied.

Writing about quantitative data is usually a more straightforward rhetorical problem than is writing about qualitative research. Quantitative research typically fits in the genre of the empirical research report. In this genre, the body of the text usually has four main divisions: (1) an introduction that provides a context for the problem (often including a review of related literature) and states the research question or hypothesis; (2) a description of the methods used, including who the participants were and what equipment or instruments were used; (3) a description of the results, which may include tables and graphs to present summaries and analyses of numerical data; and (4) a discussion of the significance of the results. Sometimes the results and the discussion of their significance are combined. This genre is very familiar in the social sciences, and it is popular for reporting quantitative research because it makes very clear to the reader how the writer arrived at conclusions. The reader can easily find the information necessary to judge whether or not the results permit you to draw the inferences you make in the discussion. The student paper at the end of this chapter is about quantitative data and is organized according to these common genre conventions.

Writing about qualitative data is more difficult for the reasons already mentioned. There is often so much varied data to be analyzed that it is usually difficult to define a focus that lets you present it all systematically—unless you write a book. Even then, including all the data you've collected in a qualitative report is nearly impossible. Usually the best strategy is to generalize and then illustrate each generalization with some well-chosen details or a telling anecdote. Another strategy is to put some of your data in appendices to your report. Sometimes, some of the data can be quantified, and tables or figures can be devised to summarize it. Because you can't display the entire weight of the evidence nor all of the inferential processes that led you to draw your conclusions, readers may be more skeptical when reading a qualitative report. Your ability to persuade them that your conclusions are valid and reliable rests in large part on your rhetorical skill. You must make your argument as logically as you can and also create an ethos in your text of a credible and careful researcher.

You can easily find models of texts reporting qualitative observations, but they cannot be summarized here as neatly as the typical four-part article reporting quantitative research. In general, however, texts reporting qualitative research also have an introduction that presents a problem or question and then describes related research. They also include some information about methods, though it may not all be summarized in one section of the report. Results and interpretations of results are often intermingled, and they are not necessarily signaled with headings. Instead, unique headings may be used that name categories used in analyzing the data. The professional example in Chapter 5 and the one in this chapter are both examples of texts describing qualitative data. By carefully studying them, particularly the annotations, you will become more aware of your options for writing about qualitative research.

A PROFESSIONAL EXAMPLE

On the following pages you will read Deborah Tannen's report of her observations of gender differences in two-person same-sex conversations that had been recorded on videotape.[1] Tannen is a sociolinguist who, since this study was first published, has written extensively about gender differences in communication. However, as she explains in this report, that was not her original focus when she began to analyze the videotapes of the conversations. Rather, she had planned to study repetition and dialogue as types of involvement strategies. As Tannen notes, however, she was so impressed by what she saw as she watched the videotapes that she decided to change her focus.

As you read, notice how Tannen creates a context for her research, how she describes her methods, how she uses headings to organize the results for the reader, how she interprets her data, and what general conclusions she comes to. Notice particularly the line drawings that attempt to capture the most important thing she observed: How males and females at different age levels exhibit similar behavior in physical alignment and eye contact. These drawings are very important in making her conclusions persuasive because they reduce to a few simple images all the positions, movements, and gazes that Tannen saw in watching about 160 minutes of videotape. As usual, the annotations in the margins point out some of the rhetorical strategies she used to create a persuasive text about qualitative data.

---

[1] Deborah Tannen, "Gender Differences in Conversational Coherence: Physical Alignment and Topical Cohesion," in *Conversational Organization and Its Development*, ed. Bruce Dorval (Norwood, NJ: Ablex, 1990), pp. 167–180. Copyright 1990 by Deborah Tannen. Permission granted by Deborah Tannen.

Gender Differences in Conversational Coherence:
Physical Alignment and Topical Cohesion[1]

Deborah Tannen
Georgetown University

INTRODUCTION

Tannen begins by referring to some of her earlier research, pointing out that she no longer accepts her previous definition of coherence in discourse.

In introducing a collection of essays entitled *Coherence in Spoken and Written Discourse*, I defined *coherence* as "underlying organizing structure making the words and sentences into a unified discourse that has cultural significance for those who create or comprehend it," as distinct from *cohesion*, which I defined as "surface-level ties showing relationships among elements in the text" (Tannen, 1984, p. xiv). These definitions now strike me as too static, perhaps more applicable to monologic discourse than to the interactive discourse of conversation. The organization of coherence in conversation must be not a preexisting structure, but an emergent one, much as Hopper (1988) shows grammar to be emergent. In other words, conversation is not like flesh shaped by a preformed skeleton, but a shape which is renegotiated in interaction, created anew by participants in accordance with shared expectations based on previous conversational experience, or what Becker (1988) calls "prior text."

Tannen borrows a concept from another scholar to present an analogy for a new definition of coherence.

Two elements of emergent coherence in conversation—that is, two elements that create an integrated activity, conversation, out of individuals' separate speech—are physical alignment and topical cohesion. By *physical alignment* I mean the ways that speakers position their heads and bodies in relation to each other, including eye gaze. With Schiffrin (1988), I take "topic" to be "what speakers talk about." *Topical cohesion* then refers to how speakers introduce and

Tannen introduces two elements that she now believes make up coherence in conversation.

---

[1] I am grateful to Bruce Dorval for the enlightening opportunity to study these videotapes and to A. L. Becker for helpful comments and discussion on a pre-final draft. I also benefited from discussion with panelists Penelope Brown, Penelope Eckert, Marjorie Harness Goodwin, and Amy Sheldon, when I presented findings from this study as part of a panel entitled "Gender Differences in Conversational Interaction" at the 1988 Georgetown University, Round Table on Languages and Linguistics, Georgetown University, Washington DC, March, 1988.

Papers presented in that panel, including a slightly revised and significantly shortened version of this one, are forthcoming in *Discourse Processes*, I3(1), 1990. My thanks to Greta Patten for drawing the illustrations.

develop topics in relation to their own and others' prior and projected talk. This chapter describes and discusses physical alignment and topical cohesion in the 20-minute videotapes of eight pairs of friends, one female and one male pair at each of four age levels: second graders, sixth graders, tenth graders, and 25-year olds.[2]

I did not approach these data with the intention of examining gender differences. Rather, I intended to analyze involvement strategies such as repetition and dialogue, in keeping with the focus of my current research (Tannen, 1987, 1988, 1989). However, watching the videotapes of same-sex pairs at each age level, I was so struck by gender-related patterns that I could not resist the drive to study them more closely. My own previous research includes only one study of gender differences, specifically, of indirectness in conversation (Tannen, 1981, 1982). But for a general book about conversational style (Tannen, 1986a), I had reviewed and discussed recent research on gender differences. Some of the patterns I observed in the videotapes of friends talking supported previous studies of which I was aware, but some were unexpected to me. Inspired, in part, by the striking impression made by these data, I decided to devote a forthcoming book to gender differences in conversational style (Tannen, 1990).

Overview of gender-related patterns in the videotapes. Watching the videotapes of the boys and girls and women and men at these four age levels, I observed that there were patterns which linked the speakers of like gender across the ages and distinguished cross-gender age-mates. At every age level, the girls and women oriented to each other with the alignment of their bodies and gaze far more directly than did the boys and men. Whereas all the pairs displayed discomfort with the experimental situation and the assigned task, at every age level, the female friends quickly established topics for talk and produced extended talk related to a small number of topics. In contrast, boys at the two younger ages produced small amounts of talk about many different topics. At the two older ages, the boys and men, like their female counterparts, produced a lot of talk about a few topics, but the level at which they discussed the topics was more abstract, less personal.

Tannen directly announces the purposes and content of this article. She also alludes to her method of gathering data.

Tannen states that she analyzed her data in a way that she felt compelled to, not the way she originally planned to.

Tannen previews for the reader what she found in this study. She concludes that female conversation partners at all age levels align their bodies and gazes more directly than male conversation partners do.

In the footnote, Tannen qualifies the age classifications of her participants and explains why one age category was omitted.

[2] I refer to the oldest pairs of speakers as "25-year-olds" in order to avoid the cumbersome but more accurate label, "24- to 27-year-olds." The fifth age level in the study, involving speakers of approximately 20 years of age, was eliminated because it was not possible to identify female and male pairs for which legible transcripts were available and which did not include speakers of radically different cultural backgrounds.

Tannen previews another conclusion this study will lead to: Men's conversational patterns are not disengaged or somehow deficient.

A cross-cultural view of gender differences. Despite these findings of gender differences, I question the conclusion made by researchers in the field of family therapy as well as by women who interact with men in everyday life that, because the boys and men are less directly aligned with their interlocutors in posture and gaze, they are not "engaged" or "involved." Furthermore, I question the conclusion that, because the boys produce small amounts of talk about each of a large number of topics, they are evidencing a failure or lack. Rather, I subscribe to a cross-cultural approach to cross-gender conversation by which women and men, boys and girls, can be seen to accomplish and display coherence in conversation in different but equally valid ways.

Tannen reports research conducted on the speech patterns of different cultural groups because she thinks it is relevant to her present research.

A model for understanding cross-cultural communication is provided by Gumperz (1982). That such an approach can be applied to conversations between women and men is demonstrated by Maltz and Borker (1982), on the basis of ethnographic research on language socialization by sociologists and anthropologists, especially the extensive work of Goodwin (see for example, Goodwin, 1980a, 1982, 1983, 1985, 1990) and others. Only a brief summary can be provided here.

Based on microanalysis of conversations among British speakers of English and speakers of English from India and Pakistan in London, as well as among Black and White speakers of English in the United States, Gumperz demonstrates that interlocutors accomplish conversational inferencing and identify the speech activity they are engaged in by means of contextualization cues: aspects of talk such as intonation, prosody, loudness, pitch, sequencing, and choice of words, that both signal and create the context in which communication is taking place. But speakers of different cultural backgrounds use different contextualization cues. In other words, they have different habits for contextualizing their talk: different ways of signalling similar speech activities. In cross-cultural communication, such cues, therefore, are likely to be misinterpreted or missed altogether.

Tannen asserts that, in effect, males and females are socialized into conversation in different cultural environments because they learn to converse mainly with their own sex.

Reviewing the work of Goodwin and others, Maltz and Borker (1982) explain that males and females learn their styles of talking in sex-separate peer groups. In this sense, they grow up in different cultural environments, so they too develop different habits for signalling their intentions and understandings. Because they learn to have conversations in same-sex peer interaction, women and men develop different norms for establishing and displaying conversational involvement. These "cultural" differences account for the differing patterns observed among girls and boys and women and men, as well as for mutual negative evaluations that often result from cross-gender interactions.

In the discussion that follows I consider patterns of physical alignment first and then move to topical cohesion.

PHYSICAL ALIGNMENT

Overview. Patterns of physical alignment which link same-gender speakers in all the videotapes studied, and differentiate pairs of speakers of different genders at similar age levels, can be instantly appreciated by watching the videotapes with the sound turned off. Even if there were no differences in how they spoke, their physical alignment, body posture, movements, and eye gaze make for very different forms of conversational involvement.

At each of the four age levels, the girls and women sit closer to each other. They sit across the chairs in order to align their bodies facing each other. They anchor their gaze on each other's faces with occasional glances away. They also occasionally touch each other, and they sit relatively still. In contrast, at every age level, the boys and men are less directly aligned with each other in terms of body posture and gaze. Their chairs are at angles to each other, and they sit aligned with the chairs and, consequently, at angles to each other. They anchor their gaze elsewhere in the room, occasionally glancing at each other, rarely if ever head on. The two younger pairs of boys are restless and seemingly diffuse in their attention; they give the impression that the chairs cannot contain them. The two older male pairs sit still but align themselves more or less parallel rather than facing each other. The tenth-grade boys in particular sprawl out from the chairs rather than sitting in them.[3]

In this section, I proceed by age level to describe the physical alignment of the boys and girls or men and women, in comparison to each other at each level.

[3] Scheflen (1976, p. 55) describes what I am calling "tight" or "direct" alignment as a "closed mutual orientation" and "full face-to-face orientation." He does not, however, address gender differences. Aries (1982, p. 127) notes that "men have been reported to assume more relaxed, open postures than women," a finding supported by her own study. These studies do not, however, address the issue of mutual orientation. Citing Exline (1963) as the pioneering source, Henley (1977, p. 160) observes, "Probably the most accepted finding in this area is that women engage in more eye contact than do men, especially with each other." Frances (1979) corroborates this and also find that male subjects in her study "made significantly more seat position shifts and leg position shifts during the experimental sessions than did female subjects" (p. 531). Thus previous research on posture and gaze has identified the patterns that I observed in the videotapes of friends talking but has not examined these patterns in terms of coherent gender-related strategies for establishing conversational involvement.

Tannen overviews this section of the article and summarizes what she found from analyzing the videotapes.

Tannen tells the reader how she has organized her analysis of the data by age groups. Each pair of conversation partners that she observed exhibits the behavior that Tannen argues is characteristic of the group.

In this note, Tannen cites other scholars whose findings support her own. This enhances the persuasiveness of her analysis.

Grade two. The second-grade boys, Kevin and Jimmy, look at each other only occasionally. They look around the room, look at the ceiling, squirm in their chairs, get up and sit down again, pummel the arms of the chair (the one whose chair has arms), rhythmically kick their feet, make faces, point to objects in the room, mug for the video camera.

The second-grade girls present a strikingly different image. At the beginning of the session, Ellen is sitting at the edge of her seat. Later she moves back into the seat, but then Jane moves to the edge of hers. Thus the space between them remains small. Finally, and for much of the session, they are both at the edges of their seats, sitting very close to each other, almost nose to nose compared to the boys. In all the positions in which they sit, they look straight into each other's faces. When they are thinking of something to say, their eyes and heads veer away, but their bodies remain facing each other throughout. At one point, Jane reaches out and adjusts the headband on Ellen's head.

The contrast in physical composure and level of physical activity is in keeping with prior research on very young boys and girls. Amy Sheldon (personal communication, September 1988) reports that her study of the videotaped interaction of 3- to 5-year-old boys and girls in same-sex triads at play yields similar findings. The boys moved around more than the girls did while playing in the same area. This difference was brought home by the video technician in Sheldon's study, who had trouble keeping the entire boys' triad in the camera's sights; no such problem arose with the girls.

Tannen includes a line drawing that illustrates the observation that male conversation partners of any age seldom look directly at each other.

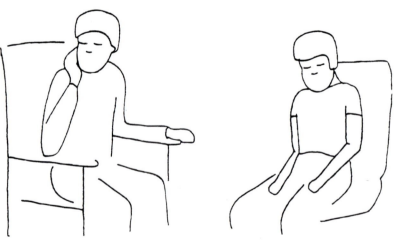

Drawing #1. Second-grade boys.

The line drawings of female conversation partners show that they align their bodies and their gazes more directly than males do.

Drawing #2. Second-grade girls.

Grade six. The diffuse physical alignment of the sixth grade boys is not as marked as that of the second grade boys, but it follows the same pattern. The sixth grade boys stay in their seats, but one boy, Walt, squirms continually. The lack of direct eye contact is reinforced by Walt's frequently rubbing his eyes and playing with his fingers in his lap, his gaze firmly fixed on his fingers. Tom is less visibly restless, but he spreads his legs out in front of him and occasionally briefly drapes his right arm behind the chair. He sits aligned with the upholstered chair and therefore at an angle to Walt.

Of the sixth-grade girls, Shannon sits quite still throughout the session, with her arms on the arms of her wooden chair. At the beginning she sits at the edge of her chair, and later she sits back in it, but she always has her body aligned to face Julia, and, although her gaze drifts away, it always returns before long to Julia. Julia sits diagonally across her armless upholstered chair in order to face Shannon head-on. Whereas the sixth-grade boy who sits in this chair spreads out across the chair, Julia draws her body up onto it. She places her left ankle on her right knee; she holds her foot and plays with her shoelaces. Although this partly occupies her gaze,

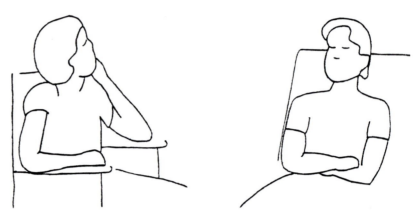

Drawing #3. Sixth-grade boys.

she frequently returns the gaze to Shannon, in contrast with the boy at the same age level whose eyes are anchored on his hands for long periods of time. The sixth-grade girls change their physical positions a few times during the 20-minute session: Julia sits back in her chair and eventually moves forward again. Having put her left leg down, she again raises and holds it at the end. But these shifts are neither abrupt nor frequent, and the girls are always tightly aligned with each other in gaze and body posture.

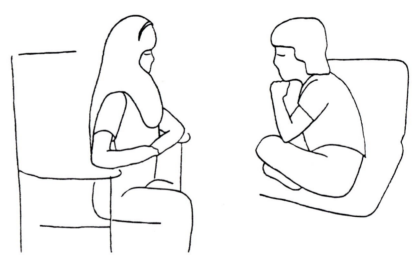

Drawing #4. Sixth-grade girls.

Grade ten. In contrast to the second-grade boys, the tenth-grade boys are relatively still; they significantly change their positions only once. But the postures they maintain are marked. They begin by sitting so that their bodies are aligned with the chairs they sit in, which are at an angle to each other, so their bodies are at angles to each other. In order to face each other, they would have to turn their heads; they rarely do so. For the most part, they look away and out; Todd, on the right in the upholstered chair, steals occasional fleeting glances at Richard, but Richard, on the left in the wooden armed chair, almost never looks at Todd, as if he has been forbidden, as Orpheus was forbidden to look back at his wife. Throughout the 20-minute conversation, Richard sits with his legs extended before him, and he is slouching, almost reclining, in the chair. For the first 5 minutes, Todd sits upright in his chair. But when the investigator leaves following his 5-minute visit, having just told the boys to talk about something intimate, Todd swivels around—*away* from Richard. He briefly places his hands, one on top of the other, on the back of the upholstered chair and rests his head on his hands, assuming a forlorn and weary posture. Immediately after, he leans back in the chair, extends his legs, and uses his feet to pull a wooden swivel chair on wheels into place as a footrest. As the conversation proceeds, Todd manipulates the swivel chair with his feet, alternately resting them on it and using them to push it around or away. But regardless of what he is doing with his feet, he maintains a reclining position, his back slid way down. Thus the two boys conduct their

Tannen describes in detail the movements that tenth-grade boys made during the time they conversed.

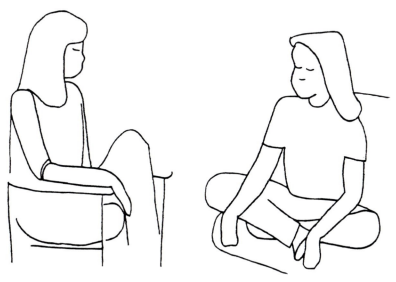

Drawing #5. Tenth-grade girls.

Another line drawing of females captures them in a pose of eye and body alignment.

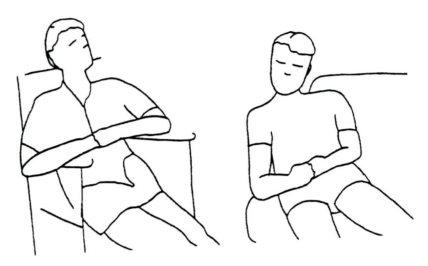

Drawing #6. Tenth-grade boys.

conversation with their bodies reclining, parallel to each other, their gazes fastened straight ahead. One person, seeing a brief clip of the two boys aligned in this way, commented that they look like two people riding in a car: side by side, each looking ahead, rarely looking at each other.

The tenth-grade girls provide a startling contrast. Like the sixth-grade girls, they sit across rather than aligned with the chairs in order to face each other. Whereas the boys at this age extend their legs, the girls both draw their feet up onto the chairs. Nancy, on the left in the wooden chair, sits fairly still, hardly changing her position. For a brief time, Sally, on the right, leans back, placing one arm on the back of the upholstered chair; at one point she takes a bottle of skin cream out of her purse and rubs cream on her elbows; but throughout, she sits firmly in the chair and looks steadily at her friend, who looks steadily at her.

Twenty-five-year olds. The 25-year-old men, like the tenth-grade boys, align themselves with their chairs rather than with each other, so they end up sitting at angles to each other. Furthermore, Winston's chair, on the left, is situated slightly forward, so he has to turn his head not only to the side but also slightly back in order to face Timothy. This he does occasionally—not as rarely as the tenth grade boys look at each other, but not often. When he listens, he looks at Timothy more often than when he speaks, but never for extended time. Timothy keeps his gaze more or less steadily ahead, which means he rarely looks at Winston. He, however, is not looking as far off in another direction as are the tenth graders.

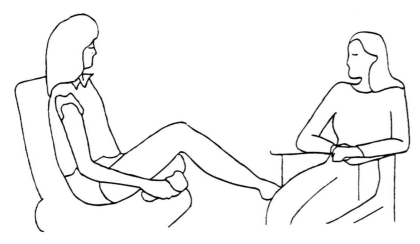

Drawing #7. 25-year-old women.

Finally, the 25-year-old women conform to the pattern. Marsha, on the left, sits across her chair so that she is facing Pam directly, with her profile to the camera, a profile which does not perceptibly change during the 20-minute conversation. At the start she has her left leg drawn up onto her chair, and her right leg bent slightly with her right foot resting on the front edge of Pam's chair. This brings her body almost or actually in contact with Pam's. Later she extends her left leg and brings it to rest on the rear left edge of Pam's chair. Throughout, she looks directly at Pam. Thus, although Marsha stretches one leg out for a time, her legs become a physical connection to the other woman rather than being pointed out and away, like the limb extensions of the boys. Furthermore, her body remains upright, not slouched down and spread out. Pam has the wooden chair with arms; she sits squarely in it, with her arms on the arm rests, facing Marsha. Both women maintain steady and rarely broken eye contact throughout their conversation.

Discussion: are males disengaged? The impression made by viewing the physical alignment of the boys and girls and women and men in comparison to each other is that the girls and women are more closely oriented to each other. They seem more involved, one might say more conversationally coherent. When I described the pattern I was observing to a practicing therapist, she commented, "Oh, yeah. When I see families in therapy, the man never looks at his wife and never looks at me. The men are always disengaged." She remarked that the family therapy literature includes descriptions of this phenomenon. But is the lack of physical and visual alignment evidence of lack of engagement?

After describing all of the data, Tannen begins a discussion of it. She first explains how others have usually interpreted these patterns.

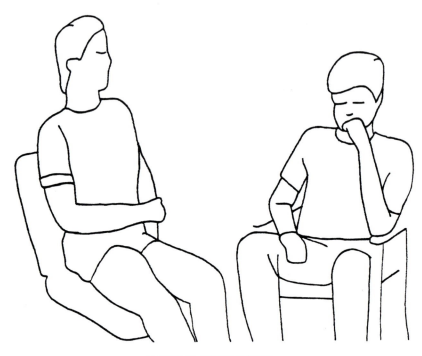

Drawing #8. 25-year-old men.

Tannen argues that a cross-cultural approach to analyzing the data supports her earlier claim that males are not disengaged just because they lack direct eye contact or physical alignment.

Tannen questions the common interpretation, setting the reader up for a new explanation.

Footnote 4 provides a little anecdote to illustrate and bolster Tannen's main claim.

If gender differences are seen in a cross-cultural framework, the evaluation of lack of eye contact and physical alignment as disengagement is taking the women's pattern of showing conversational engagement as the norm. However, the anthropological literature is rich with examples of cultures in which interactants are expected not to look at each other in particular settings and interactions. For example, in many cultures, respect is shown by casting the eyes down and never looking a superior in the face. No one would conclude, however, that this means the interactants are not "engaged." Rather, in those situations, avoiding eye contact is the appropriate display of conversational involvement. The consistency of the pattern observed in these videotapes by which the boys and men do not directly align themselves with each other physically and do not look each other in the eye suggests that there is a norm among them not to do so. A. L. Becker, commenting on my observation, suggested that, for men, head-on posture and gaze connote combativeness, so breaking that alignment signals and establishes friendly engagement.[4]

The conversation of the tenth-grade boys provides dramatic evidence that physical alignment away from rather than toward each other does not mean lack of engagement. As described above, the tenth-grade boys sit parallel to each other, stretched out in postures that could be interpreted as lackadaisical and careless, in one case occasionally and in the other case almost never glancing at the other. Viewing the videotape with the sound turned off could easily give the impression that these boys are disengaged. But turning the sound up reveals the most "intimate" talk heard in any of the tapes I observed.

In accordance with the procedure followed in the experiment, the investigator entered the room after the boys had been talking for 5 minutes and said, "Hi. I said I'd come back in 5 minutes? And ask you to talk in a serious or intimate way?" After he leaves, the boys snicker and chuckle briefly. Then the following interchange ensues:[5]

Tannen points out that the visible evidence seems to support the interpretation that men are disengaged, but the auditory evidence shows otherwise.

Footnote 5 explains how Tannen transcribed passages of conversation from the videotapes.

[4] When he sat down to join me in the conversation in which he made this observation, Becker began by moving his chair. Having found it positioned directly facing mine, he moved it slightly to the side and swiveled it slightly, so that, when he sat in it, he was sitting at an angle to me rather than facing me head-on. This he did without thought, automatically, although we both recognized the result in a flash of recognition and amusement.

Becker also pointed out that the world of animals provides numerous instances of the behavior of individuals which seems, at first glance, unrelated but turns out, upon close observation, to show finely tuned coordination. An example he offered is two geese seemingly self-absorbed in preening their feathers with movements that precisely mirror each other, as if they were performing the same dance to the same music.

Animal behavior also provides a parallel to Becker's suggestion that head-on posture and gaze may suggest combativeness: Horse and dog trainers warn that looking these animals directly in the eye will ready them for attack. The association of gaze with aggressiveness, and the analogy of primate behavior, are also noted by Henley (1977).

[5] Transcription is based on that provided by Dorval. I have, however, checked and refined transcription of passages I cite, and have laid them out in "chunks" or "lines" which I believe are easier to read because they reflect the natural prosodic and rhythmic chunking of spoken discourse. Three spaced dots (. . .) between lines of transcript indicate a small number of lines has been omitted; three unspaced dots (. . .) indicate a brief untimed pause. Numbers in parentheses show measured pause length in seconds; spaces between lines of transcript indicate segments taken from different sections of the transcript. In a number of the transcripts, the word *god* appears. I have chosen to render it with a small *g* because I believe it is a formulaic usage, not intended to refer to a deity but used automatically as a discourse marker. (See Schiffin, 1987b, for discussion of discourse markers.) In instances where the word *god* begins a sentence, I render it with a capital as I would the first word of any sentence. Colon (:) indicates elongation of preceding vowel sound. *Underline* indicates emphatic stress. /?/ indicates unintelligible word(s). Brackets show overlapping speech. = indicates latching (no interturn pause). – indicates a glottal stop (abrupt cutting off of sound.)

Tannen provides this transcript of part of the conversation between the tenth-grade boys in her study to show that males can have an emotionally intimate conversation with each other even if they do not align their bodies and gazes the way females do.

Todd: What the hell we supposed to talk about?
I mean I know what's bugging me.
Richard: What's bugging you?
Todd: [snicker] That we don't talk.
Richard: Who don't talk?
. . .
Todd: We're doing it again.
Richard: What?
Todd: Not talking.
Richard: I know. Well, go.
Todd: We're not even making small talk any more.
[laugh]
Richard: Right, okay. (3.4)
I mean you know.
What can I say? (3.6)
I mean,
if you meant everything you said last
weekend,
and I meant everything I said. (1.0)
Todd: Well of course I did.
But I mean I don't know.
I guess we're growing up.
I mean—I don't know.
I guess I live in the past or something.
I really enjoyed those times
when we used to stay up all night long
and just you know
spend the nights over someone else's house
just to talk all night.
Richard: mhm
Todd: They were kinda fun.
Richard: Yeah that *was* fun.
(2.2)
Todd: But now we're lucky if we say anything
to each other in the hall.
Richard: Oh, all right! [challenging intonation]
Todd: I'm serious.
I remember walking in the hall
and I'd say "Hi" to you
and you'd say "Hi there"
or sometimes you'll push me in the locker,
if I'm lucky.

	[laugh]
	(1.4)
Richard:	We ta:lk. [protesting]
Todd:	Not the same way anymore.
	(4.8)
Richard:	I never *knew* you wanted to *talk*.

The conversation continues in this vein until the investigator enters and ends it. Todd reveals deep feelings of hurt and disappointment that his friendship with Richard is not as close as it once was.

SUMMARY: PHYSICAL ALIGNMENT

In summary, then, my analysis of the postural and visual alignment of the pairs of friends indicates that girls and boys and men and women achieve and display their involvement with each other and with the conversation in different ways. The girls and women are more physically still, more collected into the space they inhabit, and more directly aligned with each other through physical proximity, occasional touching, body posture, and anchoring of eye gaze. The boys and men do not touch each other except in playful aggression, do not anchor their gaze on each other's faces, and spread out rather than gather themselves into the space they inhabit. The boys in the youngest pairs are more physically restless, more diffused in the room both in their movements and in their gaze. The boys and men in the two older pairs are more physically still but still less directly aligned with each other in posture and gaze. However, this does not mean that the men and boys are not engaged, not involved. It simply means that their means of establishing conversational engagement are different. These differences, however, are likely to lead to negative evaluation and the impression of lack of engagement if measured by women's interactional norms.[6]

> Tannen summarizes her findings again and repeats her assertion that it would be wrong to conclude that men's conversational patterns are somehow deficient because they aren't like women's. She implies that difference does not equate with inferiority.

[6] The suggestion, made earlier, that psychotherapeutic norms of interactive behavior may reflect women's norms is supported by a psychiatric study (reported in *Psychiatry '86*, August 1986, pp. 1, 6) which found that women are more effective therapists when they are new to the field, but that the gender difference in effectiveness fades among experienced psychotherapists. This suggests that psychotherapeutic training and experience teach men to behave in ways that women do with minimal or no training or experience.

STUDENT EXAMPLE

Following is a report of an observational study conducted by four students—Emily Gwilliam, Kyle McLaughlin, Greg Nielsen, and Susan Walley—majoring in psychology and sociology. Their initial question was whether or not patience is a gender-related trait. In order to answer this question, they devised a study in which they could observe other students who were forced to wait in line to use a campus courtesy telephone (one that can be used at no cost for local calls). Working as a team, these students made unobtrusive observations about the gender and behavior of the students who were forced to wait. One member of the team would work to the head of the line waiting to use the phone, then use it for longer than the allowed time. Another member of the team would be standing in line two or three spots back in order to hear the words and see the behaviors of the other people waiting. Still another member of the team was not in line but was close by so they too could observe the behavior of waiting people.

Before they began their observations, the team of students tried to anticipate what they might observe and created a coding system for recording the various behaviors (included in the appendix to their report). This coding sheet made it easy to standardize observations and to compare what different observers saw. They also made quantitative observations about the length of time people actually waited. In these ways, they enhanced the validity of their report. However, as they admit, they didn't have time to gather enough observations to draw reliable conclusions, and there were some flaws in their methods that make some of the interpretations shaky. Nevertheless, their report illustrates how students can plan and carry out an interesting study—one that might be replicated by other students.

A Study of Patience:
Gender-Related Differences in College Students

by
Emily Gwilliam
Greg Nielsen
Kyle McLaughlin
Susan Walley

Abstract

This study tested the hypothesis that male college students are less patient than female college students when forced to wait in line. Two observers recorded both verbal and non-verbal behavior of 12 male and 12 female students waiting to use a free telephone while a caller (member of the research team) exceeded the 3-minute limit. Men tended to behave more assertively and to react sooner than women, but more women exhibited impatient behavior. Because of the limited number of observations and other uncontrolled variables, the hypothesis was not confirmed; further research is recommended.

Many social scientists have argued that the process of sex role typing begins before birth. For example, the anticipating father may see himself giving his son instructions on how to play baseball, and the mother may imagine dressing her daughter in frilly dresses and having others comment on how cute she looks. As a result, children learn at a young age that certain activities or characteristics are associated with one sex or the other. In contrast, other experts argue that gender-specific behaviors are a result of biological differences between the sexes. Whatever the reason, there *are* differences that exist between the behavior and attitudes of males and females, not only as children but also as adults. One specific trait that may be influenced by gender is patience. We decided to research this assumption by measuring the variance in patience between male and female students on our campus.

In order to measure different levels of patience, we chose to observe the reactions of people subjected to waiting in line. Waiting in line is an ordeal that occurs frequently for students, whether they are waiting to get movie and football tickets or just to get something to eat. We felt that by observing people subjected to waiting in line to use the courtesy telephone we would get relatively accurate readings of genuine patience or irritability for those individuals. Because of our general experience, we hypothesized that male college students would become irritated more easily than female college students, showing that females are more patient in this situation.

Methods

Participant Selection

We chose to use the courtesy phones in the student union and the library copy center to make our observations. Our team observed individuals who we assumed to be college students because they are on campus in these high-traffic areas during the hours when school is in session. All students in the immediate area were given an equal opportunity to use the phone and thus were selected randomly as they stepped in line for the phone. However there was no effort to achieve *standard* randomization, and though we had a small sample (24 participants, 12 male and 12 female), we assumed that a variety of personalities were represented.

Procedures

The independent variable for our observation was a situation in which the subject had to wait in line for an extended period of time in order to use the phone. We chose to use impatience as the dependent variable. The operational definition of impatience in our observations was any expression of being irritated because of having to wait in line, demonstrated by a given set of behaviors, both verbal and non-verbal. A list of these behaviors is included in the sample observation sheet in the appendix. Waiting in line is a routine occurrence with the potential to cause irritability; thus we assume face validity for this measure.

To create the observational situation, we had two members of our research team stand in line to use the phone with up to three people in between them. The first individual on our team introduced the independent variable (forcing others to wait in line by talking on the phone for an extended period of time). The length of time on the phone was left up to the discretion of each group member, depending on the reaction of the individuals we observed. The length of each observation was between 4 and 9 minutes. Our observations were limited to the first two people waiting to use the phone. The second member of our team, because of the close proximity, was able to accurately observe both verbal and non-verbal reactions of the subjects. A third member of our team was strategically placed nearby at a pay phone. Both observers used a small coding sheet (see appendix) to record the reactions of the subjects and the time it took before the behavior appeared. One variable we controlled for was the participants' awareness of the time limit while using the courtesy phones. In both locations where observations were made, signs are posted reminding patrons of the 3-minute time limit for using the phones. Another variable we controlled for was content of the telephone conversation carried out by our team member. Though each telephone conversation was different, we tried to keep the conversations mumbled so the participants couldn't understand what was being said. We did not control for the variable of gender of the team member on the phone. We acknowledge that the gender of the offending party might have affected the reaction of the subjects waiting in line. This is a variable that should be measured in further studies of this topic.

To verify the reliability of our data, we tested the consistency of the coding of each observer on our team by comparing observations recorded on the sheet. Because the behaviors we were recording were easy to observe and classify, we found that there were no discrepancies between the different observers' notes.

Results and Discussion

Because of the small sample size and the difficulty in analyzing the eight different categories of data accurately, we collapsed the data into two different types of reactions: assertive and passive. The behaviors we considered passive were making impatient gestures, looking at a watch, giving disapproving looks, and talking to others in line about the offending party. The behaviors we considered assertive were walking away, tapping the offending party on the shoulder, making a request to get off the phone, and pointing out the 3-minute rule.

After the coded data were categorized, we grouped the data according to gender and type as illustrated in Figure 1, and according to gender and time of reaction as shown in Figure 2. This allows us to analyze the data in different ways. First, we can see who reacted more frequently and more assertively, and, second, we can compare both the variance in male and female reaction times and the variance within each gender.

We found, as illustrated by Figure 1, that although women showed a higher tendency to exhibit some form of impatient behavior than did males, the behavior exhibited was slightly more passive. Men, on the other hand, had a higher tendency to exhibit assertive behaviors than did women, even though they had a slightly lower tendency to exhibit any impatient behavior at all. So, in general, women tended to react more often, but men tended to react more assertively.

Figure 2 illustrates the reaction times for each male and female participant. The data are sorted from shortest to longest reaction time to enable comparison of the data. One female and two male participants did not react at all; thus there is no time score on this graph for those three. According to Figure 2, men tended to exhibit both

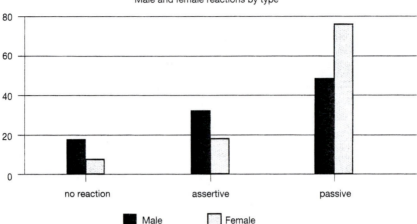

Figure 1
Male and female reactions by type

assertive and passive types of impatient behaviors earlier than did women; however, the initial reaction time for each gender did not vary greatly. One interesting comparison shown by Figure 2 is that the time variance was greater for men than for women—a 7-minute spread for men, but only a 5.33-minute spread for women. This difference in variance shows that we are not able to generalize about men's impatient behaviors as easily as women's, which appear to be more consistent. Only when we consider the time averages—5.37 minutes for men and 5.59 minutes for women—can we state that females generally wait longer to respond than men do. However, 0.22

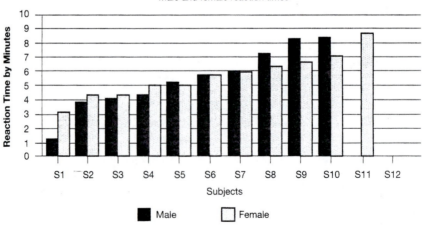

Figure 2
Male and female reaction times

minutes equates to only 13 seconds, and that is clearly not a very significant difference.

Since men in our study tended to exhibit impatience slightly more quickly than did women, and since men's reactions tended to be slightly more assertive than those of women, we conclude that our original hypothesis—that male college students more easily become irritated when forced to wait than do female college students—may have some validity. However, because our sample size was small and the variance between groups was also small, the conclusion should not necessarily be generalized yet. A much larger sample would be necessary to determine if the small variance is significant or not. In addition, there were several other factors that could have affected our results that we did not consider in making our conclusions, such as whether or not the gender, age, or physical characteristics of the person on the phone would influence the reactions of the subjects, or whether time of day is a factor. Consequently, more research is required to form a definite conclusion about the differences in levels of patience between men and women college students.

Appendix
Coding Sheet
(The observers checked the behaviors elicited and the time elapsed for each person observed.)

	Person #1	Person #2	Person #3	Person #4
M/M, M/F, F/F, F/M*				
Looks at watch				
Disapproving look				
Fidgety/impatient gestures				
Talks to others in line				
Walks away				
Taps on shoulder				
Makes request				
Points out 3-minute time rule				

* This refers to the gender of the observed person waiting in line and the gender of the person tying up the telephone.

SUGGESTIONS FOR RESEARCH AND WRITING

Note: These suggestions are well suited for collaboration. By planning an observational study with two or three classmates, you can improve the research design and increase the reliability of the results; you can then pool your analytical and composing talents to write a stronger paper.

1. Plan some kind of unobtrusive observation that will allow you to make a claim about typical human behavior. For example, this chapter repeatedly used the example of observing what people do when a stranger sits in the chair right next to them, rather than choosing a vacant chair further away. Conduct such a study by sitting next to 30–40 strangers in a public place. Have one or more collaborators unobtrusively observe and record what the people do. Or, see if you can independently confirm Deborah Tannen's observations about two-person, same-sex conversations. By unobtrusively observing in dorm lounges and public sitting areas on your campus, determine how pairs of men and pairs of women align their chairs and bodies and how they direct their eyes when involved in conversation. Keep careful notes; draw sketches if they help you remember.

2. Who buys what at the supermarket? After making some initial observations of product displays and customers at a supermarket near where you live, formulate a hypothesis about the type of person who is most likely to buy a certain kind of product. For example, who buys frozen dinners the most— men or women? old or young? What kinds of dinners do they buy? Who buys the tabloids (newspapers that typically have headlines like "Woman gives birth to two-headed child after encounter with space alien") that line the aisle leading to the checkout stand? You could observe by posing as shoppers.

3. Identify one or more words that often have an unusual pronunciation in your region of the country. For example, in some regions, "bell" and "bale" and "hell" and "hail" might be pronounced the same. Plan a structured observation of pronunciation by writing a brief passage that you ask passers-by to stop and read aloud. As they read, notice what pronunciation they give to the target words and make a record. Or choose an object that has various names in your region. For example, a soft drink might be called a "coke" no matter what brand or flavor it is; but perhaps young people are more likely to call it that than older people are. Take the object in question to a busy place and stop people to ask them what they call it. Have a collaborator record answers and ages. See what generalizations you can make based on the data you collect.

4. In an age when discrimination has become illegal, do employers and landlords still discriminate on the basis of race or gender? Working with a collaborator who is of a different race or gender than you, reply to ads for help

wanted or rooms to let. Contact the person who placed the ad, one after the other, and see if you both get the same treatment. If the person who placed the ad appears reluctant to hire or rent an apartment to a person of a particular race or gender, politely ask for reasons. Compare notes with each other after each of you makes the contact.

7

SURVEYING

Has a representative of an organization ever called you on the telephone to ask your opinion about a political candidate, a referendum on the ballot, a recent controversy? Have you ever filled out a form to evaluate a teacher, a product you've purchased, or a service you've received? Has someone ever stopped you on campus, at the mall, or as you've emerged from the voting booth to see if you would answer a few questions about a university policy, about your shopping habits, or about how you just voted? If so, you have been a respondent in a survey.

Surveying is probably the most common method of research that social scientists use, if you include oral surveys along with written ones. Oral surveys can take the form of structured interviews with well-defined questions (called the interview schedule), and they can be conducted on the telephone as well as in face-to-face encounters. Written surveys are frequently called questionnaires. They too can be structured, asking questions that offer only fixed answers for the respondent to choose, or they can be open-ended, permitting respondents to answer as they wish. Questionnaires may be given to respondents in face-to-face settings, mailed to the respondents, or personally delivered to classrooms, homes, and workplaces to be picked up later.

ADVANTAGES OF SURVEYING

Many social scientists favor the survey method because it is the best way to get large numbers of responses in relatively short periods, usually at a reasonable cost. It is usually not difficult to get people to participate in a survey, especially if it won't take long. A large set of data is important when researchers want to draw generalizations that are valid for the whole population under investigation. If a representative sample of an entire population answers a survey, researchers can then generalize the results, making valid claims or predictions about people who didn't even participate in the survey. That is why each time there is a presidential election, the television reporters covering the election can project which candidate has won in each state even when only a small percentage of the voting districts have reported results. If one candidate has a clear majority in those districts, and if the districts are representative of the state as a whole, polling experts can quite accurately predict which candidate will receive the state's electoral votes.

Social scientists, particularly sociologists, also prefer surveying because it is probably the best way to learn about people's attitudes, beliefs, and practices. Researchers assume it is fairly likely that the respondents will answer truthfully, particularly if they are sure that their identity will remain anonymous. For sensitive topics, a written survey is probably more reliable than an oral one, because respondents are more likely to answer questions candidly in writing than they are in a face-to-face interview, in which they might be embarrassed to reveal their true attitudes or opinions. With a written survey respondents are also less likely to answer the way they think the investigator wants them to. Finally, filling out a questionnaire affords the respondent more time to think, and perhaps even to consult with others or to check records in order to give the most complete and correct answer.

DISADVANTAGES OF SURVEYING

Despite its advantages, surveying has some limitations as well. Some of these are inherent in the method. What researchers gain in breadth of sampling and generalizability of results, they often lose in depth of information. The data from a survey are seldom as complex and subtle as those from observation, for example. With a survey, there is little chance to learn about the contexts that may have influenced the respondents' answers. If the survey has only fixed-response questions, there is no chance to probe and learn more about the reasons for answers.

Other drawbacks of surveying are due to the human nature of the respondents. There is a chance that the respondents may either purposefully or inadvertently report something that is false. They may give answers they think the researcher wants, or they may change their answers in order to project a more favorable image of themselves. They may choose not to answer some of the questions. If the survey is very long, respondents may become tired or bored toward the end and give rushed or incomplete answers. With a telephone survey, people may simply hang up after answering a few questions or refuse to answer any at all. With a questionnaire mailed to a home or business, the intended respondent may not fill it out but have someone else answer it instead. Often, mailed questionnaires are simply not returned because taking time to do a favor for an unknown researcher is simply not a priority in most people's lives. Those questionnaires that are returned may represent a somewhat biased sample because they come from respondents who are eager to comply and who want to make their answers known. Many of these limitations can be overcome, however, if the researcher follows some basic principles of survey design and uses care in selecting a sample of people to answer the survey.

DESIGNING A SURVEY

You can design a good survey if you will observe some basic instructions about defining your purpose and writing good questions and clear directions that help you achieve your purpose.

DEFINE YOUR PURPOSE

As with any method, the first step in designing a survey is to define your purpose. You might state it as a question, such as this: "To what extent do people's eating habits and exercise practices coincide with their knowledge about sound nutrition and good exercise habits?" Or you might state it as a hypothesis, such as this: "People who know more about sound nutrition and good exercise habits are more likely than those who don't to eat a balanced diet (daily recommended servings from the food pyramid) and exercise for at least 30 minutes three to four times a week." Notice that the hypothesis is stated more specifically than the question. Typically, beginning with a hypothesis implies that you will later do some statistical tests to determine whether or not you can confirm or must reject the hypothesis; in order to do the statistical calculations, you must have clearly defined variables to measure and relate. Whether you start with a question or a hypothesis, however, you will find that the way you state your purpose suggests the kinds of questions you must ask. There are basically three kinds of questions.

CREATE DEMOGRAPHIC QUESTIONS

A standard part of almost every survey is questions about what sociologists call the *demographics* of the respondents. These might include questions about the respondent's age, gender, race or ethnicity, occupation, income, education, political or religious affiliation, and so on. Researchers ask about these matters when they want to compare the answers of identifiable groups in order to determine whether or not membership in the group somehow influences the opinions, attitudes, or practices of an individual. So, for example, if political pollsters wanted to find out which gender, which regions of the country, and which income groups vote Democratic more often, they would create questions that allow them to sort the respondents by those categories and compare their overall answers to other questions about voting.

Demographic questions are fairly easy to ask. Normally, they are fixed-response questions because the researcher can usually anticipate accurately all the demographic categories the respondents will fall into. The researcher can then just instruct respondents to check a box or circle a word that corresponds to a particular demographic fact about themselves.

Suppose you wanted to survey students on your campus about how their knowledge compares to their practices in eating and exercising. What demographic groups might you want to compare? It might be interesting to compare men with women, dorm-dwellers with off-campus residents, or juniors and seniors with sophomores and freshmen. If your college or university has a required health and fitness course, it would certainly be interesting to see if students who have already had this course practice better eating and exercise habits than students who haven't had the course. Notice that once you start looking at your respondents by demographic categories, you create subquestions to answer or additional hypotheses to test. Be sure to write adequate demographic questions that will allow you to sort the responses according to your purposes.

CREATE FIXED-RESPONSE QUESTIONS

As the name implies, a fixed-response question has a limited number of answers a respondent can choose. It is sort of like a multiple-choice question on a test, except it doesn't have one right answer. Instead, you try to think of the range of possible answers that people could give, and you list them all. That way, people only have to check a box or circle the answer that they would give. Taking our hypothetical survey again as an example, you might ask a question like this to find out how often people exercise.

1. On average, how many times a week do you exercise for at least 30 minutes?
    (a) none

(b) 1–2 times

(c) 3–4 times

(d) more than 4 times

Notice that with just four responses you have anticipated all the possible answers respondents could give: In a week, they either exercise or they don't; and if they do, they do it 1 or more times a week. By specifying a range that each respondent would fall into, you make it easy for them to answer quickly. Not only that, but you also make it easy for yourself to later tabulate and analyze the responses—a particular advantage of the fixed-response question.

Sometimes you can't anticipate every possible response, but you can still write a mostly fixed-response question by creating categories and offering respondents the option of filling in a blank with answers you can't anticipate. Here is an example:

2. What kind of exercise do you usually do?

(a) individual (e.g., walking, swimming, jogging, biking)

(b) compete against an opponent (e.g., tennis, racquetball)

(c) play a team sport (e.g., basketball, soccer, volleyball)

(d) other (please explain)

(e) I don't exercise.

But as you will note, question 2 may be worded ambiguously. Perhaps someone who plays pick-up basketball at the gym three afternoons a week won't be able to decide if that really counts as playing a team sport or if it's just a way of getting a good workout. Another problem with fixed-response questions is that they may force respondents into a choice that they wouldn't give if the question were open-ended. In that case, respondents may choose the answer that comes closest to the one they want to give, or they may leave the question unanswered. Ideally, fixed-response questions should be pilot-tested so that the researcher can see whether respondents interpret them in ways not intended or otherwise demonstrate that they had difficulty answering the question as it is presently worded.

WRITE OPEN-ENDED QUESTIONS

As the name implies, an open-ended question does not give answers for the respondent to choose. Instead, the questionnaire simply provides a space for the respondent to write what they want to reply; or, if it's an oral survey, the interviewer writes down whatever the respondent says. Here's an example of an open-ended question from our hypothetical survey of knowledge versus practice in eating and exercise:

3. What would motivate you to be more conscientious about following healthy eating and exercise practices?

Questions like this are good for getting qualitative data, with all its nuances. But most surveys use only a few such questions because, as you might guess, they are time-consuming and difficult to analyze and categorize. Sometimes, pilot-testing of open-ended questions may reveal that respondents' answers fall into some well-defined categories. In that case, often a fixed-response question can be written to replace an open-ended one.

WRITE UNAMBIGUOUS QUESTIONS

Experienced survey designers have learned to avoid some mistakes in writing questions so they don't get confusing data. One of these mistakes is the "double-barreled" question. Although such a question appears to be asking for one thing, it is actually asking two things at once. For example, this question at first appears to be about frequency:

> Do you often suffer from anxiety or depression?
> (a) yes
> (b) no

Suppose a person who suffers often from anxiety, but not depression, reads it. How should they answer it? Suppose they answer it with a "yes." When the investigators analyze the results, they won't know whether the person suffers from anxiety, depression, or both. A muddled question will give muddled results that don't permit you to draw valid conclusions. This double-barreled question would have to be split into two questions—one about anxiety and one about depression.

But you will probably have noted another problem with the question above: How frequently is "often"? Suppose a woman who answers "yes" suffers from depression about three times a year—too often in her opinion. Suppose a man who also suffers from depression about three times a year answers "no" because three times seems infrequent to him. Words referring to time, such as *often, frequently, seldom, occasionally*, and words referring to amounts (*much* or *many*) or degrees (*extremely* or *somewhat*) must be specific enough so that people who give the same answer will have similar understandings and will be indicating similar things about themselves. A good way to offer specific choices is to give a range. For example, rather than ask the question about depression this way,

> How frequently do you feel depressed?
> (a) never

    (b) occasionally
    (c) sometimes
    (d) frequently

ask it this way,

    1. On average, how many days a month do you feel depressed?
       (a) 0–1
       (b) 2–3 days
       (c) 4–7 days
       (d) more than 8

DETERMINE THE ORDER OF QUESTIONS

Another thing you must consider is how to order the questions in your survey. Should you start with demographic questions or end with them? It depends. If the rest of the questionnaire is about sensitive issues or is actually quite dull, you could start with demographic questions because they are usually nonthreatening and easy to answer; they get the respondent involved in completing the questionnaire. On the other hand, you could end with them if the main survey questions are on an interesting topic and respondents will be motivated to begin answering them right away. In general, the main questions should follow a sequence that you have reasoned out carefully, rather than being put in a random order.

Sometimes not all questions will apply to all respondents. In that case, you can devise screening questions or directions that tell respondents which question to answer next depending on the answer they have just chosen. For example, suppose in our hypothetical survey on diet and exercise, you planned to ask five questions about exercise, beginning with the example question on frequency of exercise. If respondents chose the answer "never" on question 1, they could be directed to skip to question 6, where the questions on eating habits would begin.

WRITE CLEAR DIRECTIONS

Although directions should come first in your survey, you may wait to write them last. Most people will be curious about what the survey is for, who is conducting it, and how the results will be used; they usually want to be assured also that their answers will remain anonymous. They will be more inclined to cooperate with you if you are open about these matters. You should satisfy their curiosity with a brief, general statement about your purpose and at the same time get their informed consent to use the data they give you (see Chapter 3 and Chapter 11). Your opening statement might look something like this:

> We are conducting this survey to determine students' knowledge and practices in eating and exercise. We are three students in [name of course] and we will use the data you give us to write a paper for the course. We will not reveal the identity of any participants in our survey. By completing this survey, you signify your consent to let us use the data in our study.

Besides writing the initial explanation, you must write clear directions about how you want the respondents to answer questions in each part of your survey. For example, you might write, "Circle the answer that best describes what you do" or "Place an X next to the answer that most closely corresponds to your attitude" or "Fill in the blank with your answer."

FINDING RESPONDENTS

Once you have designed your survey—and, if possible, pilot-tested it and revised it—the next step is to find respondents for the final study. If you were conducting the study of college students' exercise and eating habits, it wouldn't be practical or necessary to survey every student on campus. Instead, you would need to survey only a sampling of the students. Professionals who conduct surveys place a high priority on getting a *representative sample* of people from the population under investigation. If they can survey a small percentage of the entire population, and if that sample is representative of the whole, then they can save the time and money it would take to survey everyone. And they can confidently generalize the results to the whole—usually allowing, however, for a small margin of error.

Undergraduate students learning how to do survey research, however, are not as likely as professionals to be able to get a representative sample because students generally lack the time and resources to identify and contact a truly representative sample. Frequently they also lack the expert understanding of sampling techniques that comes from successfully completing statistics courses. Because a complete discussion of sampling is beyond the scope of this book, only a brief summary of the main points of sampling is presented here so that you will understand what is involved in getting a representative sample.

Random Sampling

A representative sample is a *random sample*. In a random sample, every *unit* (person, family, classroom, etc.) in the entire population has the same chance of being chosen to participate in the survey. To draw a random sample, researchers must first identify all the units in the population. In our example on eating and exercise, the units would be students on your campus. Suppose there are 15,000 students in all. With the proper authorization, you might be able to obtain a master list of every student enrolled at the institution. Or you could also safely use the student telephone directory; although not every student may have a telephone, in this case the chances of bias are small. You could then randomly choose a predetermined number of students—say 100—whom you would ask to participate in the survey.

To randomly draw names from the master list or telephone directory, you could use several methods: You could number all the names and use a random number table to select 100 numbers between 1 and 15,000; then you would choose the 100 names that correspond to the random numbers. A faster and easier method would be to draw a systematic sample. Because you need 100 names from 15,000, you could take every fifteenth name from the list, after first determining a random starting point. To do this, you would again use a random number table to select a number between 1 and 15. Suppose you selected the number 2; you would take the second name; then you would choose the seventeenth name, the thirty-second name, and so on, until you had chosen 100 names. After randomly selecting names, you would be ready to contact the people chosen to ask them to participate in your survey.

As you can see, if you used random sampling, you would spend a fair amount of time identifying respondents; then you would have to spend more time phoning, writing, or visiting them to see if they would participate in your survey. If the results of your survey are to be published or if an important decision will be made based on the results, it is crucial for you to use random sampling. If time is short, however, and your purpose is mainly to gather data for the experience of analyzing it and writing a report for a class, random sampling may not be as critical.

CONVENIENCE SAMPLING

Depending on your purpose and your teacher's instructions, you may be able to conduct survey research using a nonrandom sample. This kind of sample is also called a "convenience sample." As the name implies, you would survey respondents who are conveniently available during the time you must gather your data. You could simply survey your friends or all of your neighbors in a single apartment building or dorm. However, doing so might give you very similar answers to your questions, if you choose your friends or neighbors on the basis of their similarity to you. It might be better to survey a broader cross section of the population you are interested in, one that would represent more variety than just the people you associate with most often.

For example, suppose you were conducting the eating and exercise habits survey; you could try to get a sample of students that is likely to include students from both genders and from various classes, majors, and ages. To avoid choosing mostly physical education majors for your survey, you shouldn't hand out your survey only in the P.E. building. Instead, you could approach students in the various buildings on campus to increase the likelihood of surveying students in engineering, fine arts, humanities, social sciences, and so forth. If you know some professors who would permit you to, you could pass out a questionnaire in courses that are likely to include various kinds of students. Although you couldn't be confident that your results are generalizable from a convenience sample, you could still have the experience of collecting data from a broad sample of people, then analyzing and writing about it.

SAMPLE SIZE

How big a sample do you need? There is no pat answer to this question. The size depends on several factors, including how diverse the population is, the purpose of the research, the available time and resources, and the degree of accuracy needed. The more heterogeneous a population is, usually the bigger the sample size needed to include representatives of each type. The more important the research is and the more it must be accurate and generalizable, the more it should be based on a large enough sample to minimize the margin of error. Some statisticians estimate that a random sample size must be between 30 and 100. After determining an appropriate sample size for your study, you should increase the number by five or ten to ensure that you will have enough after you set aside incomplete or improperly completed surveys.

CONDUCTING THE SURVEY

Once you have determined how to select respondents, how you actually obtain answers from them depends on whether you have planned an oral or a written survey. In either case, you will need to make written copies of your questions so that either you or the respondent can write on the copies.

If you conduct the survey orally, either on the telephone or face to face, you ask your respondents to listen to you read each question. If you have written fixed-response questions, you also read the answers and then write down the answer the respondent chooses. For open-ended questions, you write down whatever the respondent says, probably abbreviating parts of the answer to save time. When reading questions to the respondent, you must take care not to indicate by your tone of voice or body language a preference for a certain answer. The respondent may be able to sense the answer you favor and choose it just to please you. You should also not reveal your approval if the answer is one that you like or your disapproval when a respondent gives a reply that you find unappealing. You must make every effort to remain neutral about the topic during the entire process of reading the survey questions.

If you hand respondents a written copy of your survey, you don't have to worry about unduly influencing them by your intonation or body language. You should, however, not hover about, looking over their shoulders while they fill it out. Create an atmosphere in which they feel free to answer candidly. Be prepared to give simple, clear directions about the purposes of the survey and how to answer the questions when you hand the copy to the respondents. If they ask for clarification during the time they are filling it out, try to give simple answers that focus on the meaning of the question, not on how you expect or want them to answer.

ANALYZING THE DATA

When you have collected your data, you can begin tabulating it. If you have asked mostly fixed-response questions, it is not difficult to simply count the number of respondents who chose a given answer on each question. You can use a blank copy of your question form to keep a tally for each question. If you have asked some open-ended questions, you should read through the answers once quickly to get a sense of the range of answers. You may discern repeated or similar answers immediately that suggest categories you can sort the open-ended answers into. However, it may take more than one reading to see a pattern in the data provided by the open-ended questions. Perhaps only a very faint pattern will be evident if respondents' ideas or opinions are quite diverse.

The more questions you have asked and the more respondents you have included in your survey, obviously the more time you will need to spend consolidating the data onto a tally sheet and into categories of answers. Once you have total figures, you should calculate percentages of respondents who chose each answer; your readers will find percentages more meaningful than raw numbers. If your aim is simply to describe what you found, the numerical operations you need to perform can stop with percentages and averages. However, if you want to compare numbers to see if they are significantly different, or if you want to compare responses from different subgroups in your sample, you will have to have some statistical expertise. If you know how, or if you know someone who will help you, you can enter your data into computer programs designed to cross-tabulate data, perform different statistical tests, and determine the statistical significance of your findings. Again, it is beyond the scope of this book to explain statistics, but if you have learned how to use inferential statistics in other courses, by all means try to do a more sophisticated analysis of your data.

WRITING THE REPORT

Survey research is frequently, but not always, reported in the four-part format characteristic of the research report genre, which typically uses the headings "Introduction," "Methods," "Results," and "Discussion." The form you present your findings in will depend on your purpose and your audience. Even if you don't choose the standard form, however, your report should still provide a context for the problem you've investigated, describe who your respondents were and how you collected data from them, and present and interpret your results. These things might be somewhat more interwoven with each other, though, than they are in the traditional genre. If your results are complex and fall into different categories, consider creating unique headings for each section of your report where you describe a new category of findings.

A PROFESSIONAL EXAMPLE

The professional example of survey research that follows has its own unique form. It comes from the book *Middletown Families: Fifty Years of Change and Continuity* by sociologists Theodore Caplow, Howard M. Bahr, Bruce A. Chadwick, Reuben Hill, and Margaret Holmes Williamson.[1] From 1976 to 1978 they did a follow-up study of two groundbreaking studies conducted in 1924–1925 and 1935 by sociologists Robert and Helen Lynd. These first two studies were published as *Middletown* in 1929 and *Middletown in Transition* in 1937. Caplow and his associates wanted to know what had changed in Middletown during the 50 years since the Lynds did their research. So this new group of sociologists took turns living for months at a time in the small industrial city in the Midwest that the Lynds called "Middletown." There, Caplow and colleagues report, they

> read everything of local interest we could find, attended every public or private occasion to which we could gain access, interviewed the movers and shakers in business and politics and conducted cross-sectional surveys of carefully selected samples of the population: adolescents and adults, individuals and families,

[1] Theodore M. Caplow, Howard M. Bahr, Bruce A. Chadwick, Reuben Hill, and Margaret Holmes Williamson, *Middletown Families: Fifty Years of Change and Continuity* (Minneapolis: University of Minnesota Press, 198), pp. 88–96, 356–357. Copyright © 1985 by the University of Minnesota. Reproduced by arrangement with the University of Minnesota Press.

employed men, employed women with and without children, people in and out of churches, voluntary associations and government agencies. In all, we did 13 major surveys in Middletown, not counting some minor ones undertaken for special purposes. In three of these surveys—and they were the most informative—our questionnaires were largely copied from those used by the Lynds and we repeated many of their questions verbatim. (Caplow et al. 1982, v–vi)

Notice that the above description of methods comes from the preface of the book, not a separate chapter called "Methods." Note also that Caplow and his associates did not rely exclusively on the survey method, but it was their main way of gathering data. In the excerpt that you will read, they compare their findings on the work patterns of Middletown men with the Lynds' findings. As you read the excerpt, note the various headings used to organize the findings. You will see also that the authors use tables in addition to sentences to present their data. Tables are almost always an important part of presenting findings from survey research because they allow you to present numerical data concisely and in a more understandable and easy-to-reference format. Note, finally, that the researchers don't merely report their findings and leave the reader to draw all the conclusions; instead, they intersperse their reporting with comments on the significance of what they found. In other words, they interpret the data for the reader.

Work and Family Life

The authors begin by reviewing the Lynds' findings about two classes of workers in the 1920s.

The men engaged in earning a living in 1924, according to the Lynds, fell into two separate groups, the working class and the business class. The working-class men were three times more numerous. These men used their hands and backs to make things and to provide services. They wore overalls to work and came home from work dirty and exhausted. The smaller group of business-class men made their livings by selling or promoting ideas and by arranging the goods and services produced by the working class. These men wore suits to their jobs in offices, banks, and shops. They returned home from work with no more dirt than a ring around the collar of their white shirts. Ten years later, in *Middletown in Transition*, the Lynds noted that subgroups had emerged within these two classes, but they contended that the differences of life-style *between* them had increased visibly.

The Workday

The authors note how the workday was different for working and business class men in the 1920s.

The day's activities started early for the working-class family during the 1920s; more than 90 percent of them arose by six o'clock. Almost all working-class men walked to work. The normal work week consisted of five, 10-hour weekdays plus a half-day on Saturday. When the factories were producing at capacity, many of their workers were required to work night shifts, which meant that they went to bed when their families were waking up and slept through most of the daylight hours. Shift work limited the association of husbands with their wives and children. Family activities were dislocated by this routine, with some adverse consequences. The Lynds (1929, 58) quoted a father appearing before a juvenile judge who blamed his night work and lack of daily contact for his son's wayward conduct.

Life for business-class families during the 1920s was considerably more comfortable than for working-class families, and, among other things, their days began significantly later. None of them got up before six and most lingered in bed until after seven. Their breadwinners arrived at work after eight o'clock, nearly two hours after the blue-collar workers. The latter were generally required to be at work by six-thirty, and they remained there until five, eating lunch at or near their machines. The business establishments of Middletown during the 1920s opened at eight or eight-thirty and closed at five.

During the intervening years, the daily schedules converged until they met, and by 1978 the difference between them had been reversed to some extent. The working class now sleeps in later, and the business class rises earlier. Today, stores and banks stay open later and work longer hours than factories. Professionals are commonly induced by the competition in their fields to spend extra hours at their offices, while unionization and collective bargaining have reduced the factory workday from 10 hours to 8 and the workweek from five and one-half days to five, and in some industries to four days. This change in work schedules encourages closer association among the members of working-class families. The general tendency for husbands to spend more time with their families in 1978, compared to 1920, will be described in detail in a later chapter.

The authors note that by 1978, business class workers spent more time on the job, and working class men spent less.

Occupations

In 1920 the people of Middletown worked in more than 400 different occupations. About a third of the blue-collar workers were skilled craftspeople. They worked 10 hours a day blowing glass, designing molds, and shaping metal in factories and foundries. Some of them worked in the construction trades. All of the craft jobs involved a high level of skill and required some kind of apprenticeship that led to certification as a journeyman. The Lynds noted the decline of craftsmanship between 1890 and 1920 and lamented the fact that the "cunning hand of the master craftsman" was being supplanted by "batteries of tireless iron men." In 1890, 21 glassblowers assisted by two dozen boys produced 1,600 dozen quart jars per shift; in 1920, 8 men operating three machines turned out 6,600 dozen jars in the same amount time. The "batteries of iron men" made some of the old craft skills obsolete, but not all of them by any means.

The authors review the Lynds' findings that Middletown's blue-collar workers in the 1920s were one-third skilled craftsmen, one-third machine operators, and one-third laborers.

Another third of the blue-collar workers of 1920 operated the machines that tirelessly produced goods. Adolescent boys could be trained in less than a week to run most of the machines in Middletown's factories. The more difficult operations could be mastered in a few weeks or months. But the work required the speed and endurance of youth. On most assembly lines, the machines set the pace and the workers had to keep up or lose their jobs.

The rest of Middletown's factory workers were laborers. They unloaded raw materials and supplies, wheeled or carried them to stations on the production line, and loaded the finished products. They also cleaned up after other workers. The lucky ones had reasonably stable employment. The less fortunate hired themselves out daily at whatever work was available.

The business-class men were proprietors, lawyers, bankers, public officials, engineers, teachers, shopkeepers, merchants, and clerks, among other things. One out of five were in the professions. Professionals earned relatively high incomes, and, within limits, most of them set their own working hours. A much smaller number managed factories, foundries, banks, and large stores, directing the

According to the Lynds' data, business class workers in the 1920s were professionals, managers, and clerical and sales employees.

manufacture and distribution of the industrialized products that sustained Middletown's economy during the 1920s. The business class workers enjoyed the highest incomes and the widest influence in the community. The largest group of male white-collar workers were clerical and sales employees. They worked, for example, as tellers in banks, bookkeepers and clerks in factories, and salesmen in stores and shops.

The continued development of production machines and the introduction of computers has altered working-class occupations much more than business-class occupations over the intervening decades. The men and women who performed most of the dangerous and dirty jobs moved upward in the occupational hierarchy. Between 1920 and 1970, the working class shrank from 70 percent of the male labor force to 54 percent. (See Table 4-1 in Appendix A.) Within the working class, the number of unskilled laborers was reduced by automation and other factors from 20 percent of the total in 1920 to less than 4 percent in 1970 and no more than 2 percent in 1980. The attrition of craftsmen noted by the Lynds has continued. They constituted 21 percent of the male labor force in 1920 but barely 9 percent in 1970. Meanwhile, the number of machine operators (semiskilled workers in conventional terminology) has risen sharply, and their proportion of the total labor force is about the same today as it was 50 or 60 years ago, despite the relative decline in the amount of blue-collar work.

Just as the contraction of the working class has not diminished the number of machine operators in factories, so the expansion of the business class has not increased the proportion of businessmen in the labor force. A large part of the expansion of the business class has been in the increased number of professionals. The proportion of the labor force in professional occupations more than tripled between 1920 and 1970. Clerical occupations also experienced considerable growth during the 50-year period, and the number of salesmen has declined sharply during the era of self-service stores and prepackaged merchandise.

Unemployment

The threat of unemployment hovered continuously over working-class families during the 1920s. Even during a year of economic prosperity like 1923, one out of every four men in the working class was laid off for a time. During bad years, unemployment mushroomed. The consequences of being out of work were more severe in the 1920s than now; there was no unemployment insurance, little public assistance, and no aid to dependent children, and the average family's cushion of savings was much smaller.

The authors conclude that work has changed the most for the working class because of improved technology and upward mobility.

The authors conclude that though the working class has shrunk, the percentage of machine operators has risen. They refer the reader to Table 4-1. The authors report that the business class has expanded because of increased numbers of professionals and clerical workers.

In this section the authors report that their 1978 findings on temporary unemployment were very similar to the Lynds' 1924 findings.

When questioned about unemployment and its consequences, 68 percent of 122 working-class wives interviewed by the Lynds reported that their husbands had been out of work for one or more periods during the previous five years. Four out of five of these families had changed their life-styles drastically. The father's being laid off forced the working-class family to curtail family expenditures in every way possible so that their meager reserves and what credit they could muster might carry them through the siege.

When husbands were laid off in the 1920s, families cut their expenses to make their reserves last.

Surprisingly, the incidence of temporary unemployment has not changed appreciably since 1924. (See Table 4-2 in Appendix A.) The percentage of working-class men laid off at some time during 1977 (24 percent) was nearly the same as the percentage laid off during 1923 (25 percent). Although we expected to find much less change in spending patterns due to unemployment in 1978 because of present-day social-welfare programs, the reductions of spending in the late 1970s were almost the same as those of the early 1920s. During the 1920s, 76 percent of the unemployed reduced the amount spent on clothing; 73 percent cut amusements; 62 percent, food; 57 percent, gasoline; and 19 percent, life insurance; and 7 percent moved to less expensive housing. Despite social-welfare programs, the families whose principal breadwinners were unemployed in 1978 curtailed their spending patterns just as severely and in the same categories as their predecessors two generations before.

Even with social welfare programs to help them during times of unemployment, families in the 1970s cut their expenses just as families in the 1920s did.

The other way of mitigating the devastating consequence of unemployment was for wives or children to seek work. As mentioned earlier, a third of the wives who reported in 1925 that their husbands had been out of work had gone to work themselves. Indeed, almost all the married women who then worked gave the present or past unemployment of their husbands as their principal reason for being in the labor market. Today, nearly half of the married women in Middletown have jobs outside the home, but the unemployment of husbands has ceased to be the precipitating factor. The modern wife works for other reasons as well. Today, business-class wives are as likely to hold jobs as working-class wives, even though the risk of unemployment is negligible for their husbands, as it was for business-class husbands back in 1924.

In the 1920s a major reason women worked outside the home was to help out when their husbands were unemployed. In 1978, when women worked outside the home, the main reason was not likely to be the husband's unemployment.

In 1924, older children frequently dropped out of school, or were taken out of school, and tried to find work to enable the family to survive until the father was providing again. Ten percent of the wives whose husbands had been unemployed reported that they had taken children out of school and sent them to work. The physical quickness of the young sometimes enabled them to find jobs when their fathers could not. Today, child-labor laws and compulsory-edu-

In the 1920s, the authors report, children would drop out of school to work when their families needed help.

cation laws prevent children from seeking serious employment until they are close to adulthood.

The business-class men of the 1920s entered the labor force two to five years later than their working-class counterparts because of their lengthier education. They continued to increase their status and earnings as they matured and had little concern about being laid off temporarily during hard times or let go permanently when they reached their late forties. Unemployment of any kind was not a serious threat to business-class families before the depression. Only 1 of 40 business-class wives interviewed in 1924 reported that her husband had been out of work any time during the previous five years.

The business-class wives of that era not only did not work, most of them refused to be concerned with financial matters. They were often unaware of their husbands' earnings and assets. In the Middletown of the 1920s, it was considered unfeminine for business-class wives to discuss money and demeaning for them to work outside the home. The lone business-class wife in the Lynds' sample whose husband had been unemployed was the only one who had worked during the preceding five years.

The most devastating type of unemployment in the 1920s affected blue-collar workers who reached the ripe old age of 40. Most factory jobs required the maintenance of a high rate of effort for a 10-hour shift, and years of working at this pace used men up by the time they reached early middle age. Retirement programs and pensions were then unknown for manual workers in industry. A few companies kept superannuated employees on as janitors or watchmen, but they were not obligated to do so. Most workers hoped to save for their old age, but few did. The despair they experienced in the face of premature retirement comes through poignantly in the comments made by employers and working-class wives interviewed by the Lynds in 1924 (1929, 33–34).

> In production work forty to forty-five is the age limit because of the speed needed in the work. Men over forty are hired as sweepers and for similar jobs. We have no set age for discharging men [personnel manager of another outstanding machine shop].

> The age deadline is creeping down on those men—I'd say that by forty-five they are through [superintendent of another major plant].

> Whenever you get old they are done with you. The only thing a man can do is to keep as young as he can and save as much as he can [wife of a 40-year-old laborer].

> I worry about what we'll do when he gets older and isn't want-
> ed at the factories and I am unable to go to work. We can't
> expect our children to support us and we can't seem to save
> any money for that time [wife of a 46-year-old machinist].

Since that time, the obsolescence of many dangerous and
exhausting jobs and the protection afforded to workers by the unions
have virtually eliminated the threat of premature retirement for
Middletown's factory workers. Recent legislation has extended the
minimum age of compulsory retirement to 70. In addition, social
security provides a basic retirement income that for most factory
workers is supplemented by other retirement benefits from company
and union plans, veterans benefits, and insurance.

The authors report that many changes in labor practices since the 1920s have made unemployment due to aging a less frightening prospect for Middletown's working class.

Responses to our question "What seems to be the future of your
husband's job?" revealed the great strides Middletown's labor force
has made in extending the age of retirement. Even in working-class
families, a large majority (82 percent) of the wives reported that their
husbands' jobs are secure and offer opportunities for advancement.
Nearly all (94 percent) of the business-class wives in our survey
report the same.

Job Satisfaction

The Lynds were much concerned that the changes associated
with the increasing mechanization and rationalization of work in
Middletown's factories were inadvertently destroying the satisfaction that had previously been associated with productive work.
They never mentioned the Marxist notion of the alienation of
workers from their work in *Middletown*, but they clearly had it in
mind.

> The shift from a system in which length of service, craftsman-
> ship, and authority in the shop and social prestige among one's
> peers tended to go together to one which, in the main, demands
> little of a worker's personality save rapid, habitual reactions
> and an ability to submerge himself in the performance of a few
> routinized easily learned movements seems to have wiped out
> many of the satisfactions that formerly accompanied the job.
> Middletown's shops are full of men of whom it may be said
> that "there isn't 25 percent of them paying attention to the job."
> And as they leave the shop in the evening, "The work of a
> modern machine-tender leaves nothing tangible at the end of
> the day's work to which he can point with pride and say, 'I did
> that—it is the result of my own skill and my own effort'"(Lynd
> and Lynd 1929, 75–76).

The authors quote the Lynds' study to show that the factory workers in the 1920s experienced a kind of alienation in their work.

The authors relate an anecdote to show that some factory workers in 1978 weren't emotionally involved with their work.

However, the authors note this anecdote does not mean that workers are dissatisfied. The survey data summarized in Table 4-3 show little worker dissatisfaction with occupations.

We noticed a contemporary Middletown worker who was paying minimal attention to his job on a visit to an automotive plant in the spring of 1978. The worker whose task was bolting a part on a transmission had a paperback novel attached to a clipboard hung from a ceiling by a rope. His eyes never left the pages of the book as he accomplished his assigned work by touch. When a transmission approached on the assembly line, he felt it with his left hand and guided it into position against his work stand. The power wrench that had the part and five bolts attached to it was guided to the transmission by his right hand. His right foot then activated the power wrench that tightened the bolts. While waiting for the next transmission, he inserted the new part and bolts into the wrench with his right hand and turned the pages of the book with his left. Obviously, this man and many like him were performing their jobs with limited emotional involvement. But it does not follow that they were frustrated or dissatisfied. Blue-collar workers were significantly less satisfied with their jobs than white-collar workers were (60 percent versus 79 percent satisfied), but all were much more satisfied than dissatisfied. Only a small minority, 6 percent, of either business-class or working-class men in Middletown are dissatisfied with their occupations. (See Table 4-3 in Appendix A.) The Lynds were puzzled about why Middletown's people worked so hard when they *seemed* to derive so little satisfaction from their jobs. They concluded that working-class men, and at times their wives and children, worked hard because the money they earned allowed them to achieve a higher standard of living than their parents had ever known. Despite the hardships of the shop floor and the fear of unemployment, factory work offered them a better life than they could have found elsewhere.

The authors claim workers have many motivations to work besides just earning money. However, working class respondents viewed work as just a way to earn money more than business-class respondents did.

The motivation of Middletown's present work force is more complex. When we asked a sample of employed men whether they worked primarily for money, three-fourths of the business-class respondents but fewer than half of the working-class respondents rejected the notion that their work was just a way to make money. The difference between the two classes is substantial and significant, but not overwhelming. Only a third of the working-class respondents hold with that "alienated" attitude, that work is just a way to get money. For the majority, such factors as pride in one's work and identification with an enterprise are part of the motivational pattern. (See Table 4-4 in Appendix A.)

The authors conclude that labor unions, laws, and mechanization have made blue-collar work easier, more satisfying, and less time-consuming than it was in the 1920s.

There is no denying that earning a living is much easier for working-class men today than it was 50 years ago. Many of the dangerous, dirty, and routine tasks are now accomplished by machines. Labor unions and legislatures have forced employers to improve working conditions and to provide innumerable fringe benefits.

Today, if we can trust the survey evidence, the majority of Middletown's blue-collar workers enjoy their work and feel secure in their ability to provide for themselves and their families.

Family life has been favorably affected by these changes. Fathers have more time to spend with their children. Paid vacations, health insurance, unemployment insurance, and retirement plans have improved the quality of life for Middletown families. Most working-class families now live in comfortable homes, drive reliable automobiles, travel to faraway places, and provide the education their children desire, in addition to covering the basic requirements for food, shelter, and clothing.

The authors list the benefits that have come to Middletown families as the American economy has made a good life possible for more workers than in the past.

Each table below has a number to identify it. Each one also has a descriptive caption. The data are displayed in clearly labeled columns and rows. The source of the data for each table is noted at the bottom of each.

APPENDIX A

TABLE 4-1
Distribution of Middletown's Male Labor Force by Major Occupational Categories, 1920 and 1970.

Occupational Category	1920		1970		Percentage Change
	Number	Percentage	Number	Percentage	
Business Class					
Professionals	892	6	5,189	14	+8
Managers	581	4	1,811	5	+1
Clerical workers	1,662	10	7,865	22	+12
Salesmen	1,659	10	2,264	6	-4
Subtotal	4,794	(30)	17,129	(47)	
Working Class					
Craftsmen	3,404	21	3,232	9	-12
Operators	3,144	20	7,865	22	+2
Laborers	3,278	20	1,363	4	-16
Service workers	807	5	6,031	17	+12
Household workers	602	4	840	2	-2
Subtotal	11,235	(70)	19,331	(54)	
Total	16,029	100	16,460	101	

Sources: U.S. Bureau of the Census 1922a, vol. 2, Table 20; U.S. Bureau of Census 1971, vol. 16, Table 86.

TABLE 4-2
Middletown Housewives Reporting Husbands Unemployed during Previous Year,
by Social Class, 1924 and 1978.

Social Class	1924		1978	
	Total Number	Percentage	Total Number	Percentage
Business class	40	1	192	4
Working class	165	28	141	25

Sources: Lynd and Lynd 1929, 57; Middletown III, housewives' survey, 1978

TABLE 4-3
Job Satisfaction among Employed Men by Social Class,
Middletown, 1978
(in percentages)

Level of Satisfaction	Business Class (N=104)	Working Class (N=94)
Very satisfied	47%	23%
Somewhat satisfied	32	37
Mixed feelings	16	34
Somewhat dissatisfied	2	3
Very dissatisfied	3	3
Total	100%	100%

For Tables 4-3 and 4-4, the question respondents were answering is also displayed at the bottom of the table, making it easy for readers to know exactly what was asked without referring to the chapter text.

Source: Middletown III men's occupational survey, 1978.
Question: What is the level of satisfaction you derive from your job?

TABLE 4-4 Money as a Motive to Work, among Employed Men, by
Social Class, Middletown, 1978
(in percentages)

Response	Business Class (N=104)	Working Class (N=94)
Strongly agree	5%	16%
Agree	7	18
Neutral	13	20
Disagree	41	36
Strongly disagree	34	10
Total	100%	100%

Source: Middletown III, men's occupational survey, 1978.
Question: To me work is just a way of making money.

A STUDENT EXAMPLE

Following is a report by Thad Barkdull, a student majoring in sociology, who conducted a survey of students' perceptions of professors on his campus. From his own past experience working with professors as a research assistant, Barkdull had developed a hypothesis that close contact with a professor might actually decrease students' esteem for the professor. To test this hypothesis, he surveyed two groups of students, ones who had worked as research assistants and ones who had not. His sample was small and not randomly selected, so the results aren't generalizable to a larger population. Still, his report illustrates several features of this kind of research writing quite well. For example, Barkdull's report includes an abstract that summarizes the research. The introduction includes a review of related literature that creates a context for his research question. The methods section illustrates well how to describe the procedures used to collect data. The results section describes how Barkdull used a statistical test to compare the results from the two groups he surveyed. This statistical test showed that there was a significant difference between the two groups' answers on some questions; however, Barkdull set the level for achieving significance higher (0.1) than is usually the case in social science research, so his findings may be questionable for that reason. Nevertheless, assuming his results are significant, in the discussion of his paper Barkdull tries to explain the reasons for the differences, again referring to the literature he reviewed to draw the conclusion that professors should be careful about the example they set. Finally, Barkdull includes a list of references giving complete bibliographic citations for the research he cites. His report would be a good model for you to imitate if you collect data by the survey method.

The Influence of Extended Contact on Students' Perceptions of Professors

by Thad J. Barkdull

Abstract

This research examined how close contact with a professor influences students' opinions and perceptions of the professor. A survey was administered to 26 students who had been or were presently teaching assistants (TAs) or research assistants (RAs) to professors and to 24 students who had not been a TA or RA. For most variables surveyed, students' perceptions did not vary as a result of closer contact with professors. However, the TAs and RAs gave significantly more negative ratings of the professor's expertise and ethics, suggesting that their initial perceptions are tainted as contact increases and that they become more aware of the professor's limitations and weaknesses. The results suggest professors should be aware of their influence and the example they set.

College is a time when students make important decisions regarding their course of study and their future careers. Professors have a large impact upon these decisions. In a study of role model influence on students' performance in decision making and goal setting, Earley and Kanfer (1985) found that role models caused an improvement in their pupil's performance, even when the only modeling the student had was the visual cues of their mentor. Magolda (1993) reported that students were more willing to try a higher level of learning when they were acknowledged and accepted by their professors. Others, such as Pantages and Creedon (1978) and Feldman and Newcomb (1976), concur that the relationship between professor and student has a strong influence upon the career decisions and goals that students develop. Holland (1993) found that more intimate and inclusive relationships between doctoral students and their mentors had a profound influence on the performance and satisfaction of those students. A.W. Astin's (1977) longitudinal study of more than 200,000 students at 300 institutions showed that the interactions between students and faculty were more profound in their influence than any other aspect of the students' education, and if the interaction was not a good influence, the results were dramatic.

Therefore, it is important that professors play their role well in shaping their students and acting as a role model for them. Belenky et al. (1986) claim the professor's relationship to a student should be like that of a midwife to an expectant mother, because professors should help students creatively bring forth knowledge. When professors neglect this vital role, they may undermine their field by not preparing future professionals adequately or even by discouraging entrance into their field. However, Adams (1992) notes that professors often don't see their responsibility to be aware of students' needs. He says that when professors attend conferences, they "rarely venture into sessions on student issues." Instead, they are "deeply involved in the latest scientific discovery, issues surrounding technology transfer, sources for funding research, etc." (p. 8).

When professors work with their students, are they aware of what those students observe, and do they act accordingly to be proper role models? It would seem that students who work closely with professors, such as teaching assistants (TAs) and research assistants (RAs), would be in the most advantageous position to find mentors and role models in the professors they work with. But is this actually the case? I designed the following survey to measure whether TAs and RAs are more likely than other students to say that they esteem the professors they work with.

Methods

I selected a convenience sample of fifty students. They were divided into two groups: (1) an experimental group composed of 26 students who had been or were presently TAs or RAs for a professor, and (2) a control group of 24 students who were not. These students were asked to answer a questionnaire that required them to give ordinal evaluations of their relationship with and their perceptions of a professor they selected. (The questionnaire is reproduced in Appendix A.) Twenty-two male students and 19 female students participated (9 chose not to respond to the demographic information regarding sex). Although the sample was not random, respondents represented a fair cross-section of major fields, including accounting, biology, business, education, engineering, health, the humanities, psychology, and zoology.

In the survey I asked the students in the experimental group to respond to the evaluative statements about the professor they had assisted, and the students in the control group were told to respond about a professor of their choice. The statements required the students to give their perceptions of their professor as a role model, as a good exemplar of professional conduct, and as a helpful factor in the student's career preparation. Participants responded by rating their professor on a scale from 1 to 5, corresponding to their agreement or disagreement to each statement on the survey.

I tabulated the data to compare the responses between control and experimental groups. I then used a t-test to determine the relationship between the responses of the control and experimental groups. I used an alpha value of 0.1 because of the small sample size in this study, considering a difference between the two groups significant if there was less than a 90% chance that the difference was random.

Results

An analysis of the mean ratings showed that there were no significant differences between the two groups on statements 3, 4, 5, 7, 11, 12, and 13. In other words, students in both groups rated their professors similarly, regardless of closeness of contact. However, the two groups differed significantly in their mean ratings on statements 6, 8, 9, and 10. Table 1 shows the mean results for these statements.

TABLE 1. Differences Between Group Means

Evaluative Statement	Control Group	Experimental Group	t
6 Professor is expert in field	4.71	4.19	2.26*
8 Would take another class	4.50	3.73	2.64*
9 Behavior appears ethical	4.71	4.04	2.20*
10 Would rehire professor	4.92	4.42	1.98*

* $p < .10$

Discussion

Students who had been assistants for professors had a higher level of disagreement with statements 6, 8, 9, and 10, suggesting that their closer contact had changed their perception of their professor's expertise and of his or her professional and ethical conduct. This lower average esteem could be the result of many factors.

Most likely, the students who hadn't worked as assistants have had more limited interaction with their professor. They are probably not privy to his or her activities outside of the classroom. On the other hand, the TAs and RAs, because of increased interaction, are more likely to see behavior that would figure both positively and negatively in their evaluation of a professor. When students are able to see their professor performing as a researcher, they become much more aware of the limits of the professor's knowledge. This realization is not as likely to dawn on students in the classroom setting, where the professor has more control over the dissemination of material in the lecture, and thus has the tendency to appear much more credible and expert in the field. The greater opportunity to see professors up close could explain why TAs and RAs did not view their professors as experts as strongly as the control group. Also, as students excel at higher levels of study, which is typical of TAs and RAs, they are better able to see new avenues of thought and possibly to question the methods of their professors, leading to a lowered estimation of the faculty member's expertise.

Because of their increased contact with professors they work for, many TAs and RAs also may find that the information presented to them is not as scholarly as they once thought. When TAs are forced to find ways to teach the material to beginning students, they may find that the teaching methods used by their professors are inadequate or outdated (at least in the perception of the assistant), and this could lower their estimation of the professor's abilities as well as their desire to have future classes or interactions with that professor.

TAs' and RAs' lower rating of professors' ethics is difficult to explain. It may be due to the respondents' youth and idealism and to different perceptions of what is ethical. Students' perceptions of whether or not a given activity is ethical may be entirely different from the faculty member's perception of it. I myself have been aware of my professors doing things that I considered to be inappropriate for their position, yet when I discussed my concerns with them, they have had an entirely different viewpoint on their activities.

All of these factors, combined with possibly a simple dislike for the professor brought on by increased contact, may explain the different responses to statement 10. When individuals have a greater interest, as an RA or a TA does, in their professor's performance and abilities as a role model, these students may have a tendency to be more critical and find more error than students who have a reduced interest in a professor who merely lectures to them.

Although these results may not be reliable because of the small and non-random sample surveyed, the results show that, on the whole, students expressed approval of the professors they evaluated, whether they had worked as RAs and TAs or not. However, the few differences between the experimental group and the control group suggest that close contact with a professor can negatively affect students' perceptions. I began this research by focusing upon the great influence professors can have on students through increased contact. If professors neglect to be a role model, their students will have a lower image of the professor and possibly a lower image of the field of study. Because TAs and RAs have the opportunity to see the faculty more clearly in their role as professionals, professors must do their best to meet their assistants' high expectations, becoming their mentors and role models, rather than a source of discouragement and negative thinking.

References

Adams, H. C. (1992). *Mentoring: An essential factor in the doctoral process for minority students.* Notre Dame, IN: National Consortium for Graduate Degrees for Minorities in Engineering Inc.

Astin, A. W. (1977). *Four critical years.* San Francisco: Jossey-Bass.

Belenky, M. F., Clinchy, B. M., Goldberger, N. R., & Tarule, J. M. (1986). *Women's ways of knowing.* New York: Basic Books.

Earley, P. C., & Kanfer, R. (1985). The influence of component participation and role models on goal acceptance, goal satisfaction, and performance. *Organizational Behavior and Human Decision Processes, 36*, 378–390.

Feldman, K., & Newcomb, T. (1976). *The impact of college on students.* San Francisco: Jossey Bass.

Holland, J. W. (1993). Relationships between African-American doctoral students and their major advisors. Paper presented at the Annual Meeting of the American Educational Research Association.

Magolda, M. B. B. (1993). Knowing and reasoning in college. *Journal of College Student Development, 36*, 387–388.

Pantages, T.J., & Creedon, C.F. (1978). Studies of college attrition: 1950–1975. *Review of Educational Research, 48*, 48–101.

Appendix A

I am a student conducting this survey for a research assignment. I am interested in students' perceptions of their professors as they progress through college. By participating in this survey, you imply your consent to let me use your answers. Your identity will remain anonymous.

Your Age:_____   Year in school: Fr   So   Jr   Sr

Gender:_____   Major:_____

1. Have you ever worked for a professor as a teaching assistant or as a research assistant?

_____No   _____Yes

2. If yes, in which department?_____

If you answered "no" to Question 1, please select a professor from your major field of study that you have had or are now taking a course from, and evaluate that professor on statements 3 through 13, using the scale below. If you answered "yes" to Question 1, evaluate the professor you worked for on statements 3 through 13, using the scale below.

1	2	3	4	5
strongly disagree	disagree	no opinion	agree	strongly agree

3. The professor I studied under/worked with is a good role model.

       1   2   3   4   5

4. I would feel comfortable going to my professor for advice or help.

       1   2   3   4   5

5. My present perception of my professor is what it was initially.

       1   2   3   4   5

6. I see my professor as an expert in his or her field.

       1   2   3   4   5

7. I feel that my professor has adequately prepared me to function in my career.

       1   2   3   4   5

8. I would take another class from my professor if I could.

       1   2   3   4   5

9. I have not been aware of my professor engaging in activities that I consider unethical.

       1   2   3   4   5

10. If I had the power to retain my professor as a faculty member, nothing in his or her conduct would make me have reservations about doing so.

       1   2   3   4   5

11. My professor's teaching has inspired me to become more interested in the subject matter.

       1   2   3   4   5

12. My professor is interested in helping me understand the material.

       1   2   3   4   5

13. If my professor could choose to do only research, I think he or she would opt to do that rather than teach.

       1   2   3   4   5

SUGGESTIONS FOR RESEARCH AND WRITING

Note: Many of these suggestions are particularly suited for collaborative investigation and writing. By sharing the work with one or two classmates, you can gather more data quickly and pool your analytical and writing talents to create a good report.

1. There is frequently a gap between what people know they should do and what they actually do. In this chapter one of those possible gaps concerned what students know about a healthy diet and exercise regimen and what they actually do. There are many other such gaps between knowledge and action, for example in recycling and conserving resources, in time management and study habits, in smoking, or in drinking alcohol. Identify a potential gap between knowledge and action that you would like to study and plan a survey to gather data that will help you learn whether the gap exists.

2. What do students at your institution think about administrative or social and cultural issues on your campus? For example, what is their attitude toward administrative policies on admissions, enrollment, tuition and fees, grading, parking, and so forth? Or what do students think of trends in music, fashion, dating, dance, cinema, and so on? Design and conduct a survey that will identify student attitudes.

3. One of the complaints leveled at the American educational system is that students learn so little of world geography. How informed are students on your campus about geography and its relationship to international politics? To find out, you could give students a kind of survey that tests how many would be able to locate correctly on a map countries that are currently in the news. Or, taking a different approach, you could find out how many would be able to specify the continent a particular country is on.

4. What is a currently debated state or national political issue? How informed are students on your campus about this issue? What opinions do they hold about a given political candidate or a proposal that will be on the ballot? Design and conduct a survey to answer one or more questions of interest. What conclusions can you draw about the political knowledge of students on your campus?

REFERENCES

Caplow, Theodore M., Howard M. Bahr, Bruce A. Chadwick, Reuben Hill, and Margaret Holmes Williamson. 1982. *Middletown families: Fifty years of change and continuity.* Minneapolis: University of Minnesota Press.

8

EXPERIMENTING

THE PURPOSE OF EXPERIMENTS

It could well be said that the ultimate goal of science is to explain what causes things to happen. In the natural and physical sciences, humans have made great strides in understanding such things as what happens when various elements are combined under certain conditions of temperature and pressure, how plants can be crossbred or fertilized to produce better crop yields, or how genetic flaws cause certain diseases. Understanding causes and effects in nature puts humans in the favorable position of being able to partially control their environment, to produce better foods and medicines, and to intervene in some natural processes to engineer more desirable results. Many of these achievements have been made possible through the method of inquiry known as experimenting.

Not surprisingly, the experiment is also widely used in the social sciences with the goal of establishing firm results that will help us to better understand how individuals and groups function and to create more productive and healthful social environments. The experiment is sometimes considered the most scientific of methods because it aims to determine the cause-and-effect relationship, if any, between a *dependent variable* and one or more *independent variables*. One way to keep these two kinds of variables straight is to think of the independent variable as a possible cause and the dependent variable as an effect. The independent variable is manipulated; the dependent variable follows from this manipulation.

As an illustration of how an experiment can determine the relationship between two variables, consider a famous example from the social sciences, Stanley Milgram's (1974) experiments on obedience. It is important to understand that today Milgram's experiments would be considered unethical, but they provide a useful paradigm for describing the experimental method. Milgram chose willingness to obey authority as the dependent variable that he wanted to measure. He devised experiments in which he led participants to believe that they must obey a researcher's orders to administer 30 electric shocks of increasing levels of intensity to another person. (The person supposedly receiving the shocks was actually a knowledgeable confederate in the experiment, but none of the participants knew it at the time.) Milgram designed one series of experiments to see if willingness to obey varied as he manipulated an independent variable, closeness of the "victim" to the person administering the shocks.

Milgram designed four different states of proximity between participants and victim—remote feedback, voice feedback, proximity, and touch-proximity—so that the auditory and visible evidence of the victim's "pain" would vary. He found that willingness to obey decreased as the distance between the participant and the victim also decreased. That is, when the participants could actually see and even touch the confederate, they were more likely to refuse to continue administering the shocks, and the experiment ended sooner. Milgram concluded there is a cause-and-effect relationship between people's willingness to obey morally questionable orders and their ability to have an immediate and clear perception of what happens to those victimized by their obedience.

To you perhaps Milgram's experiment simply verifies common sense or confirms your experience. It seems to stand to reason that most people would not willingly inflict great harm on others. But that the participants in Milgram's experiments would obey orders up to a certain point under all four proximity conditions may tell you something you wouldn't have thought about human nature—something that believers in the experimental method would say has now been demonstrated conclusively. This cause-and-effect demonstration confers on Milgram's conclusion the status of being more definitive than a hunch, more scientific than common sense. When conclusions have this scientific status, theoretically it becomes possible to explain human nature, to make some predictions about it, and to devise ways to enhance desirable behavior and to mitigate or eliminate undesirable behavior.

For these reasons, experimenting is an important method of social science research, one that has become increasingly sophisticated, generally requiring a budget and a knowledge of intricate statistical procedures to determine the nature and the significance of relationships between variables. It's not possible in a book of this size and scope to give anything more than a basic understanding of the steps in the experimental method. These include creating hypotheses and operational definitions, designing the experiment and implementing controls, selecting participants, establishing validity and reliability, and meeting ethical standards. As you read the following, consider the usefulness of the experimental method and the scope of its applicability in social science research. Think about whether or not an experiment would be an appropriate method to answer a research question you have.

STEPS AND CONSIDERATIONS IN CONDUCTING EXPERIMENTS

CREATING HYPOTHESES

Experimenters usually begin with a hypothesis—a prediction about the outcome of the experiment that can be accepted or rejected. For example, Philip Merikle and Heather Skanes, the researchers who conducted the professional study reproduced at the end of this chapter ("Subliminal Self-Help Audiotapes: A Search for Placebo Effects") tested the hypothesis that a "placebo effect" (a belief in the efficacy of a product that is sufficient to produce a noticeable change in the believer) would occur in a group of people who listened to an audiotape they believed contained subliminal messages that would help them lose weight. If a placebo effect occurred, the participants would lose a significant amount of weight even though the tapes contained no subliminal messages. However, the participants who had the placebo tapes did not lose significantly more weight than participants who listened to tapes that *did* contain subliminal messages; nor did they lose more weight than participants who listened to no tapes at all. Therefore, the hypothesis that there is a placebo effect was not supported by the evidence. Another way of stating these findings is to say that the researchers rejected the hypothesis that there is a placebo effect. Stating in advance what claim you want to confirm or reject allows you to design your experiment accordingly.

CREATING OPERATIONAL DEFINITIONS

A key factor in being able to eventually accept or reject a hypothesis is the way you operationally define the variables in your experiment. In his experiments, Milgram had to define the abstract concept of *obedience* operationally; that is, he had to have a way to observe and measure obedience. He devised a simulated shock generator with 30 switches on it, each switch apparently corresponding to a different level of voltage (no electricity was actually used, however). In the experiment participants were ordered to "shock" a victim by pressing switches on the control panel, starting with the lowest voltage and moving toward the highest. The number of switches each participant activated was observable and measurable, so, for the purposes of this experiment, the number of switches pressed was the operational definition of obedience. The more switches a participant pressed, the more obedient to authority he was. In any experiment you design, you will have to define the variables in such a way that you can observe them and quantify them. This means that you will have to devise a task in which the independent variable(s) and dependent variable can interact so you can determine their relationship, if any.

DESIGNING THE EXPERIMENT AND IMPLEMENTING CONTROLS

Because experiments are meant to determine cause-and-effect relationships, experiments are, as far as possible, designed events. That is, an experiment doesn't just happen of its own accord in a normally occurring setting; instead, the researcher must somehow manipulate the setting and, to some extent, the people in it in order to test a hypothesis about the relationship between a dependent variable and one or more independent variables. The experimenter designs a study that is suited to the research hypothesis and to the population being studied. The design helps the researcher control for the effect of other possible variables on the dependent variable because, in the end, the experimenter wants to attribute any change in the dependent variable to the independent variable(s) instead of to some other possible cause. Control over other variables is difficult to achieve in a naturally existing setting, so the experimenter designs procedures and creates settings that will permit a restricted focus on just the variables of interest. There are various kinds of designs possible for experiments; they have become so standard that they have been given names such as the following:

- *Classical design*, in which participants are randomly assigned to the experimental and control groups, and members of the experimental group are exposed to the independent variable(s) one or more times, then compared with the control group on measures of the dependent variable.

- *One-group pretest-posttest design*, in which there is only an experimental group, which is pretested before the introduction of the independent variable(s), then tested again after the treatment to see if there is a significant change in the dependent variable.

- *The Solomon four-group design*, in which there are two experimental and two control groups, with observation of the first experimental and first control group at the outset, followed by introduction of the independent variable in the two experimental groups, and then observation of all four groups at the end.

- *The ABA or time series design*, in which the researchers collect baseline data about the participants' behavior on the dependent variable during an initial time specified as "A," after which they introduce the independent variable during time "B"; then they withdraw the independent variable to see whether the behavior induced by it during time "B" persists during the second time "A."

There are several other basic designs that you can read about in research methods handbooks; a classic one is Campbell and Stanley's *Experimental and Quasi-Experimental Designs for Research on Teaching* (1963). Because various statistical procedures can be used with these designs, it is helpful to get the advice of a statistician at the time you plan an experiment so that you will choose the right design and record the right kind of data to use in statistical tests at the end of your study.

As a result of the need for control, some experiments take place in a laboratory setting where necessary equipment is available and experimental conditions are easy to achieve. As has often been noted, however, the laboratory setting isn't a natural context and therefore might itself introduce a variable into the experiment that could cause the participants to behave in a way they wouldn't behave in a more natural setting. For this reason, some cause-and-effect relationships demonstrated in a laboratory may cause suspicion, with readers wondering if the same result would hold in a naturally occurring setting.

Sometimes researchers conduct experiments in "the field"—not in a laboratory but wherever the variables they are interested in can be studied. They might go to a school, for example, or a hospital or workplace. By giving up their ability to control the environment, however, the researchers also give up some of their ability to control some variables. In Merikle and Skanes' experiment, the participants were not observed in a laboratory constantly over the five weeks of the study; instead, they were weighed once each week. To minimize the possibility that any change in weight might be due to other variables, Merikle and Skanes implemented the following controls: They obtained the age and initial weight of each participant to determine the comparability of the three groups at the outset; they weighed each participant on the same day of the week and at the same time of day to control for natural fluctuations in weight; they administered a questionnaire at the end of the study to determine if participants had initiated any lifestyle changes (e.g., starting an exercise program or stopping smoking) during the period of the study that might cause weight change. By taking these steps, Merikle and Skanes made it easier to relate any change in the dependent variable, weight, to the independent variable used in each group.

A variable that can't be controlled for completely is sometimes called a *confound* to the design. That is, such a variable confounds the researchers' efforts to make an unambiguous inference about the cause-and-effect relationship between an independent and dependent variable. A number of possible confounds have been identified and categorized, including the following:

- **Maturation**—the possibility that a change in the dependent variable is simply due to the participants' maturing during the course of the experiment, not due to the introduction of the independent variable.

- **Attrition**—the possibility that a difference between experimental and control groups is due to some of the participants dropping out during the course of the research.

- **Instrument decay**—the possibility that the instruments the researchers are using to measure change are not as effective at the end of the experiment as at the beginning ("instrument" has a very broad meaning in this context and can include such things as the researchers' observations of the participants' behavior).

- **Testing effect**—in a pretest-posttest design, the effect of taking an initial test may be to familiarize participants with the nature of the posttest so they will appear to have changed as a result of the independent variable, when in fact they have just become more skillful at test taking.

- **History**—the possibility that an uncontrollable event (e.g., a fire alarm sounding) affects the participants in such a way that the outcome of the experiment is changed.

- **Experimenter bias**—characteristics of the researcher, such as age, race, sex, clothing, or personality traits, that may affect how participants perform in the experiment.

It is important for researchers to be aware of these and other possible threats to validity when designing an experiment. Although they can't always be controlled completely, these confounds can sometimes be minimized if the researchers plan for and take steps to reduce their effect.

SELECTING PARTICIPANTS

Experiments are a type of research that aim to permit broad generalization of the results. When researchers find a cause-and-effect relationship, they want to claim that the relationship will hold true for other similar people and events in other times and places. In order to generalize results, however, the researcher must select participants for an experiment who are representative of the entire population that the results will apply to. This means that, where possible, the researcher should select participants randomly. In random selection, every unit (a unit could be individuals, groups, families, classes, etc.) in the entire population being studied has an equal chance of being chosen for participation. The researcher should never intentionally select participants in such a way that the hypothesis will be verified or rejected according to the researcher's desires or prejudices.

Random samples are not always easy to achieve, however. In a study of children learning math with computers, for example, it would not be easy to randomly sort children into experimental and control groups because, in elementary schools, children are already grouped in classes that usually can't be broken up. A researcher could randomly sort whole classes of students into one treatment or the other, however, and could take other steps to estimate the comparability of the two groups. For example, by using personal data about the children and scores from earlier achievement and aptitude tests, the researcher could determine whether or not the classes sorted into the two treatment groups were roughly equal in all pertinent respects at the time the experiment began.

Sometimes, however, even this kind of random assignment of roughly equal groups isn't possible. Many social scientists working on college campuses recruit students as participants in their experiments. These students may participate because of various incentives: course requirements, the promise of extra credit, or small financial or material rewards. In these cases, the experimental results may not be generalizable to populations beyond college students, and sometimes they may not even generalize to all students. Often participants may simply volunteer, which could skew the results because people who like to volunteer for projects are usually different in personality traits and other characteristics from people who don't volunteer. The participants in Milgram's obedience experiments were volunteers who answered a newspaper ad. They represented a fairly good distribution of ages and social class, but they were mostly men, so perhaps the results cannot be generalized to women. Even when participants are representative, some experiments don't include enough participants to have a solid foundation for generalizing.

As a reader of experimental research, you should take note of sample selection techniques and sample size, using them to help you judge the reliability of the conclusions drawn. You may often note that experimental research is still published even when the sample of participants isn't ideal in size or representativeness. You will probably also note that the authors of this research frequently hedge their conclusions with a number of qualifiers (e.g., "suggests," "seems to indicate," "given the constraints noted," "under these limited conditions," etc.) so as not to make their generalizations too sweeping.

Establishing Validity and Reliability

Validity is a crucially important concept in experimental research. Briefly, validity means that a given research study has actually demonstrated what it purports to demonstrate. In other words, it means a claim is well supported by the evidence. As noted, the goal of experimental research is to claim precise cause-and-effect relationships between a limited number of variables. The experimenter achieves validity by carefully taking some of the steps already discussed: defining the variables operationally, designing the experiment appropriately, controlling for possible confounds, selecting participants as randomly as possible, assigning participants randomly to experimental or control conditions, and using appropriate statistical tests to analyze the data. But even with all these steps, the relationships between variables are not always so obvious that they immediately compel everyone's assent; instead, the relationships must usually be inferred from the data the experiment has generated. In every inference there is at least a slight "leap of faith" from the evidence to the conclusion, and there is seldom anything like 100 percent assurance that the leap is justified. The experimenter's goal is not only to make the leap as small as possible but also to show that a leap in only one direction is possible—one cause to one effect. Making this inference carefully will persuade others that the conclusion drawn is a valid one.

Reliability is another vitally important concept, one that contributes to validity. Reliability refers to the consistency and strength of a relationship between variables. One way to show that a perceived relationship between two variables is consistent is to replicate the experiment—that is, to do it again under similar conditions. When experimenters write about their research, they give many details about the methods they used—including who the subjects were, what instruments they used, and what procedures they followed—so that other experimenters can repeat the experiment if they choose to. If the same results can be obtained by researchers working independently, confidence in the first results is strengthened, and they are considered reliable. The professional experiment reproduced at the end of this chapter is not a replication, but it confirms evidence provided by earlier, similar experiments that subliminal messages are not effective in changing people's behavior.

Another way the experimenter demonstrates reliability is through two kinds of statistics: (1) measures of association and (2) measures of significance. A *measure of association* is a statistic that shows the strength or size of the relationship between any two variables. For example, one measure of association is a statistic called the Pearson product-moment correlation; when this correlation approaches 1.0, the researcher can be confident that there is a strong relationship between two variables. Another measure of association is analysis of variance; when this statistic shows that independent variable X explains 30 percent of the variation of dependent variable Y, for example, the researcher can be confident that X helps to cause Y.

A *measure of significance* shows how confident the researcher is that the results obtained were not due to chance. It is usually expressed as a confidence level, denoted by p, and is typically set at .05 or less. A p-value of .05 would mean that the researcher is 95 percent confident the observed relationship is significant—that is, due to a "real" causal relationship, not simply due to a chance association of the variables. In the professional experiment at the end of this chapter, you will read that the three groups differed in the amount of weight they lost, with the group that listened to no tapes losing the most weight, on average. The researchers state, however, that the differences were not statistically significant. Although the researchers don't state the confidence level they tested for, it is probably safe to assume that p was higher than .05. In other words, although there were slight differences among the three groups, the variations were not big enough to claim that they were due to the kind of treatment the participants received.

MEETING ETHICAL STANDARDS

Conducting research according to high ethical standards is important with any method of inquiry, but its importance seems to become more obvious with experimental inquiry. One reason is that experiments often require a temporary deception of participants so that they won't guess what the researcher's hypothesis is or what variables are being studied. When participants figure out what the experiment is about—or *think* they have it figured out—they may behave in the way they think the researcher wants them to, or, just to be perverse, in the exact opposite way they think the researcher wants them to. In either case, the validity of the study would be compromised because the relationship between the variables would be artificial rather than "real." Think for a moment about Milgram's experiments: If the participants hadn't believed they were really administering electric shocks to an innocent person, could Milgram have reported anything significant about obedience to authority?

There has been some debate about whether or not deception is justified. As noted in Chapter 3, using a ruse in an experiment to get participants to cooperate has generally been deemed acceptable if the deception is temporary and of a kind that is not likely to produce any lasting harmful effects on the participants. To ensure that deception is temporary, it has become standard practice to debrief participants immediately after a study to inform them of the purposes of the research; and to ensure that the participants will suffer no continuing distress from the experiment, the debriefing can also calm fears or soothe a ruffled ego. Even though the participants in Milgram's experiments were debriefed, it is still possible that they could have been upset by what happened during the experiment and haunted later by memories of themselves administering what they really believed were high-voltage shocks to a person who apparently was suffering great pain.

Since institutional review boards have been implemented, standards now require that human participants give their informed consent before they can take part in an experiment (see Chapter 11). Imagine how an IRB approval process and informed consent would have changed Milgram's experiment. An IRB, foreseeing the possible traumatic effects of the deception on the participants, would likely not have approved the study. And if each participant had signed an informed consent form prior to beginning the experiment, they might have been easily able to figure out what the experiment was about, and then the results would not have been as valid or reliable.

As you can see, experiments may give the best data about real cause-and-effect relationships when the participants are kept somewhat in the dark about the experiment's purpose. Informed consent, however, means that the participants must know enough about the goal of the experiment that they can choose intelligently whether or not they want to be a part of it. The researcher has to strike a careful balance here in order to meet ethical standards yet also produce results that will be considered valid and reliable. If you plan an experiment, you will have to create an informed consent document that adequately reveals the general nature of what you are trying to study, and you will have to submit your informed consent document and a thorough description of your planned experiment for IRB approval before you can proceed. How to do all of this is explained in detail in Chapter 11.

WRITING ABOUT EXPERIMENTS

When professionals write reports of experiments, they usually organize the report in four main parts, most often signaled by these headings: Introduction, Methods, Results, Discussion. In addition to these four main parts, there is often an abstract (a summary) at the beginning of an article, immediately after the title, and a bibliographic list of references to related literature at the end of the report. These divisions typify a genre that is part of a long tradition in the sciences. Using the genre conventions—its format and style—of the experimental report is part of writing persuasively about the experiment, part of establishing validity. Readers have come to expect that experimental results will be communicated in a certain way, and meeting these expectations is one way researchers can enhance the persuasiveness of their conclusions.

In the introduction, the writer usually begins by focusing on the general topic of investigation and by reviewing what previous research on this topic has already shown. The writer next typically shows how there is a need for a certain kind of additional research on this topic by stating what previous research hasn't found. The writer then states the hypothesis that was tested in the present study.

In the methods section, the writer describes the participants and tells how they were selected, identifies any instruments used, and describes the procedures that were followed to gather data. As noted earlier in the chapter, the details in this section are meant to help any reader who wants to replicate the experiment. Even if no one replicates the experiment, however, readers want to know how the experiment was done because methodological correctness contributes to the validity and reliability of the findings.

In the results section, the writer presents the findings, showing the numerical values for the variables that were studied and the results of the statistical tests that were performed. This part of the report often uses tables and figures to present results in a compact visual form that is easy to understand at a glance. Providing statistical evidence that the variables were measured reliably is an important part of the rhetoric of experimental research. The right numbers, achieved by correct procedures and calculated accurately, are highly persuasive to readers who accept the assumptions of experimental research.

Finally, in the discussion section, the writer interprets the findings, showing how they do or do not support the hypothesis. Frequently, the discussion refers again to previous research, showing how the present study corroborates, contradicts, extends, or modifies what previous researchers have already demonstrated. In this section, too, the writer might note ambiguities and problems with the present research or additional questions that the research now raises and then propose further research that would resolve these problems and answer these questions.

A PROFESSIONAL EXAMPLE

As you read the professional report of an experiment on the following pages, you will see that it contains the four parts typical of the genre, including the usual headings.[1] The annotations in the margins draw your attention to features of the report that illustrate the genre's characteristics. Notice how, in the introduction, Merikle and Skanes demonstrate a need for their study by identifying a gap in previous research on the effectiveness of subliminal messages. Take special note of how carefully the authors, in the methods section, explain the unique design of their study and the procedures they followed to eliminate or minimize the possibility that the results of the experiment could be due to other factors than the kind of treatment the participants experienced. Their care in explaining their methods contributes to the rhetorical persuasiveness of their report. Notice also how the table and bar graphs in the results section reduce the complexity of the data to a form that lets the reader make quick comparisons among the three groups of participants. The writing style could be characterized as "objective" and "detached." Compared to the style of Deborah Tannen's article (see Chapter 6) or Caplow and colleagues' chapter (see Chapter 7), where the personal pronouns "I" and "we" are sometimes used in describing methods, the style of this article is very impersonal, even though the researchers carried out the procedures described in the methods.

[1] Philip M. Merikle and Heather E. Skanes, "Subliminal Self-Help Audiotapes: A Search for Placebo Effect," *Journal of Applied Psychology* 77 (1992): 772–776. Copyright © 1992 by the American Psychological Association, Inc. Reprinted by permission.

Subliminal Self-Help Audiotapes:
A Search for Placebo Effects

Philip M. Merikle and Heather E. Skanes
University of Waterloo

The article begins with an abstract summarizing the purpose, methods, and results of the study.

Subliminal self-help audiotapes to aid weight loss were evaluated to determine if their apparent effectiveness is due to a placebo effect. All subjects were female students or staff who were both overweight and believed in the possible effectiveness of subliminal audiotapes. Three different groups of subjects were tested: One group listened to subliminal audiotapes purchased directly from a manufacturer, the 2nd group listened to comparable placebo tapes, and the 3rd group did not listen to any tapes at all. Each subject in each group was weighed once each week for 5 weeks. All 3 groups of subjects lost weight, and the average amount of weight lost by each group was approximately equivalent. These results provide no evidence that regular use of subliminal audiotapes leads to a placebo effect. Rather, the results suggest that regular use of subliminal audiotapes may simply make subjects more conscious of their weight.

The authors provide a context for their study by noting that tapes with subliminal messages are widely marketed.

Within recent years, audiotapes with embedded subliminal messages have been widely marketed by a number of different companies in North America. The distributors claim that these tapes can modify many different behavior patterns, and each company involved in the distribution and sale of subliminal audiotapes markets a variety of cassettes covering a wide range of common problems that an individual may wish to overcome or skill that an individual may wish to develop. Some of the most popular tapes are the ones marketed by distributors to help individuals stop smoking, lose weight, and reduce stress. There are also subliminal audiotapes on the market to improve such abilities as reading comprehension, visual acuity, exam performance, skill at tennis (or golf or baseball, etc.), and even psychic abilities such as "past life regression."

Most of the commercially available subliminal audiotapes share a similar format. When the tapes are played, all that a listener consciously perceives are background sounds consisting of music, ocean waves, and even the occasional cricket or sea gull. Although each company's tapes are distinguished by a unique mix of background sounds, different tapes produced by the same company are often indistinguishable. Presumably, what distinguishes the many different tapes produced by each company are the embedded subliminal messages that are impossible for a listener to hear consciously in the context of the background music or ocean waves.

Distributors often justify their claims that subliminal audiotapes are an effective means for modifying behavior by referring to
scientific findings that suggest that subliminal perception is a valid
phenomenon. What the distributors fail to understand, however, is
that the scientific evidence actually suggests that their subliminal
audiotapes cannot possibly be effective. The scientific evidence for
subliminal perception does not imply the existence of some "super-
sensitive" unconscious perceptual system, as suggested in the promotional literature for subliminal audiotapes. Rather, both older and
more recent studies show that subliminal perception is simply the
perception of stimuli that people claim were neither seen nor heard
(see Cheesman & Merikle, 1986; Dixon, 1981; Kihlstrom, 1987;
Merikle & Cheesman, 1987; Merikle & Reingold, in press). A proto-
typic demonstration of subliminal perception may involve demonstrating that subjects can discriminate between different stimulus
states when they are forced to guess (e.g., the presence or absence of
a stimulus), even though their descriptions of their subjective experiences indicate that they neither saw nor heard a stimulus. Thus, the
scientific evidence indicates that subliminal perception can be
defined by a discrepancy between one's ability to detect a stimulus
and one's subjective experience of seeing or hearing the same stimulus. Given this evidence, the minimal stimulus conditions necessary
to demonstrate subliminal perception should lead to some stimulus
detection when subjects are forced to guess.

> The authors establish that sellers of the audiotapes claim that there is scientific evidence for subliminal perception. Using research and reasoning, however, the authors show that no experiments have yet demonstrated that people have the ability to perceive subliminal messages. The authors state that to demonstrate subliminal perception, an experiment would have to show that people could correctly guess which of two tapes contained a subliminal message.

When subliminal audiotapes have been evaluated to assess
whether they meet the minimal stimulus condition necessary for
demonstrating subliminal perception under controlled laboratory
conditions, the results have been uniformly negative. Merikle (1988)
studied subliminal audiotapes supplied by a major distributor and
found that when subjects are forced to guess in a forced-choice discrimination task, they cannot distinguish between a tape containing
subliminal messages and an identical placebo tape containing no
subliminal messages. Similarly, Moore (1991) used matched pairs of
audiotapes from different manufacturers and found that subjects
cannot distinguish between tapes that contain ostensibly different
subliminal messages. Given these results, the inescapable conclusion
is that subliminal audiotapes do not satisfy the minimal condition—
stimulus detection—that is a necessary prerequisite for demonstrating subliminal perception.

> The authors cite two experiments that show people were unable to distinguish between tapes that contained subliminal messages and those that didn't, or between tapes that contained different subliminal messages.

In addition to the scientific evidence, testimonials from satisfied
users are another type of evidence often cited by distributors to support their claims for the efficacy of subliminal audiotapes. Many
users claim that the tapes were useful in helping them to lose weight,
stop smoking, and so forth. Given the pervasive nature of placebo

> Besides citing scientific evidence for subliminal perception, sellers of subliminal audiotapes often use testimonials from satisfied customers to promote their product, the authors point out.

effects (see Ross & Olson, 1982, for an excellent review) it is not at all surprising that some proportion of users may experience positive effects after using subliminal audiotapes for a period of time. For some users, a strong belief in the efficacy of subliminal audiotapes may be sufficient to produce positive effects. Thus, even though subliminal audiotapes may not contain any messages that can conceivably influence behavior, the tapes may be beneficial to at least some proportion of users, because of the placebo effects that can follow from regular listening to these tapes.

The authors summarize the findings of recent studies of subliminal and placebo tapes. They point out that the findings demonstrate no benefit from subliminal messages. They also point out that none of these studies has unambiguously shown that there is a placebo effect. One study suggested a placebo effect was at work, but the results could also be due to a practice effect.

Recent studies in which the efficacy of subliminal and placebo audiotapes has been compared are unanimous in showing no advantage for subliminal tapes relative to comparable placebo tapes (Auday, Mellett, & Williams, 191; Greenwald, Spangenberg, Pratkanis, & Eskenazi, 1991; Russell, Rose, & Smouse, 1991). However, even though these studies are unambiguous in demonstrating the ineffectiveness of subliminal tapes, the results are ambiguous as to whether regular listening to these tapes actually leads to a placebo effect. For example, Greenwald et al. (1991) evaluated the effectiveness of subliminal audiotapes designed to increase self-esteem or memory by comparing the performance on pretests of self-esteem or memory with performance on comparable posttests administered after the subjects listened to the tapes for several weeks. They found improvements in performance following regular listening to either subliminal or placebo tapes. In addition, they also found that memory improved even when subjects listened to placebo tapes labeled *self-esteem* and that self-esteem improved even when the subjects listened to placebo tapes labeled *memory*. Greenwald et al. suggested that these results reflected the operation of a nonspecific placebo effect. However, they also recognized that the results may not reflect a placebo effect at all and may simply reflect a practice effect from the pretests to the posttests. This latter interpretation is completely consistent with the results of the Russell et al. (1991) study in which no pretests were used and no placebo effects were found.

The authors explain the "placebo effect," a strong belief in the usefulness of a product that really has no beneficial ingredients. This belief may itself produce a positive effect in the user.

Because of the ambiguity of the previous research, the authors decided to conduct their study to determine whether listening to subliminal audiotapes can produce a placebo effect.

The present study was a direct attempt to evaluate possible placebo effects that may occur following regular listening to subliminal audiotapes. Relative to previous studies, the experimental design had several unique features. First, the possible effects of audiotapes marketed to facilitate weight loss were studied. Weight loss was selected as the target behavior because it can be measured very accurately and it is a relatively easy behavior to modify. In contrast, many of the behaviors studied in previous studies are ones that are either difficult to measure accurately (e.g., anxiety, self-confidence) or difficult to modify (e.g., recognition memory). A second feature of the present study was that the selected behavior pattern was measured weekly over the 5 weeks that the subjects listened to the tapes. Thus, rather than simply comparing each subject's weight before and after listening to the tapes, it was possible to monitor each subject's weight during the entire time that she listened to the tapes. Finally, three different groups of subjects were used so that any effects found in the study could be interpreted unambiguously. One group of subjects listened to subliminal audiotapes purchased from a major distributor, the second group of subjects listened to comparable placebo tapes, and the third group of subjects did not listen to any tapes at all. By comparing the average weight lost by each of these groups it was possible to determine if any observed effects were a true placebo effect produced by regular listening to an audiotape believed to contain relevant subliminal affirmations.

The authors describe the unique features of their experiment: (1) a focus on weight loss tapes; (2) measurement of the participants' weight over a five-week period to monitor the weight lost during the time they listened to the tapes; (3) use of three different groups of participants to determine if there is a true placebo effect.

Method

Subjects

Forty-seven female University of Waterloo students and staff were selected to participate in the study. The subjects ranged in age from 18 to 56 years, with a mean age of 29.7 years. All subjects who completed the experiment received either $15 or a subliminal audiotape.

The subjects were solicited through announcements posted on the University of Waterloo campus and through advertisements placed in campus newspapers. To ensure that the sample was representative of subliminal audiotape consumers, all subjects selected to participate in the study had a desire to lose weight, a belief that it is possible to change behavior through subliminal perception and a body weight that exceeded the suggested range for their height and body frame according to the *Metropolitan Height and Weight Tables* (1983). In addition, no subject was currently involved in any other weight loss program.

The subjects were selected following an initial meeting at which their body frame and weight were measured and a questionnaire was completed. The questionnaire was designed to assess each potential subject's desire to lose weight and her belief in the possible effectiveness of subliminal audiotapes. Each subject's average level of weekly exercise, use of tobacco products, and use of oral contraceptives were also determined at this initial meeting. Each of these factors is known to influence weight loss or gain, and for this reason it was considered important to monitor these factors during the study.

In the Methods section of their report, the authors describe in detail how the participants were recruited and selected. They describe how they controlled for other possible influences on weight gain or loss.

Research Design

The authors describe the three treatment groups the participants were randomly assigned to.

Once the 47 subjects were selected to participate in the experiment, they were randomly assigned to one of the three following groups.

Subliminal. Each of the 15 subjects assigned to this group was given an audiotape that was claimed by the distributor to produce weight loss. The cassettes given to the subjects in this group were exactly as purchased from the distributor, Adventures in Learning, Inc.

Placebo. The audiotapes given to the 15 subjects assigned to this group were identical in appearance and packaging to the tapes given to the subliminal subjects. However, each tape was altered so that the original recording was replaced by a recording from a tape that the distributor claimed contained affirmations to relieve dental anxiety. The background music and sounds were identical on the weight loss tapes and the dental anxiety tape. Thus, on the basis of conscious perceptual experience, it was impossible to distinguish placebo from subliminal tapes.

Waiting list. The 17 subjects assigned to this group were told that the maximum number of subjects was currently participating in the study and that for this reason, they had to be placed on a waiting list. These subjects remained on the waiting list for the duration of the experiment. In this way, they provided baseline data that were used to evaluate any changes observed in the subliminal or placebo groups. At the completion of the experiment, the subjects in this group were given a subliminal audiotape to use so that the promise of being in the experiment was fulfilled.

The authors describe how they ensured randomization and protected against experimenter bias.

To ensure that subjects were assigned to the subliminal and placebo groups in a double-blind manner, Philip Merikle, who had no direct contact with the subjects, placed a randomly selected number on each subliminal and placebo tape. In addition, he assigned subjects to the subliminal or placebo groups and assigned specific, numbered tapes to the subjects in those groups. Heather Skanes, who was responsible for working with the subjects, was given a list of subjects' names and associated tape numbers; she had no knowledge of which tapes were subliminal and which tapes were placebo.

Procedure

The authors describe the procedures they used to collect weight data for each participant.

Before the beginning of the experiment, each subject met with Heather Skanes. Each subject's baseline weight was measured, and each subject was told whether she would receive a subliminal audiotape immediately or whether she had been placed on the waiting list. The subjects in all three groups were told that they would be weighed once each week for the next 5 weeks. The subjects assigned to the waiting list group were also told that it was important for us to monitor their weight on a weekly basis, even though they would not receive a subliminal audiotape until the end of the 5 weeks. To minimize any influence of daily or hourly fluctuations in body weight, each subject in each group was assigned a particular day and time to be weighed each week.

The subjects assigned to the subliminal and placebo groups received their tapes at the initial meeting. All tapes were identical except for a randomly selected number that was used for identification purposes. The experimenter, who was completely unaware of whether a tape was subliminal or placebo, simply gave the tapes to the subjects according to a predetermined list. Given the importance of each subject believing in the efficacy of her assigned tape, no subject was told about the existence of placebo tapes before the beginning of the experiment. In addition, even though all subjects were told about the subliminal and placebo tapes when they were debriefed at the end of the experiment, no subject was told which tape she had received.

The authors describe how each participant received a subliminal or placebo tape at random, but how each one believed that she had a subliminal tape. This deception was revealed in debriefing at the end of the experiment.

The subjects in the subliminal and placebo groups were asked to listen to the tapes between 1 and 3 hrs. per day, and they were told that they could listen to their tape during most activities. Each subject was also asked to record the number of hours that she listened to her tape each day. Finally, each subject was given an instruction booklet and a list of the subliminal weight loss affirmations. These additional materials were supplied by the distributor, and they are typically included with each tape that is sold.

The instructions that the participants followed are described.

The subjects in all three groups were weighed on Weeks 1, 2, 4, and 5. Because of a study week (i.e., a vacation week to many students), it was not possible to weigh many of the subjects during Week 3. After each subject was weighed on Week 5, she was asked to complete the same questionnaire that she had completed during the initial selection process. The primary purpose of this post experiment administration of the questionnaire was to determine if any life-style changes had occurred during the study (i.e., exercise, use of tobacco).

The authors explain how a vacation interfered with their ability to weigh the participants during Week 3.

Once the subjects in the waiting list group had completed the post-experiment questionnaire, they were given either a placebo or a subliminal audiotape. At this point in the study, it was no longer necessary to monitor each subject's weight on a weekly basis. For this reason, each subject in the waiting list group was simply asked to weigh herself once each week for 5 weeks.

The authors show how they controlled for the possible effects of other events that could have influenced the results.

Results

The data for 8 subjects were not analyzed. Four subjects did not return for the initial session after they were selected to participate in

The authors describe the attrition of some participants and how many were left in each group at the end of the experiment.

the study. Two of these subjects had been assigned to the subliminal group and one subject each had been assigned to the placebo and waiting list groups. Four additional subjects were not included in the data analysis because they failed to attend at least three of the four weight-measuring sessions. Two of these subjects were in the waiting list group and one subject each was in the subliminal group and the placebo group. After these 8 subjects were dropped from the study, a total of 39 subjects remained, with each group containing the following number of subjects: subliminal = 12, placebo = 13, waiting list = 14.

The authors describe the characteristics of each group to show that they were comparable by the end of the experiment.

In general, the three groups were very comparable. The average age of the subjects (subliminal = 29.1, placebo = 30.5, and waiting list = 29.4) and the average baseline weights (see Table 1) were similar across the three groups. In addition, the answers that the subjects gave on the post experiment questionnaires indicated that the three groups were roughly equivalent in terms of listening habits and life-style changes during the course of the study. The subjects in the sub-liminal group reported an average listening time of approximately 1.4 hr/day, whereas the subjects in the placebo group reported that they listened to the tapes for approximately 1.7 hr/day. Furthermore, a similar number of subjects in each group reported an increase in the number of times they participated in weekly exercise (subliminal = 4, placebo = 3, waiting list = 6), and no more than 1 subject across all three groups reported a decrease in weekly exercise, a cessation in the use of tobacco, or a change in the use of oral contraceptives. Given these statistics, there do not appear to have been any systematic differences across the three groups.

The authors explain what they did to make up for the missing data from Week 3.

Before the mean weights for each group were computed, it was necessary to estimate the weight of 6 subjects at one of the four weight-measuring sessions. These subjects missed one of the four sessions, and to keep these subjects in the study, their weight at the missed session was estimated by computing their mean weight across the immediately preceding and immediately following sessions. For example, if a subject missed the Week 2 weight-measuring session, her weight at Week 2 was estimated as her mean weight averaged across Weeks 1 and 4. The resulting mean weights for each group of subjects at baseline and at each week during the study are shown in Table 1.

The authors describe in words what Table 1 presents graphically and numerically.

Three aspects of the data presented in Table 1 are important. First, relative to the baseline weights, the mean weights of all three groups are consistently lower at each week of the study. Second, the weight loss experienced by all three groups was modest, and third, there are no apparent differences in the patterns of weight loss across the three groups. The data shown in Table 1 were evaluated by a 3 x

5 (Group x Time of Weight Measurement) analysis of variance (ANOVA). This analysis revealed neither a significant main effect of group, $F(2, 36) < 1$, nor a significant Group x Time of Weight Measurement interaction, $F(8, 144) = 1.18$. However, the analysis did reveal significant changes in weight across the different times of weight measurement, $F(4, 144) = 3.3.1$, $p < .012$. Thus, on the basis of this analysis, it appears that significant weight loss was experienced by the subjects but that the three groups did not differ in the amount of weight lost.

The authors explain the results of an ANOVA, a statistical test that showed no significant differences in weight loss among the three groups.

TABLE 1

Mean Weight and Standard Deviation for Each Group at Baseline and Each Week During the Study.

	Time of weight measurement									
	Baseline		Week 1		Week 2		Week 4		Week 5	
Group	lb	kg	lb	kg	lb	kg	lb	kg	lb	kg
Subliminal (n=12)										
M	166.5	75.5	165.2	74.9	165.5	75.1	166.2	75.4	166.1	75.3
SD	29.3	13.3	28.5	12.9	28.7	13.0	28.6	13.0	29.4	13.3
Placebo (n=13)										
M	167.1	75.8	166.8	75.7	166.7	75.6	166.5	75.5	165.8	75.2
SD	22.4	10.2	23.0	10.4	23.0	10.4	22.7	10.3	23.2	10.5
Waiting list (n=14)										
M	164.9	74.8	163.3	74.1	163.5	74.2	164.6	74.7	163.9	74.3
SD	27.9	12.7	27.0	12.2	27.4	12.4	27.5	12.5	27.7	12.6

To obtain more stable, reliable estimates of overall weight loss, the data for each subject were collapsed and averaged across the four weight-measuring sessions. The resulting mean average weights across Weeks 1 to 5, as well as each group's mean baseline weight, are shown in Figure 1. Inspection of Figure 1 confirms that all three groups lost approximately equivalent amounts of weight during the study. To evaluate these data, we used a 2 x 3 ANOVA to assess time of weight measurement (baseline vs. Weeks 1 to 5) and group. This analysis revealed that the overall decrease in weight between baseline and Weeks 1 to 5 was significant, $F(1, 36) = 7.22$, $p < .011$. The

By reading across this table, you can see that there were no big fluctuations in weight for any group from the first to the fifth week. You can also see that there were no big differences between the three groups at any given week in the study.

The authors explain how they combined the data for all participants at all weight measurement points to get average amounts of weight loss for each group. As Figure 1 shows, all three groups lost a significant amount of weight, but no group lost significantly more than any other group. Another statistical test was used to demonstrate this.

analysis also revealed that neither the group difference nor the Group x Time of Weight Measurement interaction was significant, both Fs(2, 36) < 1. This analysis of overall weight loss confirms that the subjects in all three groups experienced some weight loss during the study and that there is no evidence to suggest that the different groups lost different amounts of weight.

Figure 1.

Mean weight for each group at baseline and averaged across Weeks 1 to 5.

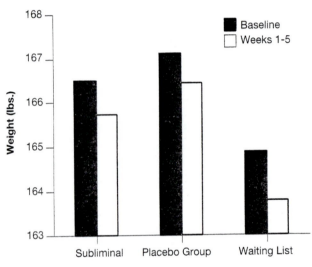

Discussion

The results of the present study provide no evidence whatsoever that subliminal audiotapes are an effective means for modifying behavior. If subliminal affirmations were effective in aiding weight loss, then the subliminal group should have lost more weight than either the placebo or the waiting list groups. However, as the results indicate, all three groups lost small but approximately equivalent amounts of weight. Thus, the present results are completely consistent with the results of previous studies demonstrating the total ineffectiveness of subliminal audiotapes (Auday et al., 1991; Greenwald et al., 1991; Russell et al., 1991).

However, the present results also indicate that the weight loss experienced by the subjects during the study cannot be attributed to a placebo effect produced by regular use of the audiotapes. If a true placebo effect had occurred, then the placebo group would have lost significantly more weight than the waiting list group. However, the results indicate that the waiting list group actually lost slightly, but not significantly, more weight than the placebo group. Thus, the present results provide no evidence that either listening to the tapes or believing in the tapes' effectiveness increases weight loss. Furthermore, given the slightly greater weight loss for the waiting list group, our failure to find an advantage for the placebo group cannot be attributed to a lack of statistical power, because no amount of statistical power would reverse the direction of the difference between these two groups. This complete absence of any placebo effect suggests that the improvements in performance that Greenwald et al. (1991) attributed to a nonspecific placebo effect probably reflected a practice effect from the pretests to the posttests used in their study.

The most interesting result found in the present study is the fact that the waiting list subjects, who did not even listen to audiotapes, experienced as much weight loss as the subjects assigned to the subliminal and the placebo groups. This finding suggests that all subjects may have become more conscious of their weight just by participating in the study. Thus, the subjects in all three groups may have lost weight simply because participation in the study increased the likelihood that they would attend and think about weight-related issues during the course of the study. The paradox that is suggested is that regular use of subliminal audiotapes may make users more conscious of their problems. If so, then the benefits experienced by satisfied users are not produced by subliminal or unconscious influences, as implied by the promotional literature, but by conscious attention to the problem or behavior that they are trying to change.

Even though the present study and previous studies provide considerable evidence that subliminal audiotapes cannot and do not change behavior through subliminal perception, the pessimistic conclusion for anyone who believes in rational decision making is that many individuals will continue to purchase and to use subliminal audiotapes. Both the present study and previous studies (e.g., Greenwald et al., 1991) demonstrate that regular use of subliminal audiotapes can be followed by improvements or changes in certain behavior patterns. As long as users continue to attribute these behavioral changes or improvements to subliminal affirmations that they believe are contained on these audiotapes, there is every reason to expect that many people will continue to purchase this widely promoted and distributed product.

In the Discussion, the authors interpret their findings, arriving at three main conclusions: (1) Subliminal messages do not aid in weight loss, and this conclusion is consistent with previous research on the ineffectiveness of subliminal messages; (2) there is no placebo effect for participants who believe they are listening to a subliminal audiotape because participants who listened to no audiotape lost about the same amount of weight as the placebo group; (3) just thinking about trying to lose weight may be enough to bring about some weight loss because all three groups lost some weight. Thus, the benefits some people claim to find with subliminal tapes may come just because they are focusing on changing their behavior.

The authors conclude that their research is not likely to change some people's belief in the value of subliminal messages, even though there is no evidence for perception of subliminal messages.

References

Auday, B. C., Mellett, J. L., & Williams, P. M. (1991, April). *Self-improvement using subliminal self-help audiotapes: Consumer benefit or consumer fraud?* Poster presented at the 71st Annual Meeting of the Western Psychological Association, San Francisco.

Cheesman, J., & Merikle, P. M. (1986). Distinguishing conscious from unconscious perceptual processes. *Canadian Journal of Psychology, 40,* 343–367.

Dixon, N. F. (1981). *Preconscious processing.* New York: Wiley. Greenwald, A. G., Spangenberg, E. R., Pratkanis, A. R., & Eskenazi, J. (1991). Double-blind tests of subliminal self-help audiotapes. *Psychological Science, 2,* 119–122.

Kihlstrom, J. F. (1987). The cognitive unconscious. *Science, 273,* 1445–1452.

Merikle, P.M. (1988). Subliminal auditory messages: An evaluation. *Psychology & Marketing, 5,* 355–372.

Merikle, P. M., & Cheesman, J. (1987). Current status of research on subliminal perception. In M. Wallendorf & P. Anderson (Eds.), *Advances in consumer research, volume XIV* (pp. 298–302). Provo, UT: Association for Consumer Research.

Merikle, P. M., & Reingold, E. M. (1992). Measuring unconscious perceptual processes. In R. S. Bornstein & T. S. Pitman (Eds.), *Perception without awareness: Cognitive, clinical, and social perspectives* (pp. 55–80). New York: Guilford.

Metropolitan height and weight tables. (1983). *Statistical Bulletin of the Metropolitan Insurance Co., 64,* 2–9.

Moore, T. E. (1991). *Evaluating subliminal auditory tapes: Is there any evidence for subliminal perception?* Unpublished manuscript, York University, Glendon College, Department of Psychology, Toronto.

Ross, M., & Olson, J. M. (1982). Placebo effects in medical research and practice. In J. R. Eiser (Ed.), *Social psychology and behavioral medicine* (pp. 441–458). New York: Wiley.

Russell, T. G., Rowe, W., & Smouse, A. D. (1991). Subliminal self-help tapes and academic achievement: An evaluation. *Journal of Counseling & Development, 69,* 359–362.

A STUDENT EXAMPLE

As a student conducting experimental research, you may not be required to write about your research in quite the same way as professionals do. For example, your professor may not require you to do a thorough search of related literature. The student example of an experimental report on the next few pages does not contain a detailed review of literature; instead it refers generally to studies that show people are not helpful to others when they assume someone else will take the responsibility to help the person in need. Rhett Neuenschwander and Paul Rose, two students in psychology, devised an experiment to see if this general finding was true of students on their campus. They tried to determine whether or not busy students in high-traffic areas of campus would take the time to pick up and mail a lost envelope. Their operational definition of helpfulness was putting the lost envelopes in the mail. They decided to measure not only how many envelopes were mailed (actual helpfulness) but also how helpful students believe they are (perceived helpfulness). So they included a short survey in their study that gave them a way to compare actual with perceived helpfulness.

As you read the students' paper, you will note that it is brief, factual, and to the point. It contains enough information about methods to allow someone to replicate the study. However, you may note that a future experiment could change the procedures. Since Neuenschwander and Rose did not know how many students walked past their lost envelopes before someone picked up each one to mail it, future investigators might station someone to unobtrusively observe and count how many people pass by each envelope before someone picks it up. Adding this step to the method would give a more accurate indication of helpfulness.

A Study of Helpfulness:
Reported versus Actual Helpfulness Among Students

by
Rhett Neuenschwander and Paul Rose

Abstract

This research was designed to measure and compare perceived helpfulness of students with their actual helpfulness. To measure actual helpfulness, stamped letters we addressed to ourselves were left in various locations on campus. We measured actual helpfulness by counting the number of letters that were mailed back to us. We simultaneously conducted a survey to find out what students deemed the best course of action when confronted with a lost letter. The survey results were compared to the number of returned letters. The results can be interpreted in two different ways. If alternative ways of being helpful are considered, students are actually less helpful than the survey indicated. However, according to the operational definition of helpfulness, students returned more envelopes than they claimed they would in the survey. By this interpretation, students are more helpful than they perceive themselves to be.

Introduction

Several psychologists have conducted studies to determine how willing people are to help or offer assistance to others. These studies have proven that when people are in large groups they are less likely to offer assistance to someone. This occurs because the individuals fail to accept personal responsibility for the situation by assuming that someone else will help. On our campus, the approximately 30,000 students sign an Honor Code pledging, among other things, to "be honest" and "respect others." We decided to conduct a simple test to measure whether or not students were actually living these standards. Are students willing to perform a simple act of kindness to help a fellow student, or will they fail to accept personal responsibility and confirm previous studies? We hypothesized that students perceive themselves to be more helpful than they actually are.

Methods

We chose to answer the research question two different ways. We began our research by placing 20 letters around campus which were addressed, sealed, and stamped. (Ten of the letters had fake names with the first researcher's address and the return address of the second researcher. The other 10 also had fake names, but with the second researcher's address and the return address of the first researcher. No name was given on the return address.) Each letter was placed in a high-traffic area in different buildings on campus, thus making it appear as if the letter had simply been dropped, forgotten, or misplaced. The letters were placed at the different locations during peak school hours, which made them visible to hundreds of students. The passing students who saw each abandoned letter were now in a situation to make a choice as to what course of action to follow. The ideal course of action would be to help or assist the person who lost the letter by picking up the letter and placing it in a mailbox. Obviously, the student encountering the letter could have done a number of other things, including ignoring the letter, throwing the letter away, or opening the letter—none of which would be considered a helpful response. We reasoned that this scenario placed each student passer-by in an actual situation where they had the opportunity to help another student. Helpfulness could then be measured by the number of letters returned by the students.

The second part of our research was a survey asking 20 students to respond to the following question: "Imagine yourself on campus one day. On a table you see a fully addressed, stamped envelope that has clearly not yet been processed by the postal service. What, in your opinion, is the best course of action?" The respondent could then select one of five responses that were provided, or state their own unique response (see Appendix A). Twenty students, 10 male and 10 female, were randomly asked to answer the survey. (Obviously, the twenty students who actually found the envelopes were not specifically selected, either.) The purpose in conducting the survey was to determine how helpful students perceived themselves to be. By comparing the number of students who said they would mail the letter to the number of students who actually mailed a letter, we could compare the perceived helpfulness of students to their actual helpfulness.

Results

Seventeen of the 20 abandoned envelopes arrived in our mailboxes. Therefore, 85% of the envelopes were mailed, suggesting that actual helpfulness on campus is very high. Figure 1 summarizes the responses to the survey of students' perceived helpfulness. Fifteen students said that the best course of action would be to simply deposit the abandoned envelope in a postal delivery box. One student said he would take the envelope to the Lost and Found; another would attempt to contact the sender of the envelope by phone using a directory; and another said she would simply ask people standing around her if it was theirs. Only two students responded that the most correct thing to do was to ignore it. Thus, according to the results of the survey, 75% of the students would deposit the envelope, 5% would place it in the Lost & Found, 5% would attempt to contact the sender by phone, 5% would ask bystanders if it was theirs, and 10% would ignore the envelope.

Figure 1

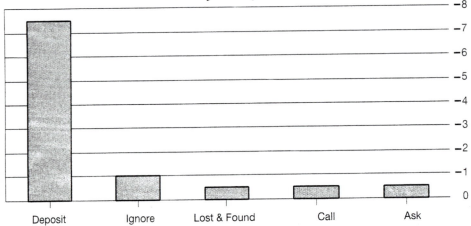

Survey Responses

Deposit   Ignore   Lost & Found   Call   Ask

Discussion

Contrary to our hypothesis, students were actually far more helpful than we expected. Considering the results of the survey alone, one would expect that only 75% of the envelopes would eventually arrive in our mailboxes, but the actual number was 10% higher.

We should point out, however, that our interpretation of helpfulness was narrower than that of the students who participated in the survey. That is, by our definition, the only helpful course of action was to deposit the letter for mailing. A closer look at the other answers given to the survey, however, indicates that there are other responses that are also helpful. Putting a letter in the Lost & Found, for example, is certainly more helpful than ignoring the letter entirely. If we assume that the only "unhelpful" response given by those surveyed was to ignore the letter, then actually 90% of the students surveyed said that they would do something helpful. Only two students said that they would ignore the envelope.

Assuming that all the answers given to the survey are helpful except "Ignore it," then 90% of the students chose a course of action that was a helpful one. With this assumption, the actual results are mildly disappointing, because only 85% of the abandoned envelopes were mailed to us. Considering our operational definition of helpfulness, it was difficult for us to measure the choices proposed by the students who may have been helpful in an alternative way. For example, we didn't check the Lost & Found for any of the envelopes, and because we didn't put a name above the sender address, it was impossible for a student to contact the sender by phone. We did not have a way to measure any alternative methods of helpfulness, then, and we are only assuming that the three envelopes that were never mailed were actually ignored and eventually discarded. We also don't know how many students passed by each envelope before someone picked it up, so we are only assuming that the students who did return the envelopes are representative of the whole campus population.

If our assumptions are valid, we can draw two possible conclusions from our research: (1) Students are more helpful than they claim to be, because in the survey only 75% of the students said they would mail the abandoned envelope, but 85% of the envelopes actually arrived. (2) However, if we consider the alternative responses to also be helpful, then 90% of the students surveyed perceived themselves to be helpful. But because only 85% of the envelopes arrived in our mailboxes (the only method of helpfulness we measured), students are not as helpful as they claim. Figure 2 combines these two

Figure 2

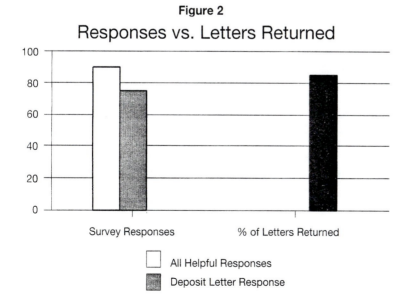

Responses vs. Letters Returned

interpretations by comparing the number of letters returned with all helpful responses from the survey and the "deposit letter" response. All things considered, our study suggests that the majority of students are indeed helpful and try to follow the standards prescribed in the Honor Code.

Appendix

This survey is part of a study the investigators are conducting to meet a course requirement. Please answer the questions as honestly as possible. Completing the survey implies your consent to let the data be used in a report. You will remain anonymous. Thanks.

Please write a unique, fake name in this blank: _____

Imagine yourself on campus one day. On a table you see a fully addressed, stamped envelope that has clearly not yet been processed by the postal service. What in your opinion, is the best course of action?

A. Ignore it.
B. Open it.
C. Deposit it in the nearest mail box.
D. Throw it away.
E. Other (please explain)

_____

_____

SUGGESTIONS FOR RESEARCH AND WRITING

1. What foods do college students generally consume often? How important is price to them? Peanut butter, pizza, chips, and soft drinks are all possible candidates for an experimental taste test. Design an experiment that would let you conclude whether or not students on your campus judge the more expensive product as better tasting than the inexpensive one in a blind taste test.

2. Do students automatically assume that male professors are more competent than female professors who work in the same discipline and have the same qualifications and rank? Design an experiment in which you test the hypothesis that students do make this assumption. One way to do this would be to find or write a brief article on an academic topic and reproduce it for a selected number of participants. On half of the copies of the article you could attach a description of a hypothetical male professor who you would say wrote it; on the other half, you could attach the same description but say that a female professor wrote it. You could randomly assign participants to read a version of the article and then rate it on a list of qualities related to academic competence. By comparing the ratings, you could determine whether or not your hypothesis was supported.

3. To what extent do an attractive face and figure influence people's judgments of someone's qualifications for a job? Design an experiment in which you could test the hypothesis that when other qualifications are equal, the more attractive person in a pair of people will be preferred for a job. (This experiment could be done by having participants look at pairs of pictures, in which one member of the pair is more attractive than the other, but accompanying descriptions of each one's qualifications show them to be equally suited for the hypothetical job.)

4. Look in the professional journals in your major field to find a simple experiment that you could replicate—one that doesn't require a lot of expertise, time, equipment, or money to do. Conduct the experiment and write a report, using the earlier study as a model.

REFERENCES

Campbell, Donald T., and Julian C. Stanley. 1963. *Experimental and quasi-experimental designs for research on teaching.* Chicago: Rand McNally.

Milgram, Stanley. 1974. *Obedience to authority: An experimental view.* New York: Harper & Row.

III

FINDING AND USING EXISTING KNOWLEDGE

The next two chapters discuss how you can find and use knowledge that has already been created and published by other scholars. Your two main sources of such information are libraries, discussed in Chapter 9, and the Internet, discussed in Chapter 10. Knowing how to use these sources well to locate information about your field is vital as you prepare to write research papers or reviews of literature for college and professional papers.

The development of libraries as places for categorizing, storing, and retrieving information has been of immense importance in the progress of human civilization, allowing scholars to build on the work of previous ones. Without libraries to organize and store the bodies of knowledge each discipline develops, the collaborative enterprise of science would be more difficult to carry out. In the twentieth century, libraries have had to cope with an amazing explosion of knowledge as various university disciplines have become increasingly specialized and as technologies for producing printed texts have improved. The proliferation of publications has increased costs for libraries, as they have attempted to continue buying the latest books, subscribing to the ever-increasing number of periodicals, and adding to their shelf space.

Now, as electronic information is beginning in some ways to supersede printed texts, libraries face new challenges in storing and retrieving information. Libraries are no longer places that simply catalog and shelve books, journals, and other documents to read; increasingly, they are places where you will find new computer technologies that can help you locate and retrieve information that may not even be on the library's shelves. One increasingly important source of new information is the Internet, particularly sites on the World Wide Web that are created and maintained by researchers and organizations that aim to share the latest findings, statistics, evidence, data, or arguments that other scholars can make use of in their research. Without up-to-date library research skills and a knowledge of how to navigate the Internet, you will be seriously handicapped in joining the conversation of your discipline.

9

LIBRARY RESEARCH AND WRITING

WHY DO LIBRARY RESEARCH?

Professors frequently assign a library research paper in order to involve students more deeply in the subject matter of a particular course. It is a unique academic genre whose closest professional cousins are a review of literature and a review essay. Completing a library paper requires you to read books and periodicals that are likely very different from the textbooks you read for your courses. The reading you do for a library research paper can also acquaint you more intimately than a textbook does with the community of scholars in your field—with the kinds of knowledge your field values, the methods it uses to create knowledge, and its ways of organizing and expressing that knowledge in written form. As you read the articles published in your field's latest journals, you will begin to see what important questions are driving the current research; you will notice who the major researchers are; you will begin to discern how one study incorporates findings from other studies and then spawns even more studies; and you will notice the rhetoric typical of your field. In short, if you are observant as you do library research—if you think of it as getting acquainted with the members and practices of an intellectual community you want to join, instead of as a hoop you must jump through for a grade—you can learn much about becoming a professional in your field.

Library research is a kind of prewriting, but because it is much more involved and time-consuming than other prewriting techniques such as brainstorming, clustering, or freewriting, this entire chapter is devoted to how to do it. Where applicable, the focus of this chapter is on doing research in the social sciences. As detailed as this chapter is, however, it is not a complete guide to all of the sources you can use for social science research. You should also take advantage of whatever classes and instructional aids your campus library offers to help you become better acquainted with its holdings and its research tools. Regardless of local differences, however, library research papers always require you to take these four steps: (1) *find*, (2) *evaluate*, (3) *record*, and (4) *synthesize* information from sources. In this chapter you will learn about what is involved in each step.

FINDING INFORMATION IN THE LIBRARY

Most library research starts with a question you want to answer. At first your question might be rather broad and ill-defined, but you will be able to narrow and focus it as you learn more through your research. To answer your question, you must first locate sources that contain pertinent information. Library sources can be categorized into two broad classes:

- *Directional sources*, such as indexes, card catalogs, on-line catalogs, bibliographies, thesauruses, and databases
- *Informational sources*, such as books, periodicals, and microform records

Directional sources point you to informational sources. There may be some overlap between these two categories; for example, an encyclopedia can be both an informational source about a topic like psychotherapy (though it is likely to be general and perhaps out of date), and it can also be a directional source if the entry on psychotherapy includes a bibliography of works you could consult for more information. Because you ultimately want to locate the best informational sources for your question, you must first understand how to use the many directional sources available discussed below.

SUBJECT HEADINGS LISTS

A productive search for information begins with defining the terms that will help you locate sources. One very commonly used directional source that provides you with search terminology is the *Library of Congress Subject Headings List (LCSH)*. The volumes of this large, red-bound book can be found in the reference area of the library. Say, for example, that your overall goal is to answer the question, "What are the factors that cause teenagers to join gangs?" As you look in the *LCSH* under such headings as "crime" and "gangs," you will see other terms that you can use to locate information that will answer your question.

The *LCSH* uses several abbreviations to classify the terms it lists. Some of the most important ones include the following:

> UF means "use for"
>
> BT stands for "broader topic(s)"
>
> RT stands for "related topic(s)"
>
> NT stands for "narrower topic(s)"
>
> SA directs you to "see also"

So, under the subject "crime," for example, the abbreviation UF tells you that "crime" is used for the terms *crime and criminals, delinquency,* and *urban crime.* Under BT, the *LCSH* lists *social problems.* Under RT, it lists *criminals* and *criminology.* And under NT it lists such terms as *juvenile delinquency, organized crime, drug abuse and crime,* and *education and crime.* All of these other terms would be useful starting places for researching your question on teenagers and gangs.

In addition to the *LCSH,* most disciplines (for example, education, psychology, sociology, and political science) have specialized thesauruses that you can use to define search terms. Ask your librarian where to locate thesauruses for your field.

CARD AND ON-LINE CATALOGS

Once you have search terms for your topic, you are ready to use additional directional sources to begin locating informational sources. The first you will probably turn to is the list of the library's holdings, which might take the form of either a card catalog or an on-line (computerized) catalog—or, in some libraries, both. On-line catalogs are often called OPACs—short for Online Public Access Catalogs. You are probably familiar enough with these catalogs that you know you can search them by author, title, or subject, because every book the library has will be listed under all three headings.

An advantage of most on-line catalogs is that you can also search the library holdings with keywords. If you enter the keyword search command and the search terms you've already chosen at the computer terminal's prompt, the computer will search the on-line catalog for any documents that contain the designated terms. The librarian should be able to show you how to connect search terms with words like "and" and "or" in order to expand or limit your search.

PERIODICAL INDEXES

In addition to books, which are listed in the card or on-line catalog, libraries have many periodicals. Periodicals, as the name implies, are publications such as newspapers, magazines, and journals that are published at regular intervals: daily, weekly, monthly, quarterly, or semiannually. As you can readily see, the sheer number of periodicals and the frequency of their publication means that there is an immense amount of periodical literature to select from. To retrieve relevant information from periodicals you must use periodical indexes which are available in several formats.

Periodical indexes in print. You are probably already familiar with the *Reader's Guide to Periodical Literature*. This guide, updated about every six weeks, provides a regular index to the contents of over 170 popular magazines by listing the various topics they give information about and then listing the titles and authors of articles on those topics. There are many other indexes designed like the *Reader's Guide*, but they index specialized journals rather than popular magazines. For instance, the *Social Sciences Index* regularly surveys approximately 900 journals, then catalogs their contents under descriptive headings that allow social scientists to locate the latest articles of interest to them. If you were researching the subject of gang-related crime, for example, you could go to the *Social Sciences Index*, say the March 1994 issue, and under the subject heading "gangs" find the following reference:

"Gangs, drugs, and delinquency in a survey of urban youth" [Denver Youth Study] F. A. Esbensen and D. Huizinga. bibl Criminology v31 p565 89 N '93.

This reference uses abbreviations that are explained inside the front cover of each issue of the *Social Sciences Index*. Using the key to the abbreviations, you would know this article is published in the journal *Criminology*, volume 31, and begins on page 565. You could then locate the article and evaluate its usefulness.

General computer periodical indexes. There are also several computer indexes that aid general social science research. These are often accessible from the same library terminal used for searching the library's book catalog. One such index is the *UMI Periodical Abstracts Index*. It covers material published since 1986 and is used to find articles on all subjects in general periodicals and scholarly journals. In some libraries, through *UMI Periodical Abstracts*, you may also be able to access the full texts of selected periodical articles. The *Reader's Guide to Periodical Literature* is also on-line, indexing material dating from 1985. It covers general periodicals rather than scholarly publications. Most of these general periodical indexes can be searched using the same commands used to search OPACs.

Specialized computer databases. There are a number of other specialized computer databases that are excellent resources for library research in the social sciences. The following list includes many of the important ones. This list is not comprehensive; your library may not have some of these, or it may have others not listed here.

ABC Poli Sci

Indexes articles dating from 1984 from over 300 journals in political science, public administration, and international relations. Updated three times a year.

CD Sourcebook of American History

Indexes a database containing the full texts of many American history documents such as the Mayflower Compact, the Declaration of Independence, the Constitution, the *Federalist Papers*, and many first-hand accounts of American history from Columbus through WWI. Also contains some interpretive histories of the United States and some biographies.

Census CD ROM

Contains summary statistics dating from 1990 for U.S. population, farms, businesses, manufacturing establishments, per capita income, and so on.

Constitution Papers

Indexes a database containing full texts of important U.S. government documents such as the Constitution and the *Federalist Papers*.

EconLit

Indexes a bibliography and selected abstracts of world economic literature since 1969. Covers over 350 scholarly journals, dissertations, conference proceedings, collected works, and books.

ERIC (Educational Resources Information Center)

Started by the U.S. Department of Education in 1966, indexes periodicals (EJ numbers) and microfiche documents (ED numbers) of interest to educators, such as conference papers, project descriptions, research reports, teaching ideas, curriculum guides, creative works, statistical data, tests, annotated bibliographies, and state-of-the-art studies. Since late 1980s also mentions books on educational topics.

Government Information

Contains full texts of information from the U.S. federal government on subjects including demographics, legislative histories, agriculture, health, patents, economics, trade, imports/exports, toxic waste, and so on.

Historical Abstracts

Indexes scholarly articles, books, and dissertations written since 1982 on international history (excluding the United States and Canada) since 1450.

LEXIS/NEXIS

Legal and business research database containing general business and current news information. Contains full texts of many daily and weekly periodicals. It also has a database of current federal and state appellate court decisions, including retrospective coverage of decisions from various jurisdictions and lower federal court opinions not published in any printed source.

MARCHIVE

Contains bibliographic index to publications issued by the U.S. government since 1976. This is a key resource for searching government documents.

PAIS (Public Affairs Information Service)

Indexes a selective list of the latest pamphlets, government publications, agency reports, and periodical articles relating to business, economics, public administration, international relations, political science, and other subjects. Includes entries from 1972 to the present.

PC Globe/PC USA

Contains atlas and statistical database of the world and U.S. maps. Displays elevations, major cities, and geographical features. Also gives population and age distributions, health statistics, educational data, trends, political leaders, and more.

PsychLit

Indexes articles from over 1,500 psychology journals since 1974.

Social Work Abstracts

Contains citations and abstracts from 400 social work-related journals since 1977.

Sociofile

Indexes articles dating from 1974 in over 700 periodicals in sociology.

SUPERMAP

Contains data from the 1980 U.S. population and housing census as well as a wide variety of other social and economic data.

OTHER USEFUL SOURCES

There are at least three other sources you should be aware of: government publications, microforms, and interlibrary loan. Finally, don't forget to ask librarians to help you.

Government publications. Besides books and periodicals, you may need to locate government publications, maps, statistics, and the like. Most libraries have an area devoted to government resources, usually staffed by librarians who specialize in government research and who should be able to guide you. For general research of government resources, you can consult both print and computer indexes. The most widely used print index for government research is the *Monthly Catalog of U.S. Government Publications*. This index is similar to other indexes you may have used: It indexes government documents by author, title, and subject. Government documents produced since 1976 are also indexed on computer databases, and most libraries have access to one or more of these databases. (They have various names, so ask your librarian to show you your library's government document databases.) Using the computer database, you can perform searches with author names, titles, subjects, and keywords. The databases are an easy way to search government documents if you are not interested in anything older than 1976. If you are, however, you should consult print indexes.

The government documents area is a lot like a separate library within a library because, for most specialized government research, you need to use research strategies that are often different from the strategies you would use for general library research. Searching for government statistical or census information, for example, requires you to consult very specialized indexes that differ from other government document indexes. The best thing you can do when researching government documents is ask the librarian for guidance.

Microforms. The term "microform" refers to all library material stored on microfilm (rolls of microfilm on a reel) or microfiche (small card-like pieces of microfilm) and viewed with some sort of a magnifier. Microform material often consists of microfilmed copies of valuable historical artifacts and documents. But artifacts are not the only things put in microform. Journal articles, back issues of newspapers and other periodicals, government documents, and unpublished academic papers are also commonly available in microform. Libraries use microform for two general reasons: (1) to make copies of valuable or delicate archival material available to the general public, and (2) to store in compact form documents that would otherwise be too voluminous to store.

Most libraries list much of their microform material in their main on-line catalog, so that is a good place to start your search for microform resources. Libraries also often purchase microform collections (for example, a popular collection for historians is "The Evans and Shaw-Shoemaker Collection of Early American Imprints," a microform collection of material from early American commercial printers), and these collections usually come with their own printed guides or indexes. Consult a librarian to find out which microform collections your library has.

One specialized computer index that is particularly useful for locating microform resources is ERIC (for Educational Resources Information Center). In addition to indexing educational journals, ERIC indexes unpublished scholarly papers that are available in microform. ERIC microform documents have their own numbering system—numbers of microform texts begin with the letters "ED." If you have an ED number, ask a librarian to help you locate it.

Interlibrary loan. No library can afford to buy all the new books printed or subscribe to all the periodicals issued. By agreeing to share their holdings through interlibrary loans, libraries can serve their patrons more effectively. If you need a book or journal article that is not available in your library, consider requesting it through interlibrary loan. It usually takes from one to two weeks to obtain items through interlibrary loan, depending on how far away the lending university is, so you need to determine if the item will still be useful to you by the time you would get it. There may also be a small fee for this service, which will vary depending on how much the cost of interlibrary borrowing is subsidized by your university.

The librarian. With all of the technology for locating sources in today's libraries, it is sometimes easy to overlook the most valuable directional source available to you—the librarian. Librarians are highly skilled at locating information. After listening to you describe your research question for just a few minutes, they can often help you define your search terms better and point you to the indexes, computer tools, and other resources that can best help you answer your question. Don't be shy about asking for the librarian's help.

EVALUATING SOURCES

Once you have used directional sources to identify the books, periodical articles, government documents, microforms, and other printed material that may help you answer your research question, you begin the process of sifting through everything you have located to judge its reliability and its usefulness to you. These two qualities—reliability and usefulness—are related but distinct. Reliability refers to the quality of the source, whereas usefulness refers to the extent to which it helps you answer your question. A source might be reliable but not useful. Conversely, a source might at first appear to be useful, but if you determined it was unreliable, its usefulness would be questionable. Obviously, you want to use sources that are both reliable and useful, so here are some criteria to use in judging each.

SOURCE RELIABILITY

By this point in your education you have no doubt come to realize that not everything in print must be true. As Chapter 1 explained, the production of knowledge in academic disciplines is a social process that uses peer review frequently throughout the process to ensure that the most valid and reliable knowledge is created and disseminated. But not all books and articles are peer reviewed, and some are not as rigorously reviewed as others.

Political dimensions of peer review. Even when rigorous peer review takes place, it is carried out by humans, who can't entirely escape the way their background, education, and values influence their reading of a manuscript. Peer review therefore has a political dimension because politics, simply defined, is the use of power to gain or offer advantage. There are various points in the process of producing knowledge where some people—particularly reviewers, editors, and publishers—have the power to advance or stall the publication of someone else's ideas. Reviewers, editors, and publishers have the power to decide what ideas will gain the stamp of approval in a particular discipline and therefore to help determine which researchers will come to be considered authorities.

Ideological dimensions of research funding. It is also important to remember that much social scientific research requires funding before it can even be started. Social scientists seek funding from universities, government agencies, and private foundations or institutes. These funding agencies also exercise power in determining what counts as knowledge because they may favor some kinds of research projects and not others. In fact, some foundations and institutes have been established to support research that certain groups believe is needed because this research isn't likely to be supported by other funding agencies. For example, according to Carey (1994), some of the data used to support the main argument of *The Bell Curve*, a 1994 book arguing that African-Americans have lower average IQs because of genetic predisposition, comes from research supported by the Pioneer Fund Inc., established in 1937 to finance studies of human genetics and to "encourage reproduction of 'white persons who settled in the original thirteen colonies'" (36). If you question the ideology of a research fund that exists to help "'conserve the population quality of the U.S.'" (Weyher, as cited by Carey 1994, 36), you might also question the reliability of the data used in *The Bell Curve*.

How to evaluate sources. The political and ideological dimensions of the funding and publishing processes should make you properly cautious of swallowing whole the arguments of any documents you locate in the library. You should evaluate the reliability of every document you locate by considering each of the following.

1. **The author's credentials and reputation.** Most books and articles give brief biographical information about the author. In books, this information is often given at the back of the book. In periodicals, it is frequently given in a note on the first or last page of the article. By scanning this information, you can often assess the author's education and current status and learn something of his or her research interests and previous publications. As you gather more documents to answer your research question, you can also check to see if a particular author is cited by others writing on the same topic. If an author's research has earned the respect of his or her peers, you can be more confident about using it yourself.

2. **The publisher's reputation, aims, and emphases.** There are many kinds of publishers, each having different aims and emphases. University presses are among the foremost publishers of academic research; that is usually their reason for being. However, some commercial publishers also define themselves as outlets for certain kinds of academic books. Books from either university presses or academic commercial presses are generally peer-reviewed and likely to be reliable sources. In contrast, many other large commercial publishers are interested in serving the everyday interests of the public and in marketing books that will attract large numbers of readers. Other smaller commercial presses want to fill niches by publishing books that might not otherwise be printed and that meet the special needs of different groups of readers. Books from either of these two kinds of publishers may be reliable sources for academic research, but you should be aware they are not primary publishers of academic research.

    There is one kind of publisher you should especially watch out for—the vanity press. As the name implies, these publishers satisfy the vanity of some authors who want to see their books in print but have not been successful in publishing with a commercial or university press that requires favorable peer review. These authors then pay to have their own books published. Even though your library may have some books from vanity presses on the shelves, their reliability is questionable because they have not been subjected to rigorous peer criticism.

    It's impossible to list all the reputable publishers for the social sciences, but you can start to form impressions of who they are by noticing names of publishers that crop up again and again in the bibliographies of your research sources. You can also ask a professor in your major to name some of the most reputable publishers in your field.

3. **Date of publication.** In most of the social sciences, the publication date can be an important factor in determining the reliability of a source. As research methods are refined and new questions are investigated in a discipline, new findings frequently replace or at least modify older ones, and the general theories of a particular field change accordingly. Therefore, in order to make your own research as reliable as possible, you may want to restrict your research to the most recent publications—or at least view older documents through the perspective of more recent ones.

    If, however, your research is about the historical development of a particular theory, you would want to deliberately choose older sources because they would be considered reliable—even essential—for your purposes. Also, some landmark texts by great innovators in a discipline maintain their relevance over the years, and it is often important to show familiarity with these texts in your writing. (For example, even though the theories of Sigmund Freud are not uniformly regarded as credible today, because his theories were groundbreaking and highly influential, people in many social science disciplines still learn about Freud's work and mention it in their writing.) So you must make decisions about the reliability of older documents based on your purpose, your audience's expectations, and the general regard in which the documents are held.

4. **Type of publication.** There are basically four types of documents you will use to do research in the social sciences: books, periodicals (in both print and electronic formats), government documents, and microforms. These will not be equally pertinent for a given topic. Because recency of publication is frequently an important indicator of reliability, periodicals are likely to be the type of publication you draw on most. But not all periodicals are equal; in most cases, you will want to use professional journals rather than popular magazines and newspapers. Professional journals are refereed, and they contain accounts of original research written by the researchers themselves. Popular magazines and newspapers, on the other hand, contain secondhand information about the latest findings in the social sciences and are usually written by lay reporters. They frequently omit discussion of the methods, and they do not usually qualify and hedge the conclusions the way the authors of the original research do. (There are certainly occasions to use popular magazines and newspapers for research, however; for example, if you were investigating how the news is reported to the public or public reaction to current events, you would have to use popular magazines and newspapers.)

   While periodicals are an important source, you should not overlook the potential of books from reputable publishers that serve academic interests. Books may not be as current as periodicals, since it takes longer for a book to be written and published than it does for a journal article. But authors of books have the advantage of being able to take a wider perspective on their subject and more space in which to develop it. One kind of book that you should particularly consider is the edited volume. Edited volumes, as the name implies, have one or more general editors who assemble a collection of essays on related topics. Each essay is written by an expert on the particular topic. Edited volumes can be an excellent resource if the information in them is still timely.

   Government documents can also be important sources for research questions in several of the social sciences, particularly political science, economics, sociology, and history. Government documents are generally considered reliable because various government agencies have methods and networks for data gathering that can't usually be duplicated by private entities. Microforms can also be an invaluable source of primary data or of information that is not likely to be available in periodicals or books.

5. **Soundness of research.** Even when you have determined that a particular document comes from a credible researcher and reputable publisher and

that it is scholarly and up to date, you must still read it critically. Consider the definitions of key terms and note the methods the author used to create his or her findings: Are they sound and rigorous? Are they well chosen for the question or hypothesis? Have the right statistical tests been used? Scrutinize as well the conclusions the author comes to: Are the conclusions justified on the basis of the evidence? Has the author overlooked other possible interpretations? As you read your sources critically, you will be able to judge how much weight to give them in constructing your own argument.

6. **Reviews and citations.** If you feel somewhat unqualified to judge the reliability of sources, you can relax knowing that people more experienced than you have often made those judgments. Most new books in a field are not only peer-reviewed during the prepublication process, but shortly after publication as well. Most journals print brief reviews of new books, and there are special bibliographies for locating these reviews. Reading the reviews of a book will at least alert you to what reviewers saw as the book's strengths and weaknesses, and it will also make you familiar with the criteria that experts use to judge each other's work.

   By paying attention to which books and articles are cited in the bibliographies of the sources you locate, you will also see what others have considered to be good research. Articles and books that are frequently cited are generally well-regarded. There is even an index, the *Social Sciences Citation Index*, that gives you information about how many times articles and even some books have been cited in a given year. This index will also lead you to the authors who are citing those articles or books.

SOURCE USEFULNESS

While you are determining the reliability of your sources, you should also check their usefulness to you. You do this by skimming the sources to judge whether or not they contain information that will help you answer your research question. This is not to say that you will already have definite ideas of what your paper will be like. You probably won't, and you should remain open to all points of view rather than automatically rejecting certain ones at the outset. Nevertheless, you can begin making decisions about the scope and content of your paper by noting which of your sources contain the facts, evidence, data, and reasoning that seem most pertinent.

Evaluating books. As you scan the books you've located, check each of the following:

The book's index. Look in the book's index for the same terms with which you began your search in the on-line catalog and computer databases. Look for synonyms and related terms as well. Then turn to the pages the index directs you to and skim them to see if they have the kind of information you are seeking.

The preface or introduction. The author of a book frequently gives an overview or summary of the entire book at its beginning, usually in the preface or introduction. Reading this overview can be very helpful to you in judging whether it will be worth your time to read more of the book. Sometimes a book's title sounds very promising, but on closer inspection, you find that the book's focus is too narrow or too broad to be helpful to you.

The table of contents. Look at the chapter titles to determine which ones most closely relate to your topic. Turn to those chapters and skim them quickly.

Headings within chapters. If the author has used them, headings within chapters may allow you to scan even more quickly to locate the kind of information you are seeking.

Evaluating Articles. There are also some quick methods of sizing up a journal article's usefulness to you. Pay attention to the following:

The abstract. Many social science journals require articles to have an abstract, which is simply a summary of the article's contents. The abstract is usually printed directly below the article's title. By reading it you know the purpose or hypothesis of the study, something about the methods, and the major findings and their implications.

The headings. Most articles are divided into sections with descriptive headings that allow you to find what you are seeking. Typical headings are *Introduction, Methods, Results,* and *Discussion.* The *introduction* will tell you the aims of the research and summarize related studies. The *methods* section will tell you how the investigation was conducted. The *results* section describes the findings in words and often includes tables and graphs as well. The *discussion* section interprets the results and makes generalizations about their implications. Sometimes the results and discussion sections are combined. After reading the abstract, you should probably read the discussion section next to see whether the article has implications relevant to your own research. You may also find that it is easier to scan the discussion than the results, where the findings can be presented in language and numbers so technical and complex that you may lack the necessary training to read them easily. Because the discussion interprets the results, you will find that it gives you a grasp of the significance of the research more quickly.

The references. Check the bibliography at the end of the article. From this you can see whether the author of the article has drawn on reputable sources and also whether sources are mentioned you haven't uncovered in your own research. By considering the sources your sources cite, you improve your chances of finding something useful.

As the ideas above suggest, when you are evaluating sources, you should not read them straight through from beginning to end. Rather, you should try to focus on those parts that will help you judge the usefulness of each source. After skimming the books, articles, and other sources you've turned up, you may reject half or more of them as not useful. So it's best to start with a longer list of potential sources than you can really use, given the time and length constraints your teacher has imposed on your paper. For example, if your teacher has assigned a 15-page paper that must be based on a minimum of 10 sources, try to locate 20 or more sources at the start, as you will surely find some of them not useful or reliable. You should aim to make your paper one that includes the best information you can find, not just one that meets the minimum requirements for the number of sources.

RECORDING INFORMATION

After choosing the most reliable and useful sources you can find, you are ready to read them more carefully and decide what you will use in your paper. When you find something useful, rather than trust your memory, you should have a system to record the information. You will need to record two kinds of information: (1) bibliographic information and (2) notes on the facts and ideas you want to borrow from each source.

RECORDING BIBLIOGRAPHIC INFORMATION

As you use directional sources to locate good informational sources, you will find titles (and sometimes abstracts) of books and articles that seem relevant to answering your research question. When you do, write down authors, titles, and call numbers or other information that will help you to retrieve the sources you need. A small pack of 3x5 cards is a handy means to record this information for three reasons. First, cards are small and light, and with a rubber band around them, they are easy to keep in your pocket, backpack, or purse. Second, cards are a uniform size and are therefore easy to shuffle through in order to look for ones you want to keep or discard, or in order to put your sources in alphabetical order for your bibliography. Third, a card is just the right size for writing down the bibliographic information for one book or one article, and if you write it down according to your discipline's documentation style, you won't need to worry about finding that information later when you are finishing your paper's bibliography. Also, you need to write the bibliographic information only once; then, as you take notes, you can simply indicate that the note comes from a certain author and page number. Some students number their bibliography cards and then identify where a note comes from by simply writing the number of the source on the note.

Taking Notes

There are different ways to borrow from your sources, and there are different methods of recording what you borrow, each with its drawbacks and advantages. Regardless of the recording methods you use and how you present what you borrow, you must be careful to avoid plagiarism, so we address this topic first.

Avoiding plagiarism. To *plagiarize* means to use an author's *words or ideas* without acknowledging that you have borrowed them, implying that they are your own. The word *plagiarize* comes from the Latin for "kidnaping." Metaphorically, the etymology is apt because, if you plagiarize, you are kidnaping someone's brain child—claiming to be the originator of something that someone else took the time and trouble to conceive, bring forth, and give their name to. The copyright laws regard plagiarism as the theft of intellectual property, similar to the stealing of real property, such as jewels or furnishings. Legal protection against plagiarism extends not only to written documents but also to sound and video recordings and computer software. There are not only serious legal penalties for plagiarism, but also severe social and professional penalties. Occasionally the news media report on government officials, researchers, academics, and others in the public eye who have had past acts of plagiarism revealed, much to their embarrassment. Such revelations result not only in the loss of credibility and reputation but sometimes in the loss of one's job. For students, the discovery of plagiarism is usually grounds for receiving a failing grade for the plagiarized paper and often for the course in which the plagiarism occurred. Extensive and repeated plagiarism may even be grounds for additional disciplinary action from your college or university.

But fear of repercussions should not be your primary motive for avoiding plagiarism. Your own integrity should motivate you to avoid this form of theft, just as your obligation to the communities you belong to should motivate you to respect the rules that make communal life possible. The temptation to plagiarize will be minimized if you remember that producing knowledge is a social, not solitary, endeavor. By carefully acknowledging what you have borrowed, you demonstrate that you recognize and are grateful for the contributions of earlier researchers. Far from indicating that you are unable to come up with your own ideas, when you document your use of others' ideas, you show that you are well read in your field. By citing your sources, you also point the way for your readers to locate more information, should they desire to. Finally, a carefully documented paper shows the limits of your borrowing and makes your original contributions stand out more clearly against the ground of previous research that your ideas grow from. Your readers will be better able to recognize the extent and judge the value of your own thoughts as you carefully distinguish them from what you have borrowed.

Common knowledge.   There is one qualification of the rule against plagiarism: You are not required to cite a source for "common knowledge." Determining what is common knowledge is often difficult, however, as it depends not only on who the writer is but who the audience is as well. The more educated and specialized both a writer and an audience are, the more likely it is that they can draw particular facts and figures from their store of knowledge without looking them up in other sources. Even though those facts originated with someone, after a period of time these ideas have become so commonplace that their origin is seldom mentioned. As you read your sources, you may see some facts mentioned with no source cited. If you see them mentioned repeatedly, you may assume that these are common knowledge for both the writer and the intended audience.

When you see specific facts mentioned without a citation, however, you need to consider whether they are common knowledge for you and your intended audience. Ask yourself these questions: Did you already know these facts before you began your research? Is it likely that your audience already knows them? If so, you may include them in your paper without a citation. But if you find it necessary to take notes on particular facts, the very act of writing notes suggests that they were not common knowledge for you. You ought to cite at least the source where you first learned them, even if you can't cite the original source. When in doubt, it is safer to cite a source than to assume that something is common knowledge.

TYPES OF BORROWING

There are basically three ways to borrow from your sources: summarizing, paraphrasing, and quoting.

Summarizing.   To summarize is to distill the original source down to its essence, by capturing the main points and ignoring the details. A summary is therefore much shorter than the original. It is also written in your own words, though it might include a few quoted words that you can't adequately express in your own words. Although you write a summary in your own words and style, you still must attribute the ideas to the author from whom you borrowed them.

Paraphrasing.   To paraphrase is to restate the original in your own words and syntax, while still capturing the entire meaning of the original. A paraphrase is thus about the same length as the original, and it parallels the original by following the same order and giving the same emphasis to ideas as the original. A paraphrase might contain a few quoted words or phrases you can't find appropriate synonyms for. When you paraphrase, you do not distort the intent of the original by leaving out ideas or by enlarging minor points or downplaying major points. The value of paraphrasing is that you can give your paper a more coherent voice and point of view by putting source information in your own words. But you still must attribute what you have borrowed to the original author.

Quoting. When you were younger, you may have "written" research papers by simply finding and quoting the exact words of many different writers. Hopefully by now you have learned that quoting is the type of borrowing you should do least; in fact, only about 10–15 percent of your paper should consist of direct quotations. Papers that consist mainly of many quotations strung together with a few transitional sentences tell your reader that you have failed to digest your sources well enough to present the information in your own voice and as support for your unique point of view. Research papers are much more effective if you translate most of your sources into your own words and recombine them in a way that allows you to make your own argument—always documenting your borrowings, of course. That being so, you should quote only under the following circumstances:

1. **When the words of the original are open to several interpretations.** For example, the First Amendment to the U.S. Constitution has been interpreted differently by various groups and at different times by the Supreme Court. If you were writing a paper about the disputes surrounding the First Amendment, it would be important to quote it rather than paraphrase it, since by paraphrasing you might inadvertently favor a particular interpretation.

2. **When the words of a document are the topic you are writing about.** If you are writing about the language of a treaty, a trade agreement, a letter, a diary, or some other primary source, it is essential to quote actual excerpts from it, both to establish what is under discussion and to make your claims about it credible to the audience.

3. **When the words of the original are especially striking and a paraphrase or summary would diminish their impact.** Occasionally one of your sources will provide a phrase, sentence, or paragraph that is particularly well said and memorable. If quoting it verbatim will add strength, insight, and color to your own argument, by all means quote it. But note that you can be selective about how much you choose to quote by paraphrasing or summarizing some of the original and quoting only those words that are particularly striking.

4. **When a quotation will help bolster the authority of the argument you are making.** If you are writing about a controversial topic, trying to persuade a

hostile audience, you and your argument may gain some credibility if you judiciously choose some quotations from respected sources that support your position. Be sure you don't distort the intentions of the original authors, however, by lifting supportive quotations out of their original context and using them in a rather different context.

FIGURE 9-1 Original Passage from Source

Since Malinowski's time, the "method" of participant-observation has enacted a delicate balance of subjectivity and objectivity. The ethnographer's personal experiences, especially those of participation and empathy, are recognized as central to the research process, but they are firmly restrained by the impersonal standards of observation and "objective" distance. In classical ethnographies the voice of the author was always manifest, but the conventions of textual presentation and reading forbade too close a connection between authorial style and the reality represented. Though we discern immediately the distinctive accent of Margaret Mead, Raymond Firth, or Paul Radin, we still cannot refer to Samoans as "Meadian" or call Tipioka a "Firthian" culture as freely as we speak of Dickensian or Flaubertian worlds.

Examples of summary, paraphrase, and quotation. To understand the difference between summarizing, paraphrasing, and quoting, read the passage in Figure 9-1, from James Clifford's Introduction to *Writing Culture: The Poetics and Politics of Ethnography* (1986, 13). Figures 9-2, 9-3, and 9-4 show various ways of adapting this information for use in a paper.

Figure 9-2 shows one possible way the above passage could be presented as a summary in a research paper (with a reference to the source in parentheses).

FIGURE 9-2 Summary of Original Passage

Clifford points out that the distinctive voice of the anthropologist is always present in a classical ethnography, yet the conventions of participant observation since Malinowski have dictated that subjective elements be held in check by objective ones. Thus, the worlds represented in ethnographies are not considered to be the author's creation, as they are in novels (1986, 13).

FIGURE 9-3 Paraphrase of Original Source

Clifford states that the careful balancing of subjective and objective elements has been a part of the "method" of participant-observation since Malinowski's day. It is conceded that ethnographers can't exclude their own experience from their research, since they participate in the culture they are studying and feel empathy for it, yet they are also required to meet "impersonal standards of observation" and maintain an aloofness that will enable them to be "objective." The author's voice could always be heard in the "classical ethnographies," but these ethnographies were written and read in such a way that no one seriously believed the culture described was a function of the author's way of writing. We instantly recognize the unique voice of Margaret Mead, Raymond Firth, or Paul Radin, but even now we don't say that Samoans are "Meadian" nor that the Tipiokan society is "Firthian" in the same way we would call the world represented in a novel "Dickensian" or "Flaubertian" (1986, 13).

Figure 9-3 shows how the same passage could be paraphrased in a research paper. Note that the paraphrase is longer than the summary; in fact, it is about the same length as the original. Note also that it tries to capture every idea of the original, but uses different words and sentence structures. Words that could not be adequately paraphrased are placed inside quotation marks.

The same passage could be quoted in whole or in part. Most likely, though, elements of summary, paraphrase, and quotation would be combined to use the original in a research paper, as Figure 9-4 shows.

FIGURE 9-4 Combined Quotation, Summary, and Paraphrase of Original Source

Clifford notes that "since Malinowski's time, the 'method' of participant-observation has always enacted a delicate balance of subjectivity and objectivity." Because ethnographers can't divorce themselves from their own experience, their research is influenced by their "participation and empathy," but it is simultaneously constrained by "the impersonal standards of observation and 'objective' distance." Thus we can discern an author's voice in a "classical ethnography," but the way it is written doesn't lead us to think that the author's style creates the reality described. We don't call the Samoans Margaret Mead wrote about "Meadian" in the way we would call the world of a Dickens novel "Dickensian" (1986, 13).

As you can see from these examples, summarizing and paraphrasing call on you to comprehend the meaning and structure of a passage before you can put it in your own words. Summary and paraphrase are therefore the preferred ways of borrowing from your sources, because they will allow you to present information knowledgeably and compactly to support your own unique argument.

METHODS OF RECORDING NOTES

As you find useful information in your sources, you will need a method of recording what you wish to borrow. Since you must not deface library materials by marking in them, you have basically three options: photocopying, writing on notecards, and taking notes with a computer.

Photocopying.   Most libraries have several photocopy machines, conveniently permitting you to make your own copies of source material. However, you should observe the copyright laws, which are intended to protect authors by ensuring that they receive fair compensation for their work. These copyright laws include "fair use" guidelines that permit you to make photocopies for your own use (but not to sell or otherwise disseminate) without first seeking permission from the copyright owner and paying a fee for the right to make a copy. Under the fair use provisions, you may make a single copy of the following:

- A chapter from a book
- An article from a periodical
- A short story, short essay, or poem
- A chart, graph, diagram, picture, or cartoon from a book or periodical.

The advantage of making photocopies is that you may then underline, highlight, or write in the margins. You may even cut up your photocopies to rearrange source information as you organize your paper.

One disadvantage is that photocopying can be expensive. Another disadvantage is that you may head home from the library with a stack of photocopies thinking that you have already accomplished much of your research, when in fact the work of reading and digesting, summarizing and paraphrasing still lies ahead of you. Nevertheless, photocopying is a convenient way of gathering information that you can't check out of the library so that you can read it later. Make sure, however, that you get all the information you will need to write a complete citation for the source later, because you must give credit to the author for any material you eventually use.

Writing notecards.   The time-honored method of writing your notes on 3x5 cards is still a good one, if you have the patience to do it. One advantage of notecards is that you must come to grips with your sources as you write the notes. If you choose what you will summarize, paraphrase, and quote as you read, your notes will be all ready to use when you begin drafting your paper. A second advantage is that, because you put one piece of information on each card, you can then shuffle your cards into the order you will use them when drafting your paper.

Some students combine photocopying with notecards. They cut out of their photocopies pieces of information they want to use and then glue these pieces on the cards. That way, they save the time of hand-copying a source yet still have the information in a form that is easy to organize. Whatever you do with note cards, be sure to indicate on them what source you have borrowed the note from. If you have made complete bibliography cards for each of your sources, all you need to write on your notecards is the name of the author (or number you have assigned the source) and the page number you are borrowing from.

Using a computer. Some students avoid the expense of photocopies and save the time it takes to write notecards by typing notes directly into a computer, saving the notes in clearly labeled files. (Some word processing programs have notecard functions that make this easy to do.) If you have a portable computer, you can even take it to the library and take notes from sources you are not permitted to check out. Then in the drafting phase of the paper, you can simply retrieve notes from the files and incorporate them into the text of your paper. The advantages of this method are clear: It saves time, and, if you summarize and paraphrase your sources as you take the notes, it will be easy to fit the borrowed information into the paper later. One disadvantage may be, of course, that you must have enough money to afford your own computer. But even if you don't own a computer, it may be possible to use this method if your campus provides computers that you can use free or for a small fee. That way, your only expense would be for a computer disk and possibly rental time.

SYNTHESIZING INFORMATION

When you have finished taking notes—perhaps even before you are quite finished—you will start to draft your paper. During this final step in creating a research paper, it is useful to know how to make an outline to guide you in drafting; and it is essential to know how to attribute and document the information you have borrowed from your sources. It is also important to understand and follow the format your instructor has specified.

OUTLINING

Since a library research paper is typically longer than other academic writing assignments, you will probably find it helpful to make an outline to guide you as you write a draft. Your outline doesn't have to be a formal one (unless your teacher requires that), but it should show the major divisions of your topic, including the subtopics to be covered in each division, and also the order you will present your ideas in. With an outline, you can organize your notes according to where you will use them in creating your draft. This step will help you see if you have enough information in your notes to create each section of your planned paper. You may find that you have too little information for a certain part; this might mean that you need to go back to the library to find more information, or it might mean that you will have to de-emphasize or even eliminate that section of your paper. On the other hand, you may find that you have too much information for some parts of your planned paper. In that case, you should be selective about what to include or what concepts to focus on. Don't force every note you took into your paper; be willing to discard some of your work, especially if it doesn't fit well anywhere.

DRAFTING

Once you have planned which notes to use where, you begin writing. You don't need to start at the beginning, though most people do. If you have a bit of writer's block about what to say first, start in the middle. Often, writing other parts of your paper will help you see what you need to say at the beginning to set up your main points and the conclusion. Don't be reluctant to change your outline, either, if you find in the middle of drafting that a different organization of your material will improve the paper. You should see the entire paper as somewhat fluid and subject to change because what you write in one part of it will affect what you can or need to write in other parts. Keep working through the various parts of the draft until you feel they have the right connections and emphases.

ATTRIBUTING AND DOCUMENTING

During the drafting phase, as you incorporate borrowed information into the text, be sure to indicate the boundaries of each item you have borrowed. You must do this to differentiate your own ideas and sentences from those that are based on borrowed information. The best way to do this is to give the name of the person from whom you are borrowing as you open the summary, paraphrase, or quotation. This is called *attributing*. Refer again to Figures 9-2, 9-3, and 9-4; notice how each instance of borrowing is introduced with Clifford's name (the attribution) and ended with a parenthetical reference (the documentation). Documentation almost always comes at the end of a borrowed piece of information. By first attributing and then documenting, you can indicate the limits of what you have borrowed and clearly differentiate your own thoughts and words from those of your sources.

If you want to incorporate a particularly long borrowed idea or passage into your paper, such as a paraphrase, you can use the author's name or a pronoun for the author at one or more points in the passage to indicate you are continuing to borrow. At the point you stop borrowing, place the parenthetical reference or the footnote or endnote number that tells your reader more about the source you have borrowed from. (Some common documentation styles used in the social sciences are defined and illustrated in Chapter 20.)

Kelli Boren's research paper, reproduced on the following pages, illustrates how source information can be incorporated into the text by summary, paraphrase, or direct quotation. As you read it, note not only its clear focus and coherent organization, but also pay attention to how Boren has synthesized her sources carefully to make a clear and forceful argument. Note how she presents the research in each major division of the paper and then summarizes its significance for her overall thesis.

FORMATTING THE FINAL DRAFT

The student research paper is a genre that varies from department to department, course to course, and professor to professor, particularly in details of formatting. Although Kelli Boren uses the APA documentation style (see Chapter 20), the format of her paper does not conform strictly to the format prescribed by the APA *Publication Manual*. The reason is that the APA manual is a submission manual for professionals preparing copy manuscripts for publication in a journal. The copy manuscript is a peculiar genre that has a very short life and is not seen by very many people. It is read only by the editor, the reviewers, and the typesetter. Once the copy manuscript has been turned into a typeset article, the copy manuscript is discarded. The typeset article looks very different from the copy manuscript.

Student papers are usually not copy manuscripts. They are final documents, and they reach their intended audience in the form in which they are submitted. This means that, as the APA manual states, for student papers "a number of variations from the requirements described in the *Publication Manual* are not only permissible but also desirable" (p. 332). So, while the format of Boren's paper conforms in many ways to the APA manual's guidelines (principally in its abstract, headings, parenthetical references, and list of references), some of its other features (for example, the title page, the table of contents, and the pagination) were required by her professor.

For any writing assignment you are given, you should learn what special requirements the professor has for you in addition to following documentation specifications of a professional style manual. Your instructor may want you to make your paper look different from Boren's, so keep that in mind as you read her paper. But pay close attention to the annotations in the margins of Boren's paper. They will help you understand some basic principles of citing sources and organizing information in research papers that transcend the boundaries of particular disciplines and style manuals.

A STUDENT EXAMPLE

Maternal Employment and Child Behavior:
Compensating for Negative Effects

The title page is divided
into thirds, with the title in
the top third, the author's
name in the middle, and
the class, teacher, and
date at the bottom.

by

Kelli A. Boren

English 315
Prof. Harker
April 14, 1996

Table of Contents

These divisions of the paper are used as primary and secondary headings in the body of the paper. This table of contents grew out of the outline.

These dots are called "dot leaders."

Prefatory pages are numbered with lower case Roman numerals. The title page is "i" but it is not numbered.

Abstract

This paper analyzes the literature on the effects of maternal employment on child behavior, and it recommends steps mothers can take to minimize any negative effects. The following factors were found to increase negative behavior in children: parenting styles that were overcontrolling, rejecting, or punishing; mothers working between 10–20 hours a week or more than 20 hours a week; inconsistent care or babysitter care for boys; father care for girls or boys; and mothers entering the work force before the child was at least 9 months old. The following factors were found to decrease negative behavior in children: parenting styles that were warm, less controlling, supportive of self-government, and less reliant on physical punishment; mothers who worked less than 10 hours a week; high quality child care; consistent care or care by a relative for boys; mothers entering the work force after a child was 9 months or older. The increasing numbers of working mothers can lessen the impact of their employment on their children's behavior by compensating for any negative factors.

An abstract is a summary of a paper. It states that purpose and thesis of the paper and summarizes each main point. It generally has a neutral, impersonal tone. It is best written after the paper is completed.

Maternal Employment and Child Behavior: Compensating For Negative Effects

Introduction

The title is repeated at the top of the first page of the body.

In 1988 the Bureau of Labor Statistics stated that half of mothers with infants one year or younger were in the work force, and two-thirds of mothers with toddlers between the ages of two and three worked outside the home. Furthermore, experts estimated that by 1995, two-thirds of all infants and toddlers would have an employed mother. These figures represent an increase in the number of working mothers with children under the age of 6 from 2.3 million in 1960 to 7.1 million in 1988. Because of the significant increase in the number of mothers who work, there has been growing concern about the effects of maternal employment on children (Baydar & Brooks-Gunn, 1991).

This parenthetical citation indicates what source the summary of information comes from. Note that the period comes after the reference.

This concern has focused around many topics including child/parent attachment, academic achievement, self-esteem, and child behavior. Of these topics, one of the most significant is whether a mother's employment affects her child's behavior. Parcel and Menaghan (1993) indicate that behavioral difficulties in children pose significant problems because they not only impact a child's immediate circumstances, but may also have long term effects on their ability to positively interact in society. The researchers state that

Long quotations (over 40 words) are indented 5 spaces on the left.

Boren uses ellipses twice to show omission of words from the quotation.

> children who are aggressive, or undercontrolled, during early childhood often persist in this pattern...with long-term repercussions including negative labels from teachers, academic difficulties, and rejection by peers. These consequences disrupt opportunities to develop better social skills, thus encouraging the persistence of aggression.... The anxiety, fearfulness, and social withdrawal that characterize overcontrolled behavior also tend to persist because such behaviors impede normal assertiveness in social situations. (Parcel & Menaghan, 1993, p. 120)

This parenthetical reference has a page number because Boren quoted. Note the period comes before this reference.

These behaviors feed upon each other and then repeat themselves as part of a destructive cycle which affects children not only early on, but throughout their entire lives. To ameliorate any negative effects of maternal employment on child behavior, we must first identify what those effects may be and then find ways to counteract them.

Maternal employment may improve how a child behaves under certain circumstances (Crockenberg & Litman, 1991); however, a significant number of studies have shown that, in general, there is a significant link between mothers who work and problem behavior in their

1

children. These problem behaviors, however, do not stem exclusively from maternal employment but are influenced by many factors: parenting style, the amount of time mothers work each week, the type of child care received by boys versus that received by girls, and child age. Research findings suggest that the negative effects of maternal employment on child behavior are not inevitable and may be lessened if not eliminated. Mothers who work may decrease the negative impact of their employment upon child behavior if they learn which factors may be harmful and then learn how to compensate for those factors.

This sentence overviews the paper.

These sentences are Boren's thesis.

Parenting Style

A level-one heading is centered. The first main division of the paper begins here.

Relationship of Child Behavior to Parenting Style

A level-two heading is flush left and underlined.

The parenting style of mothers was found to be one of the most significant factors in determining how employment affected child behavior. In 1991, MacEwen and Barling conducted a study designed to measure the effect of employed mothers' different parenting styles on child behavior. They measured child behavior by having the mother complete the Revised Behavior Problem Checklist (RBPC) which measured conduct disorder, attention problems/immaturity, and anxiety/withdrawal. Children's anxiety/withdrawal behavior was shown to increase when mothers' parenting style was rejecting, or when mothers avoided interacting with their children. Additionally, when working mothers had a high level of punishing behavior, children's conduct disorders and attention/immaturity behaviors also increased (MacEwen & Barling, 1991). Conversely, when mothers had a strong sense of mastery (feeling of control) in their own lives, they were better able to help their children take responsibility for their actions; as a result, behavior problems decreased (Rogers, Parcel, & Menaghan, 1991).

Effects of Mothers' Work Environment on Parenting Style

Rogers, Parcel, and Menaghan (1991) found that a mother's work environment also influenced parenting style and child behavior. Kohn explained that the complexity of the work in which mothers were engaged and the opportunities that their occupations allowed them to work independently affected "parents' child-rearing values and the kinds of behavior they encourage[d] in their children because they encourage[d] the styles of behavior most conducive to success in their own type of work" (cited in Parcel & Menaghan, 1993, p. 122).

These brackets indicate that Boren changed the verb tense from what it was in the original.

2

Mothers who spent most of their time dealing with people in their occupations reported fewer behavioral problems in their children. In their working environments, these mothers' managers expected them to internalize company rules and standards, develop consistent work habits, and maintain loyalty to the company. Additionally, these mothers had less direct supervision and more freedom to govern themselves. They expected these characteristics of themselves at work, and so they also expected their children to implement many of these same characteristics at home. Mothers working in this environment emphasized internalization of family rules and standards, a high level of personal responsibility, and a low level of parental control. They also relied more heavily on reasoning and explanations than on physical punishment to control their children (Parcel & Menaghan, 1993; Rogers, Parcel, & Menaghan, 1991).

In contrast, mothers who spent most of their time dealing with technical equipment or "things" in their occupation reported the most incidents of uncontrolled child behavior. In their working environment, they learned to follow orders exactly and to match their behavior to the specific demands of the job. Mothers working in these fields were given less opportunity to make their own decisions and come up with creative solutions to problems. At home, these mothers expected the same behavior from their children that they were required to exhibit at work. Mothers working in this environment were more likely to demand strict obedience and conformity, exert too much control, limit their children's independence, use a greater amount of physical punishment, and create an oppressive home atmosphere (Parcel & Menaghan, 1993; Rogers, Parcel, & Menaghan, 1991).

All of these studies point to important factors that may indicate how the parenting styles of working mothers affect the behavior of their children. It is important to note, however, that the researchers' purpose in these particular cases was not to compare the effects of mothers who were employed and mothers who were not. These same parenting styles in mothers who were not employed might have affected child behavior in much the same way.

Effects of Mothers' Use of Positive and Negative Controls

In 1991, Crockenberg and Litman conducted a study which did attempt to compare the effect of parenting styles in mothers who were employed with mothers who were not. They divided parenting styles into positive styles (having a low level of negative control) and

Two sources are cited here.

Boren draws a conclusion from the research cited so far.

Boren begins to summarize here by attributing.

3

negative styles (having a high level of negative control). Negative control was generally defined as control that expressed negative feelings towards the child or intruded upon the child's self-image. Examples of feelings that indicated this type of control were anger, annoyance, criticism, and lack of empathy. Mothers exhibiting this type of control were also more likely to use force or restraint, undermining, spanking or slapping, threatening, restricting freedom of choice, or bribing to obtain their child's obedience.

In the laboratory setting, Crockenberg and Litman found that children of employed mothers who had a high level of negative control were more defiant (refused to follow or did the opposite of their mothers' request) than children whose nonemployed mothers had a high level of negative control. These differences may have occurred because mothers who were not employed were likely to spend more time with their children; consequently, the children may have had more opportunities to share "good times" with their mothers. Perhaps those "good times" compensated for the more stressful situations in which mothers exerted a higher level of negative control. On the other hand, the children of mothers who were employed had fewer "good times" to fall back on during stressful interactions (Crockenberg & Litman, 1991).

There was an interesting difference, however, between employed and nonemployed mothers who exercised a low level of negative control. Children of employed mothers who exercised low levels of negative control were less defiant in the home setting than children of nonemployed mothers. These results indicate that employed mothers can lessen or eliminate the negative effects of their absence by "accommodat[ing] to the circumstances of their [children's] lives by avoiding conflict and increasing their responsiveness when they are with their children" (Crockenberg & Litman, 1991, p. 951). These findings suggest that the quality of maternal care may be more important in determining child behavior than the quantity of time mothers are able to spend with their children (Crockenberg & Litman, 1991).

Mothers must be aware of how their parenting style affects their children's behavior. Regardless of what their work environment may be, mothers must make a conscious effort to adopt parenting styles that will reduce the negative effects that their children may experience because of their employment. Working mothers whose parenting style is negative, overcontrolling, rejecting, or punishing tend to increase bad behavior in their children. However, if mothers allow their children to govern themselves, are less controlling, use

> Boren uses the authors' names again to show she is continuing to summarize from the same source.

> Boren uses brackets again to change a verb tense and to clarify the pronoun "their."

4

Boren draws a conclusion that supports her thesis and ends the first main division of the paper.

less physical punishment and more reasoning, their children will have fewer behavioral problems. When working mothers' parenting styles are positive and constructive, child behavior may be as good as, if not better than the behavior of children whose mothers do not work.

Amount of Time Mothers Work Per Week

The first sentence of this main division of the paper makes an explicit transition from the preceding section. Do not use headings as your only form of transition.

In addition to parenting style, the amount of time that mothers work each week has been shown to affect a child's behavior. Baydar and Brooks-Gunn (1991) found an interesting relationship between these two variables. Children of mothers who worked less than 10 hours per week showed no significant behavioral differences from children whose mothers did not work. However, children whose mothers worked more than 10 hours per week did show more behavior problems. Interestingly, the children who showed the highest number of behavior problems were not the children whose mothers worked full-time, but rather the children whose mothers worked 10 to 20 hours per week.

There are several possible explanations as to why a mother's working 10 to 20 hours may more significantly impact child behavior than a mother's working more than 20 hours a week. Perhaps mothers who know that they will be spending significantly more time away from their children make a greater effort to find their children high quality care, whereas mothers who work only part-time might be less cautious in their child care choices (Baydar & Brooks-Gunn, 1991). It may also be that mothers who work more hours a week are simply better able to afford higher quality care for their children (Parcel & Menaghan, 1993). Spending more than 20 hours a week in an alternative care setting may also provide children with greater opportunities to develop strong and healthy attachments with their care givers, which in turn may reduce the incidence of problem behavior (Baydar & Brooks-Gunn, 1991). On the negative side, mothers who work fewer hours and have a lower household income may also feel a higher level of anxiety than full time working mothers. This higher anxiety level in part-time mothers may negatively affect their parenting styles resulting in greater behavior problems in their children (Rogers, Parcel, & Menaghan, 1991).

Boren again interprets the significance of the research cited in this section, showing how it relates to her thesis.

Regardless of the number of hours that mothers work each week, they should be aware that the quality of care that their child receives while they are away is of extreme importance. Choosing a less expensive, lower quality care facility for children is far more detrimental to the child than it is advantageous to the budget. Mothers should seek out warm and caring environments where their children will be well attended and have the opportunity to form strong attachments with their care givers, even if it costs a little more.

Gender and Type of Child Care

<u>Boys' and Girls' Responses to Day Care</u>

A child's gender has also been shown to be a significant factor in how maternal employment may affect child behavior; boys and girls respond differently to working mothers. Crockenberg and Litman (1991) found that boys whose mothers were employed exhibited a higher level of defiant behavior than boys whose mothers were not employed. Their behavior was also more defiant than the behavior of girls, regardless of whether or not the girls' mothers worked. Several other studies cited by Crockenberg and Litman also concluded that boys have a more difficult time adjusting to maternal employment than girls. For example, Brofenbrenner and Crouter (1982), and Hoffman and Nye (1974) both found that boys' ability to interact with adults and children their own age was affected by whether or not their mothers worked. Vandell (1989) also found that boys whose mothers had worked extensively during their first two years of life had more difficulty interacting with their parents, teachers, and peers (cited in Crockenberg & Litman, 1991).

Other studies further indicate that boys may be more sensitive than girls to the type of childcare they receive when their mother is at work. Baydar and Brooks-Gunn (1991) found that girls responded favorably to baby-sitter care, but boys responded more favorably to care by a grandmother or other relative. Additionally, Crockenberg and Litman (1991) found that boys were less able than girls to adapt to a "multiple care arrangement" (p. 951), and responded best to consistent care given by a relative (Crockenberg & Litman, 1991). Baydar and Brooks-Gunn (1991) concluded that boys were more vulnerable than girls to low quality child care, less attentive or less attached care givers, and inconsistent environments.

<u>Effects of Being Cared for by Fathers</u>

Results conflict, however, concerning the effect of a father's full-time care of his children. Crockenberg and Litman (1991) found that father care was beneficial to children of mothers who worked

Boren cites three secondary sources here, giving authors and dates. She read about them in Crockenberg & Litman, so they are not in her list of References.

A brief quotation is embedded in this summary, so a page number follows immediately.

6

full-time in regards to the attachments that children were able to form. They found that children who were cared for by their fathers developed secure attachments and had high levels of quality care. However, Crockenberg and Litman only analyzed the level of attachment children had with fathers in these situations and did not consider the effect of such child care arrangements on child behavior. Baydar and Brooks-Gunn (1991), however, did specifically study the effects of father care on child behavior. They found that children who had been cared for by their fathers scored higher in behavioral problems on the BPI (Behavioral Problems Index)[1] than children who received other forms of child care throughout the day. The researchers concluded that "fathers who were the main care providers were probably unemployed, with associated problems in emotional well-being and self-esteem" (p. 943). Because of these problems, the researchers concluded that the children might be better off in some other form of child care (Baydar & Brooks-Gunn, 1991).

Although it is essential to all children that mothers seek out the highest quality care possible, it is important to note that boys may be more vulnerable than girls to lower quality care. Boys benefit best from care by a relative. When relative care is unavailable, mothers should find one care giver who will provide her child with individual attention, an opportunity to form strong attachments, and a consistent environment. Full-time father care is usually not beneficial for children of either gender and should therefore be avoided.

Child Age

Another significant factor in determining the effects of maternal employment on a child's behavior is the age of the child when the mother begins work. Crockenberg and Litman (1991) cited studies by Farber and Egeland (1982), Rubenstein and Howes (1983), and Schwartz, Strickland, and Krolick (1974) which found that children whose mothers placed them in child care before two years of age were more angry and aggressive towards adults and peers and were less likely to comply with care giver requests (Crockenberg & Litman, 1991). Baydar and Brooks-Gunn (1991) also found that there were significant negative behavioral effects on children whose mothers worked during the second or third quarter of a child's first year. They did find, however, that these negative effects were minimal if the mothers only worked during a child's first three months (although they found only a few instances where mothers limited their employment to this period). Negative behavioral effects were

7

Boren gives an endnote number here to alert the reader to a content note at the end of the paper.

Boren draws more conclusions at the end of this section to support her thesis.

also lessened if the mothers delayed employment until the last quarter of the child's first year or if mothers waited to return to work until the child was two or three. They concluded that the negative effects of maternal employment were lessened after these times because of one of three reasons: the children would have been allowed more time with their mother, child cognitive and emotional level would be more developed, or mothers who delayed employment had some other characteristic that was significant (Baydar & Brooks-Gunn, 1991). It should be noted, however, that Baydar and Brooks-Gunn's findings may need to be qualified because they failed to show the effects of the intensity of maternal employment during infancy and the effects of employment when it continues past infancy (Greenstein, 1993).

The best way to eliminate any negative effects of maternal employment on child behavior that result from a child's age is simply to delay a return to work until the child is at least nine months old. By this time, a child has developed a greater sense of self and of the mother's presence. Such a child may be better able to deal with temporary separation than a child who is less cognitively mature.

Boren again interprets the research and relates it to her thesis.

Conclusion

While research indicates that all of the above elements may adversely affect a child's behavior when mothers work, it is important to note that these negative effects can be lessened or eliminated. Although factors involving work may contribute to misbehavior, work in and of itself is not the problem. The behavior of children whose mothers work can be just as good as or better than the behavior of children whose mothers do not. If working mothers make a conscious effort to counteract the factors that may negatively impact their children's behavior, they may avoid many behavioral problems.

Boren's conclusion restates the thesis. By this point the reader should have been persuaded to agree.

Endnotes

1 *"Behavior Problems Index (BPI).* The BPI was developed for children ages 4 to 17 by Zill and Peterson (cf. Peterson & Zill, 1986), with items drawn primarily from the Child Behavior Checklist (Achenbach & Edelbrock, 1981) as well as from other problem checklists (Graham & Rutter, 1968; Kellam, Branch, Agrawal, & Ensminger, 1975; Rutter, Tizard, & Whitemore, 1970). Consisting of 28 items of maternal report, the BPI has six subscales: antisocial, anxious-depressed, headstrong, hyperactive, immature dependency, and peer

This endnote is called a "content endnote" because it gives an explanation rather than a bibliographic citation. Boren wanted her readers to know about the BPI, but she didn't think this information belonged in the body of the paper.

conflict-social withdrawal." (Chase-Lansdale, Mott, Brooks-Gunn, & Phillips, 1991, p. 922)

References

Baydar, N., & Brooks-Gunn, J. (1991). Effects of maternal employment and child-care arrangements on preschoolers' cognitive and behavioral outcomes: Evidence from the children of the National Longitudinal Survey of Youth. *Developmental Psychology, 27,* 932–945.

Chase-Lansdale, P. L., Mott, F. L., Brooks-Gunn, J., & Phillips, D. H. (1991). Children of the National Longitudinal Survey of Youth: A unique research opportunity. *Developmental Psychology, 27,* 918–931.

Crockenberg, S., & Litman, C. (1991). Effects of maternal employment on maternal and two-year-old child behavior. *Child Development, 62,* 930–953.

Greenstein, T. N. (1993). Maternal employment and child behavioral outcomes: A household economics analysis. *Journal of Family Issues, 14,* 323–354.

MacEwen, K. E., & Barling, J. (1991). Effects of maternal employment experiences on children's behavior via mood, cognitive difficulties, and parenting behavior. *Journal of Marriage and the Family, 53,* 635–644.

Parcel, T. L., & Menaghan, E.G. (1993). Family social capital and children's behavior problems. *Social Psychology Quarterly, 56,* 120–135.

Rogers, S. J., Parcel, T. L., & Menaghan, E.G. (1991). The effects of maternal working conditions and mastery on child behavior problems: Studying the intergenerational transmission of social control. *Journal of Health and Social Behavior, 32,* 145–164.

In APA style, the bibliographic entries are called "References."

REFERENCES

American Psychological Association. 1994. *Publication manual.* 4th ed. Washington, DC: American Psychological Association.

Carey, John. 1994. Behind the bell curve. *Business Week*, 7 November, 36.

Clifford, James. 1986. Introduction: Partial truths. In *Writing culture: The poetics and politics of ethnography*, eds. James Clifford and George E. Marcus, 1–26. Berkeley: University of California Press.

Herrnstein, Richard J., and Charles Murray. 1994. *The bell curve: Intelligence and class structure in American life.* New York: Free Press.

10

USING THE INTERNET AS A SCHOLARLY RESOURCE

In addition to print sources of information found in libraries, scholars are increasingly turning to electronic sources—electronic mail, journals, archives, discussion lists, bulletin boards, and other locations—to gather data, look up information, query colleagues, or otherwise carry out research. All of these sources are available on the Internet, a computer network that is becoming an increasingly important research tool, one that few scholars can afford to ignore if they look forward to staying alive professionally. This chapter will give you a brief introduction to this important resource.

Because the Internet is constantly changing and expanding, however, some of this information may be out of date by the time you read it. If you are already an Internet user, you will probably find this chapter elementary. But if you are a beginner, it should help acquaint you with some of the characteristics and functions of the Internet. Even though you can learn a lot about the Internet by just logging on and starting to browse, this introduction may help make your browsing a little more purposeful and informed. (Terms in boldface type are defined in the glossary at the end of this chapter.)

HOW THE INTERNET WORKS

The Internet evolved out of a government experiment called ARPAnet, which was started 20 years ago. Government experimenters created ARPAnet by connecting several computers located in different parts of the western United States in order to form a small network. These networked computers were able to send messages to one another, and they were linked in such a way that messages between computers could travel any of several different paths. That way, if part of the network became disabled, messages between computers could simply follow another path and still arrive at their destination.

Government agencies and computer scientists then began setting up small networks similar to ARPAnet around the country, and they soon realized that all of these small networks could be linked together to form one large network. Many people and organizations started using this growing supernetwork, and it became known as the Internet. Now virtually anyone who has the proper equipment and is willing to pay the necessary fees can access the Internet.

The Internet works much like the United States interstate highway system—hence the term *information highway*, a common nickname for the Internet. Just as interstate highways connect all the major cities in the nation, the Internet connects all the computers that access it. But, just as there are very few direct routes between any two major cities on the interstate highway system, there are very few direct links between computers. For example, to get from Portland to Denver, you could take Interstate 84 to Interstate 80, and then take Interstate 25. In much the same way, to go from one computer to another on the Internet, you would have to travel several connected paths, perhaps passing through many computers along the way. Just as there are several different possible ways to get from Portland to Denver on the highways, there are many different ways to get from one computer to another on the Internet.

ACCESSING THE INTERNET

There are various ways to gain access to the Internet. Some ways provide more access to Internet services and information than others. You should learn what the options are on your campus for gaining access to the Internet, what kinds of services you can expect to have, and what fees, if any, you may have to pay.

ACCESS THROUGH A PROVIDER

The most limited form of access is through what is called an access provider. A commercial access provider, such as America Online, Compuserve, or Prodigy, provides you a connection to the Internet from its computer network. Typically, with this form of access, you cannot use all Internet functions—just the ones made available to you through your access provider.

ACCESS THROUGH A HOST COMPUTER

Another way to access the Internet is through a **host computer**. Most colleges and universities have computers that are linked directly to the Internet for 24 hours a day, seven days a week. As a student, you can usually purchase an account on one of these host computers for a relatively small fee. With an account, you can log in to the host computer from various locations, either on campus through the school's computer network or from home with a **modem**. After you've logged in, your terminal acts just like a terminal hooked up to the mainframe. At this point, you will not be using software on your system; you will be using the host's software, giving you access to as much of the Internet as the host computer has.

Accessing the Internet through either a provider or a host computer gives you ample opportunity to use its services and information, some of which are explained next.

USING THE INTERNET AS A SCHOLAR AND RESEARCHER

There are several important services the Internet can provide that are likely to help you in your research. These are E-mail, **OPACs**, electronic journals, and electronic conferences.

E-MAIL

Electronic mail, or "E-mail," is becoming a popular way to communicate because it is very quick and virtually free to anyone who has paid the initial fee to purchase an E-mail "box" on a host computer. With E-mail, you can send a message from one word to several pages long, and it will arrive at your addressee's E-mail box in a matter of minutes, whether your addressee is across town or across the ocean. E-mail makes possible the following kinds of participation in scholarly conversations.

Joining discussion lists. A discussion list is simply a group form of E-mail. Lists are organized to allow people who share in an interest in a particular topic to discuss their interest with others electronically. People interested in joining a particular discussion list add their name and E-mail address to the list by sending a short E-mail message to the list's central address. Then, whenever any member of the list sends an E-mail message to the list's central address, the message is automatically sent to each name and E-mail address on the mailing list. In this way, the members of the list can exchange ideas, ask questions, respond to queries, or debate any issues that come up on the list.

There is an amazing variety of discussion lists. People have formed lists to discuss everything from fly-fishing to psychobiology. Some lists are more serious than others, and many are centered on academic topics. You can find lists devoted to both general and very specialized fields of academic inquiry. Many scholars use these lists as places to exchange ideas, get feedback about projects, and give advice to others about their academic questions and pursuits. Discussion lists have made it much easier for scholars and researchers to include people from all over the world in their research communities.

One of the best things about electronic discussion lists is that virtually anyone can join or leave them at anytime. You can find a relatively complete index of discussion lists in the *Directory of Electronic Journals, Newsletters, and Academic Discussion Lists*, which should be available in your campus library or in a local bookstore. Search this directory for lists in your field; then, if you find an interesting one and if you have an E-mail address, you can subscribe by following the instructions given with the address. Once you have subscribed, you will receive messages that other members post to the discussion list. You don't have to post messages to a list in order to be a member of it. Reading messages but seldom or never sending any is generally referred to as "lurking." Although it sounds devious, it is acceptable Internet behavior, and you can learn a great deal simply by reading the postings to a discussion list. However, if you feel you have something to add to the conversation, you should certainly post messages too.

Gathering data and information. E-mail can be a very efficient tool for gathering data, especially survey data. Because any message you post is automatically circulated to every member of the list, you could use a discussion list to send a questionnaire or some other call for response to many people—possibly hundreds. However, before posting any sort of survey to a discussion list, get permission from the list's manager or mediator (you can do this easily through E-mail).

Because E-mail is a quick, inexpensive, and far-reaching form of communication, it can be a good way to collect information from people in other regions or nations. For example, from the United States, you could contact someone in Russia and ask him or her about the political or social situation there, getting valuable, first-hand information about a topic you might be researching.

Contacting or collaborating with other scholars. You can also use E-mail to contact a scholar personally, perhaps to ask a question about that scholar's area of expertise (assuming, of course, that the person has an E-mail address). The chances are good that someone you contact will respond to your message because E-mail is so quick and easy to use—a person can type a response in a matter of seconds and then simply press a key to send it. In fact, you may have more success getting a response using E-mail than you would by leaving a phone message or sending a letter.

E-mail also makes it possible for two or more people to collaborate with one another on a research and writing project, though they may be hundreds of miles apart. They can insert or attach drafts of a document to E-mail messages and get much quicker feedback from each other than if they used conventional mail. This method of collaboration is also less expensive than using long distance telephone calls to discuss the project.

Accessing OPACs (On-Line Public Access Catalogs)

With **telnet** you can access the computerized card catalogs (or "OPACs," as librarians refer to them) of over a thousand libraries from all over the world. Once you have accessed the OPAC of another library, you can search that OPAC just as if you were sitting at one of that library's terminals.

The Denver Public Library, for example, has an OPAC that is accessible through telnet: the Colorado Alliance of Research Libraries, or CARL. This OPAC's address is *pac.carl.org* and its log-in word is *pac*. It is a favorite OPAC of librarians, and with it you can explore all of Colorado's libraries or you can access other OPACs in the United States that are linked to CARL (and there are many). You can access other OPACs all over the world. Your librarian should be able to tell you what those addresses are and give you more information about using the Internet to search remote OPACs. Other libraries' OPACs can be valuable research resources, because by searching them, you may turn up titles that your school's library doesn't carry and then request those titles through interlibrary loan.

Electronic Journals

Increasingly, scholars are publishing their work in paperless electronic journals. Electronic journals are similar to the traditional paper journals you find on the library shelves, except they exist as files on a computer, rather than as bound, printed pages, and you read them on a computer screen.

Unfortunately, there is still no complete on-line index of electronic journals, so, in order to find electronic journals, you should consult a print index such as the *Directory of Electronic Journals, Newsletters, and Academic Discussion Lists*. There are few indexes that organize electronic journal articles by subject or author, so you have to browse through journal issues to find what you need. However, you should watch for developments in this area of Internet technology—computer scientists and librarians are close to developing computerized indexes that search electronic journals by subject or keyword, much as specialized databases on local area networks in libraries search print journals.

There are four basic ways to access electronic journals: through E-mail lists, gophers, **File Transfer Protocol** (FTP), or the **World Wide Web** (these access methods are all described later in the chapter). Many electronic journals are accessible by more than one of these methods—some are accessible by all four. Indexes listing electronic journals will contain the address or addresses of both current and back issues.

ELECTRONIC CONFERENCES

Researchers in the social sciences regularly hold professional conferences at which they present papers to each other about their most recent research. These conferences are usually held in various large cities to which the participants must travel and then stay in hotels for several days. With the advent of the Internet, scholars are beginning to hold on-line conferences, either in place of or in addition to actual conferences. To participate, they post their papers, or abstracts of them, to a given address; then a **home page** is set up on the World Wide Web (discussed later in this chapter) that interested readers can log in to and retrieve these papers to read on their own computers. This method of interaction obviously saves people the time and expense of attending the conference; or even if they do attend, it can allow them to read papers they may not have had the opportunity to hear.

RETRIEVING INFORMATION FROM THE INTERNET

There are several ways of exploring the Internet and accessing the information it offers. Besides documents, you can find pictures, videos, graphics, and sound clips. The following descriptions of Internet functions will give you a general overview rather than specific details about how each function works.

TELNET

With the Internet function known as telnet, you can log in to distant host computers. Telnet is a very simple function to use: Simply type *telnet* at your computer's **prompt**, or select *telnet* from the menu. Then type the address of the distant host computer you want to log in to. Since logging in to a computer often requires a password, many telnet addresses include the necessary password. For example, the telnet address for one computer that holds online history databases looks like this:

Address: *ukanaix.cc.ukans.edu*
Login password: *history*

To access this host computer, you would type *telnet ukanaix.cc.ukans.edu* at your computer's prompt, and after establishing a connection, you would type *history* when the host asked for a password or log-in word.

Pay careful attention to any commands required to access a host computer, because those are the only commands that computer will respond to. You should pay special attention to the commands that let you exit or disconnect, like *escape* or *quit*, because you may get stuck or lost in the remote computer. You should jot these commands down when you find them.

GOPHERS

Until recently, it was very hard to find information or resources about specific topics on the Internet because everything was so unorganized. It was a lot like trying to find things in a library without using indexes or card catalogs. However, finding information on the Internet has become a bit less daunting with the creation of Internet gophers. Gophers organize information and resources on the Internet and display them in menu form. (Of course, because not all Internet information can be accessed through gopher menus, you may need to use other methods besides gophers when searching for information.)

You can select text files from gopher menus, in which case the gopher retrieves the file you selected and displays it on your screen, or you can select connections to other computers, in which case the gopher establishes the connection for you in a matter of seconds. Gopher menus are often connected to other gopher menus so that, by starting from one gopher menu, you can connect to another and another and another, going on indefinitely.

Most Internet host computers maintain their own gopher menu. If you access the Internet through a host, your host's gopher may be a good place to become familiar with gophers and start exploring the Internet. To get to your host's gopher menu, either select "gopher" from the opening menu or type "gopher" at the computer's prompt. Gopher is very easy to master and the best way to learn about it is simply to log on and start using it.

FILE TRANSFER PROTOCOL (FTP)

The abbreviation *FTP* refers to "file transfer protocol," a popular Internet function that transfers files from one computer to another. Many computers on the Internet have archives of data and text files available for public access that you can copy to your own computer's memory using FTP. For example, there is a public FTP archive at the address *ftp.loc.gov* giving a directory of files which contain the minutes of top-secret Soviet government meetings. You could use FTP to copy these files to your computer, where they might be useful in a research project on Soviet government.

The World Wide Web makes FTP simple to use. The next section explains what the World Wide Web is and how you can use it to transfer files with FTP.

WORLD WIDE WEB

The World Wide Web (WWW or "the Web" for short), as its name implies, is an interconnected collection of information "sites." Anyone with the proper access can set up a site on the Web to provide information for other users to access. Each of these sites has a **home page** that provides a starting point into a hypertext, a type of document that you don't have to read in a linear pattern, that is from top to bottom and left to right. Instead, you can read associatively, jumping from one part of a text to another, following the path of your curiosity, rather than some predetermined route through the information. Using a **mouse** to point and click, you can select highlighted words or images, called **links**, in a hypertext that will connect you to other files not displayed on the screen you are looking at. These other files may be texts or images or sound. By going from hypertext file to hypertext file, you can browse the Internet indefinitely (this is called "surfing the Web" by experienced Internet users).

The World Wide Web is very easy to use if you are familiar with a few key concepts and terms. The Web is accessible in various formats, depending on the type of **browser** installed on your host computer. One popular, easy-to-use browser is *Netscape*. Netscape is based on the **Windows operating system**, a system which allows you to use a mouse to select links and navigate the Web.

In addition to surfing randomly, you can navigate the Web more purposefully. Home pages and other hypertext pages on the Web have addresses called **URL**s, for "Uniform Resource Locator." A typical URL looks like the example below, the URL for a social sciences-related hypertext document:

http://doradus.einet.net/galaxy/Social-Sciences.html

Rather than "surfing" the Web searching for information, you can type in a particular URL and have WWW retrieve the corresponding document.

Locating information on the World Wide Web. If you don't have time to surf the Web and if you are not sure what URL to type, Netscape allows you to do keyword searches of the Web. To do a keyword search on Netscape, for example, simply select the function "Net Search" from the **toolbar** and type in your keyword or words. Netscape will then search the Web and display a list of hypertext documents that contain your keyword(s).

Another Web tool that is valuable for locating information on a specific topic is a search engine, such as WebCrawler or Yahoo!. Yahoo! is a hierarchically organized directory to thousands of Web sites. The URL for Yahoo! is *http://yahoo.com*. By typing in this URL, you can zero in on the kind of information you're hoping to find. You will first see a list of very general categories of information, such as "Arts," "Science," or "Social Science." Using a mouse to point and click on a word in this list, you will get another list of more specific terms. For example, if you select "Social Sciences," you will get a list of subdisciplines, everything from "Aboriginal Studies" to "Women's Studies." Then by selecting one of these terms, you will get the various divisions of each subdiscipline. Eventually, you will get to home pages and the addresses of discussion lists on the specific topic that interests you.

Using FTP and Gopher with World Wide Web. You can use FTP and gophers with the Web by converting the FTP or gopher address into a URL address. To convert an FTP or gopher address, put it in the format *ftp://[FTP site address]* or *gopher://[gopher site address]*. For example, you could access the FTP site at *ftp.loc.gov* through the World Wide Web by using *ftp://ftp.loc.gov* as the URL address. Or you could access the gopher site at *gopher.stat-usa.gov* through the World Wide Web by using *gopher://gopher.stat-usa.gov* as the URL address.

Once you type in an FTP or gopher URL, World Wide Web browsers such as Netscape display the gopher menu or the directories of FTP files as hypertext links. You can then select interesting links and the browser will quickly retrieve and display the documents you select.

THE PROS AND CONS OF USING THE INTERNET FOR RESEARCH

Up to this point, the tone of this chapter has been rather enthusiastic about the potential of the Internet as a research tool. However, you should understand that there are some drawbacks to this exciting technology. Two of these have to do with the rapidity of technological change and the reliability of Internet information.

RAPID TECHNOLOGICAL CHANGE

The fact that the Internet is constantly growing and changing makes it both a valuable and a challenging resource—valuable because it is constantly adding more services and information, yet challenging because it is difficult to keep up with changes that occur so rapidly. One advantage of the Internet's instability is that people are always creating ways to make it easier to use—in other words, it keeps changing for the better. For example, finding information on the Internet is becoming less and less difficult, thanks to tools like gophers and World Wide Web browsers.

However, even with organizers like gopher and browsers like Netscape, Internet information remains rather poorly organized when compared to printed information in libraries. The Internet is like a giant encyclopedia that is constantly growing and changing yet one that has no general editor to make its contents uniform in quality or appearance and has only a partial table of contents or index. We are not far from having more advanced indexing methods that will allow us to more easily search electronic journals and other Internet resources by keyword, subject, title, or author. Now, however, except for some electronic journals, much of the information on the Internet is not organized for easy retrieval. Much of it is also not refereed—which brings up the second problem, the questionable reliability of information on the Internet.

RELIABILITY

Since just about anybody with the right access and tools can put information on the Internet, it is important to evaluate the reliability of data on the Internet. Just as you do with printed information, you can best determine whether Internet information is trustworthy by learning something about its source. If you have found an article in an electronic journal, for example, you should find out if its author is considered credible and if the article was reviewed by authoritative peers in the field before electronic publication. You can usually locate this information rather easily—reliable electronic journals include a file containing their editorial policies and a list of people on their editorial board, or they give this information in each issue.

Just as you can evaluate books for reliability by knowing something about the publisher, you can sometimes determine the reliability of Internet information by evaluating the site where you find it—the home page, the sponsor of the database, or the owner of the discussion list. You should be able to learn easily who created the site and how you can contact them. If the information you've found comes from a government-sponsored site, or if it comes from a university-sponsored site, it is likely to be reliable. However, you should check to see whether information at a particular electronic site is comprehensive and updated periodically. By checking the links in a particular hypertext, for example, you can find out whether they lead to other apparently credible hypertexts, or whether they lead you to links that are no longer there or that are of questionable value.

Finally, you can simply read the information you find on the Internet to try to judge the politics and ideology—and therefore the agenda—of the person or persons who created the information and put it on the Internet. Remember that anyone with an ax to grind can create a home page or start a discussion list as a way of trying to put biased information out for public consumption. Just as you do with printed information, you should read Internet information critically, analyzing the assumptions and the motives of its authors.

At this point, scholarly print sources tend to be more reliable than electronic ones because of the careful peer review process they are put through. University librarians scrutinize print sources and use their budgets to acquire the books and journals they consider most reliable. However, librarians do not systematically scrutinize and categorize electronic information to determine its reliability. Not only do they lack the time and training to do so, but also the criteria for judging the reliability of Internet information are still being developed. Despite these problems, librarians realize that the Internet has great potential as a scholarly resource, and they are working to make it more accessible and useful for researchers. Their goal, however, will not be to acquire and store electronic information (this information is already available outside of libraries to any user with access to a computer); rather, they are more likely to work on identifying paths to good collections of electronic information and then make those paths known to researchers.

ETHICS AND ETIQUETTE ON THE INTERNET

The Internet is relatively unregulated by the government or any other organization, which makes it very important that Internet users adhere to some rules of etiquette so that the Internet will continue to be a valuable resource for everyone. These rules are not imposed by any authorities; instead, they were developed democratically, coming from the users of the Internet themselves as they have collaborated in creating research and archival tools that will serve a wide range of users. You should be aware of the following rules as you use the Internet.

Use E-mail Conscientiously and Respectfully

When posting messages to discussion lists, remember that you are writing to a large group of people who may interpret your message differently from how you intend it to be interpreted. You should therefore avoid using sarcasm because people may not realize you are using a sarcastic tone. You should never post abusive or obscene messages to discussion lists. If you do, other members of the list may write to the administrator of your host computer, who in turn may deny you access to the Internet.

Finally, remember that any E-mail message you send, whether to a discussion list or a friend, could potentially become public knowledge. Your host administrators may be able to read your mail, or your mail may be misdirected and end up in the wrong E-mail box. Even after an addressee has deleted your message, it may remain on a host system's backup tapes. It is best to avoid writing anything that you would not want read by the public.

Respect Your Host Computer

If you access the Internet through a host computer (as a student, you most likely will), you can help your host continue to provide you and other users with the same level of service at the same price if you remember a few things. First, if you have an electronic mail box, you should make sure it doesn't get overfilled. Delete unwanted mail messages regularly, and, because your host has a limited amount of disk space for each user, keep the number of messages you save to a minimum. Remember that you can **download** messages to your own computer in order to free up space in your host computer's memory. And if you are going to be away from your E-mail box for more than a week, you should temporarily unsubscribe yourself from discussion lists so that your mail box doesn't overfill.

Limit Internet Traffic

When using services such as telnet and FTP, remember that other users may be trying to access the same computer site as you. Since computers can allow access to only a limited number of users at one time, don't remain logged in for longer than you need to. Finally, when using FTP to copy files, try to copy large files after business hours; it will be faster for you and more convenient for others that way.

Obey Copyright Laws

You should not assume that information available on the Internet is exempt from copyright laws. Check for any copyright information included with files and observe any restrictions on the use of copyrighted information.

CONCLUSION

The Internet's importance as a research tool is likely to grow as the technology improves and as scholars, particularly librarians and information specialists, devise better ways of judging and indicating the reliability of information and of identifying paths to the most reliable information. As you participate in the virtual community of scholars linked electronically, you can contribute to the definition of standards and practices that are likely one day to make the Internet as important as libraries now are for information storage and retrieval.

GLOSSARY

Browser: A program that is used to look at different Internet resources. A browser organizes and displays Internet information in the form of text, graphics, and even sound and video. A browser allows users to "navigate" the Internet, locating and viewing Internet resources.

Download: To copy a file or set of files to one's personal disk or terminal.

File Transfer Protocol (FTP): A program that is commonly used to move files between two Internet sites. FTP allows users to log in to remote computers in order to send or receive files.

Home page: A screen of information and links that serves as a starting point for accessing the World Wide Web.

Host computer: A central computer on a network that acts as a repository of services available to other computers on the network. A host computer will commonly provide several different services. For example, a host computer for university students may provide Internet access, E-mail access, and access to the university's on-line library catalog.

Link: Sometimes called a "hyperlink" or "hot button," this is a highlighted word or phrase on a Web page that, when selected, will connect to and display another Web document. Users who create Web pages use links to give other users access to Web documents that seem interesting or are relevant to the information on the original Web page. For example, a Web page on the subject of jazz might include the highlighted name *Louis Armstrong*, which users could select in order to go to a Web page with more information about Louis Armstrong.

Modem: A device used to connect one computer to another over a phone line.

Mouse: A common pointing device. It allows a computer user to move and control a pointer on the computer screen. A mouse has one or more buttons that are used to select whatever the on-screen pointer is touching.

OPAC: A common acronym used by librarians to stand for On-Line Public Access Catalog. In other words, an OPAC is a computerized catalog of a library's general resources.

Prompt: The symbol that a computer displays to show that it is ready for a user to type in a command.

Select: To activate a computer function or hypertext link. A mouse is the most common selecting device; it is used to position the on-screen pointer on the desired link or menu item, after which pushing the mouse button will activate the function or link.

Telnet: A program that allows users to get from one computer on the Internet to another. Telnet allows users to log in to remote computer systems.

Toolbar: In graphical browsers such as *Netscape,* the toolbar is a display of functions, usually located at the top of the screen. The toolbar resembles a panel of buttons, and each button is selected with the on-screen pointer and the mouse. When a toolbar button is selected, its corresponding function will be activated.

Windows operating system: Currently the most popular computer operating system, Windows is an operating system that displays both text and graphics. Windows-based programs commonly have toolbars and other icons that make computer functions easy to execute. Windows-based programs usually require a mouse.

IV

COMMON SOCIAL SCIENCE GENRES

In Part IV of this book, you will learn about some common genres that are related to the main genres (illustrated in Part II) that social scientists write in to present their research findings. In Chapter 11, you will learn about proposals, which social scientists write to seek funding or permission to carry out their research. You will also learn about prospectuses, detailed and formal rationales and outlines of what will be included in a long document.

Chapter 12 presents examples of two kinds of writing social scientists sometimes do for a public audience, rather than the specialized audience of their peers. These are position papers and opinion pieces. In these genres, the writers draw on their specialized knowledge to offer a solution to a problem or a professionally informed opinion about a current issue to the general public. Instead of following the rhetorical conventions of their more scholarly genres, the authors use a simpler, more general vocabulary and write in a form that will keep their audience's interest and hopefully persuade them to act for the general good.

Chapter 13 describes and illustrates abstracts, critiques, and reviews. Knowing how to write in each of these genres is important because each one plays an important role in constructing the shared body of knowledge in any field. Writers of critiques evaluate documents for their peers to help improve them before they are published. Abstracts and reviews, written after documents are complete, offer members of a field an efficient way to keep up with the endless flow of new books and articles as well as a way to evaluate their usefulness.

11

Proposals and Prospectuses

Planning ahead is crucial to success in any kind of venture, including writing. Sometimes your plans for completing a writing assignment are so brief and simple that you can work them out and store them all mentally. Other times, you may need to at least scribble a brief list or informal outline to remind yourself of the things you want to include in your paper and the order you want to follow. Sometimes your planning may extend to making a formal outline of what you intend to write; your professors may even require that you submit such an outline. The longer and more complex the writing task is, the less likely you are to be able to succeed with simple mental planning. In such cases, prior planning becomes especially important and sometimes very complex itself.

For example, if you have ever tried to write a 15-page library research paper just two or three days before it is due, you know that the best-laid mental plans can be frustrated: You find the books and articles you hoped to use are still checked out or they've simply disappeared from the library shelves. Or you discover that so few people have written on your chosen topic that you can't find enough information to write even 5 pages, let alone 15. Or, even if you have enough sources, you find at the eleventh hour that you are still struggling to understand them and to figure out how to integrate them into a focused, coherent paper. Or you realize at 2 A.M., when the library is closed, that you don't have all the information you need to write the bibliography for a paper that is due six hours later. Any number of other things could also go wrong. But by systematically planning several weeks before the paper's due date, you could avoid most of these problems.

An excellent way of systematically planning long, complex writing tasks that involve research is to write a proposal or prospectus. While these two words are often used interchangeably, a distinction will be made in this chapter. The word *proposal* will be used for research plans that primarily involve methods other than library research and for other kinds of formal written plans, such as bids and grant proposals. The word *prospectus* will be used for plans to write a paper based primarily on library research. Prospectuses mainly contain information that helps the reader imagine a finished written product—a research paper, a dissertation, a book. Proposals are like prospectuses in that they typically entail a written document, although in the proposal, the final document is usually not described in much detail. With proposals, usually something else besides your plans for a document is at stake—and that something else is almost always money or permission.

PROPOSALS

Proposals are a very common genre in the worlds of education, business, and government, where innovative solutions to new problems are constantly sought and where funds and other resources are limited and must be used in the wisest way. Before committing money, time, personnel, or other resources to a project, people in charge of an organization want to be persuaded that the investment will be worthwhile. That is why a proposal must often compete with other proposals, either for funds from a research foundation or for the go-ahead from the leaders of an organization.

Typically, competitive proposals are written to respond to a need announced by an organization. The organization considers all proposals submitted by a given deadline and then rewards the best one—or several excellent ones—with cash or approval. Even proposals that are not in competition with others must usually comply with various specifications or measure up to standards predetermined by those with power to approve the proposal. Therefore, proposals usually stress the researcher's qualifications, the writer's plans, and the writer's preparation to complete the proposed task—including whether the writer has the necessary expertise, a detailed budget, and a reasonable time line—much more than they describe any documents that will result.

PROPOSALS COMPETING FOR MONEY

Proposals that compete for money are generally called *grant proposals* or *bids*. A key part of a grant proposal or bid is an itemized budget, showing how every dollar will be spent. Grants are sums of money that corporations, philanthropic organizations, and government agencies give away, usually to scholars, so that the scholars will be able to pursue research that will benefit society in general. Usually for a grant proposal, the funding agency announces that a certain amount of money is available for a specified purpose or kind of research, and proposal writers compete for a portion of the total. Often more than one grant is awarded, as several proposals may be judged to merit support.

In a bid, however, a business, government agency, or other institution has a specific need that it wants filled, either for a product or a service. The organization publicly describes the need and sets a deadline when it will stop taking bids and choose whom to award a contract to. In bids, the proposers try to demonstrate that they can provide the requested product or service at a lower cost than other bidders. The organization accepting the bids will generally award the contract to the bidder who seems able to provide the most value for the least money. Because organizations that award grants and contracts want to give their money to people who know what they are doing, bids and grant proposals include much detail about processes as well as eventual products.

Proposals Seeking Permission

Proposal writers who seek permission rather than funds also have to be very clear about the procedures they will follow. They must demonstrate that they have planned how to comply with all the criteria that approval is based on. Before writing this kind of proposal, then, it is important to know all of the requirements your proposal must meet. Usually someone in the office that will review the proposal issues a description of what the proposal must include and a list of the criteria by which it will be judged. Sometimes this officer even provides one or more forms for you to fill out to guarantee that your proposal will contain all the necessary information.

Because proposals can be written for many diverse purposes and can take many different forms, it is not possible in this chapter to describe or illustrate all kinds of proposals. In the course of your education, your career, and your civic involvement, you may have to write many different kinds of proposals. Teachers and co-workers will be able to help you with some aspects of preparing individual proposals. Beyond that, the best things you can do are ask a lot of questions about what the organization is looking for in the proposal and study other proposals that were successful in situations similar to yours.

The rest of this chapter will teach you about one kind of proposal that, as a student in the social sciences, you are likely to write—a proposal seeking permission to conduct research with human participants. Because federal law has established ethical and professional guidelines for such research, nearly all campuses have an Institutional Review Board (usually abbreviated IRB) that must review and approve all research projects, including student projects, that include human participants. (What IRBs are and the ethical standards for research are explained in detail in Chapter 3.)

Below you will read the proposal that one group of students prepared to gain permission to conduct research with persons who have disabilities. (The paper the students eventually wrote about their research is included in Chapter 5.) By noticing how the students described their research and complied with the IRB's requirements, you should be able to plan and write a similar proposal for conducting your own research with human participants. Please note that the authors of this proposal were complying with requirements in effect on *their* campus. The actual forms or lists of criteria may be different on your campus. Requirements for this kind of proposal may also change as government agencies issue new regulations.

EXAMPLE STUDENT PROPOSAL

The four students who prepared the proposal on the following pages were majoring in either sociology or therapeutic recreation. They were all interested in the challenges faced by persons with disabilities, and they were aware that terminology for talking about different disabilities seems to change often. Although it was once considered completely acceptable and natural, for example, to speak of the crippled or the handicapped, in recent years new names have been proposed and adopted. These students wanted to learn what people with disabilities thought about various labels for their disabilities. Because the students lacked enough time to find and survey a large sample of people with disabilities, they decided that in-depth interviews with a few people would be the best method of answering their research questions.

The forms the students filled out or followed to create unique parts of their proposal are shown as Figure 11-1. Figure 11-1 has four parts; Figure 11-1, Part C shows both the instructions the students followed and also the documents they created to comply with the instructions.

Figure 11-2 shows possible components of a consent form. Because the students did interviews and kept the identity of their informants anonymous by using pseudonyms, they were not required to have a consent form.

Consent forms are generally required only for experiments. If you were to conduct an experiment, you would have to create a unique consent form and make copies for each participant in your research to sign. That is, you would not use the model in Figure 11-2 in its present form; instead, you would decide what, if anything, would need to go where the blanks presently are, and you would write a new form that contains appropriate information about you, your institution, and your particular study. You might leave out some parts of the model. However, you must include some version of the parts that indicate what the research is about, its known risks or benefits, the participant's right to decline or withdraw, the statement that the participant complies freely, and the date and signature lines.

FIGURE 11-1 Part A

APPLICATION FOR HUMAN SUBJECT REVIEW COMMITTEE APPROVAL
USE OF HUMANS SUBJECT PROTOCOL

Part A

TITLE OF STUDY: Labels: What Individuals with Disabilities Prefer

Principal Investigator: Ashley McMaster (student in sociology)
(Name, Title, Department)

Co-Investigator(s): Melissa Lundmark, Charmaine O'Donnal, Jemma Williamson (students in therapeutic recreation), Dr. Kristine Hansen, Prof., English Dept.
(Name, Title, Department) (If the PI is student this should be responsible faculty member)

Full Address:	Phone Number:	Date:
224 South 335 West	224–0853	8 Feb. 1995
Orem, UT 84058		

This research
is originated by   _Faculty   _Staff   XXXStudent   _Other

                     _Thesis   _Dissertation   XXXCourse Project   _Other

SIGNATURES:

Principal Investigator: *Ashley McMaster*

　　　If student research:

　　　Committee Chair/Faculty Sponsor: *Kristine Hansen*

　　　Thesis/dissertation—Date of approval by proposal review committee:

RECORD OF INSTITUTIONAL REVIEW BOARD ACTION

Date of Review:

_APPROVED AS SUBMITTED   TYPE OF APPROVAL: _Full Board   RISK: _Minimal

_TABLED   _Expedited   _Moderate

_DISAPPROVED   _Exempt   _High

_Approved with conditions (see attached letter)

DATE APPROVED: **ANNUAL REVIEW DATE:**

Chair, Human Subjects Review Committee   Expedited Reviewer   Date

FIGURE 11-1 Part B

HUMAN SUBJECTS REVIEW PROTOCOL
Part B

Study Title: Labels: What Individuals with Disabilities Prefer
Principal Investigator: Ashley McMaster
Duration of Study: From 14 Feb. 1995   To 28 Feb. 1995

Is this a multicenter study?   ___yes   xx_no
(If yes list other institutions participating and attach a
page which explains the responsibilities and obligations
of each center and/or each investigator.)

Will you be seeking external funding for your research?   _yes   xx_no
(If yes, list to what agency you are applying and the
approximate dollar amount.)

**Does this study involve subjects located outside
of the United States?**   ___yes   xx_no
(If yes please submit both the English consent form and
the translation in the appropriate language.)

Does this study involve subjects who are not fluent in English?   ___yes   xx_no
(If yes please submit both the English consent form
and the translation in the appropriate language.)

Are the investigators requesting not to use a consent form?   xx_yes   ___no
(If yes please explain the rationale for the request.
Attach another page if necessary.)
The method is interviewing. Identity of respondents will not be revealed.

Number of Subjects: 4   **Gender of Subjects:** 3 male, 1 female
Ages of Subjects: 22, 24, 25, 26
Health Status of Subjects:
    Are subjects healthy volunteers?   xx_yes*   ___no
    Are subjects mentally competent?   xx_yes   ___no
    (if no explain)
    * each subject has a disability but they are all otherwise healthy

Vulnerability of Subjects:
    Are subjects younger than 18 years of age?   ___yes   xx_no
    Are subjects older than 65 years of age?   ___yes   xx_no
    Are subjects pregnant women?   ___yes   xx_no
    Are subjects prisoners?   ___yes   xx_no
    Are subjects institutionalized?   ___yes   xx_no
    (if yes explain rationale for selecting vulnerable subjects)

Is this research: ___therapeutic?   xx_non-therapeutic?
Note: Therapeutic research includes study of the efficacy of a therapeutic or diagnostic/assessment method
        when the intervention is not designed *solely* to enhance the well-being of the subject who is seeking a
        health benefit.
        Non-therapeutic research has no likelihood or intent of producing a diagnostic, preventive or therapeu-
        tic benefit to the subject.

FIGURE 11-1 Part C—Instructions

HUMAN SUBJECT REVIEW PROTOCOL
Part C
Instructions: Please address these areas in a concise, informative manner.

I.   Specific Aims and/or hypothesis/questions to be tested should be stated briefly and succinctly and should logically derive from the summary of background and significance.

II.   Background and Significance should contain a brief review of appropriate literature and a statement of how the proposed project will relate to or differ from what has been accomplished previously. Place the reference list at the end of this section.

III. Description of subjects and the specific criteria that will be used to include or exclude persons from taking part in the study. If vulnerable subjects are included justify their inclusion. Describe how subjects will be recruited into the study, how consent will be obtained, and how confidentiality will be maintained.

IV.   Method or Procedures including research design should be described in detail. Instruments, questionnaires, surveys, etc. should be attached in Appendix A. Include here a description of all instruments and questionnaires to be used. Any interventions, drawing of blood, or other procedures should be described including who will be doing the procedure and their qualifications. Be very specific about methods for obtaining the data.

V.   Data Analysis should be described in relation to each question/hypothesis.

VI.   Risks and benefits should be described as well as protection measures used and method(s) of handling any potential adverse reactions to the data collection techniques.

VII. Qualifications of the Investigator(s) should be described.

The following appendix should be attached:

    A. Instruments and/or questionnaires

    B. Consent form(s)

    C. Other documents which the investigator considers necessary

FIGURE 11-1 Part C—Answers

I.   **Specific Aims.** The aim of our study is to learn what labels people with disabilities prefer to have others use to refer to the disabilities.

II. **Background and Significance.** The background of our study lies in our joint interest in working with people who have disabilities. We believe in order to comprehend the issue of labeling such people, it is important to understand the feelings of those who are most affected. By questioning people with disabilities about various labels that have been and are now used, we can understand how the various labels affect these people; then we can be more sensitive in our use of labels as we work with people who have disabilities. We haven't reviewed literature on this topic.

III. **Description of Participants.** The participants in the study will be four people with disabilities who are personally known to one or more of the investigators. Two have spinal cord injuries, one is blind, and one is deaf. Although they are potentially vulnerable, our investigation is non-therapeutic. We will obtain the verbal consent of each before proceeding with our interviews. We will maintain confidentiality by using pseudonyms in our report.

IV. **Method.** Our method will be to ask the same questions of each participant (see Appendix). The interviews may also include questions arising spontaneously in the course of each interview.

V.   **Data Analysis.** We will simply summarize the respondents' answers to our questions.

VI. **Risks and Benefits.** There are no known risks or benefits from participating in this study.

VII. **Qualifications of the Investigators.** The investigators are students majoring in sociology and therapeutic recreation. All of us have taken courses about disabilities and worked with people who have disabilities. One of us is fluent in American Sign Language. We are conducting the study to meet the requirements of an assignment in our English 315 course.

FIGURE 11-1 Part C—Appendix

We are students conducting interviews for a class research assignment. In general, we are interested in how individuals with disabilities prefer to be labeled. By going ahead with this interview you are giving us permission to use your answers in our research paper. Your name will be kept anonymous.

Demographic Information
Age:
Gender:
Have you had this disability since birth? Yes or No
If not how long?

Questions
1. What label would you like people to use in reference to your disability? Why?
2. Have you noticed people who are uncertain about how to refer to your disability?
3. How do most people refer to your disability?
4. How do you refer to yourself when you need to describe your disability to others?
5. What kind of labels do you use to refer to others with disabilities?
6. We are now going to read a list of words. We want to find out how these terms make you feel.

	Prefer	Offend	Don't Care
handicapped			
disabled			
(Why do you prefer, feel offended, or do not care?)			
Person with handicap			
Person with disability			
Physically challenged			
If applicable:			
wheel chair bound			
confined to wheel chair			
uses a wheel chair			
paraplegic			
quadriplegic			
spinal cord			
blind			
visually impaired			
visually challenged			
deaf			
hearing impaired			
hard of hearing			
hearing loss			

7. Are there any that particularly offend you or you prefer?
8. Is it important to you what labels people use? Why?
9. How do you think labels affect you in general?

FIGURE 11-1 Part D

ASSURANCE DOCUMENT

Part D

The attached investigation involves the use of human subjects. I understand the University's policy concerning research involving human subjects and I agree:

1. To obtain voluntary and informed consent of subjects who are to participate in this project.
2. To report to the IRB any unanticipated effects on subjects which become apparent during the course of, or as a result of, the experimentation and the actions taken.
3. To cooperate with members of the Committee charged with the continuing review of this project.
4. To obtain prior approval from the Committee before amending or altering the scope of the project or implementing changes in the approved consent form.
5. To maintain documentation of consent forms and progress reports as required by institutional policy.
6. To protect the confidentiality of research subjects on the data collected.

Ashley McMaster   8 Feb. 1995
_____   _____
Signature of Principal Investigator   Date

FIGURE 11-2 Sample Consent Form

Consent to Participate in Research

The purpose of this research is to determine _____.

The researchers are students in _____ [name of course]

at _____ [name of college or university].

As a participant in this research, you will be asked to _____.

The total time you will be asked to volunteer is _____.

In order to complete the research you will have to go to _____

[location of laboratory or research site] between the hours of ____ and ____.

The person in charge of this research is _____.

Any questions or concerns should be addressed to him/her at _____

[phone or address].

Your participation in this research is strictly voluntary. You have the right to

refuse to participate, and you have the right to withdraw from the research

at any time without jeopardizing _____ [reputation, status, grades,

employment, etc.].

There are no known risks or discomforts resulting from participation in this
study. There are also no known benefits.

*I have read the above form, and I hereby signify that I am voluntarily participating
in the study. I accept whatever risks and benefits may come from participation.*

_____   _____
        Date   Signature

THE PROSPECTUS

A prospectus is a detailed rationale and outline for a long document. Publishers typically ask for a prospectus, rather than a complete manuscript, when an author contacts them with an idea for a book. By writing a prospectus, authors are forced to be as clear as possible about their plans, distilling their ideas persuasively in a very few pages. After reading a prospectus (and often having it reviewed by others), publishers can determine whether a project is interesting and promising enough to encourage the author to complete the manuscript. Often, on the strength of a rhetorically effective prospectus, the publisher will offer the author a contract. Similarly, a prospectus for a long academic paper helps both the student writer and his or her instructor come to an agreement about the worth and feasibility of the student's plans. Rather than being offered a contract, however, a student either receives permission and encouragement to proceed with the planned paper or receives advice on how to strengthen or redirect the prospectus.

A prospectus is commonly required in graduate school for a master's thesis or doctoral dissertation. Its primary audience is a committee of professors who must approve the project before the student can proceed. The committee members are not likely to approve a project that is trivial or uninteresting, one that would merely plow over old ground, or one that would be too difficult or even impossible to complete. So the student typically must persuade the committee that he or she has answered these questions:

- What is proposed?
- Why is it proposed? What contribution to knowledge will the student make?
- What will the finished work include?
- How, where, and when will the proposed work be accomplished?
- What qualifications are required to accomplish the proposed project?
- Are the necessary resources available?

By answering these questions well, the student assures the committee that he or she will undertake a project that is worthwhile, original, well planned, and feasible. For the same reasons that a prospectus is desirable in graduate school, it is advisable for undergraduates to write one before completing an extended research project.

PARTS OF THE PROSPECTUS

Exploring what is involved in answering the above questions will help you better understand what a typical prospectus contains.

What is proposed? You undertake a research project in order to answer a question or a set of related questions, solve a problem, or address an issue in a new way—perhaps because it has been addressed inadequately in the past or perhaps because there are new methods to be applied or new evidence to be examined. In a prospectus, then, you should state at the outset what the purpose of your research will be—what question, problem, or need your research will resolve. It is also helpful to locate the problem in a context—for example, to show what historical, social, or individual issues it relates to. Providing this context will also help you establish a rationale.

At the time you write the prospectus, you may not know exactly what answer you will find to your question, what solution you might propose to a problem, or all the new information you might turn up about your topic. But you should know enough to state very clearly the aim and the scope of the research you want to undertake. For example, suppose a new therapy, validation therapy, has been created for helping elderly persons with dementia, and you wish to know more about it. After considering how little you know about it, you determine that some good questions to start with would be, "How does validation therapy differ from reality orientation, the standard therapy used in hospitals and residential care facilities? What are the merits of validation therapy? What evidence is there that it has been used successfully?" These questions already imply a scope for the paper—limits that will make it manageable because you will focus on answering these questions and not any of several related questions you could also answer.

Why is it proposed? Always intertwined with the *what* of any prospectus is the *why*. Explaining why it is important to research the topic you have chosen constitutes giving a rationale or justification for your project. Your reasons may be partly personal. Continuing the example above, you may have a grandparent who suffers from a form of dementia. Or you may have worked with such persons or plan to work with them in the future. You will no doubt be more interested in researching a topic that draws you personally, and that alone is a good justification.

But remember that you will be writing your paper for an audience too, so you should be able to come up with some more "public" reasons. What will help your readers believe that it is important to do this research? What other reasons justify the time and effort you will spend researching it? What will be the value to your audience and others of the knowledge you will collect and write about? You don't want your audience to read your prospectus and say, "So what?"

For the therapy project mentioned above, for example, you could justify your research by noting the widespread incidence of dementia among elderly people, its debilitating effects on them, and the difficulties that caregivers face in responding adequately to the confusion and disorientation that these patients experience. Perhaps the current therapy is based on faulty premises or it is unsatisfactory in the way it works for some patients. Any research that promises to shed some light on a vexing health issue should be welcome to most audiences because it is possible that many people or their loved ones may be affected by such problems.

The rationale of a prospectus doesn't have to be long, but it ought to be presented carefully. You want your project to be approved, so give some good reasons why it should be. Check with your instructor, however, to learn whether he or she deems it appropriate to bring up personal reasons in the rationale. No doubt all researchers have a personal interest in the research they conduct, but sometimes they do not expressly state their personal reasons in their justification for the research.

What will the finished work include? Your prospectus should give evidence that you have thought about the paper you will eventually write. Because you have already stated the question or the problem and rationale in the introduction of your prospectus, in this part you can show how you plan to present the answer or the solution that meets the need implied in the rationale. To write this part, ask yourself these questions:

> What overall thesis will you argue for?
>
> What parts will you divide your finished research into?
>
> What order will you put these parts in? What should come first, second, or third? Last?
>
> How much space will you devote to each part—how much emphasis will each receive?

In prospectuses for graduate theses, this part of the prospectus usually takes the form of a list of chapters and a summary of what each chapter will cover. In an undergraduate prospectus, a more suitable form might be a preliminary outline of the eventual paper. This outline could be done in the traditional way, with Roman numerals and indented subheadings. Or it could be less formal, in paragraph form, with sentences describing the subtopics you intend to address.

Obviously, to write this part of the prospectus you will have to locate at least some of the library sources you plan to use and become familiar with what is in them. It won't do to simply imagine what your eventual paper will contain, hoping that you will later find just the sources you need to fill in the projected parts. What if no such sources exist or they are difficult to get? By going to the library as you prepare your prospectus, you can determine if your project is even feasible and avoid a last-minute attempt to find usable, reliable sources. And by skimming several of your sources weeks before your paper is due, you will already have begun your research, eliminating the need for frantic, late-night reading.

As you can see, a prospectus demands that you "get serious" about your topic early enough to explore it meaningfully. By showing your reader how you have limited the scope and contents of your project, the overview of your proposed research adds greatly to the persuasiveness of your prospectus and enhances the possibility that your project will be approved.

How, where, and when will the work be accomplished? In addition to describing the eventual paper you will write, for many audiences you may need to describe the process you will go through to write it. This description can take the form of a task breakdown showing how and where you will conduct the research. This task breakdown can also include a time line showing what phases of the work you will have completed by intermediate dates before the final deadline.

Including a task breakdown in your prospectus can be very helpful if you plan to conduct complicated research, requiring you to travel to more than one library, for example, or to procure documents through interlibrary loan, or to interview an authority on your topic. Also, if you need to manage your time carefully because of other commitments, planning a reasonable schedule and then sticking to it can help you meet the ultimate deadline without panic. Here are some intermediate steps you could use to create a timeline that will help you finish your research project on time:

- Begin research
- Create preliminary bibliography
- Start note taking
- End note taking
- Write first draft of research paper
- Get feedback from peers, teacher, or others
- Write final draft of research paper

The task breakdown in your prospectus might be very brief if your research will be limited to simply reading in your campus library. Similarly, creating a time line might be a perfunctory step if your instructor has already imposed intermediate deadlines. However, you should not underestimate the time that will be required to do good work, and you should make careful plans for fitting each step of the research process into your personal schedule.

What qualifications are required to accomplish the proposed project? In addition to showing that you can complete the work within the constraints of time and location, you may need to persuade your readers that you have the required background, expertise, and training to accomplish the goal of your research. This would be especially true if you were planning to supplement your library research, say, with some interviews or with statistical data that you would need to collect, analyze, and interpret. Briefly describing your education, your previous experience with your proposed methods, and your other qualifications for completing the task is sufficient for this part of a prospectus. In cases where no especially difficult or unusual research techniques are involved, however, your readers are likely to take for granted your ability to complete the project, and you won't need to demonstrate it.

Are the necessary resources available? Beyond time and expertise, research often requires materials, instruments, and sometimes money to be completed. In more elaborate prospectuses, you would have to show that these necessary resources are available. A library research paper, however, typically requires only access to documents. You can usually use library materials at no or very little cost, so the important point to argue in this part of your prospectus is that the documents you need are relevant to your purpose and available for your use. You should also demonstrate that they are reliable and useful (see Chapter 9).

Together with the part of your prospectus that outlines the eventual form and contents of your paper, this part is probably the most important in persuading your audience to approve your project. It usually takes the form of a review of literature—so named because it surveys and summarizes the sources (the "literature") you have already located and shows how they can help you accomplish your research goals.

One possible way to organize the review of literature is to follow the preliminary outline you have already created. For example, if you have planned a paper that has four main divisions, you could similarly divide your review into four parts and summarize the sources that should help you write each part of your proposed paper.

Since your research and reading will continue after the time you write and submit the prospectus, your readers do not expect the review of the literature to be extensive or detailed. In fact, it can be appropriate to indicate that you intend to read sources you haven't yet been able to check out from the library. Your goal in writing this part of your prospectus is to persuade your audience that you have made significant progress toward finding, reading, and organizing information that will eventually be a part of your final paper. It is usually not necessary at this point to quote or paraphrase your sources extensively; instead, you should summarize in a sentence or two the main points of the books and articles you've skimmed, explaining how they will contribute to your project.

Another part of the prospectus that shows available resources is a selected bibliography of works you have identified as relevant to your research. This selected bibliography is usually attached as a separate section at the end of the prospectus, and it should be labeled and formatted according to the documentation style used in your discipline (see Chapter 20). It should include documents you have reviewed in the prospectus as well as documents you still intend to review. If you are required to use a minimum number of sources, obviously your list should contain at least that many. If no minimum was specified, you ought to list as many sources as you can find that show real promise of contributing to your project, without padding the bibliography just to make it impressive.

Note that any readers of your prospectus will review your selected bibliography carefully to determine whether you have used sound criteria to select your sources. These criteria include the following:

- Are the sources relevant to the proposed purpose?
- Are the authors and publishers of the sources credible and scholarly?
- Are the publication dates of the sources appropriate? For some topics, recency of publication is vital; for other topics, older sources may be particularly relevant.
- Are the authors and sources sufficiently varied so that the biases of individual works are balanced by works with different assumptions and approaches?
- Have you included all potentially useful sources?
- If appropriate, does the list contain a variety of kinds of publications? For example, does it include journal articles, particularly in fields where articles are the primary medium for disseminating information?

As you can see, preparing a prospectus that has all these parts will carry you far along the road toward a finished research paper. Your final paper will be stronger because of the careful planning you will have to do to prepare the prospectus. By starting early and answering the questions outlined above, you will avoid the stress of trying to write your paper in a few rushed days. You might even experience the pleasure—and relief—of finishing your paper ahead of schedule.

ORGANIZATION OF THE PROSPECTUS

Although the parts of a prospectus described above don't vary much, how they are organized in a particular prospectus can vary a great deal, depending on the requirements of the professor or department you are writing for. In most cases, the purpose and rationale of the proposed research project comprise the introduction. After that you may be required to use prescribed headings and subheadings in a specified order so that readers can check the completeness of the prospectus and read or reread parts as they desire. If you are required to follow an organizational plan, it is likely based on current genre conventions in your field. The organization below is suggested mainly for pedagogical reasons—to teach you one way of writing a prospectus that includes the necessary parts. Your instructor may ask you to modify this organizational scheme to meet other objectives he or she has for you. A complete prospectus can be divided into these four main sections:

1. **Purpose and Rationale.** In this section, you describe the general context of the problem, state the narrowly defined question, problem, or issue you propose to research, and justify its importance.

2. **Plan of Work.** In this section, you outline the thesis, organization, and contents of the eventual paper you will write; you provide your qualifications as a researcher (if required); and you outline the schedule you will follow, including how, where, and when you will accomplish the various phases of your research (if necessary).

3. **Review of Literature.** Finally, you summarize what you have learned from your research so far, showing how the sources you have read help you achieve your purpose and fit into your plans for the eventual research paper.

4. **Selected Bibliography.** Attach to your prospectus a list of the works you have consulted so far and still intend to consult. Write this list according to the specifications of your field's documentation style. Label it appropriately (that is, the APA style and Turabian parenthetical reference style call it "References"; the Turabian note style calls it "Selected Bibliography.")

In addition to following this suggested organizational pattern, remember that the proposal is a formal document; therefore, you should take care to do the following as you compose it:

- *Make the tone formal to match that of the proposed paper.* The prospectus is not like a chatty letter to your teacher, so avoid writing in a casual tone.

- *Revise and edit your prospectus carefully.* Its purpose is to persuade your audience that you have the ability to conduct the proposed research and write the research paper, so you should demonstrate that you can write well.

- *Write the bibliographic citations in the correct format.* Getting the bibliographic citations right at this point will save you time as you prepare the final draft of your paper. If you are using the APA style or the Turabian reference list style, note that when you write the titles of books and articles within the *body* of the prospectus, the titles should be capitalized according to standard conventions, even though they are capitalized sentence style at the end in the list of references.

- *Follow principles of good document design when formatting your prospectus.* Use headings that correspond to the parts of a prospectus described here, or use other headings that your instructor may specify. Use letter-quality printing and a good grade of paper. The professional appearance of the prospectus should enhance its persuasiveness and indicate that you take pride in your work.

EXAMPLE STUDENT PROSPECTUS

The prospectus reproduced on the next pages, by Kelli A. Boren, was written several weeks before she wrote the research paper reproduced at the end of Chapter 9. As you read her prospectus and compare it to the research paper she later produced, you will note that she adhered closely to her original outline. This high degree of correspondence is probably due to Boren's very thorough search of the literature for her prospectus. By identifying most of her sources early and digesting their contents carefully, she had a very clear idea of what her paper would finally contain.

Not everyone is able to produce a research paper that corresponds so well with the prospectus. If, after submitting your prospectus and continuing to do further research, you discover materials that alter your initial focus and plans, or if you begin to think differently about the topic and want to change your basic position, you should change your research paper accordingly rather than adhere rigidly to your previous outline. It would be a good idea to consult with your instructor, however, about any substantive changes in your plans. If you find that very broad changes become necessary, your instructor may advise you to write a new prospectus.

Prospectus for Research Paper:
Effects of Maternal Employment on Children

by

Kelli A. Boren

English 315

March 15, 1996

Effects of Maternal Employment on Children

Purpose and Rationale

In 1988 the Bureau of Labor Statistics stated that half of mothers with infants one year or younger were in the work force, and two-thirds of mothers with toddlers between the ages of two and three worked outside the home. Furthermore, experts estimated that by 1995, two-thirds of all infants and toddlers would have an employed mother (Baydar & Brooks-Gunn, 1991). Because of the significant number of working mothers, there has been growing concern about the effects of maternal employment on children.

One specific topic of interest is whether a mother's employment affects her child's behavior. Parcel and Menaghan (1993) assert that any negative effects on behavior are significant because problem behavior in children not only impacts their immediate circumstances, but may also have long term effects on their ability to positively interact in society. The researchers state that poor early child behavior may lead to lasting consequences such as poor performance in school, inability to form relationships with peers, aggressiveness and social withdrawal (Parcel and Menaghan, 1993). These behaviors feed upon each other and then repeat themselves as part of a destructive cycle which affects children not only early on, but throughout their entire lives. To ameliorate any negative effects of maternal employment on child behavior, it is essential that we first identify what those effects may be and then find ways to counteract them.

A significant number of studies have shown that there *is* a link between mothers who work and problem behavior in their children. These problem behaviors, however, do not stem exclusively from maternal employment but are influenced by many factors, including parenting style, the amount of time mothers work each week, the type of child care boys receive compared to that received by girls, and child age. Research findings suggest that the negative effects of working mothers on child behavior are not inevitable and may be lessened, if not eliminated. In my research paper I propose to show that mothers who work may decrease the negative impact of their employment upon their children's behavior if they learn which factors may be harmful and then try to compensate for those factors.

Plan of Work

Scope of Project

There is much literature about the effects of maternal employment on children. However, I have chosen to limit my study specifically to how working mothers may adjust circumstances to compensate for being absent from their children. I will not consider whether a mother should work or what effects her employment might have on other aspects of childhood such as self-esteem, ability to form positive attachments, or ability to achieve in school.

So far, I have limited my research to journal articles more current than 1990. However, recent interest in this subject seems to have decreased significantly since the 1980's, and there is less current literature available. As a result I have been unable to find an adequate amount of information in the journal articles I have consulted to this point. In order to supplement areas where I found little research, I plan to consult additional articles published as early as 1985.

In my paper I will explain the factors which may increase negative behavior in children of working mothers as well as possible means of lessening the effects of these factors. The factors my paper will discuss will be limited to the following: parenting style, the amount of time mothers work each week, the relationship between type of child care and child's gender, and child age. My paper will follow the outline below.

Outline of Proposed Paper

I.   Introduction
II. Mothers' parenting style
     A. Parenting styles that increase negative child behavior
         1. Rejecting style
         2. Punishing style
         3. Style of mothers involved in technical work
         4. High negative control
     B. Parenting styles that decrease negative child behavior
         1. Style of mothers involved in bureaucratic work
         2. Low negative control
III. Amount of time mothers work each week
     A. Amount of time mothers work that increases negative child behavior
         1. Work over 20 hours
         2. Work 10–20 hours
     B. Lessening negative effects of amount of time mothers work
         1. Work less than 10 hours
         2. Provide high quality child care
IV. Relationship between type of child care and child's gender
     A. Relative lack of effect of type of child care on girls
     B. Factors that increase boys' negative behavior

      1. Inconsistent child care arrangements
      2. Care by non-relatives
      3. Care by father
  C. Lessening negative effects on boys
      1. Consistent child care arrangements
      2. Care by relatives
      3. Alternatives to care by father
V. Child age when mothers work
  A. Negative impact of mother working the second or third quarter of infancy
  B. Lessening negative effects due to child age
      1. Delay employment until child is two
      2. Work only during first quarter of infancy

Timeline

In order to complete my research paper by the April 15 deadline, I have created the following schedule for completion of the intermediate steps:

Begin notetaking	March 1
Complete notetaking	March 20
Write first draft	March 21–31
Submit draft to classmate for peer review	April 2
Revise first draft	April 9–14
Submit final draft	April 15

My research plans and my work habits don't require a more detailed task breakdown than this.

Review of Literature

The literature I have reviewed so far provides me with information to use in the four main divisions of my proposed paper: parenting style, the amount of time mothers work each week, the type of care boys receive compared to that received by girls, and the child's age when the mother works.

Parenting Style

In 1991, MacEwen and Barling found that children's anxiety/withdrawal behavior increased when mothers' parenting style was rejecting towards their children. Also, when working mothers had a high level of punishing behavior, children's conduct disorders and attention/immaturity behaviors also increased. Rogers,

Parcel and Menaghan (1991) found that when mothers had a strong sense of mastery (feeling of control) in their own lives, they were able to help their children control their own behavior. Rogers, Parcel, and Menaghan (1991) also found that a mother's work conditions influenced parenting style and child behavior.

Crockenberg and Litman (1991) divided parenting styles into positive, or having a low level of "negative control," and negative, or having a high level of "negative control." They found that children of employed mothers who used a lot of negative control were more defiant than children whose nonemployed mothers had a high level of negative control. However, children of employed mothers who exercised low levels of negative control were *less* defiant in the home setting than children of nonemployed mothers.

Amount of Time Mothers Work Per Week

Baydar and Brooks-Gunn (1991) found that children of mothers who worked less than 10 hours per week showed no significant behavioral differences from children whose mothers did not work. Children whose mothers worked more than 10 hours per week, however, *did* show more behavior problems. However, the researchers found that the children who showed the highest number of behavior problems were not the children whose mothers worked full-time, but those whose mothers worked 10 to 20 hours per week.

Type of Child Care and Gender

Crockenberg and Litman (1991) found that boys whose mothers were employed exhibited a higher level of defiant behavior than boys whose mothers were not employed or than girls in either category. Several other studies cited by Crockenberg and Litman also concluded that boys have a more difficult time adjusting to maternal employment than girls do.

Other studies indicate that boys may be more sensitive to the type of child care they receive when their mother is at work. Baydar and Brooks-Gunn (1991) found that girls responded more favorably to baby-sitter care, but boys responded more favorably to grandmother care. Additionally, Crockenberg and Litman (1991) found that boys were less able than girls to adapt to a "multiple care arrangement" (p. 951) and responded best to consistent care given by a relative. Baydar and Brooks-Gunn (1991) found that children who had been cared for by their father scored higher in behavioral problems on the BPI (Behavioral Problems Index) than children who received other forms of child care throughout the day.

Child Age

Crockenberg and Litman (1991) reported that children whose mothers placed them in child care before two years of age were more angry and aggressive towards adults and peers and were less likely to comply with care giver requests. Baydar and Brooks-Gunn (1991) also found that there were significant negative behavioral effects on children whose mothers worked during the second or third quarter of infancy. They did show, however, that negative effects were minimal if the mothers worked during the first quarter of infancy, if the mothers delayed employment until the last quarter of infancy, or if mothers waited to return to work until the child was two or three.

References

Baydar, N., & Brooks-Gunn, J. (1991). Effects of maternal employment and child-care arrangements on preschoolers' cognitive and behavioral outcomes: Evidence from the children of the National Longitudinal Survey of Youth. *Developmental Psychology, 27,* 932–945.

Crockenberg, S., & Litman, C. (1990). Autonomy as competence in two-year-olds: Maternal correlates of child compliance, noncompliance, and self-assertion. *Developmental Psychology, 26,* 961–971.

Crockenberg, S., & Litman, C. (1991). Effects of maternal employment on maternal and two-year-old child behavior. *Child Development, 62,* 930–953.

Greenstein, T. N. (1993). Maternal employment and child behavioral outcomes: A household economics analysis. *Journal of Family Issues, 14,* 323–354.

MacEwen, K. E., & Barling, J. (1991). Effects of maternal employment experiences on children's behavior via mood, cognitive difficulties, and parenting behavior. *Journal of Marriage and the Family, 53,* 635–644.

Otto, L. B., & Atkinson, M. P. (1994). Maternal employment experiences and children's behavior: A reanalysis and comment. *Journal of Marriage and the Family, 56,* 501–506.

Parcel, T. L., & Menaghan, E. G. (1993). Family social capital and children's behavior problems. *Social Psychology Quarterly, 56,* 120–135.

Rogers, S. J., Parcel, T. L., & Menaghan, E. G. (1991). The effects of maternal working conditions and mastery on child behavior problems: Studying the intergenerational transmission of social control. *Journal of Health and Social Behavior, 32,* 145–164.

SUGGESTIONS FOR WRITING

1. After reading Chapters 3 through 8, plan a research project you could carry out on your campus using one or a combination of the methods described. Find out what approval procedures you must comply with on your campus and what forms, if any, you must fill out and submit to an IRB or a committee designated by the IRB to approve research projects. Write a proposal to do the research, including the following: who your co-investigators are, if any; the qualifications of the researchers; the time frame in which you will conduct the research; your research objectives; the significance of the research; what methods you will use; how you will analyze the data; who the participants will be; what the risks and benefits will be to the participants; how you will gain informed consent. Attach a consent form the participants will sign, if one is needed. If you are planning an interview or a survey, attach the questions you will ask.

2. After reading Chapters 9–10, write a prospectus for a research paper you have been assigned to complete during the current academic term. Describe your purpose and tell why it is important to research the topic you have chosen. Describe what the eventual research paper will contain by telling how you have limited the scope of your topic and by outlining the eventual contents of the paper. Summarize the library and Internet sources you have located that will help you write your planned paper. Attach a bibliography of sources, formatted in the style appropriate to your field (see Chapter 20). Submit the prospectus to your instructor to get approval and advice before proceeding to write your research paper.

12

PUBLIC POSITION PAPERS AND OPINION PIECES

As a student of the social sciences, you are learning about social and cultural institutions such as governments, the justice system, schools, hospitals, churches, charitable organizations, youth groups, and families. In general, these institutions aim to promote a just, harmonious society and the development of productive, healthy individuals. It's probably clear to you by now, however, that these and other institutions are not always successful in reaching these goals. After more than 200 years of government under the United States Constitution, for example, there is still not complete harmony and equity among various groups in the United States, and some well-intended government programs and policies do not always promote justice or help individuals be productive. Similarly, as hard as they try, schools, churches, and charitable groups do not always succeed in enhancing individual development. Some families can be dysfunctional, too, not fostering the kind of relationships and individual growth that healthy families do.

As social scientists study these and other institutions, they often point to flaws in them that they believe could be corrected through taking some appropriate action. When social scientists make recommendations that affect public life, their purpose for writing changes from informing their peers about their research to participating in civic discourse. They turn from the professional realm that normally absorbs most of their time and interest to the public realm, a decidedly political realm in which their recommendations might have real consequences in the lives of real people.

There are several genres in which social scientists might write about their opinions and recommendations. One would be an article for a popular magazine (as opposed to a professional journal). Another would be a newspaper article or editorial, often called an "opinion piece." Still another possible genre is called the "position paper," typically written for government officials and sometimes the public to influence them to adopt recommendations the writer might make.

Although position papers are often identified mainly with the writing that political scientists do, other social scientists—including economists, anthropologists, sociologists, social workers, psychologists—all might have occasion to make important contributions to the formation of public policies and programs. For example, suppose a state has the luxury of a budget surplus and its legislature is debating what to do with the extra funds. An economist might prepare a position paper recommending a reduction in the state property tax or sales tax, showing how the reduction would affect future state revenues and the general economy of the state. A social worker might write a position paper recommending increased funding for state agencies serving unemployed and homeless persons and people whose job skills need to be upgraded. A psychologist might argue for creating and staffing more public mental health clinics. An anthropologist could plead for a bigger budget to preserve sites in the state where remnants of prehistoric cultures have been discovered. The expertise of social scientists can sometimes magnify their voices in the political process and persuade legislators and the public to take actions they might not otherwise think of. By writing effective position papers, then, social scientists can use rhetoric in the way that it was first designed to be used—as a way of influencing the body politic.

As you prepare for your career, it is important for you to consider how you could apply your knowledge to the analysis of real problems that we face as members of the various overlapping communities we belong to. As you learn to create solutions to problems and recommend those solutions persuasively to the people who can implement them, you will see how your developing expertise in a field could have an impact in the lives of other people besides yourself and professional peers. In this chapter, you will learn some basic steps for writing position papers and opinion pieces to be read by the general public. You will read examples of two professionals' public discourse: a position paper by a medical doctor recommending changes in the U.S. health care system and an opinion piece by a political science professor concerning a public debate on the separation of church and state in his community.

WRITING A POSITION PAPER

DEFINE AND LIMIT THE PROBLEM

The first step in writing a position paper is to define and limit the problem carefully. Most social problems are complex and therefore require multifaceted solutions. Consider, for example, the problem of violent juvenile gangs in urban areas. The factors that might lead youth to join gangs are many, including lack of strong family ties, low self-esteem, unemployment and economic despair, peer pressure, racial discrimination, learning disabilities or low motivation to succeed in school, and lack of wholesome leisure time activities. Once youth have formed gangs, other factors could contribute to their destructiveness, including such things as too few police officers, easy access to firearms, inadequate detention and reform facilities, crowded court dockets, or laws with lenient penalties for adolescents. When you see how complex the problem of gangs is, you realize that it would probably take volumes to write a comprehensive position paper recommending solutions that would even start to scale back this problem, let alone get rid of it. Making a problem like this manageable obviously will require the efforts of a number of professions, all working together to attack it from different angles.

The complexity and intractability of most social problems means that writing an effective position paper will usually require you to limit your definition of the problem. So, for example, rather than defining the problem as "gangs," you could define it more narrowly by focusing on one of the factors that lead to the formation of gangs or contribute to their destructiveness. It will be most helpful, too, to focus on factors that could be affected by a public policy or program. For instance, you could focus on the shortage of police officers or the easy availability of firearms, since government officials have the power to appropriate money for hiring more officers and to write laws regulating access to firearms.

However, if you see these measures as striking at the branch rather than the root of the problem, you might instead focus on factors that make some youth susceptible to the pressure to join gangs, such as low self-esteem, lack of success in school, or lack of constructive leisure time activities. You might choose these because you think it is possible to create educational and civic programs that could ameliorate the factors that predispose youth to join gangs. By selecting one part of this problem to study and take a position on, you would make your task manageable and you would be more likely to propose a clear and workable solution for decision makers to consider and act on.

RESEARCH THE PROBLEM

Once you have defined the problem, the next step is to learn more about it. Your two most likely sources of knowledge are documents and people who are experts on the subject you plan to write about.

Read documents. You may find most of what you need to know about the problem in documents, either at a library or at an institution that has something to do with the problem, such as a government agency, a workplace, or a charitable organization. Since doing research in the library is already covered at length in Chapter 9, little more will be said here, except to remind you again to establish the reliability of any documents you read as you try to understand the problem or develop solutions. The recency of publication, the carefulness of the research, the generalizability of any findings, and the political agenda of the writer could all be important for you to consider as you determine how much faith to place in any documents you use.

Documents from another institution could well become an important source of information as you work on defining the problem and developing solutions. For example, suppose your city council is debating whether or not to continue contributing a fraction of its budget to a privately run organization in your area that provides food and shelter to homeless persons. In the past, the city has chosen to make a contribution to this private organization rather than establish its own food and shelter operation, but now some citizens have objected that it is not the proper role of city government to contribute to private welfare services. To study this problem in order to write a position paper about it, you could check the records of the food and shelter organization (with permission of course) to determine how much of its total operating budget comes from the city; how many people it serves each year; how many people it could not serve if it didn't have the city's contribution; and who else contributes to the organization and how much. With facts like these, gleaned from the organization's own documents, you would be in a better position to analyze the nature of the problem and to think about possible solutions.

Consult experts. In addition to reading pertinent documents, it is important to learn from people who are close to the problem and therefore know a lot about it from their experience with it. If these experts are local, you may be able to interview them. For example, you could easily interview the directors of the food and shelter organization; you could also interview the mayor and members of the city council to learn about their reasoning in voting funds for the organization in the past. If the experts you would like to interview are more distant, you may still be able to reach them by phone, letter, or E-mail. (See Chapter 5 for more information about planning and carrying out an effective interview.)

EVALUATE POSSIBLE SOLUTIONS

Once you have limited and defined the problem in a manageable way, you are ready to begin formulating solutions. But clearly it won't do to formulate easy "pie-in-the-sky" solutions that have no chance of being accepted. This means you will also have to evaluate the solutions you formulate so you can offer those that have a good chance of being accepted. Obviously, solutions have a higher chance of being chosen and implemented if they are feasible (that is, they *can* be implemented and are likely to work); if the benefits are worth what it will cost to obtain them; and if the public can be persuaded to go along with implementing the solution. Let's examine these three interrelated criteria for evaluating solutions.

Feasibility. Solutions must actually be workable, given the power and resources that public officials or other administrators possess and are willing to use to solve a problem. If you identify part of the gang problem as poor parenting, you might decide that a solution would be to require all people who plan to have children to take college courses in how to be parents, courses such as one to teach their children to be able to resist negative peer pressure. Some reflection on this solution, however, would probably lead you to decide that this solution is simply not workable. How would you identify the people who should take the courses? How would you pay for creating and staffing the course? How would you ensure that people took it, or if they did, that they learned what they were supposed to? Even if you could achieve the initial steps, how could you guarantee the course would have the desired effect? This solution simply would not be practical.

If, however, you identify the most important part of the problem as a lack of constructive leisure time activities for children and teens to engage in, you may decide that a solution is locating or constructing more sports facilities, creating more after-school drama, music, and special interest groups for young people to be involved in, and getting people to work as coaches for sports and leaders and teachers for other activities after school. This solution might be feasible, provided there are funds and people, either paid employees or volunteers, that can be employed in this cause, and provided that the right officials and the public could be persuaded to see the solution as feasible.

Cost-effectiveness. A very good way to demonstrate that a solution is feasible is to determine what it will cost to implement the solution and then to estimate the value of the benefits that should come from the solution. If the value of the benefits is greater than the cost, then the cost of implementing the solution may be attractive to decision makers. Suppose you decided to propose that your city should provide two recreation facilities where young people could engage in sports or other activities that would keep them off the streets. After some research, you could calculate the cost of building, renovating, or renting existing facilities, providing them with equipment, and staffing them with leaders, coaches, and teachers. Then you would attempt to determine the monetary benefits of this solution. It would be difficult, but with some research you might determine the city would eventually save some money now being spent on police patrols, repairs of vandalized property, the creation of juvenile detention facilities, the juvenile justice system, and social service workers. If you could show that the costs would lead to measurable financial benefits, your solution would probably stand a better chance of being accepted. In this example, you might not be able to show that the city would save a lot of money, but you could argue that the money currently being spent on apprehension and punishment of gang members could be better spent on preventing gang activity in the first place.

Political Persuasiveness. Although it is important to argue for the feasibility and the cost-effectiveness of a solution in a position paper, these arguments may not count for much if you have misjudged the political climate and the attitudes of the people to whom you will be presenting your solution. Many people inside as well as outside government, for example, are simply not convinced that government can do much to prevent the gang problem. They do not view it as part of government's role to sponsor recreational facilities and hire people or seek volunteers to work with youth. They believe such activities are the proper role of churches, schools, private organizations, and the family. With beliefs like these, they are more likely to see solutions to gangs in stricter laws, more police officers to enforce the law, and more public spending for jails and prisons. You must always carefully analyze your audience and determine whether or not your proposal will be persuasive to them, given the political beliefs and assumptions they have.

RECOMMEND ONE OR MORE SOLUTIONS

As you analyze the problem, you will probably think of more than one solution that could be proposed. As you evaluate each solution, you should identify one that you think will be most feasible, most cost-effective, and most likely to win favor in the given political climate. However, you may believe that more than one of your solutions is workable, and you might consider offering ranked recommendations in the event that the audience for your position paper will be able to implement more than one solution. Remember, however, that you should argue forcefully for the solution you deem best. The whole aim of a position paper is to take a position, not to waffle after you have carefully researched the problem and evaluated the possible solutions.

DRAFT THE POSITION PAPER

After you have analyzed the problem carefully and chosen one or more workable solutions, the final step in producing a position paper is to write it. Two considerations are of prime importance in planning the paper: level of language and organization. As with other writing, your purpose and your audience will determine what you should do.

Level of language. Consider your audience carefully as you compose the sentences and paragraphs of your position paper. Remember that they may not share your expertise and the vocabulary that people in your field generally use. You may need to find synonyms for specialized terms or at least define and illustrate terms carefully before using them repeatedly in your paper. Use shorter sentences than you would generally use in writing for peers in your field. If you are writing for the general public, make your tone less formal as well; it may even be appropriate to use some anecdotes, even personal ones, in addition to the statistics or other data you use to make your point. You want to move your audience to action, so in some cases it may be helpful to appeal to their emotions as well as their ability to reason, as long as the appeal is not manipulative. After completing a draft of your position paper, seek feedback from someone who knows the intended audience well or is already a part of that audience to see if the language you have chosen is understandable and makes the impact you desire.

Organization. A position paper can take many forms. If it is to be read by the public, a brief, simple, clear organization is probably best, since many will not likely have the patience to puzzle out a long, complex structure. If it is to be published in a magazine or newspaper, the paragraphs should be short because they will be displayed in narrow columns. The scholarly apparatus of footnotes or parenthetical references can usually be omitted for publication in popular periodicals, although you should be prepared to name your sources of information if asked. You may also work them into the text of the paper; for example, you might write, "A recent survey sponsored by a coalition of local businesses has shown...."

For a more formal position paper that will be read by legislators or heads of organizations, the structure might be longer and more complicated, but it should use organizational devices to make the information accessible. For example, it would be wise to use headings that increase the accessibility of the desired information. Document design features such as numbered or bulleted lists or boldface and italic print can also help draw attention to key points (see Chapter 16). Important numerical data can often be presented in tables or graphs that let the reader quickly grasp relationships between different bits of data (see Chapter 17). The longer the paper is, the more helpful it is to provide a summary of your position and a table of contents to your document at the beginning to help busy readers get an overview of your position. In most cases, if you cite published sources, the position paper should have a list of references giving bibliographic citations for any printed materials you have consulted (see Chapter 20) and names of people you have interviewed or contacted for information. Finally, if there is extra information that you did not put in the body of the paper but that would bolster the argument you make, it is appropriate to include it in one or more appendixes, so that readers who have the time to study your argument carefully can see all the data that led you to the solution you proposed.

A PROFESSIONAL EXAMPLE OF A PUBLIC POSITION PAPER

The example of a position paper on the following pages was written by Regina Benjamin, M.D.[1] Her article outlines the problems of the working poor, who earn too little to afford health insurance but earn too much to qualify for the government health care programs Medicare and Medicaid. The working poor also tend to live in rural areas and inner cities, where doctors are in short supply. After outlining the problem, Benjamin proposes a three-pronged attack on this problem. This position paper was originally published in *National Forum* in Summer 1996, a magazine for members of a national honor society, Phi Kappa Phi. Although the readers of this magazine probably have more education than the average American, Benjamin makes no special presumption of their expertise in medicine and workings of the health care system, and she writes in a way that could be understood by the general adult public. Her paper is not written expressly for public policy makers, but it contains recommendations for members of Congress that their constituents might endorse and pass on to them.

As you read, notice how Benjamin uses headings to, first, characterize the problem, and, second, to draw attention to the major points of her proposal. Notice also the vivid, engaging level of her language and her use of personal examples to gain the reader's trust and interest at the beginning before she introduces some of the statistics that describe the magnitude of the problem. Although she includes some factual data in the article that, under most circumstances, would require documentation, she does not provide it, since formal documentation is not one of the usual conventions of the genre of popular magazine articles. However, Benjamin's explanation of her education and her work, along with her sure grasp of the problem, inclines the reader to trust her and perhaps to believe that, if she were asked, she could provide the references for the statistics without hesitation. She keeps her paragraphs short and to the point, making the article easy to read. Imagine how her words, sentences, paragraphs, and use of evidence might differ if she had written about this problem in a scholarly paper to be published in a professional journal for an audience of other doctors.

---

[1] Reprinted from *National Forum: The Phi Kappa Phi Journal,* Volume 76, Number 3 (Summer 1996). Copyright © by Regina Benjamin, M.D. By permission of the publishers.

Feeling Poorly:
The Troubling Verdict
on Poverty and Health Care in America

Regina Benjamin, M.D.

It has been said that a country can be judged by how it treats its neediest citizens. If that judgment extends to health care, the United States and its people may not want to hear the verdict. Today, millions of Americans who need medical attention cannot afford it and therefore must go without. Many millions more have some health coverage, but not enough. As a physician in one of America's poorest communities, I see these shortfalls firsthand.

Benjamin opens with general statistics about the shortcomings of the American health care system.

I practice medicine in Bayou La Batre, a community of 2,500 residents on Alabama's Gulf Coast. During the 1970s, Bayou La Batre was among the top ten seafood producers in the country but has since fallen on hard economic times. Life here used to be a bit more difficult to describe, but since 1994, I have been able to tell people that Bayou La Batre is the town where Forrest Gump made his fortune as a shrimper.

The author describes where she practices medicine and why she chose this locale for her work. She draws the reader in with her reference to Forrest Gump and details of her life.

Like Gump, many of our residents today depend on the Gulf to provide their living—whether out on its waters harvesting seafood, or back on the shore packing and canning the day's catch. Unlike Gump, however, few are getting rich doing it. Whether it is bacteria in Mobile Bay or overseas competition, the fishing industry is failing here. Today, 80 percent of the residents live below the federal poverty line.

I grew up across the bay in Daphne. After medical school, I came back to the south Alabama area to fulfill my commitment with the National Health Service Corps, which had paid my medical school tuition in exchange for three years of practice in an underserved area. Nearly a decade later, I am still here.

I opened my private practice in Bayou La Batre in 1990. Although I probably see a few more shark bites than most doctors I meet, the majority of health problems I see are no different here than from anywhere else. They run the gamut from minor emergencies to life-threatening conditions. As the only private physician in town, I treat them all. Some of my patients can afford to pay for care, some cannot. Most pay me what they can, when they can. It is not uncommon for payments to come in five, ten dollars at a time—if at all. My ledger can wait, but my patients cannot.

The author describes her patients and why she treats them regardless of their ability to pay.

Why do I do what I do? Because too many Americans already go without needed medical care, or wait until they are much sicker

The author points out that people who lack health insurance wait until they are very sick before seeking help, then choose the least cost-effective source of help—the emergency room.

before seeking care. All told, some forty million lack insurance. Without it, many wait until they are desperate and then wind up in the emergency room of their local hospital—one of the least efficient and cost-effective places to receive or deliver care. The inappropriateness of this pattern was expressed best by one long-time health care observer, who said that giving primary care in an emergency room is "equivalent to tending a rose garden with a bulldozer."

The Underserved Poor

In this section the author describes the neglected poor—those who earn too much for Medicaid and Medicare but too little to afford health insurance.

Not surprisingly, economic circumstances drive the problem. This country's most medically underserved individuals are also among its poorest. The link between health-care status and socioeconomic status is well documented. Our poor have a premature death rate that is three to seven times higher (depending on race and sex) than those who are not poor. Of course, poor is a relative term, and it is worth noting that those with the least access to health care services are not necessarily our poorest citizens. Many of these truly indigent individuals are covered by Medicaid and Medicare.

No, the sad truth of the matter is that many of our neediest citizens, in terms of health care, are hardworking people who hold down jobs—America's working poor. They earn too much income to qualify for Medicare or Medicaid, but not enough to afford private insurance.

How much income is too much? The answer is "Not much at all." This year the federal government has set the poverty line for a family of four at $15,600. Subtract from that figure just the bare necessities of life—such as housing, food, and clothing—and that does not leave much for "added luxuries" such as health care and medicine.

The author asserts that in the United States people should not have to view medical care as a luxury, but many are forced to.

Of course, health care and medicine are not luxuries, but that is how some families in this country are forced to view them. It is a viewpoint that is more easily understood after you have seen—as I have seen—patients struggle with the decision of whether to spend their last dollars on food or medicine. Such circumstances are tragic, particularly in a country as prosperous as ours. In so many ways, the United States is the envy of the world when it comes to the medical services we can provide and the complex procedures we can perform. Unfortunately, too many Americans stand worlds apart from these services and procedures.

My work in Bayou La Batre brings a small handful of people closer to receiving the kind of care most of us enjoy—but I practice here mainly because I like the people and feel I am needed. I did not enter medicine for its financial rewards, so money has never been an important consideration in how or where I practice. Still, good intentions are not enough to sustain a medical practice. I need to pay for equipment, supplies, and a small, but vital staff.

To make practice here viable, I went back to school to get my MBA and learn more about the business side of operating a medical practice. During that time, I was fortunate to discover a little-known 1977 provision that provides government funding to health clinics and offices operating in underserved areas. This new-found provision, along with my newly acquired understanding of business principles, has allowed me to continue my work in Bayou La Batre.

The author describes how she has managed to sustain a practice despite her patients' poverty.

This country's poor and underserved, however, should not have to depend on altruism, MBAs, and the chance discoveries of old statutes to get the health care they need. Communities like Bayou La Batre exist throughout our country. As a member of the American Medical Association's Board of Trustees, I am acutely aware of the national scope of the problem. Today, some seventy-two million people live in areas designated by the federal government as underserved—thirty-four million live in rural areas and thirty-eight million in inner-city neighborhoods. Of these, forty-three million do not have access to a private-sector primary-care physician at all.

Unless we act now, the health-care plight of these individuals will only grow worse. Many hospitals, especially those in the inner city, are feeling the fallout from this country's shift to managed care. As managed care cuts into hospital revenues, many say they can no longer provide free care to those who cannot afford to pay their way. Making matters worse is the fact that Congress stands ready to cut billions of dollars from the Medicare and Medicaid budgets over the next several years. In addition to the obvious loss of funds to finance programs for the poor, these cuts will decrease funding to medical education programs—a critical source of charity care.

The author asserts that the health care problem is going to get worse if action is not taken soon.

What the Medical Community Can Do

I am proud of my medical profession and the effort that it puts forth in addressing the needs of the medically underserved. A recent AMA socioeconomic survey indicates that approximately seven out of ten physicians donate free or reduced-cost care to the poor and underserved. On average, these physicians devote about 7.2 hours a week to charity care, or thirty-six days a year. But charity care, in some ways, is like shrimping. Where it is good, the harvest feeds everyone. Where it is not, you had better be prepared to look elsewhere.

In this part of the paper, the author describes steps the medical profession can take to help the underserved poor.

That is why lawmakers and concerned citizens must join with the medical community in addressing this problem. Just as the health-care problems facing our underserved citizens are not one-dimensional, neither are the solutions. It will take a concerted effort by all groups to improve the current situation.

Our medical community is working to address this problem, but it must do more. Present shortcomings in meeting the needs of our rural and inner-city underserved are illustrated in two recent studies. The first reports that only 9 percent of medical school graduates practice in rural areas—where 25 percent of Americans reside. The most severe shortages are in the Midwest and Deep South. In my home state of Alabama, for example, the health department estimates that the state needs about 110 more physicians to serve patients in rural counties.

The author cites two studies that show doctors are scarce in rural areas and in low-income urban areas.

A second study, by the Community Society of New York, is just as alarming for urban residents. The study found only twenty-eight properly qualified physicians serving a population of 1.7 million people in low-income neighborhoods in Harlem, north central Brooklyn, and the south Bronx.

These two studies are only microcosms of a much larger problem. Clearly, we need to attract more physicians to these areas. And we can start by exposing more young medical students and residents to the needs of underserved communities. At least one medical school here in Alabama is trying to address its rural physician shortage by sending medical students into remote areas of the state to work with primary-care physicians for a month. The hope is that some of these students will be inspired to stay.

Other programs are targeting our inner cities. The New York County Medical Society, for example, has a Physician Community Services program that helps put physicians in touch with underserved communities to provide care at clinics, help with disease-prevention drives, and serve as health consultants.

The author calls for incentives to motivate young doctors to practice in the most underserved areas.

Efforts like these could be bolstered substantially by providing to physicians modest incentives to work in these areas. One suggested strategy includes additional loan-forgiveness programs, like those used by the National Health Service Corps. Such incentives not only are needed, but are necessary. Today, some 80 percent of medical school graduates face significant debt—$60,000 on average. Few can afford to serve poor or indigent patients without at least some kind of financial support.

What the Congress Can Do

In this section, Benjamin calls on Congress to stop dawdling and face up to the social and moral responsibility of developing sound solutions.

Meanwhile, in our nation's capitol lawmakers must step up their attempts to address the health-care needs of the poor and underserved. They have been debating health-care reform for some four years now with little to show for their efforts.

Medicare and Medicaid are prominent examples of issues that wait for resolution. Some reports indicate that the Medicare trust fund, which pays hospital bills for the elderly and disabled, could be bankrupt by the year 2001. Meanwhile, Medicaid, which serves poor children, remains in limbo while politicians decide whether to maintain it as a federal entitlement program or turn it over to states in the form of block grants.

The lives and health care of the poor must not be left to hang in the balance while Washington struggles to balance its budget. The time has come to end political bickering and to develop solutions that are socially, morally, and economically responsible. Finding these solutions is not a matter of politics; it is a matter of necessity.

What You and Your Community Can Do

Locally, communities must assess their needs and make it a priority to address them. If all politics is local, then so are many of the solutions to America's social problems. Nonmedical institutions and organizations can serve as important links in addressing the needs of the poor and underserved. In Washington, D.C., for example, the Archdiocese of Washington coordinates more than 200 private consultants to serve as a referral network for indigent patients.

In this section Benjamin describes how communities and individuals can devise local solutions to helping the poor.

But above all, each of us—as individuals—must remember that one person can make a difference. It may sound like a cliché, but hardly a day goes by that I do not see the truth in this philosophy.

Of course, how we choose to make a difference is up to us, and the possibilities are limitless. For me, it is practicing here in La Batre and doing what I can to provide health care to our residents. But you do not have to be a doctor to help. We can start by familiarizing ourselves with the health-care problems existing in our own communities. Follow up by investigating how to become part of the solution. You may volunteer your time at a local clinic, take time to shuttle sick patients, or pick up medicine and food for shut-ins.

Benjamin suggests specific ways individuals can help.

Or if direct care is not for you, consider forming a local coalition to raise needed funding for clinics, equipment, supplies, or yes, even the recruitment of a physician to an underserved community.

Granted, these are simple, straightforward solutions for a complex problem, but if we work at them seriously, they can have a tremendous impact. I know, because I see firsthand the difference one person can make. Addressing the health-care needs of our poor and underserved not only will improve their health, but also the health of the country as well.

Working together, we can take pride not only in the health care this country provides, but also in the compassionate manner in which we provide it. The solutions are in front of us. The verdict is in our hands. It is time to stop feeling poorly—and make Americans well again, one and all.

Benjamin concludes by stating her conviction that it is possible to solve this problem.

WRITING OPINION PIECES

An opinion piece is in some ways like a position paper because it deals with an issue or problem that concerns the public. However, a typical opinion piece is not as long as a typical position paper, especially if the opinion piece is published in a newspaper, where space is limited. Popular magazines usually afford more space for opinion pieces, though. Often, an opinion piece may not be as thoroughly researched as a position paper. In fact, social scientists who write opinion pieces may not have to do much more than draw on the knowledge they already possess as a result of their daily immersion in their field. An opinion piece also may not propose a very definite solution to a problem; rather it may simply state how the writer thinks the public should regard the problem or issue.

In organization and style, the opinion piece is meant to engage the audience's attention quickly and keep it. An opinion piece is like a well-crafted essay: In the opening sentences the writer should define the issue or problem under discussion and state his or her opinion about it. In the next few paragraphs, the writer should give reasons that support the opinion, drawing on his or her expertise. In the concluding paragraph the writer usually reiterates the opinion and asserts its broad importance for the public. Throughout the piece, the paragraph length is typically short, since newspapers and magazines publish articles in narrow columns, and short paragraphs are easier to read in that format. The sentence length also tends to be shorter than in professional journal articles. The vocabulary must be accessible to the typical reader of the newspaper or magazine that will be publishing the piece. Generally, no specialized jargon is used. The following opinion piece, written by David Magleby, a university professor of political science, for a large newspaper in his state, illustrates these characteristics of organization and style.[2]

2 David B. Magleby, "Upholding the Rule of Law: A Lesson Not Learned at the West High Graduation," *Deseret News* 18 June 1995, A9. Reprinted by permission.

A PROFESSIONAL EXAMPLE OF AN OPINION PIECE

Upholding the Rule of Law: A Lesson Not Learned at the West High Graduation

by
David B. Magleby

Much attention has been focussed on the recent disturbance at the West High graduation, where in defiance of a ruling of the U.S. Tenth Circuit Court of Appeals, many students and their parents sang a song that had been found by the appellate court to violate the First Amendment separation of church and state.

The merit of the case for and against permitting the choir to sing the disputed songs is not an easy call. The district court judge ruled that the songs could be sung while the appellate court decided the other way. Neither the students who wanted to sing the disputed songs, their parents, nor the school district chose to exercise their right to appeal the 10th Circuit Court's decision to U.S. Supreme Court Justice David Souter, the justice assigned to hear urgent appeals in our region.

Much of the discussion in the media, in a statewide public opinion survey, and by the students and parents who participated in the civil disobedience focuses on the majority's "rights" to sing songs at a public school graduation deemed religious by some students, parents and federal judges. Defenders of this civil disobedience contend that people were merely "standing up for their rights"; presumably they mean their right to freedom of expression. What has been missing from the discussion of the West High civil disobedience is a recognition that in a constitutional democracy rights are often in conflict, and there is rarely an unlimited right to speech, religion, assembly, press and bearing arms. Rights often conflict with other rights or with the obligations and duties of the government as described by the Constitution. We do not have an unlimited right to speech. We may not commit slander, incite a riot, or disrupt a public meeting by heckling, chanting or singing. Similar reasonable limits exist for other rights and freedoms. It is generally the job of the courts to place limits on rights when rights are in conflict as they were in this case. This balancing of competing rights is necessary in a civil society.

The students who defied the court's decision and the parents who supported them in their defiance apparently think they can pick and choose which court orders to follow. How would they differentiate this behavior from those who purvey pornography in the name of free speech even though the Supreme Court has clearly ruled that some forms of communication are not protected by the Constitution? In a constitutional democracy we are not free to interpret the Constitution ourselves and pick and choose the laws and court rulings we want to uphold.

Parents and school officials apparently did not teach the graduates a valuable lesson—it is usually best to uphold authority even when you think the law or decision to be in error. Instead they taught the students to defy or ignore a decision that they personally found objectionable. That is a dangerous message. The most fundamental principle of a free society is the rule of law. The adults who encouraged the graduates to sing subverted the rule of law. The school authorities who failed to anticipate the response lost a great opportunity to teach this principle.

Some will contend that all that really happened at West High was a legitimate exercise of civil disobedience like that of the anti-war and civil rights movements. This case is different from those because the objective was not part of a sustained effort to effect change and because the protesters are not willing to accept the legal punishment that generally follows civil disobedience. They wanted to flirt with civil disobedience while not being willing to accept the consequences.

In a pluralistic society, where there are students and parents of many faiths in attendance at a celebratory event like high school graduation, civility dictates that the program not promote any particular religious faith or practice, particularly when there is evidence that doing so is offensive. Graduation should have been an occasion for accommodation and civility and not for defiance of the rule of law.

Rather than defy the court, as many of the West High students and parents did, they should seek to change the law through means prescribed by the Constitution. They could constrain the courts in interpreting the Constitution by amending that document to permit offering prayers or singing religious songs at graduations, school assemblies, or other events. Such a response would have taught their children respect for the law and for the Constitutional means to achieve change in policies and interpretations you disagree with.

In a state where one religion is predominant as in Utah, the majority ought to be especially sensitive to the feelings of minorities. Sometimes the majority will not even recognize that it is injecting its perspective into non-religious activities like high school graduations. Our Founding Fathers were especially concerned about the tendencies of majorities to trample the rights of minorities in all matters, including religion. Indeed, the Constitution has, as one of its principal aims, the protection of minority interests. Our system permits individuals who feel their rights are being violated to seek recourse in the courts. Striking a balance between the conflicting rights of citizens is never an easy task and rarely one that we will always agree with. It is however, the basis for civility, community, and a constitutional democracy.

SUGGESTIONS FOR RESEARCH AND WRITING

1. In the 1970s most states enacted "no-fault" divorce laws, which allowed a couple to divorce without proving there were grounds for the divorce, such as adultery or cruelty. Some politicians believe that because these laws made it easier to divorce, the divorce rate climbed, creating a number of undesirable side effects, including displaced homemakers without job skills, children living in poverty, and increased demands on state welfare agencies. Some governors and state legislatures are now considering repealing no-fault divorce laws, making it more difficult for couples to divorce, on the premise that it is in the state's best interest to encourage couples to stay together. After researching this issue, prepare a position paper for the legislature of a state considering the repeal of no-fault divorce laws.

2. Some savings-minded legislators in Washington would like to cut federal funding for a number of social programs they deem costly, ineffective, or not part of government's proper role. These are just a few programs they would like to axe or reduce: Headstart; Women, Infants and Children food supplements; Medicare; Medicaid; the National Endowment for the Humanities; the National Endowment for the Arts. Choose one of these or another program that is related to your field of study and research its effectiveness. Prepare a position paper that you could send to your Congressional representative recommending a solution, such as a complete cut, a partial cutback, or a revision of the program.

3. Bilingual education has been touted as the best way to help youngsters whose native language is not English succeed in school. Critics argue that bilingual education is too costly and unnecessarily delays children's mastery of English. Research the effectiveness of bilingual education programs in your state and write a position paper making a recommendation to the state superintendent of education.

4. Violence in public schools is a growing national problem. What are some ways to curb it? Research this problem and recommend solutions to the principal of a school in your area who is searching for ways to deal with this problem.

5. A "flat" income tax has been proposed as the best way of revising the complicated federal tax code and simplifying what citizens have to do in paying their income tax each year. Such a tax would require that all citizens earning above a certain amount pay the same percentage of their income in tax. Study what would happen if this proposal were enacted and write a position paper for your Congressional representative making a recommendation for or against the flat tax.

6. Should adoptions be sealed or public? That is, once a child has been adopted, who should have the right to know about the child's biological parents,

including their names and how to locate them? Many adopted children are curious to know about their biological parents and spend a lot of time, money, and effort on a search to locate them. However, some biological parents do not want to be contacted by the child they gave up for adoption. Write a position paper to help lawmakers in your state write a fair law.

7. Choose a local problem that you are aware of in your community, your church, or another institution that you are associated with. Study the problem and recommend a solution to your mayor or city council, your clergyman, or the leader of the institution. Or write an opinion piece about a current issue for the "op ed" page of your local newspaper.

13

ABSTRACTS, CRITIQUES, AND REVIEWS

The abstract, the critique, and the review are genres that you will have occasion to write both as a student and as a professional. These three kinds of writing have one thing in common: Each one requires you to size up and state succinctly what a document is about. In an abstract, that's all you do; no evaluative comments are included. In a critique or a review, however, you not only summarize the parts of an article, book, or other document, you also offer your opinion about their value. Knowing how to write in each of these genres is important because each one plays an important role in constructing the shared body of knowledge in any field. The critique does this by evaluating documents before they are published. Abstracts and reviews do this by offering members of the field an efficient way to keep up with the endless flow of new publications and to evaluate their usefulness. Because of their importance in shaping knowledge and making it accessible, this chapter will show you some examples and give you guidelines for writing abstracts, critiques, and reviews.

WRITING AN ABSTRACT

Abstract is another name for a summary. Most social science journals require the author of an article to submit an abstract with the article. The abstract is not only printed with the article; it is also included in print sources and electronic databases that students and other scholars can search when looking for information on a particular topic. A well-written abstract is

- Brief, usually only a paragraph
- Dense with information encoded in key words
- Comprehensive in scope, summarizing each section of the document

These characteristics make it more likely that a computer will match the user's search terms with key words in the abstract and retrieve it. They also make it more likely that readers will be able to read the abstract and judge at a glance whether or not the entire article is pertinent to their research and worth reading in its entirety.

To write a good abstract, you have to have a good sense of your main point and of the structure of your document; you need to be able to state precisely what each part contributes to the whole. This means that the best time to write an abstract is after you have completed the entire document. If your document is a report of empirical research, it will likely have the following parts:

- An introduction that states a problem, question, or hypothesis to be investigated
- A description of methods, including participants, procedures, and materials
- A description of results
- A discussion of the significance of the results.

For this type of document, the abstract should have one or two sentences that sum up the important points of each section. For a professional example, see the abstract at the beginning of the research article entitled "Subliminal Self-Help Audiotapes: A Search for Placebo Effects" in Chapter 8. Figure 13-1 student example of an abstract from the student research report entitled "A Study of Patience: Gender-Related Differences in College Students" by Emily Gwilliam, Greg Nielsen, Kyle McLaughlin, and Susan Walley (see Chapter 6). As you read the students' abstract, judge whether or not it presents concisely what you need to know about the purpose, the methods, the participants, the results, and the implications of the research.

Another common kind of document that generally has an abstract is a theoretical article or a review essay. These genres do not report primary research results; instead, they usually have the following traits:

FIGURE 13-1 Student Abstract for an Empirical Research Report

This study tested the hypothesis that male college students are less patient than female college students when forced to wait in line. Two observers recorded both verbal and non-verbal behavior of 12 male and 12 female students waiting to use a free telephone while a caller (member of the research team) exceeded the 3-minute limit. Men tended to behave more assertively and to react sooner than women, but more women exhibited impatient behavior. Because of the limited number of observations and other uncontrolled variables, the hypothesis was not confirmed; further research is recommended.

- Focus on a limited topic
- Statement of thesis or purpose
- Support drawn from the literature, from data, and from sound reasoning
- General conclusions or implications

An abstract for a theoretical article or review essay would provide one or two sentences about each of these. As a student, the genre you will write in that comes closest to a theoretical or review article is a library research paper. Figure 13-2 is the abstract of Kelli Boren's research paper, printed at the end of Chapter 9. As you read this abstract, judge whether it tells you precisely and concisely about her topic, thesis, findings, and conclusions.

FIGURE 13-2 Student Abstract for a Library Research Paper

This paper analyzes the literature on the effects of maternal employment on child behavior, and it recommends steps mothers can take to minimize any negative effects. The following factors were found to increase negative behavior in children: parenting styles that were overcontrolling, rejecting, or punishing; mothers working between 10–20 hours a week or more than 20 hours a week; inconsistent care or babysitter care for boys; father care for girls or boys; mothers entering the work force before the child was at least 9 months old. The following factors were found to decrease negative behavior in children: parenting styles that were warm, less controlling, supportive of self-government, and less reliant on physical punishment; mothers who worked less than 10 hours a week; high quality child care; consistent care or care by a relative for boys; mothers entering the work force after the child was 9 months or older. The increasing numbers of working mothers can lessen the impact of their employment on their children's behavior by compensating for any negative factors.

In sum, an abstract should do the following:

- Make sense by itself; it should be a miniature version of the paper, not omitting important points, not adding things that aren't in the paper, and not distorting the emphasis given to any part.
- Be specific; it should give details about the purpose, the scope, the methods used or the literature surveyed, the results, and the conclusions or implications.
- Be coherent and concise; it should move from point to point in a way that the reader can follow, with no wasted, empty words.
- Avoid evaluating; the author should present as objectively as possible what the entire paper is about and let the reader draw his or her own conclusions about the usefulness of the research.

WRITING A CRITIQUE

In Chapter 1, you learned that a researcher's new contribution to the literature of a field generally goes through a process of peer review before it is accepted for publication. The goal of this process is to ensure that writers will meet their disciplines' high standards for following research methods, analyzing and interpreting data, reasoning, and writing. Typically, a manuscript will be reviewed by at least two reviewers in the writer's field as well as by one or more editors at the journal or press that receives the manuscript. After review, the manuscript is usually returned to the writer with suggestions for revision. These suggestions might take the form of both marginal notations on the manuscript and written critiques in which the reviewers and editor describe in some detail the strengths and weaknesses of the manuscript and suggest ways to improve it. These critiques are meant for the writer only, not for a broader audience. After reading the critiques, the writer usually makes substantial revisions, sometimes negotiating details of content, organization, and style with the editor. Criticism of this kind is positive and helpful because it strengthens a document before it is finally published.

While you are still in college, probably very little, if anything, of what you write will be published in professional journals or by academic presses. (However, many campus departments and organizations sponsor undergraduate writing contests and occasionally even journals, so you could very well aim to submit some of your best papers for judging or publication in local forums.) Even though most of your academic writing won't be published, it will be made public in the sense that it will be read by others besides yourself. Your primary audience in most academic writing tasks is the instructor who assigned the writing. Your goal obviously is to submit quality work, and one way you can improve your written work is to solicit feedback from knowledgeable peers—your classmates, for example, or tutors in your campus writing center. Your teachers may even require that you show early drafts of your writing to others to receive feedback that will help you make your final draft stronger.

Just as you may solicit feedback from peers, you should be prepared to give helpful criticism, oral or written, to others about their writing. Because writing assignments vary widely, the kind of criticism you give to a classmate will depend on what the student has been asked to do; it will also depend on the criteria the instructor will use to evaluate each student's performance. The best place to begin any critique, therefore, is with careful scrutiny of the assignment's requirements and the evaluation criteria. If these are unclear, ask the instructor for more information. Most teachers want to get good writing from their students and therefore should be willing to clarify their instructions. Many instructors will also provide models of the kind of writing they are seeking with a given assignment. By studying the model, you can usually answer your own questions about appropriate format, organization, length, level of detail, and style.

As you evaluate an early draft of a classmate's paper, you will usually need to think about the following characteristics of the writing.

1. Focus. Depending on the type of assignment, the focus might be called the "thesis statement," the "purpose," the "claim," the "point," the "theme," or some other name that indicates that a piece of writing is generally *about* something—it is generally limited to a particular aspect of a broad topic and the writer generally takes a particular position or point of view. No paper can say something about everything, and a paper that just wanders about, touching on this and that, but never asserting anything in particular, leaves you wondering what the reader is supposed to learn from it. To help you criticize the focus of a paper, ask questions such as these:

- Is the writer's focus clearly stated in a prominent position?
- Is the focus limited enough for the kind and length of paper?
- Is the focus evident throughout the paper, or does the paper seem to wander?
- How could the writer sharpen the focus?
- Could you state the thesis in your own words?
- Is the position the writer takes a significant and valid one?

2. Support. Once you have determined the focus of a paper, you should check how the writer supports his or her point of view. Support for a particular focus might take the form of general reasoning, of evidence drawn from authoritative sources, of data created by research methods, or of personal experience. To determine the relevance of the support, ask yourself such questions as these:

- Is the support appropriate for this kind of paper? (For example, has the writer used personal experiences when the assignment requires library research?)
- Is the support relevant?
- Is it credible and reliable?
- Is it sufficient to make the writer's point?
- Has the writer taken into account contradictory evidence or simply ignored it?
- Does the support go into enough detail or is it too general?
- How could the writer make the support stronger?

3. Organization. The organization of a paper will depend on a lot of factors, including any directions the instructor gave in the assignment (or implied in the model, if one is given). The organization of a particular paper might be chronological if the paper is about the past or steps in a process. The organization might proceed from a problem to a solution, from a cause to an effect, or from an effect to a cause. It might compare two things point by point, or it might consider all the points related to one before proceeding to the other. It might divide something into its parts or classify a number of related things. Whatever it does, the organization of a paper should be congruent with the purpose and focus of the paper and help to advance the claim the writer is making. The reader should be able to discern the organization and should feel that the paper moves smoothly from part to part. To help you criticize the organization of someone's writing, consider these questions:

- Could you outline the paper?
- If the writer has outlined the paper, does the outline match the text?
- Has the writer chosen the best order in which to present points?
- Are major points obscure, not given enough emphasis or space?
- Are less important points given too much emphasis?
- Would some points fit better somewhere else in the paper?
- Should some parts be deleted because they don't really fit in?
- Does the writer show connections between parts?
- Where could the writer strengthen the connections?
- Are headings appropriate? Would they improve the reader's ability to perceive the organization?
- How could the writer improve the organization?

4. Audience. All good academic writing is for somebody, and it is pitched at an appropriate level for the intended reader. All of the preceding elements—

focus, support, and organization—must be considered when you evaluate the appropriateness of the writing for the audience. Ask yourself questions such as these:

- What real readers are addressed by the paper?
- What are the audience's expectations and needs?
- Has the writer taken the audience's knowledge, background, and experience into account?
- Will the audience find the particular focus appropriate and interesting?
- Will the audience find the support sufficient, relevant, and reliable?
- Will the organization help the audience understand the writing?
- What improvements in the paper would help the audience understand it better?

5. Format, style, and mechanics. The format of a paper includes such things as the overall appearance, the line spacing, the margins, the page numbering, and so forth. The format will vary with the genre assigned and the instructor's requirements. For example, some professors want a cover sheet on each paper with the title, course name, and your name in designated places. Others want your name, the course number, and the date in the upper-right-hand (or upper-left-hand) corner of the first page. Some want the pages numbered at the top, others at the bottom; still others don't care. Some professors are sticklers for one-inch margins; others are less fussy. Be sure you understand the instructor's preferences and instructions, if any, before proceeding to criticize the format of a classmate's paper.

If the instructor expresses no preferences and if the genre doesn't require any particular changes, check to see if the paper follows these general conventions:

- Is the text double-spaced?
- Does it have one-inch margins? (the default margins on most word processors)
- Does it have a ragged (unjustified) right margin?
- Has the writer paginated according to some consistent plan? (word processors offer several conventional choices)
- Is the body of the text in a 12-point serif font for the body of the paper? (see Chapter 16)
- Are headings used correctly and appropriately?

Style refers mostly to the elements of writing at the sentence level, including choices about usage and punctuation. It can also refer to the institutional style a writer is expected to follow in a particular field (see Chapters 19 and 20). Writers have many choices to make in creating the style of a particular paper. Depending on the audience and purpose, some choices are better than others. *Mechanics* refers to those elements of writing that are purely arbitrary. It includes such things as using capitalization and italics correctly or following a particular style guide's rules for writing numbers, citing sources, and creating bibliographies. In evaluating style and mechanics, once again, you should do all you can to learn the instructor's requirements and preferences. (No checklist of questions will be given here.)

Usually the best way to note problems with format, style, and mechanics is to mark them directly on the draft of the paper you are criticizing, rather than devote a section of a formal written critique to these matters. It's important to note, however, that matters of format and style belong to the part of the writing process called editing, and they may not be as important in the early stages of writing as focus, support, organization, and appropriate adaptation for the audience. There is usually little point in editing writing that still needs a lot of work on focus and organization, for example.

To suggest a delay in criticizing the style, however, is not to imply that correctness in format, style, and mechanics is unimportant. In the end product correctness is very important, because a lot of small mistakes can interfere with the reader's ability to see the focus of a paper and to appreciate its support and organization. So, as a critic of others' writing, be sure that you do point out any serious problems or patterns of error that you notice in your peer's writing, especially if you are criticizing a near-final draft. But it usually isn't necessary to copy-edit someone's paper line by line. Unless you have been asked specifically to edit the paper, in most cases you can simply point out the problems that you see and let the writer assume the major responsibility for correcting them.

A NOTE OF CAUTION

The above criteria are intended to describe writing in general—something that doesn't really exist. Writing is always for a *particular* situation: A paper is written by a particular person for an identified audience in response to a specific assignment about a particular topic. So you must always consider the particulars any time you are asked to offer a verbal or written critique of a classmate's work. One thing that will remain constant, however, is the need to offer criticism with grace and tact. Most people feel possessive about their writing, and even when they want to make it better, they sometimes feel attacked and defensive if their critics take a domineering or sarcastic approach. Imagine yourself on the receiving end of your critique. Would you be offended by it, or would you be able to accept it because it is offered in a kindly way? Be as honest as you must in offering criticism, but be as gentle as you can, too.

EXAMPLE OF A STUDENT CRITIQUE

On the next few pages you will read a critique by Kelly Welker of a library research paper written by her classmate, Greg Nielsen. Welker wrote the critique of Nielsen's next-to-final draft to help him improve the final draft, which the instructor would read and grade. This critique follows an organization suggested by the instructor's evaluation criteria, which both Welker and Nielsen were given at the time they were assigned to do their research papers. As you will note, the critique takes the form of a memo. (How to write a memo is explained in Chapter 15.)

Obviously, you would not want to imitate this critique unless you knew that the paper you were criticizing would be evaluated by the same criteria. Any critiques you write of classmates' papers should take into account the particular assignment and grading criteria that are relevant in your case. Nevertheless, this model should help you see how thorough a critique should be and how the tone of a critique can be critical yet still polite and encouraging.

MEMORANDUM

To: Greg Nielsen
From: Kelly Welker
Date: 11 December 1995
Subject: Research Paper Critique

This memo is a critique of your paper entitled "The Effects of Music on Learning and Recall," which you will soon submit for grading to Professor Henninger. In what follows, I will outline both the strengths and weaknesses of your paper, and I will recommend changes I think you should make before submitting your paper for final evaluation.

Focus and Organization

Your paper has a very clear title that informs the reader of what topics the paper will cover. The introduction is interesting to read, as it appeals to the uses of music that the reader is already familiar with, and builds upon those by stating in your thesis the additional uses you hope to discover. You also establish your focus well so that it is easy to understand.

Your overall organization is quite effective, with your ideas being clearly stated and logically organized into topics. Coherence is weak in a few places (as marked on your paper) where the flow from one idea into another is not quite as smooth as in the rest of the paper. I have noted where a sentence or two might help make a smoother transition. To improve the clarity of your paper, I suggest that you add a brief summary paragraph at the end of each section. By simply restating what the research suggests in each section, you can give the reader more of a sense of closure and an adequate base of information to build upon for the next topic. I noted several sentences in the section called "Memorization and Learning a Skill" which would make a great conclusion to that section.

Use of Research Sources

Overall, you have used the research very well. All of your research comes from authoritative scientific journals. You have effectively represented all views through a proper balance of paraphrasing, summarizing, and quoting. Through checking your sources, I have found you to be generally accurate in summarizing and paraphrasing and honest in quoting. You did, however, misquote Wallace on page 3 by changing the tense of a verb without using brackets; you also left out a parenthetical citation that appears in the original passage you quote. I'm sure these little mistakes were due to haste, and they can easily be corrected.

For the most part you cited your sources completely, but there are times where ideas are not cited, or where the boundary of what you have borrowed from one author is not distinguishable from that which you've borrowed from another author (see my notes on pages 6, 7, and 8). You also often assume that the audience is familiar with such ideas as Pavlov's classical conditioning experiment with his dogs (page 7), and you provide no citation to this experiment for further reference. I'm not sure this is common knowledge. Also, ideas such as "Brower's Associative Theory" and "associative trigger" are not attributed to anyone. You sometimes state that "it has been shown many times that…" without stating where such evidence has been shown, and again you fail to give the source of the "fact" on page 5. Remember to credit all ideas to the original authors. You also stated on page 7 that "the results were the same as the first experiment's," without stating what these results were. Because the reader is most likely unfamiliar with these results, it is wise to restate them or summarize them to refresh the memory of the reader.

Your research paper is very informative, but you could go into more depth. I note that in your References you list 20 sources, but you used only 11 in the body of your paper. From checking the library for additional sources and by looking at the extra 9 sources, I know more research is available on this very interesting topic. After taking a psychology of music course, I realize that this topic is new, but that much research has been done to link music to learning. Perhaps you could include research from a few more sources to strengthen your sections called "Learning a Skill" and "Learning Information and Concepts." You could also cite some of your authors more times, as you seem to cite Wallace more than any other author. With these improvements, your research will be very strong.

Format and Appearance
The overall neatness of your paper is very good. However, the table of contents and abstract should be paginated with lower case Roman numerals, as the teacher instructed. Otherwise, as far as format and appearance are concerned, your paper is ready for submission. Both the table of contents and the headings make your paper very clear, so that it is easy to quickly locate information. The headings also provide a good breakdown of your research to make the various topics you discuss more understandable in relation to one another.

Style and Mechanics

Your writing is clear and concise, well adapted to the audience for which it is intended. As I've noted, you need to add transitions to make the sentences in paragraphs more coherent. In a few instances (indicated on your paper), it is hard to follow your line of thought. Transitions are also needed between topics; remember that our teacher instructed us that a transition is made through connecting sentences and ideas, not simply through heading changes. Your choice of vocabulary is vague on only one occasion, in your abstract. When you state that the effects of music have been largely overlooked, it is not clear who is doing the overlooking. Is it the researchers or people in general? It will help if the reader understands who is overlooking the effects of music upon learning.

The style and mechanics of your paper need only a few minor adjustments. For the most part, you have used correct punctuation and spelling, but I have made a few revisions on your draft that point out minor spelling, punctuation, and syntax errors. Overall, your style and mechanics can be improved with little effort, and these adjustments will make your paper more readable and logical. It is almost final draft quality already.

Copy: Prof. Karla Henninger

WRITING A REVIEW

The process of peer review that you learned about in Chapter 1 does not end with publication. Once an article or book appears in print or on-line, it is subject to the scrutiny of all readers who take an interest in the topic. Although an article or book has already successfully passed prepublication review, it will continue to be reviewed in both indirect and direct ways. The most common indirect way that publications continue to receive peer review is through other writers' references to and citations of the publications. As one writer uses the work of another in creating a new document, the later writer may disagree with the earlier one; they might also praise the work of earlier ones, using it as a foundation for their own work, or extending an idea from the earlier books or articles. In these indirect ways, the writing of an author continues to undergo a type of review.

Another common way of responding to new publications is through directly commenting on them. Many professional journals have a section that is something like the letters to the editor of a newspaper. Readers can write a formal response to a recently published article and submit it to the journal. In their comments they might praise the article, ask for clarifications, or question the methods, analysis, or interpretations of an article. Sometimes journal editors invite the writer whose work is under scrutiny to reply to these critiques. By reading such comments and responses in the current professional journals of your field, you can gain a good sense of what the important issues are and how scholars disagree with and challenge each other. You will see how writers defend their thinking or concede the validity of their peers' criticisms. This give-and-take illustrates well how knowledge is socially constructed through the process of offering, receiving, and responding to criticism.

Another direct method of evaluating someone's work is the formal review. For recently published books, editors of most journals invite reviews from knowledgeable peers, to be published in a section of the journal devoted just to book reviews. Each reviewer summarizes and evaluates an assigned book in a brief format of often less than 1,000 words. By reading these short reviews, others in the field can learn a little about new books appearing in the field and determine whether or not they should get a copy of a particular book and read it for themselves. Book reviews are a good source of information for students completing research projects as well. By reading a brief review, you can determine at least three things about a book: (1) What the book's topic and basic argument are; (2) whether a professional peer judges the book to be reliable; and (3) whether it will be worth your time to read the book at length for the information it might add to your research project.

As you near graduation and become more familiar with your major field's body of knowledge and its standards for evaluating new knowledge, you may be assigned to write formal reviews of published works. This is a valuable assignment, both because it requires you to read new books in your field and because it gives you practice in writing in a professional genre. You will learn to read for the main ideas, to separate the generalizations from the details, to think critically about what you are reading, and to apply your field's standards in evaluating the importance of new ideas and research. Writing a review takes practice, especially because the genre typically gives you only a small space in which to sum up and evaluate what you have read.

The best way to approach writing a review is to gain an overall conception of what this genre of writing usually includes. If you are writing a review for a class, your instructor will usually outline what your review should include and a maximum length. If you are writing a review for a journal, the editor will supply specifications. In either case, your review would typically have these parts:

- The facts of publication
- A statement of the book's purpose and scope
- A summary of the book's contents
- An evaluation of some of the book's strengths and weaknesses
- Your general recommendation of the value of the book

It's important to note that, with the exception of the facts of publication, these parts would not necessarily be found in a review in the order given here. They might be intermixed in various ways. For convenience, however, they will be discussed as listed above.

THE FACTS OF PUBLICATION

The first elements in any book review are the title, author, place of publication, publisher, and year of publication for the book. In addition, the total number of pages and the cost of the book are usually included. If the book is available in both hard cover and paperback editions, the price for each may be given. These details give readers of the review information they can use to order the book if they decide they want to purchase a copy. Or, if they don't plan to buy it, they have enough information to find it in a local library.

STATEMENT OF THE BOOK'S PURPOSE AND SCOPE

The usual way of beginning a book review is to describe as objectively as possible what the author or authors of the book have attempted to do. Don't fault the author or authors for not writing the book you would have written. Try to understand the book in terms of what the author stated he or she was attempting to do. A good place to locate a statement of the author's purpose is in the preface or introduction to the book. State for your readers the book's purpose and its major claim or claims. It would also be appropriate to state any assumptions that underlie the claims.

Describing the particular genre the book belongs to can also help readers understand its purpose; for example, if a book is based on a survey or several interviews, saying so at the start of the review will help readers better evaluate the judgments you make later in the review. It is also helpful to describe briefly the major divisions or the general organization of the book. For example, if the book has three main divisions, you might give their titles and briefly tell what each part includes.

SUMMARY OF THE BOOK'S CONTENTS

In summarizing the book's contents you must be selective, mainly because the typical length limit of a book review forces you to be brief. One way to be selective is to summarize the book's main points at a very general level, giving just enough of the details or examples the authors use to illustrate how the points are supported. It may be appropriate to give a few brief quotations that state very clearly important ideas or focuses of the book. Your summary should substantiate your own overall opinion of the book.

Another way of being selective is to focus on summarizing only some parts of the book, describing the rest in only a sentence or two. This kind of selective review is common when the reviewer and the reviewer's audience have an interest in only one or two aspects of the total book. For example, *A Midwife's Tale*, a history from which there is an excerpt in Chapter 4, was widely reviewed in various kinds of journals from different fields. One review published in the *American Economist* focused on the book's contribution to our understanding of women's role in the economy of eighteenth-century New England; another review published in the *New England Journal of Medicine* focused on what the book tells of midwifery and nursing practices in that time and place.

EVALUATION OF STRENGTHS AND WEAKNESSES

The foregoing parts of a review all tell readers what a book is about, but readers will also want to know what the reviewer thinks of the book. They will want to see praise for specific strengths and criticism of identifiable weaknesses—and usually a book has both strengths and weaknesses, though it might have more of one than the other. As you read a book you've been assigned to review, you should be thinking critically about what the author has done in writing it as well as about what the book actually states. Here are some questions that may guide you in evaluating the strengths and weaknesses of a book:

- Is the book based on methodologically sound research?
- Does it deal adequately with the issues it raises?
- Is the book's scope as inclusive as it should be?
- Is it written clearly and persuasively?
- Has the author drawn on credible sources?
- Has the author overlooked information that would have contributed something worthwhile to the book?
- Is the book suitable for the audience it is intended for?

You might devote one or two paragraphs of your review to strengths and another paragraph to weaknesses. Or you might comment on the strong and weak points of the book as you summarize it. If your overall recommendation of the book is positive, it is important not to give undue prominence to its faults. The amount of space you devote to discussing strengths and weaknesses ought to be consistent with your general assessment of the book's value.

General Recommendation

The reviewer's general recommendation usually appears twice in the review: at the beginning and again at the end. Readers want to find out in the first few sentences of the review if your overall evaluation is positive, negative, or mixed. Be forthright in stating an opinion that you will then support through your summary and evaluation of specific strengths and weaknesses. At the end of the review, you can state your overall opinion again, this time knowing you have supported it with the facts you've included in the body of your review. If your overall opinion is a mix of positive and negative feelings, you should write a carefully qualified statement, balancing praise with criticism.

For example, you should let your readers know if the book is technical and difficult to read but would still have value for a certain group of readers who should take the time to struggle through it. If the book largely repeats what is already known but contributes a few important new ideas, then say what those ideas are. Your readers may ultimately disagree with your evaluation, but that is not a problem. By being a responsible critic, you perform a valuable service in perpetuating the ongoing conversation about a field's knowledge. Your review is like a turn in the conversation, which itself should invite still other responses.

As you read the following two book reviews, one by a professional and one by a student, you will see how each summarizes and evaluates the book.

A PROFESSIONAL BOOK REVIEW

This professional example by Mary Anna Lundeberg is part of a review that focused on two books on the same general theme.[1] The excerpted part reviews *Women's Ways of Knowing*, a selection from which appears in Chapter 5 of this book. As you read it, you will note that the reviewer has a somewhat mixed opinion of the value of the book. Lundeberg announces her overall opinion early, then summarizes the book while also evaluating its strengths and weaknesses. Her conclusion is that, despite some problems, the authors have made a significant contribution to their field, and the book has value for particular audiences and purposes.

[1] Mary Anna Lundeberg, Review of *Women's Ways of Knowing: The Development of Self, Voice, and Mind* by Mary Field Belenky, Blythe McVicker Clinchy, Nancy Rule Goldberger, and Jill Mattuck Tarule, *Psychology of Women Quarterly*, 13 (1989): 127–130. Reprinted with the permission of Cambridge University Press and Mary Anna Lundeberg.

The reviewer gives the facts of publication and prices of the book.

Women's Ways of Knowing: The Development of Self, Voice, and Mind, Mary Field Belenky, Blythe McVicker Clinchy, Nancy Rule Goldberger, and Jill Mattuck Tarule, New York: Basic Books, 1986, 256pp. $19.95 (cloth), $10.95 (paper).

Changing Our Minds: Feminist Transformations of Knowledge, Susan Hardy Aiken, Karen Anderson, Myra Dinnerstein, Judy Nolte, and Patricia MacCorquodale (Eds.), Albany: State University of New York, 1988, 171pp. (+xxiv). $10.95 (paper).

The reviewer opens with provocative questions.

The reviewer alludes briefly to the method used by Belensky et al.

Are there "ways of knowing" unique to women? Are feminist scholars transforming knowledge? Will the academy be transformed through curricular integration of feminist scholarship and feminist pedagogy? These questions, of vital interest to feminists, especially feminists in higher education, are raised in these books. The authors of the first book present their findings about the ways of knowing described to them through intensive interviews with 135 women from 9 academic institutions. The editors of the second book describe their reactions to a feminist curriculum transformation project at the University of Arizona and present a collection of essays written by a few of the participants in the project. The reader might expect that the theory proposed in *Women's Ways of Knowing: The Development of Self, Voice, and Mind* would be tested or somehow applied in *Changing Our Minds: Feminist Transformations of Knowledge*—a book published two years later. If so, the reader will be disappointed, as I was. Both titles promise more than they deliver.

The reviewer gives an initial, somewhat negative assessment of the book.

The reviewer states the authors' main research goal and compares their findings to William Perry's, with which her readers would be familiar.

Women's Ways of Knowing explores the possibility that there may be cultural and developmental reasons for women's varied intellectual perspectives or ways of knowing. The researchers' sample contained women of diverse class and ethnicity. Thus, although the authors compare their findings with Perry's (1970) research on white upperclass Harvard males, these differences may be attributed to race and class as well as gender. Nonetheless, some interesting differences emerged: the women in this study identified with authorities less than did the college men at Harvard, doubted their intellectual competence more, and sought to integrate abstract theories into their lives.

The reviewer notes a major division of the book and describes its contents.

In Part 1, the authors describe each perspective: silence, received knowledge (listening to others' voices), subjective knowledge (listening to an inner voice), procedural knowledge (acquiring the voice of reason), and constructed knowledge (integrating the voices). The biggest contrast to Perry's stages is the first perspective—silence—heard in voices of the youngest, poorest, and least educated women. These women believed themselves voiceless and mindless, incapable of learning from authority. None of the Harvard men in Perry's (1970) study had a perspective like this; however, this may be due to class and age rather than gender alone.

The other intriguing difference between Perry's (1970) research and the research reported in this book is in the distinction the authors make between separate and connected procedural knowledge. Separate knowing, valued highly in the academy, is an adversarial, impersonal approach to objective reasoning. In contrast, connected knowing is a personal, cooperative approach to learning that values tying theory to experiences and stresses belief rather than doubt. Belenky et al. indicate that women value both their relationships with other learners and their relationship with the content (attempting to ground abstractions in personal experiences). This discovery has important pedagogical implications for teaching women and warrants further research.

In Part 2, the authors speculate about the role of families and schools in developing different sequences of these perspectives. They powerfully describe a woman named Inez, initially trapped by "silence," who became angry, acted on her "inner voice," and broke away from her history of abuse, first as a child then later as a wife. Had the authors continued describing the historical contexts of women's lives in the depth they used with Inez, the text would have been much richer. However, because most of their data were limited to single interviews, questions on circumstances or contexts that might have inspired growth or changes in perspectives are not fully addressed. In the chapter on education, the book changes its tone from descriptive to prescriptive. The authors tout the writings of two men, Paulo Freire and Peter Elbow, and give several ideologically-based tenets for "connected teaching," such as confirming women's capacity for knowledge, teaching through firsthand experiences, welcoming diversity and discussion, and encouraging community in the classroom. While these pedagogical suggestions seem valuable, readers may be bothered, as I was, by the scarcity of data supporting them.

Readers also may be frustrated by the scant methodological explication and the absence of quantitative data to supplement the qualitative analyses. The lack of sufficient detail about the interview procedures and results is disappointing and may undermine the credibility of the important findings.

Although I would not use this book as an undergraduate text, I would recommend it as supplemental reading and as provocative reading for faculty development discussions. The book is written in a clear, readable style, and the absence of jargon makes it appropriate for audiences with little or no background in psychology. This book

The reviewer notes that one of the authors' categories differed from Perry's but suggests the difference may be due to age and class, not just gender.

The reviewer finds another important difference between Perry's findings and Belenky et al.'s and suggests more research.

The reviewer names the other main division of the book but mostly criticizes its contents for being more prescriptive than descriptive and for not basing claims on sufficient data.

The reviewer criticizes the author for not describing their methods in more detail.

The reviewer concludes with qualified praise for the book.

adds new information to our knowledge concerning women's intellectual development and raises intriguing pedagogical questions.

The rest of the review has been omitted.

Mary Anna Lundeberg
University of Wisconsin, Eau Claire

REFERENCES

Gilligan, C. (1977). In a different voice: Women's conceptions of self and morality. *Harvard Educational Review, 47,* 481–517.

Perry, W. (1970). *Forms of intellectual and ethical development in the college years.* New York: Holt, Rinehart & Winston.

Schuster, M. R., & Van Dyne, S. R. (Eds.). (1985). *Women's place in the academy. Transforming the liberal arts curriculum.* Totowa, NJ: Rowan & Allanheld.

Spanier, B., Bloom, A., & Boroviak, D. (Eds.). (1984). *Toward a balanced curriculum: A sourcebook for initiating gender integration projects.* Cambridge, MA: Schenkman.

A STUDENT BOOK REVIEW

The following book review was written by a college student, David Dinger, for a class assignment that permitted him to choose any book of interest to him as long as it related to his major field of study. Dinger's major is sociology, so he chose Studs Terkel's book on race relations in the United States. As you read it, note that his review conforms closely to the suggestions given in this chapter for writing a review. First, it gives the facts of publication (though it omits the price of the book); second, it offers an overall assessment of the book's purpose and scope; third, it summarizes the contents—though Parts One and Two receive more emphasis than Parts Three and Four; finally, it comments on the soundness of the author's methods of collecting information for the book and offers an overall assessment of the worth of the book.

Is Racism as Simple as Black and White?

by David Dinger

In recent years, race has emerged as a leading issue in American politics. California has declared war on illegal immigrants with its Proposition 187, affirmative action is dying, and hate crimes are increasing. Changes in the welfare program and rising prices will only worsen the problem. Americans are increasingly conscious of race, and it has become a dominant issue in our daily lives. In the book *Race: How Blacks & Whites Think & Feel About the American Obsession*, published by The New Press in 1992, author Studs Terkel examines the question of race in the 1990's. By presenting many different sides of this difficult issue, Terkel makes it clear there are as many opinions about race as there are people in the United States, and he does it in an interesting and easy-to-understand way.

In this book, interviews with nearly a hundred Americans openly reveal attitudes that few are willing to admit: opinions about affirmative action, feelings about increasing crime, and secret prejudices. The author talked to preachers and gang members, students and homeless, interracial couples, and many other black and white people. Through these interviews, Terkel discovered that questions about race in America do not have clear-cut answers; rather, they create a picture that is complicated, puzzled, and uncertain.

Race is divided into four parts, each dealing with a different aspect of the topic. The first part deals with economics—the similarities and differences between blacks and whites in the workplace, on welfare, and in housing. The author shows that economic similarities occur more along class lines than racial lines. Lower-class whites on welfare have more in common with lower-class blacks than with middle- or upper-class members of their own race. Race and class are not synonymous because there are members of all races in every social class, yet blacks are usually seen as inferior to whites and are more likely to be stereotyped as drug users, criminals, and welfare dependents. Furthermore, because blacks often live isolated in ghetto poverty, they speak a different language, with different rules of grammar and pronunciations, which only increases their isolation and causes the races to drift farther apart. Because it is becoming increasingly difficult for a black person to get a job, they exhibit frustration, anger, and hatred.

However, Terkel cites one example that indicates things may be looking up. In the Marquette Park area of Chicago an economic development program run by black, white, and Hispanic residents has transformed a neighborhood full of vacant, burned-out buildings and boarded-up shops into one where local residents run profitable businesses, children of different races play together, and women of different races chat in the grocery store. The book indicates there is still hope for improving the economic aspect of race relations.

Part Two deals with the day-to-day interaction of blacks and whites. Among other things, it focuses on blacks and whites working together in neighborhoods, schools, social situations, and crime prevention. Terkel shows although there is little blatant racism, there is distrust and misunderstanding on both sides. Although many whites may work with successful blacks and have black friends, the whites see their co-workers and friends as different from other blacks, believing they are a small minority that do not fit the stereotype. Whites see negative images of blacks through the media and many subconsciously refuse to believe that there are black people that live just like they do.

Blacks are also distrustful of whites because they believe whites do not understand how it is to be black and do not understand how racism feels. One black insurance salesman compares being black to being forced to wear an ill-fitting shoe: "It's always uncomfortable on your foot, but you've got to wear it because it's the only shoe you've got. You don't necessarily like it. Some people can bear the uncomfort more than others. Some people can block it from their minds, some can't" (p. 110). Many blacks, affected by the real or perceived racism they experience, are quick to accuse whites of racist practices. They feel that they deserve extra help in obtaining a job. They resent whites for refusing to help provide them with equality in the workplace and in society in general.

However, according to the author, whites and blacks have many similarities. A public school teacher said, "What gets you is these kids have so much potential. Except for the fact that white kids have more pimples, there's not a hell of a lot of difference. Most of the difference is in what's happened to you" (p.165). There is also not much difference between black and white adults. The book is correct in stating that whites and blacks have the same worries and concerns. Both races must work to feed their families and have a place to live. They must teach their children and keep them out of trouble. They also find happiness in the same things.

Parts Three and Four continue the discussion of racism. Part Three discusses the history of racism in America, focusing especially on how the civil rights movement has changed the way we think about race today. Part Four deals with growing up with racism—how children see themselves as members of a certain race and how they confront racism. Three very touching interviews with couples in interracial marriages describe how children feel when they belong to two races.

Although the interviews in this book were not conducted with a random sample of participants, they still give an authentic picture of people's feelings. Terkel does not attempt to prove a theory or uncover the causes of racism. Rather, he presents the general feelings Americans have about race and racism. The author is unbiased in that he interviews people with many differing points of view—those who are blatantly racist, and those who hold racist feelings but do not act on them; those who believe in affirmative action, and those who believe in reverse discrimination; those who have been the targets of prejudice and discrimination, and those who fight to stop it. The author uses the most credible source possible—the common person. The biggest strength of the book is that it does not take a specific view on racism; it simply presents the facts and lets readers draw their own conclusion.

The book is clearly written and the interviews are easy to understand. The reader may feel confused when the author jumps from one topic to the next because the lack of transitions can be difficult to follow. But this may be a strength rather than a weakness; it shows that racism does not follow an orderly pattern and may show up at any time in any part of our lives. The only other fault is that the reader may fall in love with some of the people in the book, and want to know more about their lives and what has happened to them since the interviews. The author, of course, is not responsible for this element of human nature.

Race: How Blacks & Whites Think & Feel About the American Obsession is an excellent help in understanding how the issues of race and racism affect our society. Opinions on race relations are extremely varied, and each person thinks and acts in a different way. There is no easy solution to overcoming racism, and differences will always be present. However, this book does imply that blacks and whites can achieve healthy relationships with each other individually and collectively through positive interaction and learning about each other.

SUGGESTIONS FOR WRITING

1. Write an abstract for a library research paper you have written for this course. Or write an abstract for a paper that you have created from primary sources or new data that you gathered using a method described in Part II of this book.

2. With a classmate, exchange drafts of your library research papers. Besides writing marginal comments to each other, write a formal critique of each other's research paper. Or do the same with another major paper for the course you are taking.

3. Read a recent book that has appeared in your field. Then, using the guidelines in this chapter, write a formal review of the book. Submit your review to your campus or local newspaper or to a student journal that might publish it. Compare your review to other reviews of the same book written by professionals in your field.

PART

V

CAREER-RELATED GENRES

As you prepare to graduate from college, your thoughts are probably turning either to starting a career or continuing your education in a graduate or professional school. Whichever option you choose, it will help you to have some acquaintance with genres of writing that will help you enter and function effectively in these professional settings. These genres include the resume or *curriculum vitae*, letters of application, letters of intent (also called personal statements), and memoranda. These genres differ from much academic writing in that your rhetorical purpose is usually to persuade the audience to *act*—to hire you for a job or to admit you to a graduate program, for example—in short, to do something more than simply read and think about the information. Chapter 14 presents guidelines for creating a resume or *curriculum vitae*. Chapter 15 outlines how to write letters of application, letters of intent, and memos.

14

RESUMES

TYPES OF RESUMES

The word *resume* comes from the French *résumé*. A resume is a summary of pertinent facts about you, which you will often be asked to submit with a letter of application or to bring to an interview. In the academic world, this kind of summary often goes by the Latin name *curriculum vitae* (often simply called *vita*), which means "course of life." Graduate and professional schools may ask you to submit a vita, rather than a resume. The vita typically focuses on academic achievements, such as publications and scholarly activities and awards. The word *resume* is more commonly used in the business world and other professions. It tends to focus more on work experience and skills, though education and academic honors are usually part of any resume. Since the two kinds of documents are rather similar, and since at this point in your life you are more likely to have had the kinds of experiences that are usually recounted in a resume, the name *resume* will be used in the rest of this chapter.

But even the word *resume* now has more than one meaning. Just a few years ago, visually attractive resumes printed on paper were the only kind anyone knew about. Since the advent of the Internet, however, many people are posting their resumes on the World Wide Web, and many organizations now search the Web using key words to locate possible employees. Another new development is that many organizations want printed resumes to be *scannable*.

This means they use an optical scanner to "read" the contents of each resume they receive into a computer database; in this way they can efficiently store thousands of resumes for months. Then, when they are looking for an employee with certain skills, they can search the database for all resumes that name the desired skills and retrieve the names and addresses of potential employees. Although this chapter will further describe scannable and on-line resumes, it will focus mainly on traditional printed resumes.

TRADITIONAL RESUMES

In the traditional resume, the design and visual attractiveness of the document matter much more than in most writing you do for college courses. For this reason, if you haven't yet done so, you should read about the principles of document design discussed in Chapter 16, so you can have them in mind as you view the examples of traditional resumes in this chapter and also so you can apply the principles to the design of your own resume. Computers make it particularly easy to design an effective resume, which you can then store on a disk and update or reformat as needed. As important as design is, however, you must first plan carefully what to include and how to organize the contents of your resume for greatest impact.

ORGANIZATION OF THE TRADITIONAL RESUME

The general purpose of a resume is to acquaint a reader quickly with pertinent facts about you. An employer going through a stack of resumes typically spends only 15–20 seconds scanning each one. For this reason, you should keep your resume brief (usually only a page, occasionally two), and you should organize it so that readers can easily locate the facts they seek. (A *curriculum vitae* tends to be longer than a resume, especially as a person ages and has more achievements to list; for a young person just completing college, however, a vita would likely also be one or two pages.) The specific purpose you have for each resume depends on the particular job you are applying for. You should research the requirements for each job carefully so you can tailor your resume to show how your qualifications match its specifications.

The information in resumes is typically displayed in categories identified by headings. Within these categories, the facts are displayed in list fashion, often with bullets drawing attention to particular items. Some categories of information are fairly standard on resumes, while others may vary according to your background and the immediate goals and audience for the resume. These standard and optional categories, including what each would contain, are described next. The categories often come in the order given here, but this order is not fixed, and you can vary it according to your immediate purpose and audience. Consult the example resumes given in this chapter to see illustrations of what might fall in these categories.

Contents of the Traditional Resume

Name and Contact Information (Standard). Every resume should display at the top your name, address, and telephone number(s). When listing more than one number, it is helpful to distinguish them as daytime or evening numbers and to note at which a message can be left. If you have them, you might also list a FAX number and E-mail address at which you can be reached.

Career Objective (Optional). Some people list a career objective immediately after their name and contact information. The objective can be an effective part of the resume, provided you have space to devote to it and provided you will be sending your resume to prospective employers who you are sure have available the sort of position you seek.

Trying to write a "one-size-fits-all" career objective, however, can be hazardous. For example, stating your career objective too specifically (e.g., "to work as a tax attorney in a major corporate law firm") could backfire if an employer interpreted it to mean that you would not consider a different, but related, kind of position. Stating it too broadly (e.g., "to manage personnel") might make it seem you are too vague about your career goals. Stating it too ambitiously (e.g., "to become Vice-President of International Marketing") may suggest you intend to use the available position as only a quick stop on your move up the corporate ladder. You can customize your resume for each job you apply for by stating your career objective so that it matches what the employer has advertised for. But consider your purpose and audience carefully when deciding whether or not to include this category in your resume at all. It is often a part of the resume that can be omitted without sacrificing much.

Educational History (Standard). At this stage of your life, your education will probably be the most prominent category of information after the heading. (Later, after you have worked longer, you will emphasize your work experience and give less prominence to your education.) List the schools you have attended in *reverse chronological order*. Begin with the university or college you are now attending and give the dates of enrollment. If you wish, you may list your major (and minor, if you have one) and also the date when you expect to earn your degree. If your GPA is admirable, you may list it as well. Some students who don't have an impressive overall GPA may have a respectable one for the courses they have taken in their major. If that is the case with you, consider listing your major GPA only. You could also list scholarships and academic honors in this category, or you could list them later in the resume with other awards and achievements. Continue listing other schools you have attended, but do not go further into the past than high school. In fact, if you graduated from high school more than five years ago, consider omitting that part of your education. (As a general rule of thumb for updating your resume over the years, eliminate the older and less significant facts about yourself as you add more recent and more important achievements.) Note how the resumes in Figures 14-1 and 14-2 present the educational history of their writers.

Work Experience (Standard). List the jobs you have held, again starting with your current or most recent one and moving back in time. This section of your resume can include full-time jobs, part-time jobs, internships, research or teaching assistantships, and perhaps even volunteer experience. (If you have a great deal of volunteer experience, consider creating a separate category for it in the resume.) If you have a long work history, consider an appropriate cutoff point, rather than list every position you've held since high school. Or group your part-time or summer jobs in a cluster, without giving details about each.

List the following for each significant job:

- Your job title
- The name of the organization you worked for
- The location of the organization
- The dates of your employment

You can also list your supervisor's name with each job as a way of indicating whom the prospective employer could contact for a reference; or you may list references in a separate section.

It is common to list under each job the various duties you performed or skills you acquired. However, you may also have a separate section labeled "Skills" in which you list important skills without attaching them to a specific job. Either way, make sure that the items you list are conceptually and grammatically parallel. For example, "entered data in computer," a verb phrase, is not parallel with "receptionist," a noun.

Especially when you have held few or no full-time jobs, it is important to put the best face you can on the jobs you have held—but to do so without overstating what you really did. Employers may not be as interested in the number of years you have worked or the prestige of your jobs as they are in the skills and personal attributes your work experience has given you. Emphasize how your employment has instilled in you such things as the ability to relate well with others, to communicate, to accept responsibility and follow through, to organize, to solve problems, to meet deadlines, to work with various kinds of equipment, and so forth. Describing specific tasks you did on each job will show what skills you have acquired.

Skills (Optional). You may have other skills that an employer would value but which you didn't acquire working at specific jobs. For example, through study or travel you may be fluent in speaking, reading, and writing one or more foreign languages. Through school or on your own you may have acquired skills in working with various kinds of computer software (if so, list the name of the particular software program and the version, e.g., WordPerfect 6.0). Through school or volunteer projects, you may have developed expertise in various research methods and in statistics or in writing and editing. This kind of information deserves prominence in your resume and a "Skills" section is one option for presenting it.

Accomplishments and Awards (Optional). When you are writing a resume, it is no time to be modest about your achievements. As Babe Ruth once said, "If you done it, it ain't braggin'." Obviously, you shouldn't seem vain by making more out of accomplishments than is warranted, but do state the facts. In this section, you can list scholarships and academic awards if you haven't already listed them with your educational history. This may also be the place to describe volunteer work if you haven't included it elsewhere. You may also list civic awards, special recognition from employers, membership and leadership positions you have held in societies and clubs, or any extracurricular activities that distinguish you. Don't go further back than high school and do weigh the merits of listing some of your honors by considering how impressive they are likely to be to a prospective employer. (That you were the Homecoming Queen or the Most Preferred Man in your senior year of high school is probably not relevant for most jobs.) The heading you give this section can vary depending on what it emphasizes.

Personal Information (Optional). If you have space to include some personal information about yourself, and if you think doing so will help set you apart from other applicants, list your interests, favorite pastimes, or hobbies. Be selective, however; don't overwhelm your reader with too much. In the past it was customary to list facts such as one's age, marital status, and even physical condition, including height and weight; sometimes people even included their photo with their resume. But in this age of sensitivity to the various ways employers might discriminate against applicants, it is not advisable to include such highly personal information. Federal law prohibits employers from discriminating in hiring on the basis of age, race, sex, marital status, and religion. A potential employer is not supposed to ask you about these matters in a job interview, either, so it is wise not to volunteer personal information on your resume that might work against your being chosen for an interview or for employment.

References (Standard). Once an employer becomes serious about hiring you, he or she will generally want references from at least three people who can vouch for the quality of your work, your skills, and your personal traits. You should contact former or current supervisors and professors to ask them if they will be willing to recommend you. If they agree, you can list their names, addresses, and telephone numbers on your resume. Or you can simply write "Available upon request." At some universities and colleges, you can have your recommenders write letters for you and put the letters on file in the campus Placement Center. On your resume you can provide the address and phone number of this center. Then when employers contact the center, a copy of your file of letters will be mailed to them, so your recommenders don't have to write new letters for each potential employer.

DESIGN OF THE RESUME

Layout. Think of the resume as being arranged in "chunks" of information with indented "layers" in the chunks to help readers quickly find what they are seeking. The layout should have a more vertical than horizontal feel to it. Horizontal texts, like this page, are intended for you to read from left to right, line by line, straight through from top to bottom. A resume, however, is a document that should permit random access of information; that is, a reader should be able to scan up or down it quickly, reading the headings to locate needed information. Within the major sections, the lines of text should be short and arranged in layered columns, so that left-to-right reading takes very little time. Generally, resumes have two main columns, with the column at the left containing the headings and the column on the right containing the details (see Figure 14-1). In order to keep a resume to one page, however, it may become necessary to use the width of the page for the details, with headings above each category of details (see Figure 14-2).

White space. Whether you use a one- or a two-column format, be sure to use white space to keep the resume from looking too dense or cluttered. Use indentations within columns to show how the most specific information is subordinate to more general information. Avoid creating "windows" of white space (empty spaces surrounded by print on all sides). Most of the white space should be on the sides and top and bottom but leave some between the sections of the resume as well.

Graphical devices. Use graphical devices sparingly. Typically the only ones you should use on a resume are horizontal rules and bullets (see Figures 14-1 and 14-2). Consider your audience and purpose carefully before deciding to include other graphics such as icons or vertical rules. A neat, simple appearance is preferable to one that aims to show off all your printer's fonts.

Fonts and Point Sizes. Here are some guidelines to remember when choosing fonts and type sizes:

- *Choose a typeset font.* With contemporary word processors, you can achieve a more professional look in your resume by choosing a font that is used in typesetting (e.g. "Times New Roman" or "Garamond") rather than a font that looks as if it was produced by a typewriter (e.g., "Courier" or "Letter Gothic").

- *Choose a serif font for the body (you may choose a sans-serif font for headings).* Always choose a serif font for the body of the resume, though you may use a sans serif font for your name and contact information and for the headings, if you wish. Don't use a script or novelty font.

- *Use no more than two fonts.* In general, you should not use more than two fonts on your resume, though you may put some words in boldface or italics. For example, your name and the headings can be put in boldface to give them more weight and thus visual prominence.

- *Use bigger type for name and headings.* Your name and the headings will also appear more prominent if you put them in a bigger point size.

- *Use type sizes between 9 and 12 points.* In general, other than your name and headings, the resume should be in a point size between 9 and 12. If you are faced with using a point size of 8 or smaller to fit all the information on one page, it is time to leave something out. You may also consider making the resume two pages, but you should realize that a busy reader may not have time to look at both pages.

PROSE STYLE

The information in a resume is written in telegraph style; that is, you will seldom use complete sentences. Rather, you will write words and phrases that present the information about yourself as clearly and concisely as possible. Keep punctuation to a minimum, using mostly commas. Capitalization in the resume will vary from capitalization in the accompanying letter. In the resume, you may use capital letters for degrees you've earned or expect to earn, names of courses, job titles, or other significant words. In the cover letter, however, capitalization should conform to standard rules for common and proper nouns.

Remember the importance of parallel construction in lists of related information. Remember also that a single spelling, grammatical, or typographical error may be enough reason for a would-be employer to eliminate you from consideration. When you think your resume is nearly done, print and proofread a draft of it; then ask a few people to read it for correctness before print-

FIGURE 14-1 An Example of a Two-Column Resume

Gabriel S. Waters

915 East 820 North #23 • Provo, UT 84606 • (801)373–8406 • Gabe@fsgate.byu.edu

Education	**B.S., Economics**, Brigham Young University, April '96 Minor: Business Management
Work Experience	**Computer Support Representative**, BYU, Dec. '94 to present • Support NetWare 3.11 and 4.1 networks with 400++ nodes • Integrate software packages like GroupWise, Office, Lotus, and many more • Support various platforms including OS/2, Windows, and DOS • Support both TCP/IP and IPX/SPX protocols • Implement data storage and recovery • Support Internet access across above platforms **Owner**, Gabriel S. Waters Consulting, June '94 to present • Consult, install, and support networks and other data communication needs • Research, recommend, and implement solutions to businesses' computer needs **Network Administrator**, Multi-Serve Financial Group, Dec. '93 to Dec. '94 • Administered all data communications and voice communications • Installed and supported NetWare LAN, WAN, ISDN, remote dial-up, and all hardware • Supported and maintained Toshiba DK280 PBX • Evaluated and made all computer purchase decisions within budget • Trained staff on software and voice communications systems **Teller/Computer Operator**, Tooele Federal Credit Union, June '91 to Aug. '93 • Performed all teller duties • Backed up and shut down computer system nightly • Generated annual report on Credit Union financial status for NCUA
Other Activities	**President**, Nantucket Home Owners Association, April '95 to present **Volunteer**, Boy Scouts of America, Merit Badge Counselor
References	Richard Roskelley, Director of Financial Computer Support, 173 TMCB, Brigham Young University, Provo, Utah 84602, (801) 378–4252 Donald Swain, Senior Analyst, MultiServe Financial Group, 1325 S. 800 E., Suite 322, Orem, Utah 84058, (801) 225–0800 Milford Varner, President of Tooele Federal Credit Union, 562 N. Main, Tooele, Utah 84074, (801) 833–7200

FIGURE 14-2 An Example of a One-Column Resume

Geannina Segura Bartholomew

790 N 100 W #2 • Provo, UT 84601 • (801) 371–8787 • bartholg@slkc.uswest.net

WORK EXPERIENCE

BENSON AGRICULTURE AND FOOD INSTITUTE
Translator, February 1994 to present
- translate, edit, proofread, and write articles, reports, research proposals, and papers related to the nutritional and agricultural improvement of families in developing countries
- prepare and edit articles for *Revista Latinoamericana de Agricultura y Nutrición*

BRIGHAM YOUNG UNIVERSITY HISTORY DEPARTMENT
Research Assistant, September 1994 to present
- read genealogical records handwritten in ancient Spanish
- translate documents
- search libraries for records of interest to family historians
- summarize contents of articles for research on families

EDUCATION

Brigham Young University
Bachelor of Science, Family Science and Family History Certificate, April 1996
Major GPA: 3.88   Cumulative GPA: 3.84

UNIVERSIDAD AUTONOMA DE CENTRO AMERICA, *1987–1989*

UNIVERSIDAD DE COSTA RICA, *1986*

ACADEMIC AWARDS, HONORS, AND ACTIVITIES
- International Honor Roll Student, eight semesters
- Preston G. Hughes Foundation Scholarship
- Member, Phi Kappa Phi, Golden Key, Kappa Omicron Nu
- Member, Family Science Student Association
- Member, Costa Rican Genealogy and History Association
- Volunteer, Conference on International Year of the Family
- Certified Family Life Educator by National Council of Family Relations

SKILLS

- Spanish/English translation, simultaneous interpretation, writing, editing
- Hispanic family history research and paleography
- Qualitative research skills: interviewing and content analysis
- Proficiency in WordPerfect 6.1, Excel, Harvard Graphics 2.0, World Wide Web
- Educator about family life in diverse settings

REFERENCES provided upon request

ing the final draft. If you make any changes from their feedback, proofread your resume again.

Paper and Printing

When applying for a job, internship, graduate school, or other opportunity important to your future, be prepared to spend a few extra dollars to make the best impression possible. You should have your resume laser-printed on high quality bond paper that is white, off-white, or ivory. If your resume is accompanied by a cover letter, or sent in a business-sized envelope, these should be from the same paper stock.

SCANNABLE RESUMES

A scannable resume contains the same categories of information as a traditional resume, but it differs in two important ways. First, the design of a scannable resume must be very plain so that the optical scanner can "read" it easily and store the information correctly in a database. Second, the focus of the resume is on a list of key words that name your skills and abilities, since the key words are what a computer search will look for when retrieving resumes from the database.

Design of the Scannable Resume

The design of a scannable resume is in many ways just the opposite of a traditional resume. The following list of things to do when designing a scannable resume contradicts much of what this chapter says you should do to create a traditional resume. But each of these guidelines helps to ensure that the optical scanner will store the information as you wrote it.

1. **Use a sans-serif font.** Serifs make letters a little more complicated, and the scanner might read the letter sequence *ti* as an *h*, for example.
2. **Use a typesize between 10 and 14 points.** If you use a smaller point size, the scanner may not be able to read it correctly. The optimal point size is 12, even if using it means that you must make your resume longer than one page. Headings should not be bigger than 14 points.
3. **Avoid italics and underline and limit your use of boldface type.** Too many fonts and frills will just confuse the scanner.
4. **Do not use bullets, lines, rules, graphics, or shading.** Limit your resume to words and numerals only.

5. **Display information in one column, left-justified.** Putting the information in two columns with lots of indentations and white space may cause the scanner to misread the order of information or leave something out.

6. **Send a laser-printed original on plain white paper.** The scanner has a more difficult time reading photocopies and from colored paper. Use only one side of the paper.

ORGANIZATION OF THE SCANNABLE RESUME

Like a traditional resume, a scannable resume should have your name, address, and phone number at the top. The next most important thing is a list of key words that name the various kinds of knowledge and skills you have as well as the abilities and personal traits you have developed. These key words should mostly be nouns and should include the names or labels of jobs, skills, tasks, instruments, software, hardware, or other things currently important in the career field you seek to enter. Some of the key words can be adjectives that describe your character traits and personal abilities. You should list any key words that describe you and that you think someone might conceivably use when trying to retrieve the resumes of people with desired qualifications.

After the key word summary, you should present a summary of your experience in your education, jobs, and personal life. Finally, you list the traditional headings of education, work, service, and so on with pertinent facts under each. Figure 14-3 presents an example of Geannina Segura Bartholomew's resume reformatted as a scannable resume. Comparing Figure 14-3 with Figure 14-2 will help you see how the scannable resume differs from the traditional one.

ON-LINE RESUMES

On-line resumes are written to be posted on the World Wide Web. This type of resume might include color, graphics, and links to other Web sites; it can also be updated frequently. Employers now advertise job openings on the World Wide Web, so a person looking for a job could electronically send a resume to a potential employer. In fact, people who already have jobs often keep their resumes on the World Wide Web because organizations are always looking for new employees and might contact potential employees to make a job offer. Organizations looking for employees can use a search engine to retrieve any on-line resumes that contain key words of interest to the organization. By coupling the keyword with a certain ZIP code, the employer could limit the number of resumes retrieved to people who already live in a certain area. As you can see, this method

FIGURE 14-3 An Example of a Scannable Resume

Geannina Segura Bartholomew

790 North 100 West Apt. 2
Provo, UT 84601
801 371–8787

Translator. Writer. Editor. Proofreader. Family History. Genealogy. Paleography. Family Science major. Family history certificate. Research articles. Library research. Interviewing. Content analysis. WordPerfect. Windows. Excel. Harvard Graphics. Achievement oriented. Disciplined. Team player.

Summary of Experience
Two years research assistant for History Department. Two years Spanish/English translation, writing, editing, and proofreading for Benson Agriculture and Food Institute. Proficient in IBM-compatible personal computer using WordPerfect 6.1; Harvard Graphics 2.0, Excel, and World Wide Web.

Education
B.S. in Family Science with Family History Certificate in Hispanic Sources from Brigham Young University, April 1996, 3.84 GPA
Preston G. Hughes Foundation Scholarship.
International Student Honor Roll eight semesters.
Member of Golden Key, Phi Kappa Phi, Kappa Omicron Nu.
Universidad Autonoma de Centro America, 1987–89.
Universidad de Costa Rica, 1986

Work Experience
Benson Agriculture and Food Institute, BYU, Provo, UT, 2–94 to present
      Translator, writer, editor, proofreader
      Prepare articles on nutrition and agriculture for developing nations
      Prepare and edit articles for Spanish-language journal
History Department, BYU, Provo, UT, 9–94 to 6–95
      Research assistant
      Search libraries for family history records
      Summarize articles
      Read and translate ancient Spanish genealogical records

Service
Volunteer Host, Conference on International Year of the Family
Interpret for Spanish speakers at English-only meetings
Translate official documents from Spanish to English
Teach lessons on strengthening family relationships to prisoners

of putting employers in touch with potential employees is more efficient than the present system of waiting for applicants to mail or bring in a printed resume.

It is beyond the scope of this book to describe how to create an on-line resume since it requires a knowledge of HTML (Hypertext Markup Language) or a special software program that helps you create such a resume. Designing a resume for a computer screen is also different from designing one for paper. If you are interested in seeing some on-line resumes, here are the names of three Web sites with their URLs (addresses). By logging on to the Internet and using these addresses, you can see on-line job postings and resume posting services.

Site Name	URL
Career Mosaic	http://www.careermosaic.com/cm/
Monster Board	http://www.monster.com/
On-line Career Center	http://www.occ.com/

SUGGESTIONS FOR WRITING

1. Locate an ad for a job for which you are qualified; then create a traditional resume that presents your qualifications for the job. If you haven't yet done so, read Chapter 16 to learn about document design so you can format your resume in an attractive, readable way. Write a letter of application (see Chapter 15) to accompany your resume. After getting feedback on your drafts, revise both. If now is the right time to send them, print your resume and letter on high-quality paper and mail them. Save your letter and resume on a computer disk so you can change the format and contents for the next job you apply for.

2. Take the traditional resume you have saved on a disk and reformat it as a scannable resume. When you inquire about jobs you want to apply for, find out if the employer prefers a traditional or scannable resume.

15

LETTERS AND MEMOS

As you approach the end of your undergraduate years, important decisions await you. Will you seek a job? If so, where? Will you go to graduate school? If so, what is involved in applying? The answers to these questions are likely to involve writing in some form. For example, if you are ready to apply for a job, you will generally send out letters of application. If you plan to apply for graduate or professional school, you will probably have to compose a letter of intent or personal statement to send with other required materials. This chapter outlines principles of form and content, as well as steps to follow in composing, that will help you create effective letters of application or intent.

The letter of application or intent helps you start on the path toward your professional goals. Once you are established in your profession, you will learn to write in many other genres, one of which is the memorandum. Since the memo is common in virtually all professions, this chapter also gives some brief instruction about the form and content of memos. Your instructor may have you write some memos as a way of practicing this genre and communicating with teacher or classmates about assignments in your course.

LETTERS OF APPLICATION

A letter of application is usually accompanied by a resume (see Chapter 14). In fact, the letter of application is sometimes called a "cover letter" because it allows you to draw the reader's attention to the resume and to elaborate on some of the facts listed in it. Generally your purpose in sending a letter and resume is to get an interview with the recipient or the chance to take the next step in the application process. Letters of application may be sent not only for a job, but also for internships, scholarships, grants, or other opportunities you want to apply for. Whatever their purpose, they generally take the same form as a standard business letter. That is, they have each of the parts listed below, and they incorporate the design elements described below and illustrated in Figures 15-3 and 15-4. Knowing about the letter's parts and design is not sufficient for creating a successful letter, however, so this chapter also includes advice for composing your letter.

PARTS OF THE LETTER

Heading. Except when you are writing on letterhead stationery (which is already printed with your return address), the first element of a business letter is the heading, which consists of your address and the date. Give your complete street address on the first line; the city, state, and ZIP code on the next line; and the date on the third line. The name of the state can be abbreviated using the standard two-letter abbreviation used by the U.S. Postal Service. The date should be written out completely, using the full name of the month rather than an abbreviation or a numeral (e.g., September 15, 1996, or 15 September 1996, but not Sept. 15, '96 or 9/15/96). Here is a sample heading:

726 Pleasantview Drive
Cove Village, CA 96346
August 31, 1997

Inside Address. After spacing at least twice (or more, depending on the length of your letter), write the name, title, and complete address of the person who is to receive your letter. If you don't know the name, it is acceptable to use just the title, if you know it, of the person you wish to receive your letter (e.g., Vice-President for Human Resources, or Chair of the Scholarship Committee). Here is a sample inside address:

Ms. Irene Papandreou
Director of Human Resources
National Information Systems
Longbrook, NY 20153

Salutation or Greeting.   Space twice after the inside address and write "Dear _____:" (Note that the salutation is punctuated with a colon, not a comma, unless you know the person to whom you are writing.) Fill in the blank with the title and last name of the person you are addressing. If the person goes by a title such as *Dr., Professor*, or *President*, you should use that. If no special title is used, use the standard polite forms of address. For a man, obviously, you will use the title *Mr.*; for a woman, you should use *Ms.*, unless you know the woman prefers to be addressed by *Miss* or *Mrs*. If you know the person well enough, you may use a first name.

Sometimes a person will use only their initials or they will have a first name that may be given to either sex. If you haven't met the person or can't otherwise determine which gender they are, the best option is to use their complete name in the salutation. For example, if you didn't know whether Kelly Anderson was male or female, you could write "Dear Kelly Anderson."

If you do not know the name of the person who will read your letter, you may use a title in the salutation, as in "Dear Office Manager." Or, in place of the greeting, you may write an attention or subject line, such as one of the following:

Attention: Office Manager
Subject: Advertisement for Summer Temps
Re: Management Position

So-called generic greetings of an earlier era, such as "Gentlemen," "Dear Sir," or "Dear Sir or Madam" are no longer used because they don't adequately reflect the realities or the language used in today's business world. The greeting "To Whom it May Concern" is still used sometimes, but it is rather stiff; use it only as a last resort.

The Body.   Beginning two lines under the greeting, write the body of the letter. In a letter of application, the body is generally three or four paragraphs long, each with a definite role to play in raising your reader's interest and persuading him or her to consider your application more carefully.

First paragraph.   In the first paragraph, you should name the position or opportunity you are seeking and, particularly for a job, how you learned about it. If you saw an advertisement, mention it; if you heard about it from another person, mention that. A potential employer wants to know how the news of an opening becomes known. If you do not know there is an opening and are writing on the chance that there might be, briefly explain why you want to work for the organization. End this paragraph by stating in a few words why you feel you are qualified for the position or opportunity.

Middle paragraphs.   In the middle paragraph or paragraphs, elaborate on your qualifications. You might devote one paragraph to your educational preparation and another to your work or volunteer experience. Be specific. In addition to writing, "I am a well-organized, efficient worker," provide details that *show* the reader that you are. For example, you might write, "In my last job, I was able to clear up a month-old backlog of unfilled orders by eliminating unnecessary steps from the shipping procedure, reducing the time needed by 30 percent." Be selective in what you include; you don't want to oversell yourself, and you want to keep the letter to a page. Remember that your letter works in tandem with your resume to give the reader as full a picture as possible of your experience and abilities. By presenting and elaborating on some well-chosen details about yourself in the letter, you hope to interest the employer enough to gain an interview, at which you can elaborate further.

Final paragraphs. In the final paragraph, refer the reader to your resume and politely request further action. Indicate when you will be available for an interview and express hope that you will hear from the employer soon. If the organization is in another city to which you will soon be traveling, ask to have an appointment during your stay. Sound a confident but not too aggressive tone in the closing lines of your letter.

Complimentary Close.   Two lines under the body of the letter, you will write one of several common closings that will precede your signature. For a formal letter addressed to someone you are not well acquainted with, the standard complimentary closes are listed below. Note that each is followed by a comma:

- Sincerely,
- Sincerely yours,
- Yours truly,
- Very truly yours,
- Respectfully,

If you are acquainted with the addressee, you could consider using "Cordially," or "Best regards."

Signature and Typed Name.   After the complimentary close, space down four lines and type your complete name. Write your signature in the blank space above your typed name.

Enclosure Line.   If you have enclosed something with the letter—and with an application letter you will generally enclose your resume—it is common to type the word "Enclosure" two lines after your name, flush with the left margin.

DESIGN OF THE LETTER

Layout.   There are two ways to format a business letter: full-block style (illustrated in Figure 15-1) or semi-block style (illustrated in Figure 15-2). In full-block style, all parts of the letter are aligned flush with the left margin. In semi-block style, the heading, complimentary close, and signature are aligned with each other and are placed right of the center of the page. In addition, in the semi-block style, the opening line of each paragraph can be indented five spaces.

The letter should have enough white space in it that it does not look formidable to read. Although paragraphs are single spaced, you should double-space between paragraphs. To avoid giving the letter a top-heavy appearance, center the printed matter on the page. One way to introduce more white space at the top of the letter is to space several times between the heading and the inside address. Between all other parts of the letter, however, you should leave only two lines of space. Margins on both sides and at the top and bottom of the letter should be at least one inch. Do *not* justify the right margin because doing so makes the letter more difficult to read.

Unlike a resume, a letter is not designed for random access. It is meant to be read line by line, from left to right, beginning at the top and moving to the bottom. Additional devices to draw attention to layout, such as boldface or graphics, are generally not needed. In some cases, additional indentation and bullets might be used in a letter, but not often.

Fonts and Point Sizes. As with the resume, choose a serif font that looks professionally typeset (such as Times New Roman) rather than typewritten (such as Courier). The usual point size for a letter is 12, though you could use 11 or even 10 if doing so would help you keep the letter to one page. If you would have to use an even smaller point size to make your letter fit on a page, consider trimming your letter. Only in rare cases should you send a two-page letter.

Paper and Printing. Laser print your letter on high-quality bond paper of the same stock you use for your resume. Do not use colors other than white, off-white, or ivory. The professional appearance of your letter makes an important first impression on your reader, so this is no time to be cheap or careless.

COMPOSING YOUR LETTER

Business letters have become a highly standardized genre. In a sense, this is good because the conventions to follow are quite clear-cut. However, it also could be detrimental because you may be tempted to lapse into formulaic, clichéd writing. Since your application letter is generally your first contact with an employer or someone who has the ability to grant you the internship or scholarship you are seeking, you want to make a good impression and distinguish yourself from other applicants. You want your own voice and personality to come through in your letter while still observing the conventions the genre entails.

Prewriting. As in other writing tasks, an effective prewriting strategy is the first step to a successful final draft. Using a technique such as brainstorming, listing, or freewriting, generate as many facts about yourself as you can—anything you think might even remotely interest an employer or award committee. Write much more than you can possibly use because the very act of generating material may help you think more carefully about your strengths. With a lot of material to choose from, select the facts that best represent your qualifications. Plan how you can arrange and interpret these details about yourself to show why you would be the best choice for the job, the internship, the scholarship, or other opportunity.

Drafting. Write a longer first draft than you can use, then cut it down to size. Consider the order in which you present your ideas: Is it logical and clear? Consider also how your sentences connect with each other; make transitions explicit.

Because the letter is about yourself, you will find that you need to say "I" in it frequently. There is nothing wrong or immodest about this. However, it can become monotonous if you begin every sentence with "I." Find ways to vary your syntax so you do not need to start every sentence with a reference to yourself.

To make the letter sound like you, use words you would use if you were speaking with the reader face to face. Present your qualifications in a matter-of-fact, but confident tone. You won't necessarily impress the reader by using highfalutin' and superlative language like this:

> I am possessed of the conviction that I can make a uniquely and immensely valuable contribution to your organization because my demonstrable academic success in my chosen major of social psychology and my prior assignments and accomplishments in the business field of employment constitute qualifications of a superior nature.

The reader is likely to be put off by such a pompous and wordy sentence and would probably prefer to read something simpler, like this:

> I am confident I can contribute to your organization's success because my training in social psychology and my work experience in business qualify me in unique ways.

Revising and proofreading. Revise and edit carefully to make the letter correct and concise. Show a near final draft to trusted professors, advisers, or tutors in your campus writing center. Incorporate worthwhile suggestions from them and then proofread with the utmost care. As with a resume, a single spelling, grammatical, or typographical mistake in a letter can be your undoing when the reader is looking for a reason to eliminate some contenders from consideration.

FIGURE 15-1 Full-Block Style Letter

3930 NW Witham Hill Dr.
Corvallis, OR 97330
21 January 1997

Mr. Leland Slaughter
Director of Therapeutic Recreation
Utah State Hospital
1300 East Center St.
Provo, UT 84603

Dear Mr. Slaughter:

I am writing to apply for an internship in the geriatric unit of the Utah State Hospital during the summer of 1997. I learned about this opportunity last fall when my career class, under the supervision of Dr. Gary Palmer, visited a therapeutic recreation facility similar to the one you direct. Ever since this experience, I have been interested in working with patients in a mental health care facility.

I will graduate with a BS degree in therapeutic recreation and certification in gerontology in August of 1997. Because my goal is to be nationally certified, I will have completed all of the required courses by June. Among these are classes in abnormal psychology and in assessment and programming in therapeutic recreation, both of which will help me fulfill my responsibilities as an intern. I also feel strongly that my coursework in gerontology would help me serve patients in your geriatric unit.

Because of my genuine love for the elderly, I have had several opportunities to serve this population. My first experience was at a residential care home for elders requiring 24-hour supervision and assistance with activities of daily living. At this home, I had a job serving individuals with Alzheimer's disease. More recently, I was the recreation supervisor for retired residents at an intermediate care facility for the mentally retarded and developmentally disabled. In addition to the responsibilities of planning, implementation, evaluation, and documentation, this experience deepened my understanding of how recreation improves the quality of life for elders.

Although I have not yet officially worked in the mental health field, my previous jobs and volunteer work in numerous nursing homes have allowed me to serve individuals with various mental disorders. In addition to those mentioned, I have encountered autism, bipolar disorder, depression, and schizophrenia.

I am eager to gain the experience that an internship with your facility would provide. I have enclosed my resume, and I look forward to interviewing with you soon to answer additional questions you may have. You may phone me any evening or all day Tuesdays and Thursdays at (541) 639–2713.

Sincerely,

Melissa Lundmark

Enclosure

FIGURE 15-2 Semi-Block Style Letter

218 12th Avenue East
Jerome, ID 83338
17 September 1996

Ms. Kathryn Hubbard
University of Washington
International Programs & Exchange
516 Schmitz Hall, PA-10
Seattle, WA 98195

Dear Ms. Hubbard:

I am writing to submit a proposal for the production of an ethnographic film about South American culture in the Andes. The film will be made primarily for educational purposes; it will be shot on 16mm motion picture film and will conform to standard public broadcast format. I read about your organization in a brochure that was sent to me, and I am very interested in working with the University of Washington on this project. I feel that working together we can bring a greater understanding of Andean peoples and their intricate culture to a wide audience.

Specifically, I am planning to film this project on location in Southern Peru, beginning in the summer of 1998, as part of the requirements for my MA degree. In the region surrounding Cuzco, Peru, I will document the everyday life of the Quechua and Aymara speaking peoples. My MA thesis will compare the life of the natives today, who have access to a written language, with the life of their ancestors, who depended solely on oral forms of communication.

Although I have not yet directed such a film project, I have the support of many experienced professionals, both in the fields of Latin American anthropology and archaeology, and in documentary filmmaking. I will soon complete a BA degree in anthropology, with an emphasis on the Andean peoples of South America, particularly the Lake Titicaca area of southern Peru. In June of 1997 I will travel to a village in Guatemala to study further the methods and techniques of anthropologists in the field as well as to accustom myself once again to life outside of the United States. Between the years of 1992 and 1994 I lived in the Caribbean coastal region of Colombia. I know what it's like to experience culture shock and to become accustomed to another people and their ways.

I have begun planning for the documentary film two years early so that I can put together the very best team of sponsors and crew members to work with me. I think your organization can count on my producing a film that will be highly suitable for educational purposes and public broadcast. I have enclosed my resume as well as the resume of my crew members. Also you will find our estimated production budget and schedule. I look forward to meeting with you and your staff in the near future. Please call me if you have any questions at (208) 373–4949.

Sincerely,

Tyler K. Lee

Enclosures

LETTERS OF INTENT AND PERSONAL STATEMENTS

A letter of intent or personal statement is usually part of an application for graduate or professional school. Despite its name, a letter of intent is usually not formatted as a letter: It has no inside address, salutation, or complimentary close, though it may have a heading and a signature. It is like an essay in both form and content, yet it is like a letter of application in important ways: It is about your qualifications, and its purpose is to persuade readers (usually a committee of professors) to choose you from among many other applicants for a position in the program you want to enter.

In this chapter, it's not possible to delve into how letters of intent for law school might differ from those for an MBA program; instead, this chapter provides some general advice on how to make your letter best represent you. You should be able to get more particular advice from four sources:

1. The admissions offices at the schools you plan to apply to will tell you what form your statement must take, how long it can be, and the kinds of information the admissions committee is seeking.

2. Preprofessional advisers or placement center officers on your campus may conduct workshops or tutorials on how to write successful letters of intent in your chosen field.

3. A number of books available in libraries and bookstores give helpful advice for writing letters for particular kinds of graduate programs.

4. A professor or mentor in the field you want to enter can give you helpful feedback before you print and mail a final draft of your statement.

IMPORTANCE OF THE LETTER

The letter of intent is one of the main parts of a typical application for graduate school. The other parts are usually an application form; a transcript of your undergraduate courses and grades; test scores from standardized aptitude and achievement tests such as the GRE, the LSAT, the GMAT, or the MCAT; letters of recommendation (usually three) from professors or others who can attest to your intellectual, social, and personal qualifications for graduate school; and a resume, or at least a list of work experience and extracurricular activities. Because you will be hurrying to submit all of these parts of the application by a certain deadline, you may be tempted to think you can toss off your personal statement in a few hours a couple of days before you have to mail it. Thinking that would be a big mistake.

The letter of intent is often the most important part of the application—in fact, it is the only one you still have some control over as application deadlines loom. By then your GPA is already pretty well determined, your test scores have already been calculated, and your letters of recommendation are beyond your control. But in your personal statement you can still say things about yourself that will not otherwise be apparent to the admissions committee. A strong personal statement, for example, can sometimes salvage an application that isn't distinguished by a high GPA or impressive exam scores. A poor statement, on the other hand, may sabotage an otherwise competitive application. Even when the other indicators of a successful application are strong, a highly effective personal statement may bring a bonus beyond mere admission—a scholarship or tuition waiver, for example. You should therefore plan to start several weeks early, if possible, to draft your letter of intent. Figures 15-3 and 15-4 present letters that resulted from several drafts written over a period of two or three weeks; both were successful in getting the applicants admitted to their chosen professional schools.

GENERATING SUBSTANCE THROUGH PREWRITING

Before you begin drafting your statement, generate a lot of possible material that you could use in it. Here are some questions to which you could freewrite answers:

1. What is your motivation for wanting an advanced degree? What events in your life gave you that motivation? What feelings or impulses move you in this direction?

2. What are your strengths? How are they related to succeeding in the career you've chosen? What choices have you made in school and extracurricular activities to prepare yourself for the kind of career you want?

3. What significant experiences have you had that show you have the talents to succeed in a rigorous graduate program? What unique experiences and abilities would you bring to the school you are applying to?

DRAFTING AROUND A THEME

Since the personal statement is a brief essay, it should have a clearly defined focus or theme. After generating ideas through prewriting answers to the above questions, you should be able to select a focus from all you've written and begin to draft your essay around that theme. For example, you could narrate a defining event or series of events in your life that helped crystallize why you would like a particular career. Then you could add brief descriptions of how other choices and experiences have prepared you for that career. This is largely the strategy used by David Barlow and Janiel Cragun in the personal statements reprinted in Figures 15-3 and 15-4. Notice that although Barlow was motivated to make his career choice, in part, because of pressing human needs he observed, he avoids the temptation to claim that through advanced study he will be able to single-handedly solve these problems. More modestly, he hopes through continued education to contribute to solutions. A "save-the-world-single-handed" approach is not likely to gain favor with admissions committees. Cragun also strikes a balance between confidence and humility in carefully explaining important dimensions of her preparation for a medical career.

Another way to make an argument for your acceptance is to explain strengths you have that are not measurable by test scores and GPA. Things such as work and volunteer experience, interpersonal skills, bilingual and bicultural abilities, and the ability to be independent and self-motivated count with admissions committees, if you can show how these traits are relevant to the course of study you wish to pursue. Resist the temptation to spell out everything about your life, however. There is no need to repeat information that is available in other parts of your application, and there is generally a word limit for the statement anyway. Still another approach is to explain why your particular background and talents are a good match for unique courses the program offers. This means, of course, that you will have to research the various programs you plan to apply to and learn what special emphases they offer.

REVISING AND EDITING

Plan to spend a number of hours working on your statement over a period of two or three weeks. Draft a version, get feedback on it, and let it rest a few days. Then write another version, trying ideas others have given you. Continue seeking feedback and revising until you have a draft that includes particulars that you think best describe you. Work on the organization to make it clear and cohesive; the conceptual links between paragraphs should be apparent but not obtrusive.

As you edit to make your statement the right length, be alert to empty words you could cut and to stilted words or jargon that you would not likely use if you were speaking to the admissions committee. They are not looking to be impressed by a big vocabulary; instead, they want clarity. The importance of correct spelling, usage, and sentence structure can't be overstated. The ability to write well is extremely important in all kinds of graduate work, and the committee will judge your ability to succeed as a writer in graduate school by the quality of the writing in your personal statement. Mistakes can lower your ranking in the list of applicants. You and at least one other person should proofread your statement carefully before you mail it. As with other letters, laser print the final draft on high-quality bond paper either white or off-white in color.

FIGURE 15-3 Example of a Personal Statement

David B. Barlow
Personal Statement

When I first agreed to help establish a prevention group for drug and alcohol abuse at my high school, I had little understanding of the commitment I was making. Because of my position as class president, I was approached by a social worker who was interested in establishing a substance abuse prevention group. I agreed to help, although I was not aware of a significant problem with substance abuse at my high school. Starting a drug prevention group just seemed like the type of thing a student leader should do, even if the problem seemed nebulous. Several weeks later, I received a late night telephone call that made the problem real.

Calls at two o'clock in the morning are rarely good news; this call was no exception. As I struggled to awaken, I realized two things: the voice on the other end of the line was my friend Shannon's, and something was terribly wrong. She had been abused by her drunken uncle. She was feeling worthless and wondering if she could go on with her life. Shannon and I talked for a long time that night. As we talked, I realized that anything I said to her during our conversation would have only a small effect; mostly I listened. Thankfully, at the end of our talk, she decided to give life another chance.

That conversation changed both of us. Shannon learned that she had a friend; I learned that substance abuse was a genuine problem with real victims. As the months passed and I became increasingly involved in substance abuse prevention, the original intangibility of the drug and alcohol abuse problem quickly gave way to an all-too-concrete picture of suffering. I soon met others who had suffered physical or mental abuse, lived in dysfunctional families, or lost friends or relatives because of substance abuse. For me these were no longer abstract notions of suffering; they were the painful experiences of real people, people who were my friends. Shannon's call, coupled with the aforementioned experiences, provided the impetus to dedicate myself more fully to the prevention project.

I didn't realize it then, but the national substance abuse dilemma has something in common with a novel entitled *Watership Down*. In this story, a group of homeless rabbits stumble across another colony of rabbits who agree to provide them shelter. One of the first things the newcomers notice is that fresh carrots and lettuce are left near the rabbit holes daily. They also soon realize that periodically some of their fellow rabbits turn up missing.

At first none of the other rabbits want to discuss the mystery, but the visitors doggedly persist in inquiring about their missing comrades. They eventually learn that

FIGURE 15-3 Example of a Personal Statement (continued)

a farmer who lives nearby daily sets wire traps for the rabbits, along with fresh produce. The rabbits who live in the colony realize the danger but are unwilling even to
discuss the threat of the wire traps because they love the fresh food and see no better
alternative to the arrangement.

I now see similarities in the lives of my friends. For some of them, mind-altering
substances provided quick thrills and promised easy money. For the rabbits, the free
vegetables were tasty and required no work. Yet obtaining and consuming either the
drugs or the produce was always dangerous, often destructive, and sometimes deadly.
Unlike the colony in *Watership Down*, our nation has not been afraid to talk about the
danger. Like that fictional colony, however, we have not done a good job of providing a
positive alternative.

The prevention organization I have worked with since 1986 focuses on remedying
that shortcoming. By offering drug- and alcohol-free recreational, work, and peer group
alternatives, this group has provided teens an attractive way to avoid the traps of substance abuse. I have been privileged to have the opportunity of seeing many people
benefit from this work, not only in Shannon's case, but in many others as well. In the
context of drug prevention, I have worked with teen victims of physical and mental
abuse, students who have lived at "behavior correction" schools, and children from
impoverished families. Sometimes my work with them has helped them change their
lives; sometimes it has not. Though not all of these experiences have been complete suc-
cesses, each has been a chance to make at least a small difference in someone's life.

My desire to study law stems from the same motivation that compels me to work
in drug prevention and in alleviating hunger and homelessness. No simple solution
exists for any of these intractable problems. Yet even a little progress in these areas
means improved opportunities and a better life for some of those who are currently dis-
advantaged. Though I am uncertain about the specific career path I will follow, I have a
particular interest in welfare policy and the law as well as constitutional law. Earning a
Juris Doctorate will assist me by providing rigorous intellectual training and the formal
credentials necessary to work in the judicial system and in government. I look forward
to exploring these fields in law school, as well as discovering other public service career
options.

I know that the problems the nation faces in drug abuse, hunger, homelessness,
and other areas are enormous; the difference that I will make may be small. Yet as I
learned that night when my friend Shannon called for help, sometimes a small difference is just enough.

FIGURE 15-4 Example of a Personal Statement

Janiel Cragun

Personal Statement

"It is not enough that you should understand about applied science in order that your work may increase man's blessings. Concern for man himself and his fate must always form the chief interest of all technical endeavors...."—*Albert Einstein, Address, California Institute of Technology, 1931.*

Although the study of medicine requires understanding the laws of science, the practice of medicine is guided by the *human art*—a concern for the variability and depth of human nature. As a student of human resource management and psychology, I have studied many theories of human behavior, which have shown me how to tap the human element when interacting with people. In addition, life experiences have taught me how important it is to make people the center of my profession. I feel my understanding of the human art will be a great asset as I practice medicine.

The human art is compassion and understanding. In the summer of 1994, tropical storm Alberto hit the Florida panhandle, causing severe flooding along the Choctawhatchee River. I helped a woman whose home had been submerged in the flood to retrieve her belongings. The water and silt had left many of her keepsakes ruined and contaminated. I was frustrated when some volunteers whom I had asked to come help went through her home and quickly discarded anything they thought was irreparable. To me, their behavior was callous because the old woman constantly voiced her hopes of saving her possessions. These volunteers wanted to help, but they were insensitive to the woman's emotional needs and desires. I realized that there were limits to what I could restore, but I knew she deserved my understanding and compassion, even if I believed that items were unsalvageable. I learned that service becomes an art when it combines physical help with compassion and understanding. I believe my role as a doctor will be more than stitching wounds and performing physicals; it will also be listening to people without assuming their opinions and needs are irrelevant.

The human art provides familiarity and emotion. I have thrilled to learn how the physical concepts of pressure, tension, beat frequencies, and wavelength parallel how I bow, tune, or play different notes on my cello. In theory, a computer could play the cello using the laws of physics, but in spite of its perfect technique, the computer could never reach the heart of musical performance—emotion. I have spent countless hours preparing for competitions and performances, practicing musical passages again and again just to get the right feeling. I have struggled alongside musicians in orchestras and quartets to synthesize musical opinions into one harmonic expression. It is the emotion that people respond to. When singing and playing the piano in nursing homes, I discovered that the

FIGURE 15-4 Example of a Personal Statement (continued)

best songs to sing were those from the residents' childhood, the familiar ones that brought back good memories. I believe music becomes an art when it breathes familiarity and emotion into its audience. In medicine, a patient should not feel the doctor is a computer that has been programmed to respond to certain laws of science. I want to be a doctor who can make my patients feel comfortable in a strange environment and who can communicate with genuine emotion and concern.

The human art knows its potential is guided by limits. In early fall of 1994, I found myself dangling from a rope swing 25 feet in the air. As part of a unique management training exercise, I was struggling with a difficult element of an obstacle course which demanded a great deal of upper body strength. Although I had already finished the course twice, once under normal conditions and once blindfolded, I wanted to challenge myself a third time by taking an optional route that was more difficult. Just before completing the last step, I was forced to stop. My mind and will could not overcome the exhaustion of my muscles. I felt angry and disappointed. I am not a quitter. Even when emotionally exhausted, I work hard to meet my commitments. I found it ironic that a few hours earlier I had misjudged a classmate as being a "wimp" because she had stopped short of her goal while climbing a near-vertical rockface. At the time, I did not think her exhaustion was a valid excuse. I felt that since I had made it up the rockface she could too. After my defeat on the obstacle course, I empathized with her fatigue. I realized that I had trivialized her limits by assuming they were equal to mine. This experience taught me that personal limits are like rubber bands; they can stretch a great deal over time, but if stretched too quickly, they break. The art of setting reasonable goals and demands for myself or others comes from recognizing and respecting individual limits. When practicing medicine, it will be important to recognize my own limitations of knowledge or skill. However, it will also be important to respect the emotional and physical limits of my patients when discussing sensitive issues with them and when prescribing medication or treatments.

My decision to become a doctor has evolved over several years from a simple interest to a strong commitment. I always liked the "mystery" element of medical diagnosis. Then, as I took classes in microbiology, anatomy, and physiology, my interest in medicine grew stronger. Early on, I exposed myself to many people-oriented disciplines, including psychology, music therapy, and speech pathology, and I began to feel the importance of addressing the human needs of the people with whom I work. Although I know that my love of human biology will be important in practicing medicine, I realize that medicine is more than research and knowledge. Medical practice is an art. Whether it concerns remembering a patient's name, helping a patient understand a medical term, listening to a patient, or consulting with other doctors, medicine becomes an art when it combines science with humanity. I believe my exposure to the human art has prepared me to meet the needs of my patients and therefore to be a strong health care provider.

MEMORANDA

The memorandum (the plural is memoranda), or the memo for short, is a brief written form of communication used *within* an organization. Brevity, clarity, and efficiency in reading are its hallmarks. Memos differ from letters in that they have no salutation, no complimentary close, and generally no signature (although the writer sometimes writes his or her initials next to the "from" line). Instead, the memo has a heading indicating who the reader is, who the sender is, the date, and what the memo is about. This is a sample heading:

To:	All Faculty
From:	Travel Office
Date:	16 October 1996
Subject:	New Regulations for Travel Per Diem Allowance

In many organizations, special memo paper is printed with the "To," "From," and "Date" components already supplied, each followed by a blank line which the writer can fill in. These institutions also frequently have special memo envelopes designed for routing memos from one office or department to another. Organizations that you have worked for in the past have probably had their own practices for creating and sending memos.

As electronic mail (E-mail), sent via networked computers, is fast becoming the preferred medium for communicating within an organization, special memo stationery and envelopes may be on the decline. Nevertheless, "hard copies" of memos (ones printed on paper) are still important in most organizations, particularly when a durable, portable record of the contents is needed. Memos originally composed in E-mail can be printed; memos composed for paper circulation can also be sent by E-mail. Whether the original medium is paper or electronic, the general purposes for memos and many of the principles for composing them remain the same. In this chapter, however, we focus on composing and designing paper memos, rather than electronic ones.

COMPOSING THE MEMO

As in other rhetorical situations, begin writing a memo by asking yourself who your audience is and what your purpose is. With a memo, you may have multiple readers. Usually, a memo is addressed to just one person, however, and other intended readers are named in a line that may be headed "Copy" or "cc." (The "cc" stands for "carbon copy" and dates back to the days when typewriters were the principal office technology for writing, and carbon paper was what office workers used in place of a photocopy machine.) The "copy" line may come in the memo's heading or it may come after the body of the memo.

The purposes for memos are numerous and various. Here are some typical ones:

- To propose a course of action
- To report on an action
- To report on facts discovered through research
- To give a progress report
- To record and remind others of decisions made in a meeting or conversation
- To inform of a new policy or procedure
- To make announcements of general interest
- To ask questions
- To answer questions
- To summarize something, for example, a document or meeting, for a busy person

Whatever the purpose, the goal is to say simply and briefly what you have to say. When little is at stake—when you are simply tossing out ideas for a few co-workers, for example, memos can be hastily written. Memos in government agencies, on the other hand, might become part of a paper trail that has legal or historical implications. The more important your audience or purpose, and the more important the contents are, the more carefully you should plan the wording and the design of your memo. For memos with potentially broad significance, it may take many hours of writing to achieve the right wording and the ease of reading that characterize a good memo.

DESIGNING THE MEMO

Memos usually have two parts: the heading and the body. A long memo communicating complex information might have a separate conclusion as well, summarizing the contents, drawing conclusions, or making recommendations. How much you need to design the visual structure of a memo depends largely on the length and complexity of the information it conveys.

In very brief memos of only a paragraph or two, the need for design is minimal since most readers will be able to understand the entire contents in a few minutes. For a brief memo, the most helpful thing you can do is write a clear and complete "Subject" or "Re" line in the heading. (*Re* is from Latin and means "concerning" or "about.") The subject line should sum up the memo's contents in a few memorable words. Figure 15-5 presents a brief memo that incorporates very few visual design elements.

FIGURE 15-5 A Brief Memo

To: All Faculty

From: Travel Office

Date: 16 October 1996

Re: Changes in Per Diem Travel Allowance

Because of rising expenses in cities which many of you travel to for conferences, the per diem travel allowance will be raised after October 31. When submitting claims for travel expenses after that date, please use the following new figures:

1.   For Boston, New York, and San Francisco, $75 per day.
2.   For all other U.S. cities, $60 per day.
3.   For all international travel, $85 per day.

For long memos, particularly those conveying complex information, a brief opening paragraph that gives an overview of the contents can help the reader significantly. This overview can correspond to internal headings in the memo that help busy readers locate desired information quickly. Another way to help the reader read efficiently is to use principles of document design (see Chapter 16). For example, internal headings can be placed in a separate column to the left of the text. Or they can be in boldface and underlined, then placed above sections of the text, either centered or on the left margin. Within sections of a memo, bulleted or numbered lists can present complex information in a more visual and useful fashion. White space between sections, around lists, and elsewhere also makes a long memo more readable, because it relieves the formidable impression of a densely worded page. Figure 15-6 presents a memo that makes good use of all of these design devices. (Note that this memo is written by a student to a teacher to report on a collaborative assignment. Your instructor may ask you to write memos as a way of communicating efficiently about assignments in your course.)

FIGURE 15-6 A Long Memo with Several Design Elements

Memorandum

To: Sheryl Dame
From: Danielle L. Haglund
Date: 21 December 1995
Subject: Evaluation of Collaborative Research Project

This memo summarizes information about the collaborative research project I was involved in, surveying how college students deal with stress. I describe the different parts of the paper each group member worked on, group meetings, problem areas, and my final evaluation. Having never written a group paper in my school career, I found this assignment to be both hard work and a great learning experience.

Division of Labor

Each group member passed out ten surveys in order to collect empirical data, and each wrote specific parts of the paper. All three of us worked on the table of contents and conclusion. The other parts and tasks were done by the following group members:

Michael Smaglik	Introduction, methods, and graph
Jennifer Warner	Findings and interpretations related to personal life, appendix, and printing
Danielle Haglund	Findings and interpretations related to academic life, title page, and abstract

Group Meetings

We met three times for the following purposes:

1. to tabulate data
2. to review and criticize each other's first drafts
3. to type, edit, and finalize our collaborative paper

Difficulties Encountered

The following were the most difficult problems we encountered:

- arranging times to meet that fit all three group members' schedules
- keeping the workload fair and even
- collaborating on the paper so that it had a consistent tone

Final Evaluation

Since completing our collaborative paper, I have thought about this assignment's real life implications. The field that I will be entering in the next year requires that I work with a treatment team on writing reports that will be submitted to insurance companies. Since this assignment was my first experience with working on a paper as a group, I feel that I have learned some valuable lessons regarding how to approach future group writing situations.

SUGGESTIONS FOR WRITING

1. Locate an ad for a part-time job or full-time job for which you are qualified. Compose a letter applying for the job, stressing your qualifications that come from your education or previous work experience. Show a draft of your letter to a friend, tutor, or adviser to get feedback on improving it; then revise it. If now is the appropriate time to send your letter, laser print a final copy, enclose your resume (see Chapter 14), and mail it.

2. If you are planning to attend a graduate or professional school, contact the institutions you plan to apply to (even if the time to apply is still several months away) and ask for application forms and instructions about the kind of personal statement they require. Ask also if they require a resume or *curriculum vitae* (see Chapter 14). Begin now to draft a personal statement, seeking feedback from professors and advisers, as well as your peers. When the application deadline draws nearer, take the draft out and revise it. Proofread carefully; then print your personal statement and send it with other application materials.

3. Write a memo to your instructor reporting your progress on a long writing assignment that will soon be due. Or, if you have recently completed an assignment, write a memo to your instructor reporting on what you learned and evaluating the worth of the experience to you.

PART

VI

VISUAL AND ORAL RHETORIC

To speak of visual rhetoric, as many now do, may seem at first to be extending the meaning of *rhetoric* too far. Yet, in this section of the book, you will learn that you can enhance the persuasiveness of your written documents through their very appearance and through the graphical devices you create to accompany your written words. In Chapter 16 you will learn basic guidelines for designing documents so that readers will find them inviting to the eye and easy to use. "Desktop publishing" is another name often given to the principles taught there. In our computer age, by using a few simple options of widely accessible word processing programs it has become easier than ever to produce attractive documents that look almost as if a professional typesetter had produced them. Increasingly, employers and professors will expect that you know how to use computer functions to design readable documents on the job and at school. Those who don't know how to use them will be at a disadvantage not only in getting good grades and making good impressions at work, but also in persuading their readers.

In Chapter 17 you will learn principles for creating ethical and effective graphics to display data. Computer programs have made graphics easier to produce than ever before—but they have also made it easier to produce distorted graphics, "chartjunk," and frivolous decorations. Chapter 17 will teach you that tables, figures, and other illustrations should never be merely decorative; instead, they should be simple and informative, enhancing your credibility and the persuasiveness of your argument.

If speaking of visual rhetoric seems strange, speaking of oral rhetoric seems redundant, since rhetoric originally was the art of oratory, or public speaking. Yet, with the great emphasis given to writing in college, it is important to be reminded that speech is still a vital form of communication in professional life. The effective speaker does not leave persuasion to chance but prepares carefully to make a convincing argument and a favorable impression on an audience. Chapter 18 gives you guidelines for planning, organizing, and delivering effective oral presentations.

16

BASIC PRINCIPLES
OF DOCUMENT DESIGN

ENHANCING A DOCUMENT'S READABILITY

A document's readability is either enhanced or impeded by its visual design. Regardless of how eloquent your words are, if your document is visually daunting to the reader, it will be difficult to read. Research indicates that readers use a text's visual design in order to sum up its structure and make sense of the text itself (Huckin 1983; Redish, Battison, and Gold 1985). You should therefore design your documents to be structurally clear and visually easy to navigate. Elements of document design such as page layout, typography, and headings, when used effectively, will help the reader see the structure of your document, and understand and remember it with less effort. Word processing programs have many features that make it easy to create an effective design for most documents.

PAGE LAYOUT

A page that appears crowded distracts and burdens the reader. Compare Figure 16-1 and Figure 16-2. Even though the main text is identical in each, the different layout makes Figure 16-2 more inviting and easier to read and comprehend.

FIGURE 16-1 Memo with a Poor Design

To: Joellyn Schuster

From: Tom Valdivias

Subject: Human participants in research

Date: 12 June 1997

At your request, I have reviewed the laws and ethical policies regarding using human participants in social science research and have summarized them below for you.

First, researchers must ensure the confidentiality of participants. On questionnaires, it is generally not necessary to have respondents give their names, though they may give demographic information about themselves. Most important, researchers must ensure that no answers can be traced to specific respondents. When reporting interviews, the interviewer must make a joint decision with the interviewee about whether it would be appropriate and permissible to reveal the interviewee's name.

Second, human participants involved in research must have sufficient knowledge about the purposes of the study to give their informed consent before they participate. For experiments, written informed consent must be obtained. For surveys and interviews, the subjects' consent is implied if they complete the survey, but they still must be informed about the purposes of the research so that they can choose whether or not to proceed. Unobtrusive observations of people going about their daily lives do not require informed consent.

Third, researchers must be able to show that the participants will not face risks of physical or emotional harm greater than those encountered in daily life. Surveys don't usually pose this type of risk because respondents can ignore sensitive personal questions, and the respondents' answers are kept anonymous anyway. Experiments are the most likely to pose some emotional risk because they sometimes temporarily deceive participants. There is some disagreement on whether temporary deception is justified by the knowledge gained from experiments, but social scientists generally agree that, while researchers should not tell participants something that is untrue, they may temporarily withhold some information regarding the aim of the study. Generally speaking, an ethical experiment is one in which the participants are given general, yet still accurate, information, and in which participation in the study does not pose a risk of significant emotional or physical harm. Researchers must debrief the participants afterward to fully inform them of the purposes of the experiment.

Fourth, the laws carefully regulate and insist on the strict monitoring of research conducted with the following vulnerable groups: the ill or physically disabled; the institutionalized, including people in hospitals, jails, and prisons; the mentally incompetent; those under 18 years of age (minors); those over 65 years of age; and pregnant women.

All research projects involving human participants must be reviewed and approved by the university's Institutional Review Board (IRB) before being initiated. Because most student research projects will qualify for "exempt" status, rather than requiring approval from the entire Board, student proposals will most likely be reviewed and approved by one person appointed by the IRB for such matters. In order for an experiment to receive "exempt" status, it must meet certain criteria: (1) it must be non-therapeutic; (2) the data must be recorded in a way that protects the identities of the subjects; (3) there must be no risk of criminal or civil liability to the investigator and his or her institution, should a participant's responses become known outside the boundaries of the research project itself; and (4) the research must not deal with private aspects of the participants' behavior, e.g., their sexual practices or drug use.

FIGURE 16-2 Memo with a Readable Design

MEMORANDUM
RIVER STATE UNIVERSITY

To: Joellyn Schuster
From: Tom Valdivias
Date: June 12, 1997
Subject: **Guidelines for using human participants in social science research**

At your request, I have reviewed the laws and ethical policies regarding using human participants in social science research and have summarized them below for you:

Confidentiality

Researchers must ensure the confidentiality of human participants. On questionnaires, it is generally not necessary to have respondents give their names, though they may be asked to give demographic information about themselves. Most important, researchers must ensure that no answers can be traced to specific respondents. When reporting interviews, the interviewer must make a joint decision with the interviewee about whether it would be appropriate and permissible to reveal the interviewee's name.

Informed consent

Researchers must help human participants gain sufficient knowledge about the purposes of the study so the participants can give their informed consent before participating. For experiments, researchers must obtain written informed consent. For surveys and interviews, the participants' consent is implied if they complete the survey, but they still must be informed about the purposes of the research so that they can choose whether or not to proceed. Unobtrusive observations of people going about their daily lives do not require informed consent.

Avoiding risks of physical or emotional harm

Researchers must be able to show that the subjects will not risk physical or emotional harm greater than that encountered in daily life. Surveys don't usually pose this type of risk because respondents can ignore sensitive personal questions, and the respondents' answers are kept anonymous anyway. Experiments are the most likely to pose some emotional risk because they sometimes temporarily deceive subjects.

FIGURE 16-2 Memo with a Readable Design (continued)

When withholding information is okay	There is some disagreement on whether temporary information deception is justified by the knowledge gained from experiments, but social scientists generally agree that, while researchers should not tell participants something that is untrue, they may temporarily withhold some information regarding the aim of the study. Generally speaking, an ethical experiment is one in which the participants are given general, yet still accurate information, and in which participation in the study does not pose a risk of significant emotional or physical harm. Researchers must debrief participants afterward to fully inform them of the purposes of the experiment.
Vulnerable groups	*Laws provide strict guidelines and limitations on research conducted with certain vulnerable groups, including:* • the ill or physically disabled • the institutionalized, including people in hospitals, jails, and prisons • the mentally incompetent • those under 18 years of age (minors) • those over 65 years of age • pregnant women
Approval from the IRB	*All research projects involving human participants must be reviewed and approved by the university's Institutional Review Board (IRB) before they are initiated.* Because most student research projects will qualify for "exempt" status, rather than requiring approval from the entire Board, student proposals will most likely be reviewed and approved by one person appointed by the IRB for such matters.
Getting "exempt" status from the IRB	In order for an experiment to receive "exempt" status, it must meet four criteria: 1. It must be **non-therapeutic**. 2. The data must be recorded in such a way as to **protect the identities** of the participants. 3. There must be **no risk of criminal or civil liability** to the investigator and his or her institution, should the participant's responses become known outside the boundaries of the research project itself. 4. The research must not deal with **private aspects of the participants' behavior**, e.g., their sexual practices or drug use.

The following paragraphs explain some of the document design principles that will improve the page layout of the documents you write.

Scan zones. The short headings arranged to the left of the text in Figure 16-2 form a "scan zone." By using a zone like this for short, concise headings that describe the corresponding blocks of text, you make it easier for readers to scan your document and skip over the information they do not need. Scan zones are particularly suited for documents such as guidelines, instructions, and resumes that are meant to be read quickly for specific information.

White space. White space is the space on a page that surrounds the text. White space, or the lack of it, shows relationships between items—it sets off one group from another. Whether you use a little or a lot, your goal should be to use white space for effect. In Figure 16-1 there is very little use of white space, and, as a result, the document is visually overwhelming and difficult to read. There are several ways of effectively using white space in a document.

Ragged right margins. Notice that the right margins in Figure 16-1 are justified. This justification reduces the white space on the right side of the page, making the text more difficult to read. Researchers have found that ragged right margins, like those in Figure 16-2, are easier to read (Hartley and Burnhill 1971; Gregory and Poulton 1975). As a general rule, you should use ragged rather than justified right margins.

White space as an organizer of ideas. White space should also be used to show the organization and relationships within the text. When the spacing and location of the text follow a consistent pattern, they help the reader see a text's hierarchy and order of ideas. Use white space to separate groups of ideas. Indent your text appropriately to show where different topics or ideas begin and end. Separate sections with white space. Compare Figures 16-1 and 16-2 and notice how the use of white space in Figure 16-2 makes the text less intimidating and easier to comprehend and remember.

Lists. Listing a series of items vertically rather than as regular running text can often make a page more readable and the list items easier to remember. Lists should be set off by white space in order to draw the reader's attention. Be sure to keep all the elements of a list grammatically parallel. Notice how the lists in the last two sections of Figure 16-2 help the reader see at a glance the various stipulations that researchers must meet to receive exempt status for research with human subjects.

Bullets and other graphic devices. Most word processing programs allow you to add bullets and other graphic devices such as carets, rules, and bars to your document:

- This is a bullet.
▲ This is a caret.

Bullets, carets, and other similar graphic devices can be helpful visual organizers, especially in lists. However, just because you *can* insert a bullet doesn't mean you always should. Excessive graphic devices can make a page very busy and visually overwhelming. A good rule to remember when using graphic devices is "less is more." Look again at Figure 16-2 to see how bullets are used to organize the items in a list.

Many word processors allow you to insert small novelty graphics, sometimes called "wingdings." (Here are some typical ones: ✂ ✄ ✍ ✓.) You should keep your audience in mind when you decide whether or not to use wingdings. For most academic and professional writing, they are inappropriate. However, they may be appropriate when you are writing for more familiar audiences and for less formal purposes.

TYPOGRAPHY

The term *typography* refers to the face, size, and weight of "type" or the letters printed on a page. The face, size, and weight of type are all design elements that, if used effectively, will enhance the readability of your document.

Fonts. Most computer word processors allow you to select from a large variety of typefaces, more accurately called fonts.

Serif versus sans-serif fonts. There are two basic groups of fonts—*serif* fonts, which have extensions, or tiny lines on the edges of letters, and *sans-serif* fonts, which do not use extensions. Note the difference in these examples.

This is serif type. Times, Palatino, New York, Schoolbook, and Courier are all examples of serif type.

This is sans-serif type. Avant Garde, Helvetica, Geneva, **Chicago**, and Monaco are all examples of sans-serif type.

Some fonts are neither serif nor sans-serif. These fonts can be generally classified into two categories, script fonts and novelty fonts:

This is an example of a script font.

This is an example of a novelty font.

Use script and novelty fonts sparingly because they draw attention to themselves. You should stick to serif or sans-serif fonts for most academic and professional writing.

Follow these guidelines when selecting and using a font for your documents:

- **Use a serif font as your main font.** Because serif fonts create horizontal base lines, they help the eye move from one word to the next, making reading easier.
- **Use sans-serif fonts for titles and headings.** Because sans-serif fonts have predominantly vertical lines, they accentuate individual words, making them especially appropriate for titles and headings.
- **Select appropriate fonts for headings and text and stick to them.**

Capital letters. Avoid using all capital letters for regular text. Because we read in part by recognizing the shape of a word, capital letters are less legible than lowercase letters or mixed upper- and lowercase letters because they obscure the shape of the word. Words in all capitals are especially difficult to read if they are in a sans-serif font. Compare these two examples:

COMMERCIALS ARE NOW THE DOMINANT MEANS OF CANDIDATE COM-
MUNICATION IN TODAY'S POLITICAL RACES. VOTERS ARE NOW BOM-
BARDED WITH MILLIONS OF DOLLARS IN SPOT ADS DURING THE POLITI-
CAL SEASON. THE 1990 ELECTIONS ALONE GENERATED $203 MILLION IN
SPENDING ON ADS, ACCORDING TO AN ESTIMATE BY A BROADCASTING
GROUP.

Commercials are now the dominant means of candidate communication in
today's political races. Voters are now bombarded with millions of dollars in
spot ads during the political season. The 1990 elections alone generated $203 mil-
lion in spending on ads, according to an estimate by a broadcasting group.

The first example, written in all capitals, is more difficult to read than the second example, which varies upper- and lowercase letters.

Type size. Most word processors offer a wide range of type sizes—called "point sizes"—to choose from. The larger a type's point size, the larger the type is. Note these various typesizes:

This is Times 6-point.

This is Times 9-point.

This is Times 12-point.

This is Times 18-point.
This is Times 32-point.

For regular text, you should use a 9- to 12-point type size—point sizes lower than 8 are very difficult to read and are best suited for informal documents. Point sizes larger than 12 are better suited for titles and headings.

Type weight. As a general rule, use medium-weight fonts for regular text. **Very light and very heavy fonts (such as the bold face used for this sentence) are tiring to read.** However, you may want to use boldface type to emphasize words or short passages of text. Research shows that readers notice changes in type weight more readily than they notice changes in font (Spencer, Reynolds, and Coe 1973).

Compare Figures 16-1 and 16-2 again to see how font, size, and weight can be used to enhance a document's readability. Notice that the font in Figure 16-1 is sans-serif and is therefore more difficult to read than the font of the main text in Figure 16-2, which is serif. The left column of headings in Figure 16-2 is in sans-serif, however, which causes the reader to pause appropriately. In Figure 16-2, the point size is varied to show different levels of information. Also, in Figure 16-2, boldface type is used to highlight short passages of main text.

VISUAL CUES TO TEXT STRUCTURE

HEADINGS

Headings serve as the "road map" to your document—they help readers scan the document quickly to locate information and they help readers develop a framework within which they can more easily understand and remember the text.

Heading content. Researchers have found that headings which use complete and specific phrasing, especially full statements or questions, are particularly effective in making a text easier to read (Hartley, Morris, and Trueman 1981). Compare the headings from two outlines in Figures 16-3 and 16-4.

Notice how informative and useful the headings in Figure 16-4 are compared to those in Figure 16-3. The headings in Figure 16-4 are effective because they are descriptive and specific rather than general and vague—for the most

FIGURE 16-3 An outline made from vague, generic headings

I. Introduction
II. History
III. The Pathological Perspective
    A. Definition
    B. Techniques
IV. The Cultural Perspective
    A. Definition
    B. Reforms
V. Conclusion

FIGURE 16-4 An outline made from specific, informative headings

I. Introduction
II. Early Deaf History in America
    A. Thomas Gallaudet: American Pioneer in Deaf Education
    B. American Sign Language: A Hybrid of European and Indigenous Sign Languages
    C. Founding of Gallaudet University
    D. 1817–1880: The "Golden Age" of the Deaf
III. The Tendency to Consider Deafness a Disease
    A. The "Pathological" Perspective Defined
    B. 1880–1960: The Pathological Perspective Prevails
    C. Recent Methods of "Treating" Deafness
        1. Oralism: Restoring the Deaf to Society
        2. Imposing English Grammar on Sign Language
IV. An Alternative to the Pathological Perspective: Viewing the Deaf as a Culture
    A. The Cultural Perspective Defined
    B. How Hearing Societies Can Adopt the Cultural Perspective
        1. Treating American Sign Language as a Unique Language
        2. Celebrating the Unique Values of the Deaf Community
        3. Becoming Aware of the Deaf Community's Unique Social Conventions
        4. Celebrating the Deaf Community's Literature and Traditions
V. Conclusion

part, they contain a verb rather than a single noun or short noun string. They can be read apart from the text and still make sense.

Heading design. Design your headings so that your document's hierarchy of information is visually distinguishable. In other words, design your headings so the reader can tell if a particular heading pertains to the paper in general, a large section of text, or a small portion of text. Use distinguishing elements consistently so that, at any point in the text, the reader knows which level a particular heading belongs to.

You can distinguish the level of a heading by changing various type features.

You can vary the type size:

Very Large Type

Large Type

Regular type

You can vary the type weight:

Bold-face type

Medium-weight type

You can vary the capitalization:

In This Heading, the First Letter of Each Important Word is Capitalized

In this heading only the first letter is capitalized

You can underline text or put it in italics:

<u>This is an underlined heading</u>

This heading is in italics

You can combine several of these elements:

<u>**This Heading is in Initial Capitals, is Underlined, and is in Boldface Type**</u>

Or you can use a different font altogether:

This heading is in a sans-serif font

The main text is in a serif font

You can also vary the spacing on the page. You can center a title or heading:

This Heading is Centered

The text starts here and continues...

You can keep a heading flush with the left margin:

This heading is flush left

The text starts here and continues. It keeps going in this example so you can see how it would look....

You can indent the heading above the text:

This heading is indented above the text

The text starts here and continues. These lines of text will help you see how this kind of heading would look....

Or you can indent the heading and place the text adjacent to it:

This heading is indented and next to text. The text continues from here and wraps down to additional lines....

You can also use a rule to distinguish a heading:

This Heading is Separated from the Text with a Rule

The text starts here and continues...

Notice how, in Figure 16-2, font, size, and weight are used to show different levels of headings. Larger point sizes and bold-faced type are used for major headings, while italics and medium-weight type are used for minor headings.

Additional advice regarding headings. There are a few more things to remember regarding headings: Unless your style guide says otherwise, limit the number of heading levels to four or less. If you use more than four levels of headings, your document can become confusing and difficult to read. Also, remember that readers will expect headings in larger point sizes to be more important than headings in smaller ones. And they will expect a heading in all capitals to be more important than a heading in mixed or lowercase type. Finally, don't leave a heading at the bottom of a page if the text starts on the following page. You should have at least one line of text accompany a heading.

HEADINGS AND PROFESSIONAL STYLE GUIDES

If your document must adhere to a particular style guide, such as APA or Turabian, you should follow its prescriptions for headings. When following the style recommended by the APA *Publication Manual* (1994), you should not use more than five levels of headings. The APA manual prescribes the following formats for each of the five levels (see pp. 90-93):

LEVEL 5 HEADINGS ARE CENTERED IN UPPERCASE

Level 1 Headings are Centered in Uppercase and Lowercase

Level 2 Headings are Centered, Uppercase and Lowercase, and Underlined

Level 3 Headings are Flush Left, Uppercase and Lowercase, and Underlined

    Level 4 headings are indented to begin the paragraph, lowercase, and underlined, and they end with a period.

Not every document you write will require all five levels of headings. APA offers the following guidelines for selecting level formats when you use fewer than five heading levels:

One level. When you only have one level of headings, use the format for Level 1 headings described above.

Two levels. When your document has two levels of headings, use Level 1 and Level 3 heading formats.

Three levels. For three levels of headings, use Level 1, Level 3, and Level 4 heading formats.

Four levels. When you have four levels of headings, use the heading formats for Levels 1 through 4.

Five levels. When you have five levels of headings, use Level 5 format for broadest heading, then Levels 1 through 4.

Figure 16-5 is an excerpt from a paper that follows APA guidelines regarding headings. The paper contains three levels of headings. Notice how each heading's level is easily distinguishable through its design.

FIGURE 16-5 Headings in APA Style

Our Tendency to Consider Deafness a Disease

The "Pathological" Perspective Defined

    The introduction discussed some facets of the pathological view of deafness. According to this perspective, deafness is seen as something that is missing, or as a handicap (Eldredge, 1994). Padden states that professionals such as doctors and teachers usually refer to deaf people according to their "pathological condition: hearing loss" (1980, p. 1). They are treated as medical cases, or as people with "disabilities" (Padden, 1988).

FIGURE 16-5 Headings in APA Style (continued)

Using this perspective, deafness is considered a problem that needs to be fixed. When parents discover that their child is deaf, the first person they usually consult is a medical doctor. Throughout history, physicians have used many techniques to help deaf patients regain their hearing. Eldredge describes some of these methods:

> Treatments varied from making a loud noise near the ear in order to open up the ear canal (but probably damaged the ear drum even further!) to pouring liquids down ears to wrapping deaf dog carcasses around sick children's heads. (Eldredge, 1994, p. 1)

It seems that the remedies were worse than the "disease" they were supposed to cure.

<u>1880-1960: The Pathological Perspective Prevails</u>

The years from 1880 to 1960 are known in the deaf community as the "Dark Ages." As Sacks relates, "What was happening with the deaf and Sign was part of a general (and if one wished, 'political') movement of the time: a trend to Victorian oppressiveness and conformism, intolerance of minorities, and minority usages, of every kind—religious, linguistic, ethnic" (1990, p. 24). Because of this trend to conformity, languages that didn't have a great number of users were under threat of extinction. This sentiment affected the Deaf community in America. During the "Dark Ages" the Deaf community was almost destroyed by three main thrusts—"oralist" philosophy, Alexander Graham Bell's campaign for eugenics, and the Milan Conference.
   <u>Oralism: Restoring the Deaf to Society.</u> For two centuries there had been rampant feelings that the goal of deaf education should be teaching the deaf how to speak....

Like APA, Turabian (1996) suggests that no more than five levels of headings be used. According to Turabian, the following formats may be used for each of the five levels.

Level 1 Headings are in Boldface, Italicized, or Underlined, Centered, and Capitalized Headline Style

Level 2 Headings are in Text Type, Centered, and Capitalized
Headline Style

*Level 3 Headings are in Boldface, Italicized, or Underlined, Flush Left, and
Capitalized Headline Style.*

Level 4 headings are in text type, flush left, and capitalized sentence
style.

***Level 5 headings are in boldface, italicized, and/or underlined, are
indented to begin a paragraph, and are capitalized sentence style with a
period at the end.***

FIGURE 16-6 Headings in Turabian Style

Our Tendency to Consider Deafness a Disease

The "Pathological" Perspective Defined

The introduction discussed some facets of the pathological view of
deafness. According to this perspective, deafness is seen as something that
is missing, or as a handicap (Eldredge 1994). Padden states that professionals such as doctors and teachers usually refer to deaf people according to
their "pathological condition: hearing loss" (1980, 1). They are treated as
medical cases, or as people with "disabilities" (Padden 1988).

Using this perspective, deafness is considered a problem that needs to
be fixed. When parents discover that their child is deaf, the first person they
usually consult is a medical doctor. Throughout history, physicians have
used many techniques to help deaf patients regain their hearing. Eldredge
describes some of these methods:

> Treatments varied from making a loud noise near the ear in order to open up
> the ear canal (but probably damaged the ear drum even further!) to pouring
> liquids down ears to wrapping deaf dog carcasses around sick children's
> heads. (Eldredge 1994, 1)

It seems that the remedies were worse than the "disease" they were supposed to cure.

FIGURE 16-6 Headings in Turabian Style (continued)

1880–1960: The Pathological Perspective Prevails

The years from 1880 to 1960 are known in the deaf community as the "Dark Ages." As Sacks relates, "What was happening with the deaf and Sign was part of a general (and if one wished, 'political') movement of the time: a trend to Victorian oppressiveness and conformism, intolerance of minorities, and minority usages, of every kind—religious, linguistic, ethnic" (1990, 24). Because of this trend to conformity, languages that didn't have large number of users were under threat of extinction. This sentiment affected the Deaf community in America. During the "Dark Ages" the Deaf community was almost destroyed by three main thrusts—"oralist" philosophy, Alexander Graham Bell's campaign for eugenics, and the Milan Conference.

Oralism: restoring the Deaf to society. For two centuries there had been rampant feelings that the goal of deaf education should be teaching the deaf how to speak....

If you don't need five levels of headings, Turabian suggests that you select the heading formats you prefer from those shown above, always making sure that you use them in descending order. See Figure 16-6 for an example of headings that follow Turabian guidelines.

There is more to document design than the brief pointers covered in this chapter, but these relatively simple guidelines are ones you can implement with most word processing programs. Using these principles will make the documents you create for school and on the job more readable.

REFERENCES

American Psychological Association. 1994. *Publication manual.* 4th ed. Washington, DC: American Psychological Association.

Gregory, M., and E. C. Poulton. 1975. Even versus uneven right-hand margins and the rate of comprehension in reading. *Applied Ergonomics* 6.

Hartley, James, and Peter Burnhill. 1971. Experiments with unjustified text. *Visible Language* 5, 265–278.

Hartley, James, P. Morris, and Mark Trueman. 1981. Headings in text. *Remedial Education* 16, 5–7.

Huckin, Thomas N. 1983. A cognitive approach to readability. In *New essays in technical and scientific communication: Research, theory, and practice*, eds. Paul V. Anderson, R. John Brockmann, and Carolyn R. Miller, 90–101. Farmingdale, NY: Baywood.

Redish, Janice C., Robin M. Battison, and Edward S. Gold. 1985. Making information accessible to readers. In *Writing in nonacademic settings*, eds. Lee Odell and Dixie Goswami, 129–53. New York: Guilford.

Spencer, Herbert, Linda Reynolds, and B. Coe. 1973. *A comparison of the effectiveness of selected typographic variations.* Readability of Print Research Unit. London: Royal College of Art.

Turabian, Kate. 1996. *A manual for writers of term papers, theses, and dissertations.* 6th ed. Chicago: University of Chicago Press.

17

GRAPHICS

GRAPHICS AS RHETORIC

In today's world, visual rhetoric is very important. As a consumer bombarded daily with images from advertising rhetoric, you must be alert to the kinds of hidden appeals embedded in the images so you can evaluate their messages rationally and avoid being unconsciously manipulated by this kind of rhetoric. Similarly, as a reader of social science research, you need to evaluate the graphics you find for their clarity, completeness, and appropriateness of design. As you write about your own research, you will also need to know how to create graphics so you can display complex data in a concise, readable form.

Graphics are tables and figures that you can add to your writing to clarify and illustrate the ideas or facts you are writing about. *Tables* are rows and columns of data—words or numbers or both—that display the data in a small space so that it is easy for the reader to see relationships among various parts of the entire set of data. *Figures* are all other illustrations that are not tables. Figures include photographs, line drawings, maps, diagrams, flowcharts, and various kinds of graphs—line graphs, circle graphs, and bar graphs (also called column graphs).

Well-made graphics use symbols and design principles skillfully to appeal to the reader's visual sense, enhancing and clarifying a message, making it more persuasive than it might otherwise be. Poorly designed, badly integrated, or incomplete graphics detract from the persuasiveness of a message because they call into question the writer's knowledge. Misleading graphics cast doubt on the writer's trustworthiness, detracting from the ethical appeal of the message. Illustrations, such as computer clip art, that merely decorate a document rather than add or clarify information, also call the writer's judgment into question and diminish the seriousness of the document.

Because graphics are becoming much easier to create with various kinds of computer software, it will be to your advantage to learn to use one or more graphics programs. However, some features of the available software programs are not based on sound communication and design principles, so you need to be aware of the potential flaws and ethical pitfalls in creating graphics with computers—such as needless third dimensions in bar graphs or cute but empty illustrations on tables and graphs. You shouldn't forsake simplicity and clarity to make what graphic designer Edward Tufte calls (1990) "chartjunk" simply because a computer program allows you to. In this chapter you will learn principles for creating appropriate tables and figures and for integrating them into the texts that you write so your writing is rhetorically effective.

TABLES

Tables are efficient, compact summaries of large data sets presented in rows and columns. The pattern formed by the rows and columns resembles a grid, even when the rows and columns do not have visible lines subdividing the grid into cells. Whether the lines are there or not, however, it is helpful to think of a table as containing a cell for each item of information that you want to display. Suppose, for example, that you conduct a survey of undergraduate students' reasons for reading the campus newspaper. You identify three primary reasons why students read the newspaper, as well as a few miscellaneous reasons you can characterize as "other." You also learn that the percentage of students giving each reason varies with year in college—that is, from the freshman to the senior year.

To display these 16 items of data, you would need a 4×4 grid. You could create four columns to display the reasons and four rows to display the years in college; the intersection of these rows and columns would create 16 cells. However, you would also need an extra row to label the columns and an extra column to label the rows, so you would have to make a 5×5 grid. Your table might look like Table 17-1.

This table permits your audience to read the data horizontally to see what the most important and least important reasons are for each group of students; it also enables your audience to read vertically to see how the importance of a particular reason changes as the average student progresses through college. The table would also permit the reader to quickly compare any two items of information. Besides helping the reader, this table would help you as the writer

TABLE 17-1 A Simple Table

Students' Reasons for Reading the Campus Newspaper

	Read world and national news	Learn about campus events	Read advertisements	Other Reasons
Freshman	12%	71%	14%	3%
Sophomore	18%	67%	11%	4%
Junior	34%	40%	22%	4%
Senior	49%	12%	35%	4%

to draw conclusions about the significance of the survey findings and interpret them. What trends do you notice in the data? What plausible explanations for these trends come to mind?

Imagine how much more difficult it would be for a reader to make comparisons or notice trends if the data in Table 17-1 were to be explained in paragraph form. You would have to write a very long and complex paragraph to present all of this information, and the paragraph would be much more time-consuming and tiresome to read than the table. It would be difficult for the reader to pick out any two items of information for comparison. You can strengthen the credibility of your interpretations if they are based on data that are easy to find and understand.

Tables usually present numbers, but they can also consist of words. Table 17-2 (reproduced from Chapter 3) compares the advantages and disadvantages of quantitative and qualitative research methods. It presents a handy summary of information that took several paragraphs to explain.

TABLE 17-2 A Table Made of Words

Comparison of Quantitative and Qualitative Methods

	Types	Advantages	Limitations
Quantitative methods	Experiments Surveys	Possibility of large sample size Generalizability and breadth High degree of control	Loss of particularity Possibly high costs
Qualitative methods	Interviews Observations Documents	Rich data Particularity and depth Large scope for interpretation	Low generalizability Overwhelming data Time consumption

You can create simple tables with word processing programs. Many of them have special functions to help you create tables. Even without a special tables function, however, it is not difficult to align data in columns and rows simply by setting up tabs or columns with your word processing program. There are also special computer programs called *spreadsheets* into which you can enter data and then convert the data from the spreadsheet into a table.

FIGURES

As noted above, figures are all graphics that are not tables. (In some fields, these graphics might also go by the name "illustration," "exhibit," "chart," or even "visual." In most social science journals, however, these graphics are usually called figures.) In the next few pages, some of the most common types of figures are described and illustrated, and guidelines are provided for creating these kinds of graphics.

PHOTOGRAPHS

A photograph is an especially useful kind of figure when you are writing about a person—perhaps a famous one—or place and you want the reader to be able to see what the person or place actually looks like. Photographs are also helpful when you are writing about an object or event and it is important to give a realistic and detailed image of it, rather than the abstract, less concrete image provided by a sketch. Photos can be enlarged to show more detail. They can also be cropped to eliminate irrelevant parts of a picture. Because photographs do reproduce every detail visible to the camera, however, they may cause the reader to get caught up in the little things and perhaps lose focus on the most important features of the illustration. Also, because photographs are more difficult and expensive to reproduce than drawings, you may need to limit their use.

If you decide that a photo is the best kind of illustration for a particular text, original photos must be of a high quality with high contrast between light and dark to provide the best reproductions. You will need to be skillful with a camera or hire someone to produce original photos. If you use a copyrighted photo, you will have to acknowledge the photographer and the copyright holder in the caption. You will probably have to pay a fee to others for permission to use their photos.

LINE DRAWINGS

Line drawings are simple sketches that eliminate much of the detail included in photos for the sake of simplifying and emphasizing the most important features of the illustration. If you read Chapter 6 of this book, you probably noticed that the excerpt from Deborah Tannen's research included many line drawings. These line drawings were important in helping Tannen establish her claim that pairs of female friends engaged in conversation sit with their bodies and their gazes directly aligned, whereas pairs of male friends sit at angles to one another and seldom make eye contact. The line drawing presented in Figure 17-1 illustrates very simply what Tannen saw in the videotapes of one of the conversations she studied.

This line drawing is based on videotape data that showed the research participants' every movement. Notice that the artist who created these sketches selected particular details in order to draw the reader's attention more forcefully to the facts that Tannen focuses on—body alignment and gaze. In a sense, the sketches are like freeze frames from the videos that have then been simplified even further to eliminate distracting details. Tannen's choice of line drawings for her illustrations, rather than photographs, was a rhetorically effective one, because the simplicity of the drawings allows her to emphasize the critical features of her interpretation.

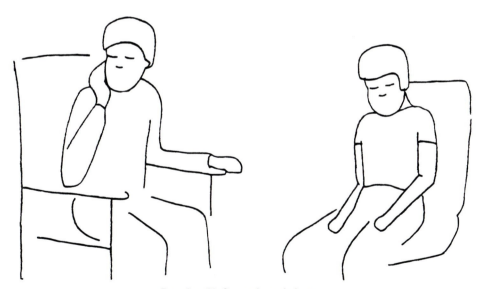

Drawing #1. Second-grade boys.

FIGURE 17-1 A Line Drawing

From Deborah Tannen, "Gender Differences in Conversational Coherence: Physical Alignment and Topical Cohesion," in *Conversational Organization and Its Development*, ed. Bruce Dorval (Norwood, NJ: Ablex, 1990), p. 171. Reprinted by permission of Deborah Tannen.

If, in your research, you find that line drawings would be the best choice to illustrate your main points, you might consider employing an artist to create the drawings if you don't feel competent to make them yourself, drawing free-hand. However, using special computer software for drawing, you should, with some practice, be able to create effective drawings of your own.

MAPS

A map is a type of line drawing because it leaves out a lot of detail that could be included in order to simplify matters and to illustrate the writer's point. For example, a road map usually doesn't include the varying elevations of the terrain that the roads cross. A contour map, however, focuses on elevations and often leaves out roads. Maps such as these, which represent geographic realities, usually include a scale showing how much real distance is represented by each unit of distance (such as an inch or centimeter) on the map. These maps may also include legends (explained later in this chapter) indicating what the various symbols on the map stand for. For example, the legend might show that various kinds of lines represent interstate highways, state highways, improved roads, and unimproved roads.

Maps can also be used as ways of making points about political, economic, or social realities. For example, a simple map of the United States outlining the boundaries of the states is a favorite way used by newspapers and magazines for making various kinds of comparisons among the 50 states. The pair of maps in Figure 17-2 is of this type. The top map shows which states have high, average, and low voter turnout. The bottom map shows which states have high, average, and low social and economic equity. The sentences below the caption explain that states with the highest economic and social equity also have the highest voter turnout. These two variables can be combined to create a measure the map makers call the "democracy index."

DIAGRAMS AND FLOWCHARTS

A diagram is a drawing that simplifies a complex object or concept. Frequently diagrams represent abstract ideas or relationships, such as parts of a theory or a conceptual model. They may consist of both words and graphical elements such as lines, circles, boxes, arrows, and the like. A particular kind of diagram is a flowchart, which generally depicts a process or the possible steps in an operation. Diagrams and flowcharts are excellent ways of summarizing visually the main points you make in words, so that the reader has a handy way to remember concepts and how they are related to each other. The flowchart in Figure 17-3 shows common stages in the grieving process that people go through when a loved one dies.

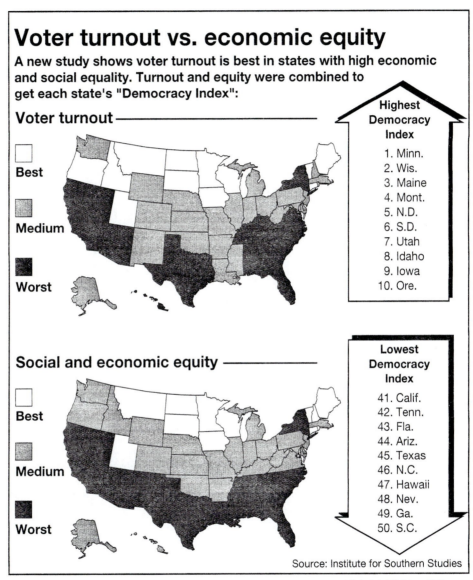

FIGURE 17-2 A Map

Source: Knight-Ridder graphic from *The Salt Lake Tribune* ©1996, Knight-Ridder Tribune.

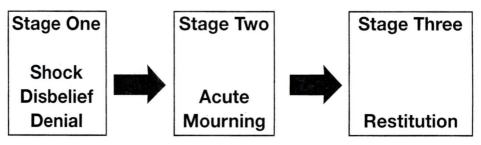

FIGURE 17-3 A Flowchart: Stages in Mourning

GRAPHS

Graphs are special kinds of figures that allow you to display the relationships between numerical and categorical variables for easy comprehension and comparison. There are three kinds of commonly used graphs: line graphs, bar graphs, circle graphs.

Line graphs. Line graphs show the continuous relationship between at least two variables. The two variables are represented as points in a space defined by two axes—an x-axis (horizontal) and a y-axis (vertical)—each of which has been divided into meaningful increments. To show the continuous relationship between the two variables, you can draw a line from one point to the next, thus showing the upward and downward trends in the relationship between the variables. For example, the fluctuations of a particular stock price over a period of months can be clearly represented by a line graph, as shown in Figure 17-4. The x-axis names the months in a six-month period; the y-axis shows the prices per share of the stock. The maker of this graph simply plotted a point to represent the average price for the stock each month, then connected the points to make a line showing the overall trend.

More than one line can be plotted on a particular line graph. For example, the line graph could have a second line showing the price fluctuation of a different stock over the same period of time. The second line could be drawn as a broken or a dotted line to differentiate it from the first one. Still more lines could be added as long as each could be clearly distinguished from the others. However, too many lines that cross each other at numerous points would clutter the graph and make it confusing and difficult to read. Instead of putting too much information in one line graph, it is better to make more than one graph.

Bar (column) graphs. Like a line graph, a bar graph also plots the relationship between at least two variables by using two clearly labeled and subdivided axes. The difference is that a bar graph is used when the independent variable is categorical, rather than numerical. The data are represented as discrete units,

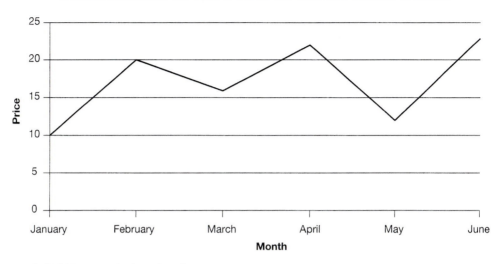

Fluctuations in the Price of Moon Rock Stock

FIGURE 17-4 A Line Graph

rather than as continuous, the way they are in a line graph. Thus, one axis is not a numbered scale; instead, it is divided into categories of data, and each bar on the graph represents a different amount or number in a particular category. Using bars with different shading, you can compare data for different groups within each category.

For example, in the bar graph in Figure 17-5 from Sipos and Hall's paper in Chapter 4, the y-axis shows three kinds of pre-trial releases granted to suspects in crimes. The x-axis shows the percentage of suspects who receive each kind of pre-trial release. Note that for each category of pre-trial release, there are two bars, a black one showing the percentage of female suspects who receive that kind of release, and a white one showing the percentage of male suspects who do. So for each category of pre-trial release you can see whether judges grant it more often to men or women suspects. The final pair of bars at the bottom of the graph show the total percentages of men and women who receive a pre-trial release.

Another important thing to notice about the bar graph is that each bar has the exact percentage (rounded to one decimal place) of suspects who received a particular kind of pre-trial release. Even though the x-axis is divided into increments of ten percent, it is important to let the reader know the exact figure in any category. The standard way to do this is to write the exact figure on the bar or at the end of the bar. Note also that the bars in a bar graph can run either horizontally or vertically. (A graph with vertical bars is sometimes called a column graph.) In this case, horizontal bars were a good choice so that the labels

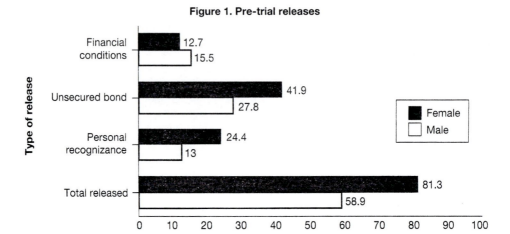

FIGURE 17-5 A Bar Graph

for the categories of pre-trial release could be written horizontally, making them easier to read than if they were written vertically.

Circle graphs. Circle graphs are also called "pie charts" because they are divided into wedges just as a pie is. They are particularly good for representing percentages and proportions. For example, a budget is commonly represented with a circle graph because the relative size of the wedges makes it easy to see how much money has been allotted to each budget category. Usually, the circle is considered to be like a clockface, and the wedges are put in descending order of size starting at 12 o'clock. Sometimes, however, the convention of descending order is not followed in order to keep similar wedges close to each other.

Like a line or bar graph, a circle graph can present too much data and become confusing. If a circle graph has very many wedges, several of the wedges are likely to be very small, and it will become more difficult for a reader to see the relative differences in size. It is also difficult to label very small wedges of a circle graph, so a bar graph might be a better choice when a lot of categories are to be compared. However, if the pie will be cut into only a few wedges, a circle graph can be a good choice to show the divisions of a whole. Figure 17-6 is a circle graph showing the budget categories for a survey research project. Note that a different kind of cross-hatching is used in each wedge to help distinguish the wedges and help you see the proportions more clearly. Note also that the budget categories are labeled inside boxes connected to the wedges.

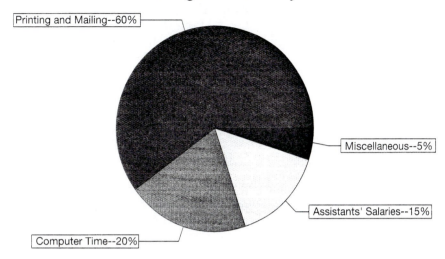

FIGURE 17-6 A Circle Graph

POSITIONING AND LABELING GRAPHICS

Position Graphics for Easy Viewing

Once you have decided what kinds of graphics will best illustrate your verbal message, you must next determine where to put the graphics in the text. If graphics are meant to illustrate and clarify a verbal text, it is important to place them as close to the relevant text as you possibly can—on the same or the following page, so the reader can easily pause while reading to glance at or study the graphic. Sometimes graphics can be made small enough so that the text can run in a narrow column right next to the graphic. Sometimes graphics are so big that they must cover two pages or even be printed on extra large paper that can be folded into the document and then unfolded when the reader is ready to look at them. Occasionally, however, graphics present information that is interesting and relevant, but not critical for the reader to see while reading the text. In this case, graphics can be placed in an appendix to the document for readers to look at or not, as they choose.

Number Graphics for Easy Reference

Although positioning a graphic in the most advantageous place is important to help the reader, position by itself is not enough to make reference to the graphic convenient. Each graphic also needs a number so you can refer to it without having to write something clumsy like "the bar graph showing the means for each year at the top of page 4" or "the table on page 2 that compares Republicans' and Democrats' responses." Usually tables and figures are numbered separately from each other. So if you created a document with two tables and three figures, they would be called Table 1 and Table 2, and Figure 1, Figure 2, and Figure 3 respectively. (In a long document, such as this book, numbering of tables and figures can start over with each chapter.)

Giving each graphic a number helps you refer to it conveniently as often as you need to. In the text of your paper, you can refer directly to a graphic by writing something like this: "As Table 1 shows, students in the experimental treatment scored significantly higher on the posttest." Or you can refer more indirectly, using parentheses: "Investments rose as inflation declined (see Figure 1)." But it is important to refer to your graphics and to discuss their significance. Don't simply put them in your paper and expect your reader to figure out why they are there and what they show.

Give Graphics Descriptive Captions

Besides numbering your graphics, you should add a descriptive caption that allows a reader to understand at a glance what kind of information the graphic displays. The more informative the caption is, the better the reader will be able to read and interpret the information in the graphic. So, rather than make captions cryptic (e.g., "Comparisons") or cute (e.g., "Sexist Sentencing"), make them long enough to be informative. For example, don't be reluctant to write a long, specific, and detailed caption like this: "Comparison of Prison Sentences for Males and Females Convicted of the Same Crimes."

Special Considerations for Tables and Figures

Besides positioning, numbering, and labeling graphics, you will have to add other information to make clear what kind of information each part of each graphic shows. For tables, you will have to label the columns and rows, and you may have to add more information in notes, depending on your purpose and audience needs. For drawings, diagrams, and flowcharts, you may need to label individual parts. For line and bar graphs, you have to label the axes. For circle graphs, you have to label the wedges. For all of these, you may need to add a legend. Each of these features is explained and illustrated below.

__Labeling parts of tables.__ In addition to a number and a caption, a table needs other information, depending on how complicated the depicted information is. Each column and each row needs a heading so that a reader can tell what particular information is given in each cell. Notice the various kinds of headings and subheadings used in Table 17-3.

As you can see from Table 17-3, a table can have footnotes besides column and row headings. A table can also have other information printed immediately above or under it to help the reader understand the context of the data. Notice how the authors of *Middletown Families* numbered and labeled Table 17-4 that presents some of their survey data. In addition, they cite the source of the information and they list the statement the respondents were evaluating.

TABLE 17-3 A Complex Table

Comparison of Male and Female Professors' Job Satisfaction and Job Performance Appraisals

Gender and Rank	Average Job Satisfaction Ranking[a]	Average Job Performance Ranking	
		Self-appraisal	Chair's appraisal
Male Professors[b]			
Asst. Profs.	4.3	4.6	4.0
Assoc. Profs.	5.2	5.7	6.0
Full Profs.	6.5	6.7	5.6
Female Professors[c]			
Asst. Profs.	3.5	4.9	5.3
Assoc. Profs.	4.3	5.4	6.0
Full Profs.	5.4	5.5	5.6

a All rankings are based on a 7-point scale, where 7 is greatest.
b *n*=46.
c *n*=24.

TABLE 17-4 A Table with Additional Information

**Money as a Motive to Work, among Employed Men, by Social Class,
Middletown, 1978
(in percentages)**

Response	Business Class (N=104)	Working Class (N=94)
Strongly agree	5%	16%
Agree	7	18
Neutral	13	20
Disagree	41	36
Strongly disagree	34	10
Total	100%	100%

Source: Middletown III, Men's Occupational Survey, 1978.

Question: To me work is just a way of making money.

From Theodore Caplow et al., *Middletown Families: Fifty Years of Continuity and Change* (Minneapolis: University of Minnesota Press, 1985), p. 357. Reprinted by permission of University of Minnesota Press.

Labeling parts of graphs. On a circle graph, you must make clear what each wedge stands for. You can do this by writing directly on the wedge what it represents. If the wedge is too small, you can write the description outside the circle and draw a line to the wedge the description stands for, as Figure 17-7 shows.

Line graphs and bar graphs plot data along two axes, the *y*-axis (vertical) and the *x*-axis (horizontal). Usually, numerical values are shown on the *y*-axis and any other variable (such as time or a category) on the *x*-axis. Remember that your reader needs to know what information you are showing on each axis, so clearly label each one, as Figure 17-8 shows. Figure 17-8 also shows the use of a *legend*. Legends are used when figures present several kinds of data on one grid; the legend helps the reader understand the figure by showing what different kinds of lines or shading stand for. For example, if you had a bar graph with several different bars in each category, you could create a legend that helps the reader understand what each bar represents. Figure 17-8 shows how a legend can be incorporated.

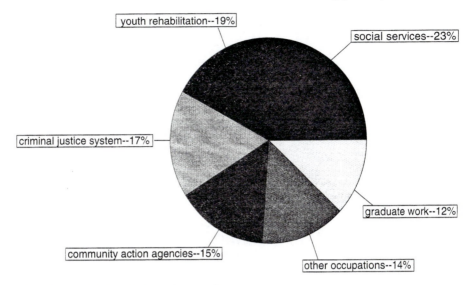

FIGURE 17-7 A Labeled Circle Graph

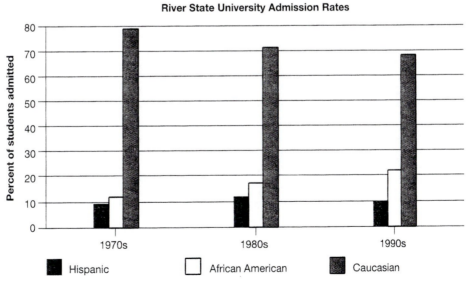

FIGURE 17-8 Bar Graph with a Legend

ETHICAL ISSUES IN USING GRAPHICS

As you learned in Chapter 1, rhetoric can be used for good or ill. Your ethical stance as a writer will be evident in the choices you make in composing and presenting information to your readers, including how you present graphical information. With graphics there are basically three areas of concern: plagiarism; omitting information or not following standard, reasonable conventions for representing variations in the data; and unfairly manipulating the impression the graphic makes on the reader by using chartjunk or distorting or cluttering the design of the graphic.

PLAGIARISM

Much of the time, graphics in your writing will present original data that you have gathered in your own research. However, graphics could present information that you have borrowed from other people's research and adapted to display in graphic form. Or they could be reproductions of graphics someone else made, which you have re-created, photocopied, or electronically scanned to use in your own documents. In either of the latter two cases—borrowed information or adapted graphics—you would need to give credit to the original source in your paper, just as you would for a quotation, summary, or paraphrase of words you have borrowed. Failing to cite the source of graphical data is a form of plagiarism. If you create a graphic out of adapted information or reproduce a graphic, the easiest way to attribute it to the source is to put a credit line in a small font underneath the graphic. You would also cite the source in the reference list of your paper.

OMITTING OR MISREPRESENTING VARIATIONS IN THE DATA

Graphics can be misleading, and therefore unethical, when they don't show all the pertinent data or they misrepresent the data, making something appear to be the case that isn't actually so. One way that the maker of a graphic might misrepresent is by using an inappropriate scale on the y-axis of a line graph or bar graph or by changing the unit of division in the scale at some point. For example, notice in the bar graph in Figure 17-9 that at first it appears that campus rapes have risen sharply in one year. But then notice the unit of division on the y-axis.

Figure 17-9 uses an inappropriate scale on the y-axis, decimal figures ascending in increments of two-tenths. But it makes no sense to think of two-tenths of a rape. In actuality, there has been one rape in a three-year period, but this graph might at first lead a reader to believe there has been a startling jump. While no one wants to minimize the seriousness of even one rape on any cam-

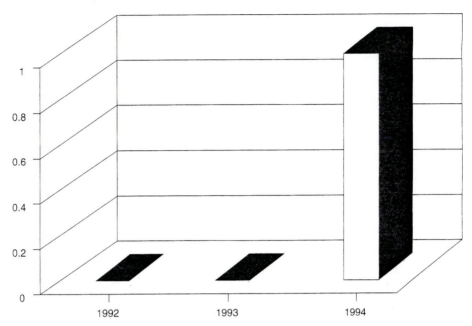

FIGURE 17-9 A Misleading Graphic

pus, it is important to give readers an accurate rather than misleading depiction of any statistical data.

DISTORTING OR CLUTTERING THE DESIGN

Graphics can also border on unethical if they distort the impression the reader gets from the actual design. There are two common sources for this kind of problem. First, using three-dimensional bars on a bar graph (as in Figure 17-9) or adding a third dimension to a circle graph can distort the data by changing the viewers' perspective of the graph and causing them to misunderstand the comparative size of the bars or wedges. Second, using "chartjunk"—often cute but unnecessary and distracting illustrations, objects, or icons—merely adds clutter to a graphic and makes the reader lose sight of the basic information the graphic should convey. Following are three illustrations that show distortion and clutter. Figure 17-10 distorts by using a needless third dimension in the bars, making it more difficult to compare the heights of the bars.

River State University Admission Rates

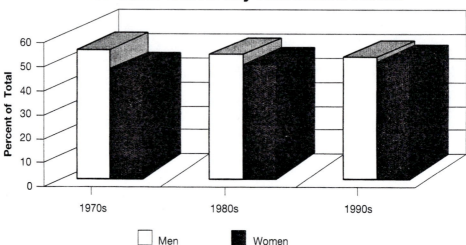

FIGURE 17-10 Distorted Three-Dimensional Bar Graph

Figure 17-11 shows how adding a third dimension to a pie chart makes the wedges in the foreground look bigger than they are.

When you use computer programs to create graphics, be careful to notice whether or not the program automatically creates three-dimensional graphics. You should be able to choose the option of creating more informative two-dimensional graphics.

Budget for Research Project

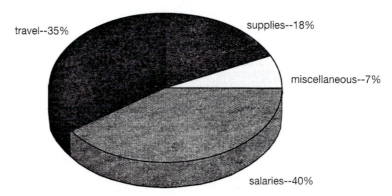

FIGURE 17-11 Distorted Three-Dimensional Circle Graph

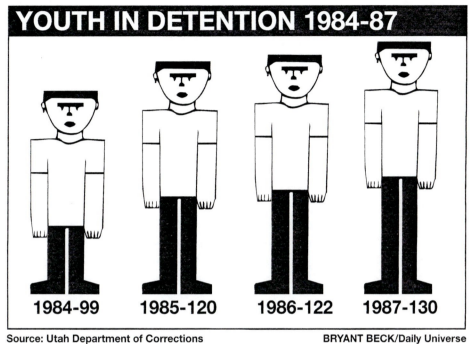

Source: Utah Department of Corrections   **BRYANT BECK/Daily Universe**

FIGURE 17-12 Example of Chartjunk
Reprinted by permission of the Brigham Young University *Daily Universe*.

Figure 17-12 contains chartjunk that draws attention away from the important information, perhaps in a misguided attempt to make the chart more sensational. When you finally locate the basic information the chart conveys, however, you may feel that the maker of the chart has favored the use of stereotypes and manipulative appeals to emotion over a direct display of the facts. By unnecessarily cluttering the chart, the designer also causes you to spend more time searching for and interpreting the basic information. Imagine how much more effective this information would have been if it had been displayed as a simple bar graph.

CONCLUSION

You will frequently see graphics in newspapers and popular magazines that violate the principles this chapter encourages you to follow. One reason may be that untrained designers create the graphics to add color and entertainment to an article. Another reason is that many computer programs for graphics actually make it easy for the user to clutter figures with junk, add needless third dimensions, or display information in a type of graph that isn't suited for the data. As you read professional journals in your field, however, you will notice that graphics are usually simpler and clearer than in popular periodicals. You are well advised to study the graphics of professional publications so that you can become both a wise consumer and producer of informative figures and tables.

SUGGESTIONS FOR PRACTICE

1. Using a spreadsheet or the table function of a word processing program, create a table that shows your personal budget for the last five months. Create six rows, one for each month and a final row for totals. Create as many columns as you need to display budget categories such as rent, food, clothing, transportation, entertainment, and school expenses. Give your table a number and an informative caption.

2. Convert the total figures from your budget table into a circle graph that shows what portion of your income went to each category. Label each wedge with the name of the budget category represented. Give your graph a figure number and a title.

3. Display in a table the following 1996 crime statistics from three urban counties: Washington County had 4 homicides, 3 rapes, and 20 armed robberies; Jefferson County had 2 homicides, 5 rapes, and 15 armed robberies; Madison County had 6 homicides, 6 rapes, and 17 armed robberies. Give the table a number and an appropriate caption.

4. Display the above crime statistics in a bar graph that compares the three counties for each type of crime. That is, create three bars side by side to show how they compare on numbers of homicides; three bars to show how they compare on numbers of rapes; and three more bars to compare numbers of armed robberies. Use shading to distinguish the three counties' bars, and use a legend to show which shade is used for which county. Give your bar graph a number and an appropriate caption.

5. Create an original table or figure to display data that you have collected as part of using one of the research methods described in Part II of this book.

6. In a library research paper display data that you have borrowed from a library source in a table or figure. Give the graphic a number and an appropriate caption. Give a credit line to the original source and give a complete bibliographic citation at the end of your paper.

REFERENCES

Tufte, Edward. 1990. *Envisioning information*. Cheshire, CT: Graphics Press.

18

ORAL PRESENTATIONS

As you learned in the opening chapter of this book, the ancient study of rhetoric focused on analyzing and teaching the art of public speaking. Two of the divisions of classical rhetoric—memory and delivery—taught students mnemonic devices to help them memorize their speeches and the art of using just the right stance, gestures, and voice inflections to make their words emphatic and memorable. In the eighteenth and nineteenth centuries, the main goal in teaching rhetoric at the university was to produce skilled orators who could take their place in society as ministers, lawyers, judges, legislators, doctors, and professors. The ability to speak eloquently and persuasively was considered a prime requirement for these professions and was the hallmark of an educated man (women did not regularly have access to higher education until the twentieth century). Some of the rituals that are still a part of traditional university life—debates, valedictory addresses, and oral exams—are a result of the strong emphasis on rhetorical training from the Middle Ages until well into the nineteenth century.

Being an effective, persuasive speaker is still vital for success in most avenues of professional life, just as it is for any citizen interested in affecting the course of local government. But in this century, what little rhetorical instruction students receive is usually limited to writing (and then only one or two courses). Courses in public speaking are still taught at most universities and colleges, but they are often no longer required. As a result, it is possible to graduate from college now without having formally studied and practiced the art of oral rhetoric. This is unfortunate because it is valuable to have the ability to get people to listen to you, to take your ideas seriously, and even to join you in action. While this chapter can't take the place of a full course in public speaking, it can offer some pointers that should be useful in your future—whether you present research findings at the meetings of professional organizations, make presentations to your supervisor or your subordinates on the job, or go to a city council meeting to influence the local zoning ordinances. You will learn how to evaluate each rhetorical situation, organize your presentation, use resources wisely, and plan and rehearse your delivery.

EVALUATING THE RHETORICAL SITUATION

Just as you do when you write, the first thing you should do when planning an oral presentation is evaluate your rhetorical situation: What is your purpose? Who is your audience? What do you intend to talk about? Whether you are writing or speaking, these are questions you must always answer when composing a text.

DEFINING YOUR PURPOSE

Your general purposes in any oral presentation will usually be to inform and persuade—though not always in equal measure. Sometimes your purpose may be to entertain (e.g., when serving as master of ceremonies) or respond appropriately on a ceremonial occasion (e.g., when receiving an award, proposing a toast, giving a eulogy). In addition to identifying your general purposes, you also need to define your immediate purpose or goal for the particular speech you are planning. For example, suppose you were presenting your research findings about a new behavior modification therapy to a group of peers. You could formulate your immediate purpose as follows:

> To inform my colleagues about the theory and practice of therapy X and persuade them that it is effective in dealing with people who display behavior Y.

By defining your immediate goal as precisely as you can, you are better able to make decisions about what information and evidence to include in your presentation and how to arrange its parts.

SIZING UP YOUR AUDIENCE

You can hardly think about your immediate purpose without simultaneously thinking about your audience. Here are some questions that will help you decide how to achieve your purpose with a given audience:

- Who are your listeners?
- What do they already know about the subject?
- What position, if any, have they already taken on the subject? Are they likely to be skeptical, favorable, or neutral to your point of view?
- What do they already know about you and how do they feel about you?
- What relationship do they have to you? Are they your peers, supervisors, students, or subordinates?

As you can see from these questions, there are many variables to consider as you plan how to address your audience. For example, if your audience knows you already and knows your background, it will not be necessary to have someone introduce you and explain your credentials—or to work that into your talk if no introduction is to be given. If the audience knows little about your subject you will have to think carefully about ways to give them a quick, basic understanding of it. If the audience already knows something about your subject, but is already inclined to disagree with you about it, you must plan ways to overcome their resistance. And if the audience members are your superiors and have the power to approve your ideas or grant money for a proposal, you must remember their need to be fully informed and to explore all the ramifications of the decisions they might make. You need to anticipate their concerns and be prepared to answer their questions.

ASSESSING THE CONTEXT AND ENVIRONMENT

As you define your immediate purpose and size up your audience, you should also assess the context and environment in which they will they be listening to you. Will you make your presentation to a class? During a board meeting? After dinner? At the end of a two-day conference? How many people will be there? What sort of mental and physical state are they likely to be in? How many minutes will you have to speak? What will the room be like in which you speak? Will it be a small classroom, a large auditorium, or a hotel conference room? Will you be standing at a podium or seated with your audience around a table? To answer questions such as these, try to learn as much as you can about the context and environment for your presentation, as they will certainly affect the strategy you will want to use. (More will be said later about how to plan for the environment.)

ORGANIZING YOUR PRESENTATION

After you have considered the above aspects of the rhetorical situation, you can begin planning what to include in your presentation and how to organize the parts. Generally, you will not have unlimited time for giving an oral presentation, so you need to limit your focus to a few aspects of the topic that you can present effectively in the allotted time. After you have decided what the focus will be, it's helpful to think about the presentation's organization in terms of the beginning, the middle, and the end.

The Beginning

The beginning or introduction of your presentation should do these three things:

1. Interest the audience in the topic and make them want to listen.
2. Provide an overview of the main points you will make.
3. Establish your credibility.

Some experts estimate that you have about a minute to make a good first impression on your audience and engage their attention. An audience that is bored or confused by the introduction is likely to give less than full attention to the rest of the talk. And they may reject the message if the messenger doesn't seem credible. In the opening sentences, then, you must simultaneously orient the audience to the purpose and scope of your presentation and make them feel you are a trustworthy, credible speaker.

You establish your credibility, your *ethos*, by projecting good will toward the audience, revealing yourself as a person of good character and being knowledgeable about your topic. You do this in part through nonverbal communication—through your dress, posture, facial expressions, and gestures—so it is important to make these work in your favor (more will be said about how to do so below under "Delivery"). But you can also establish credibility—as well as interest your audience—in the way you choose to introduce the topic. Here are some possibilities:

Begin with an anecdote that sets up a key issue you plan to discuss. Because stories deal with concrete people, places, and events, they are more memorable than abstract generalizations. They also get people's attention better than a dry statement such as, "In this presentation I will compare two therapies for eating disorders." In a well-chosen anecdote you can illustrate a problem or sketch quickly some key points of your presentation. Rather than seeming artificial, the anecdote should lead naturally to a statement of the purpose of your talk and a brief overview of the body of the talk. If you have engaged your audience's attention and shown your wisdom by framing your message through an appropriate story, the audience will credit you with the good sense and good character that wins their trust. And they will be prepared to listen to the statement of your main point before you move to the body of your speech.

Use brief, gentle humor. An audience perks up when a speaker opens with something that everyone can laugh at. A joke or witty remark suggests to them that you are relaxed and confident and that you do not want to bore them. Humorous remarks must be related to the subject of your presentation, however, and must lead easily to a preview of its contents. Gratuitous, unrelated humor might send the wrong message—that you are nervous, for example, or a frustrated comedian, rather than someone to be taken seriously.

Say something startling or unexpected. The audience will probably know the title of your remarks ahead of time and will probably have some expectations of what you will say. You will generate greater interest if you begin with a statement they *aren't* expecting. Offer a little-known statistic that points up something unusual about your topic. Or make a seemingly implausible claim that you'll support in the middle of your presentation. The audience will be curious to see how you will make the startling statistic relevant or the unusual claim plausible. Again, to win their trust, you must be prepared to move deftly from this kind of opening to a statement of the key point of your message and an overview of the facts, examples, or other evidence you will offer. You must show you can say something significant, not merely shock your listeners.

Ask a rhetorical question. A rhetorical question is one that the speaker does not expect anyone to answer out loud. But by asking the question and pausing a moment while the audience members answer it silently in their own minds, you are likely to gain everyone's involvement instantly. As you then proceed to outline and present your own answer to the question, you should have the attention of your listeners. And if your answer differs from the one they would have given, they will be particularly interested to learn why you think as you do.

Give a brief demonstration. Like a story, a demonstration immediately provokes interest and helps to make the abstract concrete. It gives the audience something to watch as well as to hear, and therefore increases the chance they will remember your main point. Granted, it is easier and more appropriate to demonstrate some topics than others, so don't stretch imagination and credulity too thin. But if the presentation is about something that lends itself to a demonstration—equipment, methods, or physical facts—consider a demonstration an excellent way to introduce your presentation. For example, suppose your speech was about the way smoking impairs health. To dramatize one health problem, the loss of lung capacity that smokers experience, you could have someone stand in front of the audience with nose and mouth taped shut, except for a small opening for a drinking straw inserted into the mouth, through which the person will breathe for 30 seconds. As the person's face grows redder, the audience will see how difficult it is to get enough oxygen when the lungs can't be inflated fully.

Involve the audience in doing something. Most people learn better when they actually do something during a presentation rather than passively listen. If your audience is small enough, if you have some flexibility with the time allotted, and if your presentation is not supposed to be very formal, consider beginning by having one or more of your listeners do something: Ask a question and then call for volunteers to answer it. Involve a few members of the audience in a simple role play, game, or demonstration that illustrates one of your main points. Have everyone write for one minute about a topic that you give them; then have some of them share what they've written. Be aware, however, that the more you open your presentation up to audience participation, the less control you will have over it because someone may say or do something entirely unexpected or use up more of your precious time than you planned. If you choose this way of beginning, you need to plan carefully for all the eventualities you can think of; then you must be flexible and think quickly on your feet to recover from an unanticipated outcome. But if you are successful in involving the audience, you will earn not only their attention, but their respect and trust as well.

Whatever you choose as an attention-getter, be sure that you keep it short and follow it up immediately with a clear and succinct statement of your main point and a quick overview of the middle of your presentation. Your audience will be able to listen for the key supporting points in the presentation if you outline them in advance.

THE MIDDLE

In the middle or body of your presentation, you elaborate on the points you previewed in your introduction. The number of points you should plan to cover depends on the time you have. In 5 minutes, you probably can do justice to only one; in 15 minutes, only two or three. Even if you have been given 45 minutes to make your presentation, you would be wise not to elaborate on more than five points.

As you compose your presentation beforehand, think carefully about the best way to order the parts of your talk. For example, if your topic is historical, a chronological order might be the most appropriate. Or, for a topic that speculates on the future, it might be useful to discuss causes and then effects. But discussing effects and then causes might be a good way to answer a question such as "How did we get to the situation we're in now?"

Because your audience is listening to, not reading, your presentation, they won't have the benefit of headings, paragraph indentations, or boldfaced type to let them know what the main ideas are. You will need to draw their attention to the fact that you are stating a main point by saying something like, "My second point is...."

You will also need to give ample illustrations, reasons, or other concrete data supporting each point. Because your audience can't reread your text, repetitions and variations of supporting evidence will help them grasp the points more firmly. For example, you might give some statistics and then make an analogy showing the significance of these statistics in a more concrete context. (Using visual aids, which are discussed below, also helps the audience to understand and remember your points.)

Avoid dwelling on a point too long, and don't assume that all your points need the same emphasis. You might, for example, spend two minutes elaborating on a simple idea so that you can have ten minutes to spend on a more complex one. You should plan the relative amount of emphasis for each point ahead of time by carefully analyzing your audience's needs. Then you can adjust your emphasis during the presentation as you notice your audience's reaction. If they seem bored and fidgety, they are probably ready for you to move on. If they seem a bit confused or anxious, they may be hoping you will say something more to clarify the matter.

THE ENDING

Rather than assuming your conclusion will just take care of itself, or that you will simply stop talking when your time is up, you should plan the ending of your presentation as carefully as the beginning. The ending is the ideal time to reassert your main points, because research shows people remember beginnings and endings better than middles. If someone missed a point or two that you made in the middle, you can still hope to reach that person with an effective summary of your points.

Although summarizing is an important part of the conclusion, you can aim to do even more. In the conclusion you can relate the significance of your presentation to a broader context, perhaps even personalize the message for audience members so that they feel its significance more strongly. For example, if you have just spoken on the 1950-era McCarthy hearings in the U.S. Senate, you could draw some comparisons between those events and current events of a similar nature. If the topic warrants it, at the end you can also issue a sort of challenge or call to action that inspires your listeners to do something with the information you have given them.

Whatever you do at the end of your presentation, provide a sense of closure that makes the audience feel they have come full circle with you in the minutes you've been talking. For example, you may allude to the anecdote, the joke, the rhetorical question, or the demonstration you began with. Say something to help the audience understand how the expectations you aroused with your introduction have now been fulfilled. In that way, they will sense that you have given the topic a full and satisfying treatment and not simply run out of time.

USING RESOURCES WISELY

Because there are important differences between listening to and reading a text, you should consider these differences as you prepare an oral presentation. Unlike written words, which are more or less permanent, spoken words vanish almost immediately. While readers can pause and reread parts of a text that aren't clear at first, in formal settings listeners usually don't have the luxury of interrupting and asking the speaker to repeat things. As you understand these differences between writing and speaking, you can prepare to capitalize on the advantages of face-to-face communication as well as compensate for the transitory nature of speech. As you plan your presentation, you should consider each of three resources that can enhance your oral message if used properly—or detract from it if you fail to take them into account. These resources are time, the environment for your talk, and visual aids.

TIME

In most cases, you will be told early on that you can speak a specific number of minutes. (If you are not told, be sure to ask how much time you'll have.) But be aware that the amount of time you are promised and what you may actually get are often not the same. For example, at meetings of professional organizations, you may be one member of a panel of three or four speakers, each of whom is supposed to talk for 20 minutes. But if you are the last speaker and the speaker just before you takes 30 minutes, you may be forced to cut your presentation. Or if one of the speakers fails to show up, you may suddenly have the dubious luxury of speaking 10 minutes longer than planned. Because of unexpected events like these, you should plan in advance where you could condense or expand your presentation if you had to. Rather than adding another point or extra detail to your talk, one good way of using additional time is to ask for questions and comments from the audience. Try to anticipate how the audience might react to your presentation so you can be prepared with good responses.

ENVIRONMENT

Before planning your presentation, it is wise to learn as much as you can about the place you will be speaking in. If you can, visit the place ahead of time to evaluate its size and other features. If it is a large auditorium, you will want to know if the acoustics are good and if a powerful enough microphone will be provided. If it is a small room, you may want to know if the chairs are fixed to the floor in rows, or if they can be moved into another arrangement. If you plan to show slides or overhead transparencies, you will need to know if the room has a projector and screen, and if the windows, if any, can be darkened with drapes or blinds. In short, what you can do in your presentation may be constrained by the physical limitations of the environment. It's better to know what those limitations are ahead of time rather than be embarrassed by not having planned for them.

VISUAL AIDS

Experts on learning agree that people will understand something better and remember it longer if you appeal to more than one of their senses. So, for important points in your presentation, it's wise to use a visual aid so that your listeners can *see* the point as well as *hear* it. The hallmarks of a good visual aid are visibility, clarity, and simplicity.

Visibility is largely a function of size, so if you plan to put a list on a posterboard, for example, the lettering must be big enough to be read easily by people in the back row. For a large audience in a large auditorium, a posterboard would be a poor choice of visual aid simply because it would have to be enormous to be visible to people in the last row. A slide of the same information would be a better choice because it could be projected onto a large screen.

Visibility can also be related to color choices. Using black lettering on a dark green background is not a good idea, for example, because there won't be enough contrast between the two colors. You also need to take care when using contrasting colors to emphasize contrasting ideas because some people are colorblind and they may not be able to discern the contrasts you intend.

Clarity and simplicity in visual aids are inextricably related. Generally, the simpler and less cluttered a visual is, the clearer it will be. Rather than try to put a lot of information into a few visuals, use more visuals with just one or two items of information on each. Don't use so many visuals, however, that you are constantly revealing a new one; your audience will start to feel overwhelmed with information and distracted by the rapid succession of visual aids.

A good visual aid should be largely self-explanatory; that is, even if a listener momentarily loses track of what you are saying, he or she should be able to pick up the thread by looking at the visual aid you have displayed. Each visual should therefore have a clear label and other cues about how to read it. On a bar graph, for example, the *x*-axis and *y*-axis should be clearly labeled.

Here is a list of some common visual aids with suggestions about how and when to use them.

Chalkboards, Whiteboards, and Sketchpads. The venerable chalkboard, the more modern whiteboard, and the portable sketchpad on an easel are all useful tools for an interactive presentation or one in which you want to present a developing progression of ideas. The physical act of portraying ideas visually on these surfaces can add energy and interest to your presentation. But because you have to turn your back to the audience to write on them, and because you may have to erase the board or turn the page on the sketchpad, you will lose some time and audience contact while using them. It's important, therefore, to limit the length or complexity of what you write or draw. Also, because what you write or draw may seem spontaneous and rough, using the chalkboard, whiteboard, or sketchpad may make your presentation seem less polished than one in which the visuals are prepared ahead of time.

Posterboards. Lists, diagrams, graphs, and tables can be prepared on sturdy posterboards in advance and displayed on an easel at the right moment in your presentation. You can use a pointer to draw the audience's attention to specific parts. If you have very many posters, it is a good idea to ask an assistant to help you with them—to remove one and reveal another as you nod your readiness.

Overhead Transparencies. Transparencies are in some ways like posterboards, and they may be easier to prepare for those whose hand lettering skills are not very good. Using a word processing program and a printer with variable fonts and point sizes, you can produce neat, legible lists, tables, graphs, and figures on a computer. You could also photocopy tables, figures, or sketches from published sources (giving credit of course). Then, using a thermal process, you can transfer the images from paper onto transparent sheets of film (any shop that specializes in making photocopies should be able to do this for you). You then lay these transparencies on an overhead projector and a large image will be projected onto a screen. You can even overlay one transparency on another, building up a series of images so your audience can see a progression of steps in a process, for example. You can also switch the projector on to focus audience attention on the visual aid, then switch if off again to return their focus to you.

Transparencies can also function like a chalkboard, as you can write directly onto blank transparencies with special pens. This method has some drawbacks, however, as the silhouette image of your hand and arm will also be projected onto the screen, and your body may block some people's view of the screen. For a small audience, writing directly onto transparencies may be a good way to keep audience attention. For a large audience, however, transparencies are probably best used like posterboards, with you standing to the side of the screen, using a pointer to draw attention to the images. If you have more than two or three transparencies, you may wish to have an assistant position the transparencies on the projector and then remove them so that you can concentrate on speaking.

Handouts. A printed handout distributed to each audience member can serve at least two functions. One is to provide an outline of your presentation so that listeners can follow along, perhaps taking notes on their outlines, and carry away a detailed record of what you have said. Another function of handouts is to supplement your presentation with visual or written information that fills in information you cannot cover completely during your presentation. Though handouts might be potentially enriching, they can also have the effect of drawing your listeners' attention away from what you are saying as they become engrossed in reading your visual aid, so be judicious in how you use them.

Photos. Still photographs of objects may be appropriate for some topics. They work best with small audiences, where the photos can be passed from person to person. To be visible to a large audience, a photo would have to be enlarged many times, and the process of enlargement usually degrades the quality of the details in a photo.

Slides. Slides overcome the drawback of photos because a tiny 35-mm slide can be projected onto a screen and be visible to all in the room. Slides are very versatile and can be of photographs, tables, graphs, lists, words, etc. Using a remote-control slide projector, you can then introduce your visuals at the right moments in your presentation. You can also use a light pointer to highlight certain parts of a slide. Some of the disadvantages of slides are the time and cost of preparation and the potential for an equipment failure. Also, because you must darken the room, you may lose eye contact with your audience. And some people may fall asleep during a slide presentation. On the other hand, a polished slide presentation can lend a very professional tone to an oral presentation.

Videos. You can use professionally produced, custom-made videotapes to create interest, illustrate a point, or analyze something in your presentation. If you use a segment from a commercially available videotape, be sure that you comply with any copyright restrictions. Before turning on a videotape, you should prepare your audience to notice the relevant details. Since videotapes are normally projected via an ordinary TV screen, they are best used with small groups. And like other visual aids, videotapes should be chosen for their relevance and not simply for their novelty or to create a change of pace. If you decide to use a video clip, you also need to make sure ahead of time that the equipment is working properly and that you know where to start and stop the videotape.

Liquid crystal display plates. With an LCD (Liquid Crystal Display) plate attached to a computer and an overhead projector, you can project onto a large screen whatever is on the computer screen. Then your audience can watch you manipulate information with the computer and see the results on the overhead screen. Be sure to tailor your use of this type of visual aid carefully to your purpose and audience.

Computer presentations software. If you have access to the necessary equipment and software, you can incorporate very sophisticated audio and visual aids into your presentation with computer presentations software. This software allows you to create a sophisticated slide presentation. You can make black and white or color overheads, 35-mm photographic slides, or on-line slides that include outlines, tables, figures, diagrams, and charts. You can also embed animated graphics and audio clips into your presentation. The software also provides clip-art or allows you to create your own figures to illustrate text. Using this software, you can prepare each component of a presentation—for example, your notes, audience handouts, and slides—and everything you create will be in a consistent format. As with any other medium, you should aim at communicating an idea clearly and simply rather than just producing a "gee whiz" effect.

Objects and models. If your presentation centers around some physical object, the actual object or a model of it can be very helpful in focusing attention and helping your listeners understand your main points. An object or model would best be used with a small group, so that all can see it clearly and perhaps even hold it. While small, inexpensive objects might be easy to bring along, a large or expensive piece of equipment may not be a practical visual aid. Models can be time-consuming and expensive to construct, too, so you need to weigh their advantages against the costs.

PLANNING FOR DELIVERY

Once you have analyzed your rhetorical situation, organized your presentation, and considered how to use the resources available, you are ready to prepare for the moment of truth—the time when you actually deliver your message.

Delivery is the most important part of an oral presentation. Even if you have prepared thoroughly, all of your hard work may come to naught if you can't deliver your message effectively. To be successful you should consider how presenting a message orally differs from giving a reader a written text. As a speaker, you can capitalize on important differences in these two types of rhetorical situations. In the oral situation, listeners have the advantage of hearing your actual voice and watching you deliver your message. You can use your voice, appearance, personal traits, gestures and body language to enhance the reception of your message in a way that you can't when you write. Planning your delivery involves deciding what method of memory support to use, choosing appropriate clothing, and rehearsing to make your voice and body movements support your message.

MEMORY SUPPORT

Although you may occasionally be called on without warning to give an impromptu speech, you usually are given time to prepare. As you look ahead to the time when you will speak, you should decide whether you will speak from memory, from notes, or from a complete manuscript. Memorizing your presentation is good mental discipline; it can also make you so familiar with your material that you feel confident and poised. For some people, however, memorizing a speech can lead to a colorless, rote presentation and inflexibility in adapting to the occasion and the audience. Others may freeze if their minds suddenly go blank and they aren't able to improvise with words other than the ones they memorized. Because of these potential pitfalls, memorizing an entire presentation is usually not the best option.

Speaking from notes is probably far more common in today's academic and professional world than is speaking from memory. Using notes permits you to sound natural and to maintain good eye contact; it may also make you feel free to move about naturally. Your notes might take the form of a simple one-page outline of your presentation that you can set in front of you and glance at, or some 3x5 cards on which you have written key words and which you can hold discreetly in one hand. Focusing your mind on concepts and key words rather than entire sentences allows you to speak extemporaneously, using the words that seem appropriate for the purpose and audience. If you are interrupted while speaking extemporaneously from notes, you can recover easily, without having to worry about exact wording.

For more formal occasions, reading from a prepared manuscript may be the best option, particularly if the audience is large and you will have to remain at a lectern with a microphone. It is also helpful if you are trying to communicate something delicate, and you have worked very carefully beforehand to find just the right words for your message. Also, if you want to create a certain mood and images with your words, you may want to read from a prepared manuscript. Reading from a manuscript is often the manner of delivery used at professional conferences where social scientists share their research findings. The scripts of their oral presentations may become the basis for eventual publications.

Reading your speech doesn't have to be monotonous and boring if you practice your delivery enough times that you can say your sentences effectively while still looking up frequently to maintain eye contact with the audience. To facilitate finding your place again easily after you look up, prepare your manuscript in a large font with wide margins and triple spacing. Don't feel so tied to what you have written that you don't feel comfortable improvising a little—tossing off a spontaneous comment related to the occasion or pausing to offer a simple explanation for something your audience seems puzzled about.

APPROPRIATE DRESS

Dressing and grooming yourself appropriately on the day of your presentation can't be overemphasized. People form first impressions about you based on your appearance, and, as unfair as it may seem, if they form negative impressions, your audience will probably not be able to judge the merits of your presentation objectively. Even though you may view your clothing, hairstyle, and jewelry as your way of making a statement about your personality, putting your individuality as your first priority can distract or even alienate your audience. Celebrities may be able to get away with eccentric dress, unusual hairstyles, and excessive jewelry, but if you are trying to establish your credibility, you would be wise to conform to the style that others follow in a given setting.

You should not dress less formally than your audience because your prominence as the speaker will make your casual clothing even more conspicuous than it would otherwise be. On the other hand, if you are dressed up a bit more than the audience, they may take it as a compliment to them; they certainly won't judge you as being careless about your dress. Often, you can adjust your clothing in simple ways to fit in. If the other men in the audience are all tie-less and in shirtsleeves, for example, a man may be able to remove his jacket and tie to be like them. Women can also remove accessories to achieve a more relaxed, understated look and blend in with how other women in the audience are dressed. If you are unsure about what to wear, ask ahead of time.

VOICE QUALITIES

Just as you want your appearance to enhance your delivery, you need to consider how you can use your voice to have the right impact on your audience. The first thing to consider is the *volume*, or loudness, of your voice. If you will be speaking into a microphone, you will merely need to be sure that you are close enough to it and that it is amplifying your voice adequately for everyone in the room. When there is no microphone, you need to speak loudly enough for people in the rear to hear you without straining. If you have a naturally quiet voice, you will need to make a conscious effort to project your voice more than usual. You can practice by rehearsing your speech for a friend in a room the size of the one you'll be speaking in.

You also need to consider the *pitch*, or high and low tones, of your voice. Interesting speakers vary their pitch rather than droning on at the same level all the time. Lowering the pitch of your voice can add a sense of drama and solemnity to what you say, while raising it can impart a sense of urgency.

The *pace* of your delivery is also important for achieving the effect you want to have on your audience. Pace is simply the speed you speak at. Most speakers average between 125 and 150 words per minute. At this rate, it takes you about two minutes to read a standard page of typewritten text. You can slow your pace down to emphasize points or to discuss complex ideas, or you can speed it up a bit to show excitement or cover some simple ideas quickly. Talking too slow or too fast all the time, however, will make it difficult for your audience to listen: Their minds will start to wander if you are too slow, and they will become confused and frustrated if you race through your presentation faster than they can comprehend it.

Finally, you must take care to articulate your words clearly and pronounce them according to common standards. Articulating "did you eat yet?" as "jeetyet?" may be acceptable in a conversation with friends, but it will convey excessive casualness in a presentation to an audience. Similarly, if you pronounce "exactly" as "ezackly," your audience may believe you are not well educated. As with your dress and grooming, you risk conveying the wrong impression if you insist on using idiosyncratic speech.

NONVERBAL COMMUNICATION

Although using your voice carefully can help make your delivery memorable, equally important are the nonverbal ways you communicate your message. A key factor here is eye contact. Speakers who seldom look into the eyes of their audience members convey the impression of being painfully shy and nervous or, perhaps worse, indifferent to the audience. On the other hand, a speaker who makes frequent eye contact with individuals in the audience reassures them that he or she is poised and prepared, keeps their attention, can assess how they are receiving the message, and can make subtle corrections as needed. Making eye contact means that you actually look into the eyes of different people in different parts of the room. You should hold one person's gaze for three to five seconds before moving on to someone else.

Gestures are another form of nonverbal communication that can enhance or detract from a message. Gestures are movements, both voluntary and involuntary, that can illustrate or emphasize a point, such as striking the podium with your fist to demonstrate your determination. (Admittedly, this particular gesture may be overdramatic, and it is certainly not one to use often.) Many people gesture naturally, using their fingers to point or to enumerate, or spreading their hands to indicate size. Others find it difficult to "talk with their hands." Too much gesturing may make you seem a bit frantic and distract your audience; too little gesturing may make you seem wooden and unnatural. As you rehearse your presentation, have a friend pay attention to your natural gestures; then make a conscious effort to eliminate distracting ones and to make the remaining ones smooth and effective. If you don't make many gestures naturally, think of appropriate ones you could make and practice them until they become natural. It is important to have some animated gestures during your presentation because they will help keep your audience alert and involved.

Your other movements, posture, and facial expressions also communicate your attitude and emotional state to your audience. Even though you may feel butterflies in your stomach, if your talk is well focused and organized, there's really nothing to dread. Move confidently to the position you will occupy as speaker. If you will be standing, keep your feet about 10–12 inches apart, relax your knees, then keep them slightly bent. Take a deep breath and let your shoulders drop naturally rather than keeping them hunched up around your neck. Pause a moment to survey your audience and smile at them. If you are not tied by necessity to a lectern, move about a little in front of your audience, but avoid pacing. Channeling your nervousness into appropriate movements as you speak will help dissipate your anxiety and will make you seem animated and at ease.

REHEARSING YOUR DELIVERY

Just as actors and singers rehearse before performing, good speakers do too. You need to practice integrating all the things you've learned in this chapter and make your presentation a seamless whole. The better rehearsed you are, the more confident you will feel and the more poised you will appear to your audience. If you practice using your visual aids, you will be able to control them and any necessary equipment smoothly, without unduly interrupting your talk and losing audience attention. Finally, if you rehearse your presentation several times you will be able to judge how well your presentation fits into the time limits you've been given and be more able to adjust its length as needed.

Asking a friend to listen to you and watch you has already been mentioned as one effective rehearsal strategy. Be sure to ask a friend who will be honest with you and critical enough of your performance to offer helpful feedback rather than simply reassure you that you're doing fine. Another rehearsal method is to practice in front of a full-length mirror. Still another is to have someone videotape you as you give a dress rehearsal; then watch the videotape several times to see where you can improve your performance.

Though all of these preparations may seem extensive and elaborate for just a few minutes on stage, after you successfully deliver your first oral presentations, you will find that you can prepare more quickly and easily for succeeding ones. Following many of the steps detailed here will become second nature, and you will become a more confident and polished public speaker.

SUGGESTIONS FOR DISCUSSION AND APPLICATION

1. Think of effective and ineffective speeches you have heard. What were the deficiencies of the ineffective speeches? What did the effective speakers do well that made their speeches memorable?

2. Attend a special lecture given by a guest on your campus or an important person in your community. Pay attention to how the speaker presents his or her message and make notes of what is done well and what could be improved. Report your findings to the class.

3. Prepare a ten-minute oral presentation based on the library research paper you complete for this class. Deliver your presentation to other members of your class and then listen as they give you feedback on your performance.

PART

VII

STYLE IN THE SOCIAL SCIENCES

Style is such an important part of rhetoric that in the past it has sometimes been the main focus of writing instruction. Although this book does not emphasize style as much as it could if there were space to do so, learning to use the right style for a given purpose and audience is one of the most important things you can do to make your rhetoric persuasive. Some elements of style are common to virtually all fields that write in the English language. Other elements of style, however, are limited to particular fields; they are an identifiable feature of the rhetoric of that field. To learn more about the elements of style common to all fields, you should consult a current handbook; there you will find guidelines for correct punctuation and mechanics and for effective sentence construction. In the next two chapters you will find some guidelines to help you with a few elements of style that are more particular to the social sciences. In Chapter 19, you will learn about current guidelines for references to yourself, for using the specialized terminology of your field, and for using unbiased language. In Chapter 20 you will find guidelines and models for documenting sources in three different documentation styles that are widely used in the social sciences.

19

INSTITUTIONAL STYLE

WHY DO STYLES DIFFER?

Style can refer to a distinctive or characteristic way of expressing oneself. For example, Mark Twain's style is very different from Jane Austen's, and both are different from Stephen King's. Novelists are not the only writers with a noticeable style; poets, playwrights, essayists, journalists, and other writers are also often noted for their unique styles. Political columnist William F. Buckley has a very erudite style that bespeaks his Ivy League education, for example, while Molly Ivins, also a political columnist, has a down-home, folksy style in which you can almost hear a Texas drawl. A writer's style is the result of all the many choices the writer makes, from deciding what to write about to selecting words, constructing and punctuating sentences, and organizing the text. Writers make their choices for many reasons, some of which they might not even be aware of, but their personal styles result at least in part from their language background, education, personal preferences, interests, goals, even their politics.

A style can be institutional as well as personal. For example, a particular publishing company, journal, newspaper, business, or professional organization will specify certain choices that a writer must make in selecting words, constructing and punctuating sentences, writing headings, documenting sources, and so on. Institutions don't specify everything a writer must do, however. Two writers writing for the same journal won't necessarily sound just

435

alike, because institutional guidelines still leave room for individual expression. But if the writer doesn't adhere to those matters prescribed by the institution, usually an editor will change the writer's text to make it conform to the
specifications before it is printed.

While it may seem that writing would be much easier if everyone, including institutions, could just agree on a common set of rules, it's not that simple.
Although there are a number of commonly shared rules for good style that
transcend the boundaries of institutions (any current handbook of style and
usage will inform you of these), like individuals, institutions have histories that
have shaped their assumptions about language. They also have an image they
want to project and even an ideology that their chosen style may help to further. A group's institutional style is, in part, its way of creating an identity and
pursuing its goals. Styles differ because people and institutions differ and
because language is an extremely flexible tool.

In this chapter you will learn about particular aspects of institutional style
in the social sciences. Though it may seem that much is prescribed for you, you
will find that there is also some room to develop your own personal style.
Indeed, as you develop expertise as a researcher in your field, you will find you
can make a more enduring mark in your profession if you also develop a
mature and confident command of the English language, which will allow you
to put your personal stamp on your prose.

STYLE IN THE SOCIAL SCIENCES

It's somewhat hazardous to generalize about the style of the social sciences,
because the social sciences do not all sanction the same styles. For instance, the
writing style of an anthropologist might vary considerably from that of an economist; in fact, two economists may write rather differently because of different
focuses in their field. Furthermore, the social sciences do not equally emphasize
conformity to a style. One field that does emphasize conformity to a style, however, is psychology. Over the years since 1929, through issuing increasingly specific editions of its *Publication Manual*, the American Psychological Association
(APA) has significantly influenced the style of not only psychology but many
other social sciences as well. The APA style manual has been adopted in many
fields, including communications, education, family science, linguistics, sociology, and social work. Professionals seeking to publish in many social science publications, including more than 30 sponsored by the APA, must conform to the
manual's prescriptions. So despite the hazards of generalizing, it is worth noting
some features of the writing style that are authorized by the current APA
Publication Manual (1994) and that are also characteristic of other social sciences,
even though they may not have adopted the APA style manual.

It is important to note here that characteristics of any institutional style can and do change. The goal of this chapter is to help you realize that style is not a constant in any field; it is always the product of choices based on assumptions about knowledge—what knowledge is, how it is created, and how it should be represented in language (see, for example, Madigan, Johnson, and Linton 1995). As these assumptions change, style usually changes as well.

THE DETACHED PERSONA

Until recently, one of the most recognizable features of the social scientific style was the detached persona. A writer's *persona* is his or her *ethos*—how the self is presented in the writing as a voice or character that the reader can judge as reliable, credible, and knowledgeable. For at least a century, the hallmark of good scientific writing was to project this authoritative ethos without revealing much about oneself. This stylistic trait is now changing, but because it has been so pervasive, it is necessary to understand what it was in order to understand how it is changing.

To create the detached persona, a writer avoided using first-person pronouns like "I" and "we." Presumably, this style gave the impression that the writer was objective and emotionally uninvolved in the subject matter. Also, by effacing him- or herself, a writer conveyed the impression that knowledge is self-existent, an object that is discovered rather than at least partially created through researchers' methods of collecting and interpreting evidence. There are two major ways writers have achieved this detached style. Both involve *not* putting human agents in the subject position of sentences (usually the first part of English sentences).

The first way of achieving the detached persona was to put nonhuman nouns in the subject position. For example, in social science writing you may still find sentences like this:

> This study investigates the relationship between marital satisfaction and the wife's employment status.

Note that "this study" is in the subject position, implying that it does the action of the verb "investigates." But only in a metaphorical sense can an inanimate thing like a study investigate something else. The APA *Publication Manual* (1994) calls this use of "study" as a subject "anthropomorphic" because it gives human characteristics to a nonhuman thing. In reality, the researcher investigates the relationship, yet only recently has the social science style begun to include sentences like this:

> In this study I investigate the relationship between marital satisfaction and the wife's employment status.

By leaving out the human agent who actually investigates, the first sentence with the nonhuman subject contributes to the impression that knowledge is objective, impersonal, and disembodied, existing apart from people who know it. By contrast, the second sentence acknowledges the role the investigator played in creating the knowledge.

Sometimes writers used sentences that acknowledged the human role in the investigation, but they used a third person noun rather than a first-person pronoun:

> The researcher investigated the relationship between marital satisfaction and the wife's employment status.

While this sentence at least puts a human agent in the subject position, it can be ambiguous because the reader can't be sure if "the researcher" refers to the writer or to someone else. The fourth edition of the APA *Publication Manual* (1994) specifically advises writers not to use anthropomorphic nouns or to refer to oneself in the third person. Instead, it tells writers to use the first-person pronoun and simply write, "In this study *I* [or *we*] investigated the relationship between marital satisfaction and the wife's employment status."

The second way of creating the detached persona was to use the passive voice. For example, instead of writing the active voice sentence,

> I conducted an experiment.

in which the pronoun "I" is in the subject position, the researcher would write instead,

> An experiment was conducted.

This second sentence is in passive voice with the words "an experiment" in the subject position. Although the researcher might have added *"by me"* at the end of the second sentence, doing so acknowledges human agency in conducting the experiment. Because passive voice allows writers to omit the agent of an action, social scientists have often used passive voice in the past, perhaps to imply that they are writing about knowledge that is objective, impersonal, and self-existent. Using this particular strategy, a writer could avoid claiming responsibility for actions performed. The APA *Publication Manual* (1994) advises against the use of passive voice unless "you want to focus on the object or recipient of the action rather than on the actor" (32). For example, if you wanted to describe your procedures in survey research, you might write, "Copies of the questionnaire were mailed to 100 people chosen randomly from the telephone directory," because this sentence would emphasize the questionnaires, not who mailed them.

The detached persona is not necessarily "bad," either in a moral or a grammatical sense. People still understand sentences with impersonal subjects and sentences in passive voice, and probably no one imagines that experiments simply happen or that studies investigate things without humans being present. Still, this style reflects an assumption about scientific knowledge—that it exists apart from people who know it, and therefore it is not necessary to refer to the human agents who invent it. This assumption is changing, however, as more scientists agree that knowledge is something humans create as much as discover, and that the style of scientific language ought to openly acknowledge the role humans play in their own research.

JARGON: WHEN IT IS AND WHEN IT ISN'T

Another major characteristic of the social science style is the prevalent use of jargon. The word *jargon* generally has negative connotations, suggesting writing that is practically unintelligible because of its technical vocabulary. But the same writing that a lay reader might label "jargon" may be completely accessible to and communicate very efficiently with readers who share the writer's assumptions, training, and knowledge. So jargon can be positive as well, when it means using specialized vocabulary and following other conventions that permit a community of trained people to communicate effectively with each other. Whether jargon is appropriate or inappropriate, then, depends to some extent on the reader. "Borderline personality disorder" may sound merely intimidating to the lay reader, but to the psychologist it communicates a concept clearly.

It must be acknowledged, however, that much writing in many fields, not just the social sciences, is needlessly difficult, even pompous, using too many unfamiliar, multisyllable words and a complex style with no gains in efficient communication to any audience. This use of unnecessary jargon often goes by such names as "gobbledygook," "bureaucratese," or "academese." In this kind of jargon, a simple sentence like "Too many cooks spoil the broth" becomes "A superfluity of culinary experts degrade the quality of the beef or poultry extract." If we agree that writing such gobbledygook is unnecessary anytime, we must still consider when there are good reasons in the social sciences (and other fields as well) to use jargon. Four kinds of sometimes necessary jargon are listed below.

New combinations of words to create operational definitions. Scientists of all kinds attempt to explain the phenomena they study as precisely as they can. Often, when they have formulated a new concept that they believe explains things well, they may create new phrases to name it. Since the social sciences are often concerned with measurements, scientists need names for their concepts that will allow them to perform precise observations and numerical operations. In other words, they must make the definition of a new concept operational. An operational definition is one that permits scientists to observe the concept with their methods (observation, experiments, surveys, and so on) and quantify it with their instruments, such as scales and tests. For this reason, social scientists don't want names with existing connotations that will make it difficult for others to accept them as operational definitions.

For example, a sociologist may want to learn something about how "happy" people are in their families or with their jobs. But "happiness" is such an emotionally loaded term that it can't be defined as precisely as needed for the kinds of measurements and statistical tests the sociologist might need to do. Therefore, the sociologist will create a more neutral name for the concept, such as "life satisfaction." While this invented phrase may seem puzzling to a lay reader, it actually increases the precision of the definition the sociologist can give to the term and allows the sociologist to measure life satisfaction, for example on a scale from one to six. And among professional peers, the term works as an efficient way of discussing an important concept.

Acronyms and Initialisms.   The social sciences are rich sources of *acronyms*—words made of the initial letters in a phrase, usually spelled in all uppercase letters. You already know and use acronyms such as AIDS, a short and pronounceable name for Acquired Immune Deficiency Syndrome that increases efficiency in writing and speaking because of its brevity. In the social sciences, acronyms like this gain currency among groups of researchers interested in the same phenomena. For example, those who study the deaf culture needed a convenient way to refer to the children of deaf adults. In order to save the time of constantly saying or writing four words, they created the acronym CODA. While that acronym may not have widespread use in the general population, it does make communication more efficient for the initiated.

Initialisms are like acronyms, shortening the way of referring to a multiword phrase. The difference is that initialisms can't be pronounced as a word; instead, the initial letters of the phrase are read off. For example, "borderline personality disorder" is often shortened to BPD in order to avoid continually writing or saying the entire phrase. And the Minnesota Multiphasic Personality Inventory is usually shortened to MMPI, with corresponding savings of space and time. With both acronyms and initialisms, however, the first use of the abbreviation should be spelled out entirely, with the short form given in parentheses immediately following, so that any uninitiated reader can learn what the letters stand for.

Sometimes an acronym becomes so common that we even forget its origin as an acronym, and it becomes, for all intents and purposes, a single word which we needn't expand into the longer phrase it stands for in order to comprehend it. *Radar* and *sonar* are such words. Most people have forgotten—if they ever knew—that radar stands for "*ra*dio *d*etection *and r*anging" and sonar for "*so*und *na*vigation *and r*anging." Note that neither is written in all capital letters anymore. The initialism HIV (for "human immunodeficiency virus") is fast becoming a term that people don't stop to recall the component words for any longer. The same assimilation of acronyms and initialisms to single words may happen in your field, though their use may not become widespread beyond the members of your field.

Neologisms. The word *neologism* may itself look like unnecessary jargon, but when you consider its Greek roots, it's not so difficult. The prefix *neo* simply means "new," and the root comes from *logos*, Greek for "word." So a neologism is simply a new word or phrase coined to represent a concept that can't be adequately represented with existing words. An example of a neologism in psychology is *affect*, a noun to refer to an emotional state as opposed to a cognitive or perceptual state. Though it has been in use for several decades now, the term is not used widely by the general public. But it has come to be a very useful name for an important concept in psychology, education, and related fields.

Multiple noun strings. One of the interesting things about the English language is that it can use a noun to modify another noun. For example, we all understand that the noun *headache* in the phrase *headache remedy* tells us what kind of remedy. Every field takes advantage of this fact of English and uses groups of nouns to create names for the concepts it studies; for example, psychologists speak of "attention deficit disorder"—a string of three nouns in a row, in which *attention* tells what kind of *deficit*, and together they both tell what kind of *disorder*. But when the jargon of a field begins to string four, five, and sometimes even six nouns in a row, the result is often sentences that are almost unreadable—even for the initiated. Here is an example quoted in the fourth edition of the APA *Publication Manual* (1994, 25):

> commonly used investigative expanded issue control question technique

It's a safe bet that only a few insiders would understand that string of four modifiers and four nouns—and they might not be sure! When that many words are strung together in this fashion it is almost impossible to tell which ones modify which other ones and in what way. It could be rewritten more clearly in any of three ways: "a control question technique that is commonly used to expand issues in investigations"; "a common technique of using control questions to investigate expanded issues"; or "a common technique of using expanded issues in control questions" (APA *Publication Manual* 1994, 26).

Even though stringing nouns together makes information more compact, it also makes it less understandable. "Unpacking" the noun strings makes sentences easier to read. In general, the way to go about unpacking a noun string is to start with the last noun in the string (the base noun) and then put the other nouns in prepositional phrases or relative clauses that modify the base noun. For example, suppose you encountered this multiple-noun string:

> a five-year hiring needs assessment plan

Starting with *plan*, you could arrange the other words as modifiers like this:

> a plan that assesses hiring needs [relative clause] for the next five years [prepositional phrase]

In your writing, particularly when your audience is not likely to understand the jargon, you should not use multiple-noun strings. For example, don't write this sentence for a lay audience:

> Although individuals typically have little difficulty in successfully monitoring the sources of their affective reality, errors or equivocations in their cognitive reality monitoring process sometimes occur.

Instead write this one:

> Although people can usually monitor the sources of their affections, they may make mistakes or equivocate when monitoring their cognitive reality.

When you are writing about the subject matter of your discipline, always consider your audience. If your readers are likely to know the jargon you wish to use, or if they can be helped to understand it with brief, simple definitions, you may feel safe in using it. When you are writing for an audience of all or mostly lay readers, however, it is important to reduce the amount of jargon you use, as the sheer abundance of it may bewilder your readers. This means that you may actually have to write five pages to say what you could say to your peers in three; paradoxically, in some cases, increased length results in more efficient communication.

INCLUSIVE AND UNBIASED LANGUAGE

Perhaps because they often study marginalized groups and unusual individuals and their behaviors, social scientists are sensitive to the processes of prejudice and exclusion that can lead to the demeaning of individuals and groups and even to discrimination against them. Perhaps also because of their quest for precise ways of describing the individuals and groups they study, the social sciences have often been leaders in using language that reduces stereotyping, eradicates bias, and promotes fairness. For example, the American Psychological Association states the following in its *Publication Manual*:

> As an organization, APA is committed both to science and to the fair treatment of individuals and groups, and policy requires authors of APA publications to avoid perpetuating demeaning attitudes and biased assumptions about people in their writing. Constructions that might imply bias against persons on the basis of gender, sexual orientation, racial or ethnic group, disability, or age should be avoided. Scientific writing should be free of implied or irrelevant evaluation of the group or groups being studied. (1994, 46)

"Political Correctness." In recent years, the phrase "political correctness" has been used rather loosely to characterize efforts such as the APA's to encourage language that respects differences and speaks of differences in nonjudgmental language. The phrase is accurate in acknowledging that language choices can indicate a political stance. But too often the label "political correctness" seems to be used negatively to mean a coercive movement to change the language of the majority to language that a minority wants to enforce as "correct." While it may be true that some efforts to change the language have been excessive or unproductive, the underlying motive in most cases has been to promote language that shows sensitivity and respect. Therefore, even though you may find some proposed language changes unnecessary or even foolish, you ought not to automatically reject efforts like those of the APA as "mere political correctness." These proposed changes only ask people to think carefully about the attitudes their language may reveal and to use words and names that avoid stereotyping or offending. Considering the professional and social penalties you might pay for ignoring such prescriptions, you should realize that compliance is often a safer choice than resistance, especially when you understand that the goal is clear communication that avoids offending others or treating them as objects. Though some terms may at first seem awkward to you, they will seem less so after you use or read them repeatedly.

References to Gender. Some of the most important changes in professional language concern the way the genders are referred to. Until a couple of decades ago, it was common to refer to human beings in general with such terms as "man," "men," and "mankind." While a few people still insist that these words are generic—that is, that they include both genders—such a claim is less credible now. Because words get their meaning from the way people use them, not from the dictionary or from some invisible authority, their meanings can and do change (for example, *fond* once meant "foolish," not "affectionate" as it does now). Today's usage and many research studies demonstrate that most people no longer regard "man" and related words as generic. To insist on using them in a generic sense can create ambiguity, since "man" also refers to a male person and "men" refers to more than one male person. Readers and listeners may not know when the specific sense or the so-called generic sense is intended. The simplest way of avoiding this confusion is to say "men and women" when you mean both genders, or to say "humankind" or "humans" rather than "mankind." Using these terms is important for greater precision. These usages also acknowledge that women constitute half the human race, and they accord women the dignity of being included in categories that are accurately named.

The increasing presence of women in the workforce, specifically in jobs that were once exclusively the domain of men, means that the suffix-*man* in certain job titles is also no longer thought to be inclusive or accurate. A number of titles have been adapted to avoid conveying the impression that only men hold these jobs and to include the women who do, too. For example, a policeman is now called a police officer; a mailman, a mail carrier; a fireman, a firefighter; a chairman, a chair or chairperson; and so on. In references to other jobs previously dominated by one gender, it is considered unnecessary and condescending to point out that a person holding a particular job is unusual because of her or his gender. For example, it is not appropriate to say or write "lady lawyer" or "woman doctor" any more than it is to say or write "male nurse" or "gentleman secretary." Qualifications such as these are generally irrelevant. The only time they are relevant is when research makes gender a variable, as, for example, in a study that compares female lawyers' attitudes with those of male lawyers. In such a case, it would be important to add distinguishing adjectives, and "female" and "male" would be the best choices because they have neutral overtones and they are parallel grammatically and conceptually.

In general, when referring to individuals or groups who are alike in all ways but gender, it is important to refer to the genders in a parallel way. For example, to call a group of 21-year-old male college students "men" but call an identically aged group of female students "girls" would not acknowledge their parallel status. Similarly, to refer to men by their professional titles but to women who hold equal credentials by their first names or their husbands' names is to imply that an important difference exists. Although no disrespect may be intended, readers may infer a subtle disparagement of individuals or groups whose equal status is not acknowledged.

Disparagement also comes from language that evokes cultural stereotypes; too often, these stereotypes are grossly inaccurate and unexamined. To use the phrase "woman driver," for example, is simply unfair to all the women whose driving ability is normal and whose behavior behind the steering wheel is safe and characteristic of that of most drivers on the road. Similarly, to say that someone behaved "like a typical man" is to offer no helpful information; it merely leaves the reader wondering what "typical" means. Stereotypes are usually generalizations based on insufficient or skewed data, and using them is inappropriate for anyone who would claim to be a scientist.

References to Racial, Ethnic, and Other Groups. Stereotypes and inaccurate labels can also be applied unfairly to other groups—racial and ethnic groups, for example, as well as elderly persons, people with disabilities, or people with homosexual orientation. The APA *Publication Manual's* advice on referring to these groups is as follows:

> Respect people's preferences; call people what they prefer to be called.... Accept that preferences will change with time and that individuals within groups often disagree about the designations they prefer.... Make an effort to determine what is appropriate for your situation; you may need to ask your participants which designations they prefer, particularly when preferred designations are being debated within groups. (1994, 48)

As you are no doubt aware, the names that some groups prefer to be called have changed more than once during the last 20 years. These name changes are often due to a linguistic process called "pejoration," in which a new word or a new name will start its life with positive or at least neutral connotations, but after a period of time, it will start to have negative connotations, often for prejudicial reasons, and will then be considered a "pejorative"—a name that is disparaging or degrading. Obviously, since no group wants to have a name that is a pejorative, the group often creates a new name for itself. Rather than look upon this process of renaming as an unnecessary nuisance, consider that each individual and group wants to be respected and take pride in their identity.

At the time this book went to press, the accepted way of identifying most racial and ethnic groups in the United States was to designate country or region of origin with the noun "American" following, as in the following illustrations:

African American
Asian American
Mexican American
Native American (also American Indian)

Another useful rule of thumb for showing respect for others is to avoid turning adjectives into nouns that become labels, suggesting that you have objectified the people you are referring to. For example, rather than write about "the elderly," "gays," and "the mentally retarded," write instead about "elderly people," "gay men," or "mentally retarded persons." In this way you acknowledge the humanity of the individuals. Another way of following this rule is to put the person first, not their condition or disability. So, rather than write "paraplegic" or even "paraplegic patient," write "person with paraplegia." This kind of phrasing separates the person from the disability, rather than identifying him or her as only the disability. Finally, avoid language that unnecessarily expresses emotion about a person's condition or disability. For example, write "persons with schizophrenia" rather than "victims of schizophrenia," which suggests that these people are doomed to a hopeless life.

References to Participants in Research.   In accord with this same line of thought, the APA *Publication Manual* (1994) also encourages writers not to think of the people who participate in their research as *subjects*. The word "subject" implies that people who agree to participate in an experiment, answer a survey, or otherwise cooperate with researchers are acted upon, rather than acting freely according to their own agency. Preferred names for those who take part in research are *participants, respondents, informants, individuals,* or some other name that accurately describes their status, such as *children, teens, college students,* or *patients.*

The APA style manual (1994) suggests further to show that individuals in research studies are actors, not subjects who are acted upon, writers should construct sentences in the active rather than the passive voice when describing what the participants did. For example, rather than write "Subjects were administered a questionnaire," researchers should write, "Respondents completed a questionnaire." Writers should also avoid using verbs that, although not passive voice in the grammatical sense, still suggest that the participants are passive rather than active. For example, writers should not say, "The participants *showed* distress"; they should write instead, "The participants *reported* they felt distress."

These recommendations of the APA *Publication Manual* (1994) indicate a significant shift in thinking for the social sciences that subscribe to that manual. However, you should be aware that the changes the manual advocates will take place gradually. Some social scientists, editors of some journals, or some of your professors may still prefer that you use the passive voice or impersonal and anthropomorphic subjects. As in other rhetorical matters, you should always learn what your audience expects and adapt your writing as necessary to achieve your goals in submitting your work. One of the most important things you can do as a fledgling social scientist, however, is to examine the prevailing style of your field for the assumptions it reveals and make informed choices rather than simply comply without thinking.

CONCLUSION

This chapter has referred frequently to the APA *Publication Manual*. If that is not the relevant style manual for you to follow, you may need to find out what other guides you should consult. Some professional journals publish or will mail to you upon request the style guidelines they require authors to comply with. You can also learn a lot about style by simply observing what authors do in the books and journals that you read for your own research. Finally, you can ask a professor in your major what guidelines have been published for your field.

This chapter began with the assertion that an institutional style is, in part, a group's way of creating an identity and pursuing its goals. At this point, you may feel that in some ways you are asked to give up your individuality or your personal convictions and simply submit to rules that you didn't help create. In a way, that's so: No one asked you what you thought, but that's because you weren't a part of the field when the institutional style was being formulated. But like styles in clothing, styles in language also change. By understanding and complying with the style guidelines of your field, you can become an insider and then have the chance to influence future changes in the style. Those with the most persuasive voices will exert the most influence. Until you have the stature to influence change, take the opportunity to observe, to learn, and to reflect on the assumptions underlying the institutional style of your field.

SUGGESTIONS FOR WRITING OR DISCUSSION

Directions: Imagine that you are the editor of a professional journal, and you find the following sentences in various manuscripts that scholars have sent to you. Edit the sentences to comply with the style guidelines given in this chapter. Be prepared to defend your choices by discussing how a given context and audience would affect your decisions.

1. The following professors collaborated in this study: Dr. Robert Jackson, Dr. Michael Parmenian, Dr. Octavio Salazar, and Mrs. David Schuster.

2. The depressives were assigned to a treatment regimen that included four doses of the experimental drug each day for two weeks.

3. This article describes and evaluates the opinions of the elderly about nursing home care.

4. In sessions with the therapist, the client acted like a typical man.

5. Mankind's quest for knowledge has led to some revolutionary discoveries in sociobiology.

6. The study included six physicians, including one woman doctor.

7. The personality is a unique configuration of life history identity items that differentiate the self from the other.

8. The 30 college-aged subjects in this experiment were all U.S. citizens; they included 10 Orientals, 15 Negroes, and 5 Indians.

9. Interviews were conducted with 10 learning disabled students, one of whom was additionally afflicted with muscular dystrophy.

10. Tom Schwartz is a male nurse.

11. While building up her clinical practice clientele, she supplements her salary by teaching a community college general education introductory psychology course.

12. The client, Mrs. Daniel Johnson, works as a foreman in a software production plant.

13. The African American subjects were randomly assigned to one of the two treatments.

14. Ironically, busy family therapists often don't spend enough time with their own wives and children.

15. The university was persuaded to create a women's resource center as part of the Counseling Service.

16. The respondents were 25 men and 25 women young professionals just starting in business. The businessmen tended to rate themselves as satisfied with their jobs significantly more often than the girls did.

17. The first two informants, Joshua and Elaine Carmichael, were man and wife.

18. I would like to thank Dr. Gloria Brunetti, the chairman of my department, for her careful reading of the first draft of this manuscript.

19. The subjects were 50 male homosexuals.

20. Since the major oil companies began using fast-pay credit card reader gasoline purchase systems, they have been able to decrease labor costs by as much as 10 percent.

21. It has been shown in clinical drug trials that these new medications are effective in alleviating symptoms for schizophrenics.

22. Stereotyping the elderly can be seen as serving an ego protection function for youth.

23. It was argued by the defense attorneys that the crime lab had contaminated the evidence.

24. The AIDS victims attributed their unusually long survival to their optimistic outlook on life.

25. Determination of veteran's benefits payments eligibility is decided by the SPE (Standards, Procedures and Exceptions) committee during its monthly analysis and review meeting.

REFERENCES

American Psychological Association. 1994. *Publication manual.* 4th ed. Washington, DC: American Psychological Association.

Madigan, Robert, Susan Johnson, and Patricia Linton. 1995. The language of psychology: APA style as epistemology. *American Psychologist* 50 (June): 428–436.

20

DOCUMENTATION STYLES

WHAT IS A DOCUMENTATION STYLE?

Part of a field's institutional style is its documentation style. A documentation style is a set of guidelines for referring to sources from which you have borrowed ideas or words so that you can avoid plagiarizing. Typically, complete documentation has two parts:

1. Parenthetical references or footnotes in the body of your paper, or endnotes at the end of it, that briefly cite the source of a particular quotation, summary, or paraphrase.
2. Complete bibliographic citations at the end of your paper for the books, articles, and other documents you used for your research. These include the author, title, publisher, and place and year of publication for any book you use; they include author, title, journal name, volume number, and pages for journal articles.

As someone preparing to enter a professional community, you should learn about the documentation style of your field so that your writing can conform to it when necessary. Various professional organizations have developed different standards for formatting documentation to provide a consistent style for their members to follow. These organizations either publish their own style guide, or adopt an existing one, that states the standards and provides examples of how to document all kinds of borrowed information—printed, oral, and electronic.

In some ways, a field's documentation style reflects its assumptions about knowledge. For example, the style of the American Psychological Association (APA) makes the year of publication the second element in a bibliographic citation, right after the author's name. This prominent position reflects the value that the APA places on recent knowledge. In other ways, an organization's documentation style simply reflects arbitrary agreements about the most efficient ways to help other readers find cited documents. Although the logic of a field's style may not always be clear, if the members of a profession use the style consistently, it facilitates easier editing, quicker publication, and more accessible information for all.

During your education, you may have learned to use more than one documentation style. Using different styles may continue in your professional life, especially if you work on the boundaries between two disciplines that each use a different style. You shouldn't worry much about why styles differ or whether you'll ever master their intricate details. In fact, probably no one but a handful of professional editors has ever memorized all the elements of a documentation style. The important thing for you to learn is what is necessary to include in documentation and how to look up the details in the relevant style manual.

WHAT THIS CHAPTER INCLUDES

It's not possible or desirable to duplicate any field's complete style manual here. Instead, this chapter provides you with basic guidelines for documenting the most common kinds of documents you are likely to cite in research papers. In this chapter you will find guidelines for using three documentation styles: (1) the APA style, (2) the reference list style found in Turabian's *A Manual for Writers of Term Papers, Theses, and Dissertations*, and (3) the footnote/endnote and bibliography style also found in Turabian's manual. The Turabian manual is closely linked to the *Chicago Manual of Style*, a prestigious style guide that scholars in many fields, including some of the social sciences, have followed for over 90 years. It is important to note that there are other styles in addition to these three that are used in the social sciences, but their use is not as widespread. The APA style is widely used in the fields of psychology, sociology, social work, family sciences, education, and public health. The Turabian reference list style is commonly used in the fields of political science, international relations, geography, economics, and communications. The Turabian footnote/endnote style is used mainly by historians.

The chapter is divided into three parts, each corresponding to the three styles. Each part provides guidelines for (1) referring to sources within the body of your paper by supplying either parenthetical references or footnotes/endnotes, and (2) creating the list of cited works at the end of your paper. Each part shows you examples of how to provide in-text documentation for borrowed information that is summarized, paraphrased, and quoted. Each part also provides examples of how to cite common kinds of documents you are likely to borrow from. You need to familiarize yourself only with the section that is relevant for you.

If you are not sure which documentation style to use, ask your writing instructor or a professor in your major what the preferred style is. If the style you should follow is not included here, a good way to learn about it is to find a journal article that uses the desired style and imitate the documentation you see there.

AMERICAN PSYCHOLOGICAL ASSOCIATION (APA) STYLE

IN-TEXT REFERENCES

When following the APA documentation style, you need to note some information about your sources—the author's name, the year of publication, and, when necessary, page numbers—within your text. This information is enclosed in parentheses and follows the excerpt or your reference to the work. There are various ways of citing sources, depending on whether you are paraphrasing, summarizing, or quoting a passage from an outside source.

Suppose you wanted to cite the following passage from pages 187–188 in Jared Diamond's book *The Third Chimpanzee: The Evolution and Future of the Human Animal*, published by HarperPerennial in 1992:

> Besides malnutrition, starvation, and epidemic diseases, farming brought another curse to humanity: class divisions. Hunter-gatherers have little or no stored food, and no concentrated food sources like orchards or herds of cows. Instead, they live off the wild plants and animals that they obtain each day. Everybody except for infants, the sick, and the old join in the search for food. Thus there can be no kings, no full-time professionals, no class of social parasites who grow fat on food seized from others.

You could summarize, paraphrase, or quote part or all of this passage in your paper. Following are examples of how you would do this.

Documenting a Summarized Source. You can document a summarized source in a variety of ways. First, you can give the author and year of publication in parentheses at the appropriate point in the sentence. Notice that the author's surname and the year of publication are separated by a comma, and that the sentence period *follows* the parenthetical reference.

Some archeologists suggest that our race's shift from hunting and gathering to farming for food may have given rise to class divisions (Diamond, 1992).

Second, you can use the author's name in the sentence and then give the year in parentheses:

Diamond (1992) suggests that our race's shift from hunting and gathering to farming for food may have given rise to class divisions.

Third, you can use both the author and the year in the sentence, thus requiring no parenthetical reference. This method is less common than the first two:

Diamond's 1992 book suggests that our race's shift from hunting and gathering to farming for food may have given rise to class divisions.

Documenting a Paraphrased or Partially Quoted Source. Here's how you would cite a passage that is paraphrased, with a partial quote included:

Diamond notes that farming may have caused the rise of class divisions. He argues that, before we as a race started farming, our hunter-gatherer predecessors each had to contribute more or less equally to the ongoing search for food and therefore didn't live off the efforts of others. Unlike an agriculturally based society, in a hunter-gatherer society "there can be no kings, no full time professionals, no class of social parasites who grow fat on food seized from others" (1992, pp. 187–188).

Although the APA *Publication Manual* does not require that you cite page numbers with paraphrases, it recommends providing page numbers so that an interested reader could locate the passage you have paraphrased in the original source (see p. 97). For one page, use the abbreviation "p."; for more than one, use "pp." Note that if the author's name is mentioned in the paraphrase, it need not be given in the parenthetical reference. Also, notice that the parenthetical reference comes before the period at the end of the sentence.

When you paraphrase material, it's important to somehow signal where your own thoughts end and where borrowed ideas begin. One effective way to mark the beginning of a paraphrase is to give the author's name and the year of publication at the beginning of the paraphrase, as is shown above. Before you return to your own words and ideas, give a parenthetical reference to the page number to mark the end of your borrowing.

Documenting Quoted Material

Brief quotations.   Brief quotations, such as the one cited within the paraphrase above, can be included as running text in the paper. This kind of quotation is sometimes called an embedded or inlaid quotation. Here is another example:

> A hunter-gatherer society is the ultimate egalitarian way of living because the lack of stored food means "there can be no kings, no full-time professionals, no class of social parasites who grow fat on food seized from others" (Diamond, 1992, pp. 187–188).

You can give the author's name before the quotation, or you can give it in the parenthetical reference. *Always* include the page numbers of all quoted material in the parenthetical reference. With an embedded quotation, the quotation marks precede the parentheses, and the sentence period follows the parentheses.

Long quotations. In APA style, long quotations must be put in an indented block separate from the running text. The APA manual defines as long any quotation that is 40 words or more. These *block quotes* are double-spaced and are indented five to seven spaces from the left margin (approximately one-half inch). If a line within the block begins a new paragraph, that line should be indented an additional five to seven spaces, or one inch. *Do not use quotation marks* with a block quote because the indentation signals that the block is quoted. You should introduce the quotation in the text before the block, usually by referring to the author; don't simply insert a block quote into the text of your paper without an introduction. Following is an example; notice that the parenthetical reference comes *after* the end punctuation of the quotation:

> Diamond (1992) argues that the rise of agriculture may not have been entirely beneficial for human society:
>
> Besides malnutrition, starvation, and epidemic diseases, farming brought another curse to humanity: class divisions. Hunter-gatherers have little or no stored food, and no concentrated food sources like orchards or herds of cows. Instead, they live off the wild plants and animals that they obtain each day. Everybody except for infants, the sick, and the old join in the search for food. Thus there can be no kings, no full-time professionals, no class of social parasites who grow fat on food seized from others. (pp. 187–188)

Special Rules for In-text References.   The above examples show the basic way of citing sources in parenthetical references. However, special cases commonly arise that call for additional guidelines. Some of the questions you may have about documenting various kinds of sources are answered below.

How do I document a work by multiple authors? When a work has **two authors**, give both authors' names every time you cite the article. Use an ampersand (&) in parentheses:

(Davis & Gillespie, 1994)

Use "and" for a citation given in running text:

Davis and Gillespie (1994) argued that...

When a work has between **three and five authors**, cite all authors, along with the year of publication, in the *first* reference:

(Evans, Coltrane, Davis, & Adderly, 1992)
Evans, Coltrane, Davis, and Adderly (1992) showed that...

In *subsequent* references, include only the surname of the first author followed by "et al." and the year:

(Evans et al., 1992)
Evans et al. (1992) stated that...

When a work has **six or more authors**, cite only the surname of the first author followed by "et al." and the year of publication for the first and all subsequent references:

Fitzgerald et al. (1988) conducted a study...
(Fitzgerald et al., 1988)

What if the author is a group—a corporation, organization, or association? If an author is a group rather than an individual, then in the first text citation, spell out the full name of the group that serves as author. In subsequent citations, if the group name is short, or if an abbreviation would be confusing, spell the name out in all text citations. However, you should abbreviate the group name if it is long and cumbersome and if the abbreviation will be familiar to your audience or can be easily associated with the group name:

The National Science Foundation (1987) found that...[first citation]
The NSF (1987) published a report...[subsequent citations]

What if the work has no author or an anonymous author? When you don't know the author of a work, give the first few words of the title together with the year. Use quotation marks around the title of an article or chapter, and underline titles of periodicals, books, brochures, pamphlets, and reports:

...appealed to many ("A New Approach," 1989).
...cited in <u>Historic Trends</u> (1985).

What if two authors have the same surname? If your reference list contains works by two or more authors with the same surname, include the authors' initials in all text citations, even if the works were published in different years:

J. Jones (1977) and B.E. Jones (1987) arrived at essentially the same conclusions.

What if two or more works were published by the same author in the same year? If you cite two or more works published by the same author in the same year, arrange the works in the references list alphabetically by title. In order to avoid confusion when citing the articles in the text, for the first alphabetized article, put an "a" after the year; for the second article, put a "b," and so on. Then refer to the articles as such in the text:

(Basie 1992a)
Basie (1992b) asserted that...

How do I cite specific parts of a source, like a chapter or table? When you cite a part of a source, like a chapter or table, indicate the number of that page, chapter, figure, table, equation, or other part after you cite it in the text. Use abbreviations for words like page, chapter, and figure:

(Hancock, 1992, chap. 4)
(Hubbard, 1983, fig. 2)
(Ellington, 1976, p. 334)

How do I cite a letter, a conversation, or an interview? Use the words "personal communication" to document information you obtain in face-to-face or phone conversations, memos, letters, informal interviews, and some forms of on-line communication (such as E-mail and discussion groups). Because personal communication is not recoverable, there is no need to cite it in the references list. Personal communication is therefore cited in the text only. Give the initials and surname of the person cited, along with a date that is as accurate as possible:

...according to S. T. Getz (personal communication, October 6, 1995)
(C. V. Terry, personal communication, September 10, 1996)

How do I cite something taken from a secondary source? If you are citing a work that you found discussed in a secondary source, mention the primary work in the text, but refer to the secondary source in both the parenthetical reference and the References list. For example, if you want to cite Wuthnow's idea, which you found in Hunter's book, you would do the following:

> Wuthnow (1988) believes that members of different religions are becoming less concerned with denominational identity and loyalty (as cited in Hunter, 1991).

You would then give *only* the Hunter work in the references list; you would not need to list the Wuthnow work.

CREATING THE LIST OF REFERENCES

When you have finished writing your paper and have included all necessary parenthetical references in the text, it is time to create a complete list of all the documents you have borrowed from. You must give complete bibliographic information for each book, journal article, or other source you have used. General information on how to create this list is given below. Specific examples follow; you may want to look at the examples as you read the following lists of general information. For an example of a correctly formatted references page, see Kelli Boren's research paper at the end of Chapter 9.

General Format

1. Entitle this section "References" and center this title at the top of the page.
2. Align the first line of each reference along the left margin. Indent all other lines five to seven spaces (approximately one-half inch). This is called "hanging indentation."
3. Alphabetize the list by the surname of the initial author of each reference.
4. Double-space the entire list of references.

Authors' Names

1. Invert all author names, giving surnames first, followed by initials abbreviated with periods. Put a space between initials. List the names of *all* authors, regardless of number.
2. Use commas to separate names of authors. Also, use commas to separate initials from surnames. Use the ampersand (&) before the last author's name.
3. Give the full name of a corporate or institutional author.
4. When no author is given, substitute the title of the work by moving it to the author position, before the date of publication. Alphabetize it by the first significant word in the title. Capitalize only the first word in the title and subtitle, if any, and capitalize any proper nouns.
5. Put a period at the end of the list of author names. If an author's initial ends the list, however, don't add an extra period.

6. If the work is an edited book, treat the editors' names as author names, placing them in the author position, and include the abbreviation "Ed." or "Eds." in parentheses after the last editor. The final period of the author list should follow the parentheses.

Date of Publication

1. List the year the work was copyrighted (or created, if the work is unpublished). For magazines and newspapers, give the year followed by the month and day.
2. Put the date in parentheses immediately after the author names.
3. If an article has been accepted for publication but has not yet been published, put the words "in press" in parentheses rather than a date.
4. End the date element of the reference with a period after the parentheses.

Titles

Articles in Periodicals

1. The title and subtitle should be capitalized like a sentence: Only the first word and proper nouns are capitalized. Do not underline the title or put it in quotation marks.
2. Put a period at the end of the complete title.

Periodical Titles

1. Give the full journal title. Capitalize the title like a headline: major words are all capitalized.
2. Underline or italicize the full title, including spaces between words. Use an underline if you are preparing a manuscript to submit for publication. Use italics if you are preparing a finished document.
3. Put a comma after the periodical title to separate it from the publication information that will follow.

Book Titles

1. The title and subtitles should be capitalized sentence style. Underline or italicize the full title, including spaces between words. Use italics if you are submitting a finished document.
2. Any additional information such as edition and volume numbers should immediately follow the title, and should be put in parentheses. Do not put a period between the title and the parentheses. Use the abbreviations "ed." and "Vol." for "edition" and "volume."
3. End this element of the reference with a period.

Publication Information

Periodicals

1. Give the volume number after the title of a journal or magazine and underline or italicize it. Do not use any abbreviations like "Vol." or "v"—just give the number.

2. For journals, if each issue begins with page 1, give the issue number in parentheses immediately after the volume number, leaving no space between the volume number and the opening parenthesis. Italicize this information.

3. Give the article's page numbers. For newspaper articles, use "pp." before the page numbers (or "p." for one page number). Do not use the abbreviation "pp." for the pages of journal and magazine articles. Do *not* underline or italicize the page numbers.

4. Separate the title, volume and issue numbers, and page numbers with commas.

5. End this element of the reference with a period.

Books

1. Give the city where the work was published and, if the city is not well known, the state or country. Use the two-letter US Postal Service abbreviations for states, and put a comma between the city and the state or country. Put a colon after this information.

2. If more than one location is given, use the one listed first, or the publisher's home office, if it is specified.

3. Give as much of the publisher's name as is necessary to make it distinguishable. Give complete spellings of names of associations and university presses, but leave out superfluous terms like *Inc., Publishers*, or *Co.*

4. End this element with a period.

EXAMPLES OF APA STYLE

The easiest way to write your reference list correctly is to imitate models. For example, if you want to cite an article with two authors, find the model in the examples that follow and write your reference in the same way. If your specific need is not addressed in the examples below, check the lists of general formatting information above for more specific guidelines.

Please note that the examples below use hanging indentation, even though the fourth edition of the APA *Publication Manual* shows its examples with paragraph indentation. The APA *Publication Manual* is a guide for professionals submitting manuscripts for publication in APA-sponsored journals. To make typesetting of manuscripts easier, APA requests that people submitting manuscripts use paragraph indentation in reference lists. However, once the article is typeset and published, its reference list will be in hanging indentation. Because the papers you will submit in college are usually considered finished documents, not manuscripts submitted for publication, you should normally use hanging indentation. To be sure, however, you should ask each of your instructors what they prefer before submitting your papers.

Books and Related Works

Book by a Single Author

Bizien, Y. (1979). *Population and economic development.* New York: Praeger.

Two Books by the Same Author

Williams, R. M. (1960). *American society: A sociological interpretation.* New York: Knopf.

Williams, R. M. (1969). *Sociology and social change in the United States.* St. Louis: Social Science Institute, Washington University.

List the works chronologically by date of publication, the earliest date first.

Book by Two or More Authors

Jackson, N. E., Robinson, H. B., & Dale, P. S. (1977). *Cognitive development in young children.* Monterey, CA: Brooks/Cole.

List all authors' last names and first and middle initials, regardless of how many authors there are. Separate names with commas and use the ampersand (&) before the last author's name.

Book Authored by a Corporation, Institution, or Organization

New York City Youth Board. (1960). *Reaching the fighting gang.* New York: Author.

Use the corporate name as the author. If the corporation is also the publisher, use the word *Author* as the name of the publisher.

An Edition

Barr, N. A. (1993). *The economics of the welfare state* (2nd ed.). Stanford, CA: Stanford University Press.

Book with an Editor or Compiler

Garcia, E. E. (Ed.). (1992). *Understanding Freud: The man and his ideas.* New York: New York University Press.

Give the editor as the author along with the abbreviation "Ed." (or "Eds." for more than one) in parentheses.

Article or Chapter in an Edited Book

Gabbert, J. B. (1992). The Mexican chief executive. In T. Tsurutani & J. B. Gabbert (Eds.), *Chief executives: National political leadership in the United States, Mexico, Great Britain, Germany, and Japan* (pp. 61–110). Pullman, WA: Washington University Press.

Multivolume Work

Barret, P. H., & Freeman, R. B. (Eds.). (1986). *The works of Charles Darwin* (Vols. 17–18). London: W. Pickering.

Book in a Series

Dudley, W. (Ed.). (1989). *Crime and criminals: Opposing viewpoints.* Opposing Viewpoints Series. San Diego, CA: Greenhaven Press.

Translation

Salazar, J. A. (1992). *Born to die in Medellin* (N. Caistor, Trans.). London: Latin America Bureau.

Government Publication

United States Congressional Senate Committee on Labor and Human Resources. (1990). *Homelessness prevention and community revitalization act of 1990: Report.* Washington, DC: U.S. Government Printing Office.

Use the complete name of the government agency as the author when no specific author is named.

Pamphlet

U.S. Congress of Industrial Organizations, Department of Education and Research. (1952). *Keep our nation prosperous.* Washington, DC: Author.

Unpublished Dissertation or Thesis

Brown, R. (1976). *The United States humanitarian aid to Third World children: The case of Bolivia.* Unpublished doctoral dissertation, Boise State University, Idaho.

Unpublished Manuscript not Submitted for Publication

Stanford, M. A. (1982). *Melting pots and matais: Stress and change among Samoans in Hawaii.* Unpublished manuscript, University of Hawaii.

Periodicals

Journal Article, One Author

Lasley, J. R. (1992). Age, social context, and street gang membership: Are "youth" gangs becoming "adult" gangs? *Youth and Society, 23,* 434–451.

Journal Article, Two Authors

Johnson, S. M., & Nelson, N. C. W. (1987). Teaching reform in an active voice. *Phi Delta Kappan, 68,* 591–598.

Journal Article, More Than Two Authors

Hunt, G. D., Riegel, S., & Morales, T. (1993). Changes in prison culture: Prison gangs and the case of the "Pepsi generation." *Social Problems, 40,* 398–409.

List all authors' names, separated by commas. Use an ampersand (&) before the last author.

Journal Article, Paginated by Issue

Tortora, P. (1973). Fashion magazines mirror the changing role of women. *Journal of Home Economics, 65*(3), 19–23.

Include the issue number, in parentheses, immediately following the volume number.

Magazine Article, Monthly

Weisman, M. (1994, July). When parents are not in the best interests of the child. *The Atlantic Monthly, 274,* 42–63.

Give the month of the publication. Give the volume number with the magazine title.

Magazine Article, Weekly

Masland, T. (1994, May 2). Voted into the history books. *Newsweek, 123,* 51.

Give the day and month after the year. Give the volume number with the magazine title.

Newspaper Article, No Author

Clinton unveils plans to trim programs. (1994, Dec. 19). *Chicago Tribune,* p. 1.

Give the date in this sequence: year, month, day.

Newspaper Article, Discontinuous Pages

Chandler, C. (1994, Oct. 31). Treasury analysis finds GOP "flat tax" too costly. *The Washington Post*, pp. 8, 12.

ERIC Microform Document

Hamner, C. J. (1993). *Youth violence: Gangs on Main Street, USA.* (ERIC Document Reproduction Service No. ED 366 706)

Electronic Media. No standard has yet been established for documenting on-line information, but APA does give a few guidelines. Follow this general format, leaving out those elements that don't apply to your particular source:

Author, I., Author, I., & Author, I. (date). Title of article or chapter [length of article in paragraphs]. *Title of full work* [On-line] *vol. number* (issue number). Available [specify format]: Specify path

Don't end a path statement with a period because a stray period will hinder retrieval. Here's an example of a reference to an **electronic journal article**:

Caporael, L. R. (1995, Jan.) Sociality: Coordinating bodies, minds and groups [51 paragraphs]. *Psycoloquy* [On-line serial], *6* (1). Available FTP: Hostname: princeton.edu Directory: /pub/harnad/Psycoloquy/1995.volume.6 File: psyc.95.6.01.group-selection.1.caporael

TURABIAN REFERENCE LIST (TRL) STYLE

"Turabian" is the name given to a form of documentation based on that in the *Chicago Manual of Style*. It is named after Kate Turabian, who first issued a short manual to help writers use this style. The Turabian style offers a choice of using either author-date parenthetical references or notes (either footnotes or endnotes). The parenthetical style with reference list will here be called "TRL" for "Turabian Reference List" style. (The Turabian note and bibliography style is explained in the next section.)

In-Text References

When following TRL documentation style, you need to cite some information about your sources—the author's surname, the year of publication, and, when necessary, page numbers—within your text. This information is given in parentheses after you cite a particular work. There are various ways of citing sources, depending on whether you are paraphrasing, summarizing, or quoting a passage from a source.

Suppose you wanted to cite the following passage from pages 187–188 in Jared Diamond's book *The Third Chimpanzee: The Evolution and Future of the Human Animal*, published by HarperPerennial in 1992:

> Besides malnutrition, starvation, and epidemic diseases, farming brought another curse to humanity: class divisions. Hunter-gatherers have little or no stored food, and no concentrated food sources like orchards or herds of cows. Instead, they live off the wild plants and animals that they obtain each day. Everybody except for infants, the sick, and the old join in the search for food. Thus there can be no kings, no full-time professionals, no class of social parasites who grow fat on food seized from others.

You could summarize, paraphrase, or quote part or all of this passage in your paper. Following are examples of how you would do this.

Documenting a Summarized Source. You can cite a summarized source in a variety of ways. First, you can give the author and year of publication in parentheses at the appropriate point in the sentence. Notice that there is no comma between the author's surname and the year of publication, and notice that the sentence period follows the parenthetical reference:

> Some archeologists suggest that our race's shift from hunting and gathering to farming for food may have given rise to class divisions (Diamond 1992).

Second, you can use the author's name in the sentence, and then give the year in parentheses:

> Diamond (1992) suggests that our race's shift from hunting and gathering to farming for food may have given rise to class divisions.

Third, you can use both the author and the year in the sentence, thus requiring no parenthetical reference. This method is less common than the first two:

> Diamond's 1992 book suggests that our race's shift from hunting and gathering to farming for food may have given rise to class divisions.

Documenting a Paraphrased or Partially Quoted Source.   Here's how you would cite a passage that is paraphrased, with a partial quote included:

> Diamond (1992) notes that farming may have caused the rise of class divisions. He argues that, before we as a race started farming, our hunter-gatherer prede-

cessors each had to contribute more or less equally to the ongoing search for food and therefore didn't live off the efforts of others. Unlike an agriculturally based society, in a hunter-gatherer society "there can be no kings, no full time professionals, no class of social parasites who grow fat on food seized from others" (187–188).

Unlike summarized sources, references to paraphrased and quoted material should include page numbers. Give only the page numbers; don't use any abbreviations like "p." or "pp." Note that if the author's name is mentioned in the paraphrase, it need not be given in the parenthetical reference. And finally, notice that the parenthetical reference comes *before* the period at the end of the sentence.

When you paraphrase material, it's important to somehow signal where your own thoughts end and where borrowed ideas begin. One effective way to do this is to give the author's name at the beginning of the paraphrase, as shown above. Before you return to your own ideas, use the parenthetical reference to mark the end of your borrowing.

Documenting Quoted Material

Brief quotations. Brief quotations, such as the one cited within the above paraphrase, can be included as running text in the paper. This kind of quotation is sometimes called an *embedded* or *inlaid* quotation. Here is an example:

> A hunter-gatherer society is the ultimate egalitarian way of living because the lack of stored food means "there can be no kings, no full-time professionals, no class of social parasites who grow fat on food seized from others" (Diamond 1992, 187–188).

You can give the author's name before the quote, or you can give it in the parenthetical reference. Always include the year of publication and the page number(s) of all quoted material within the parenthetical reference. Note that with an embedded quotation, the quotation marks precede the parentheses and the sentence period follows the parenthetical reference.

Long quotations. In TRL style, long quotations are put in an indented block. The Turabian style manual defines a long quote as a passage two or more sentences long which runs to four or more lines of text. These *block quotations* are single-spaced and are indented four spaces from the left margin (almost half an inch). If a line within the block begins a new paragraph, that line should be indented eight spaces. Double-space between the text and the block quotation. Do not use quotation marks. Introduce the quotation in your text, usually by referring to the author. Don't simply insert a block quotation in your paper without introducing it first. Here is an example; notice that the parenthetical reference comes *after* the final punctuation.

Diamond (1992) argues that the rise of agriculture may not have been entirely beneficial for human society:

> Besides malnutrition, starvation, and epidemic diseases, farming brought another curse to humanity: class divisions. Hunter-gatherers have little or no stored food, and no concentrated food sources like orchards or herds of cows. Instead, they live off the wild plants and animals that they obtain each day. Everybody except for infants, the sick, and the old join in the search for food. Thus there can be no kings, no full-time professionals, no class of social parasites who grow fat on food seized from others. (187–188)

Special Rules for In-Text Reference. The above examples show the basic way of documenting sources in parenthetical references. However, special cases commonly arise that call for additional guidelines. Some of the questions you may have about documenting various kinds of sources are answered below.

How do I document a work by two or three authors? When a work has two or three authors, cite each author's surname every time you refer to the work. For three authors, use "and" before the last author:

(Davis, Parker, and Gillespie 1994)

How do I document a work with more than three authors? When a work has more than three authors, give only the first author's surname followed by either "et al." or "and others"; however, use the same style consistently throughout the paper. Give all the authors' names in the references list:

(Evans et al. 1992)
Evans et al. (1992) attempted to show that…

If you cite two or more works with multiple authors that each have the same first author, you obviously need to distinguish the different works somehow. One way to do this is to give as many names as are needed to distinguish the two works:

(Evans, Coltrane, and others 1988)
(Evans, Parker, and others 1987)

Another way is to give a segment of each work's title in the parenthetical reference:

(Evans et al., "Politics of Remediation," 1988)
(Evans et al., *Rethinking Affirmative Action*, 1987)

(Notice that if you add part of a title to the reference, it is set off by commas.)

What if the author is a group—a corporation, organization, or association? If the author is a group rather than a person, use the group name as the author name in both the reference list and all in-text citations:

(The National Science Foundation 1987, 96–97)

What if the work has no author or has an anonymous author? When you don't know the author of a work, give a shortened version of the title together with the year. Use quotation marks around the title of an article or chapter, and italicize titles of periodicals, books, brochures, pamphlets, or reports. Alphabetize the work by the title in the References list:

...appeals to many ("A New Approach" 1989).
...as cited in *Historic Trends* (1985).

What if two authors have the same surname? If your reference list contains works by two or more authors with the same surname, include the authors' initials in all in-text citations, even if the works were published in different years:

J. Jones (1977) and B.E. Jones (1987) arrive at essentially the same conclusions.

What if two or more works were published by the same author in the same year? If you cite two or more works published by the same author in the same year, arrange the works in the References list alphabetically by title. In order to avoid confusion when citing the articles in the text, for the first alphabetical article, put an "a" after the year; for the second article, put a "b," and so on. Then refer to the articles as such in the text:

(Basie 1992a)
Basie (1992b) asserts that...

How do I cite specific parts of a source, like a chapter or a table? When you give a number after the year in a parenthetical reference, it is usually interpreted as a page number. So, if you need to refer to some other part of the work, such as a section, chapter, table, figure, and so forth, give an appropriate abbreviation:

(Hancock 1992, chap. 4)
(Hubbard 1983, fig. 2)
(Ellington 1976, sec. 5)

How do I cite a letter, a conversation, an interview, or other personal communication? Communication such as personal letters and interviews are sometimes not recoverable and therefore need not be cited in the references list.

However, you should cite the source within the text. Give the full name of the person from whom you obtained the information (unless it appears nearby in the text) and a description and the date of the communication:

(Stan Getz, telephone interview by author, October 6, 1995)
(Cecilia Terry, letter to the author, September, 10, 1996)

If you tape-recorded an interview, however, or if you deposited a letter in a library archive so that a reader could have access to the information, you would cite the interview or letter in your references list. Here is a model:

Warshinski, Paula A. Mayor of Westlake. 1996. Interview by author, 30 September. Tape recording. Westlake Public Library, Westlake, MN.

CREATING THE LIST OF REFERENCES

When you have finished writing your paper and have included all necessary parenthetical references in the text, it is time to create a complete list of all the documents you have borrowed from. You must give complete bibliographic information for each book, journal article, or other source you have used. General information on how to create this list is given below. Specific examples follow. (Victor Sipos and Trevor Hall's paper, printed at the end of Chapter 4, is documented in this style. Also, references at the end of chapters in this book follow this style.)

General Format

1. Entitle this section "References," and place the title at the top, centered. (The Turabian manual notes that the list may also be called "Works Cited," "Literature Cited," or "Selected Bibliography.")
2. Arrange references alphabetically, by author's surname.
3. The first line of each reference should be flush left. All other lines should be indented five spaces (one-half inch).
4. Single-space each reference. Double-space between references.

Format for Authors' Names

1. Give full names of all authors.
2. For works with one author, invert the author's name, giving the surname first, followed by the first and middle names. Separate the surname from the rest of the name with a comma.
3. For works with multiple authors, invert *only* the first author's name. Separate authors' names with commas, and precede the last name with "and."
4. End this element of the entry with a period.

Year of Publication

1. The year of publication immediately follows the author's name
2. End this element with a period.

Title

Book Titles

1. Give the complete title.
2. Capitalize the title like a sentence. Capitalize the first words of subtitles and capitalize proper nouns.
3. Italicize the title.
4. End this element with a period.

Article Titles

1. Capitalize the title sentence style.
2. Do *not* underline the title or place it within quotation marks.
3. Place a period after the title.

Periodical Titles

1. Give the full name of the periodical.
2. Capitalize the name like a headline, capitalizing all important words.
3. Italicize the name of the periodical.
4. Place a comma after the underlined name.

Publication Information

Books

1. Give the city where the work was published and, if the city is not well known, the state or country. If more than one city is listed, you may list them all, or you may list only the first one. Use the two-letter U.S. Postal Service abbreviations for states and countries. Put a comma between the city and the state or country. Place a colon after this information.
2. Give the full name of the publisher.
3. End this element with a period.

Periodicals

1. For journals, give the volume after the title. Give the month of publication in parentheses. Use a colon after the final parenthesis.

2. For journals that use issue numbers rather than volume numbers, simply give the issue number followed by a colon.

3. For magazines, give the publication date. Give the day first, then the month. Do not include the year, because it is given after the author's name. Use a comma after this information.

4. Give the page numbers of the article.

5. End this element with a period.

EXAMPLES OF **TRL** STYLE

If your specific question is not addressed in the examples below, check the lists of general formatting information above for more specific guidelines.

Books and Related works

Book by a Single Author

Bizien, Yves. 1979. *Population and economic development.* New York: Praeger.

Two Books by the Same Author

Williams, Robin M. 1960. *American society: A sociological interpretation.* New York: Knopf.

_____. 1969. *Sociology and social change in the United States.* St. Louis Social Science Institute, Washington University.

The author's name need not be repeated; it should be replaced by an eight-space line. Arrange the author's works alphabetically by title.

Book by Two or More Authors

Jackson, Nancy Ewald, Halbert B. Robinson, and Philip S. Dale. 1977. *Cognitive development in young children.* Monterey, CA: Brooks/Cole.

Give the full names of all authors and invert only the first author's name. Separate the names by commas and use "and" before the last author's name.

Book Authored by a Corporation, Institution, or Organization

New York City Youth Board. 1960. *Reaching the fighting gang.* New York: New York City Youth Board.

Use the corporate name as the author. If the corporation is also the publisher, use the corporate name as the publisher.

An Edition

Barr, N. A. 1993. *The economics of the welfare state.* 2d ed. Stanford, CA: Stanford
University Press.

Book with an Editor or Compiler

Garcia, Emanuel E., ed. 1992. *Understanding Freud: The man and his ideas.* New
York: New York University Press.

Use the editor's name as the author, followed by a comma and "ed." (or "eds."
for more than one).

Article or Chapter in an Edited Book

Gabbert, Jack B. 1992. The Mexican chief executive. In *Chief executives: National
political leadership in the United States, Mexico, Great Britain, Germany, and Japan,*
eds. Taketsugu Tsurutani and Jack B. Gabbert, 61–110. Pullman, WA:
Washington State University Press.

Multivolume Work

Darwin, Charles. 1986. *The works of Charles Darwin.* Edited by Paul H. Barret and
R. B. Freeman. Vols. 17–18. London: W. Pickering.

Book in a Series

Dudley, William, ed. 1989. *Crime and criminals: Opposing viewpoints.* Opposing
Viewpoints Series. San Diego, CA: Greenhaven Press.

Translation

Salazar, J. Alonso. 1992. *Born to die in Medellin.* Translated by Nick Caistor.
London: Latin America Bureau.

Government Publication

U.S. Congress. Senate. Committee on Labor and Human Resources. 1990.
Homelessness prevention and community revitalization act of 1990. Washington,
DC: U.S. Government Printing Office.

Use the name of the government agency as the author if no other name is given.
You can refer to the publisher in one of the following styles as long as you use the
same style consistently throughout the paper:

Washington, DC: U.S. Government Printing Office.
Washington, DC: Government Printing Office.
Washington, DC: GPO.

Pamphlet

U.S. Congress of Industrial Organizations. Department of Education and
Research. 1952. *Keep our nation prosperous.* Washington D.C.: U.S. Congress of
Industrial Organizations, Dept. of Education and Research.

Unpublished Dissertation or Thesis

Brown, Ray. 1976. The United States humanitarian aid to Third World children:
The case of Bolivia. Ph.D. diss., Boise State University, Idaho.

Periodicals

Journal Article, One Author

Lasley, James R. 1992. Age, social context, and street gang membership: Are
"youth" gangs becoming "adult" gangs? *Youth and Society* 23 (June): 434–51.

Journal Article, Two Authors

Johnson, Susan Moore, and Niall C.W. Nelson. 1987. Teaching reform in an active
voice. *Phi Delta Kappan* 68 (April): 591–8.

Journal Article, More Than Two Authors

Hunt, Geoffrey, Stephanie Riegel, and Tomas Morales. 1993. Changes in prison
culture: Prison gangs and the case of the "Pepsi generation." *Social Problems*
40 (August): 398–409.

List all author names, inverting only the first one. Separate the names with commas; use "and" before the last name.

Journal Article, Paginated by Issue

Tortora, Paula. 1973. Fashion magazines mirror the changing role of women.
Journal of Home Economics 65, no. 3: 19–23.

Include the issue number immediately following the volume number.

Magazine Article, Monthly

Weisman, Mary-Lou. 1994. When parents are not in the best interests of the child.
The Atlantic Monthly, July, 42–63.

Magazine Article, Weekly

Masland, Tom. 1994. Voted into the history books. *Newsweek*, 2 May, 51.

Newspaper Article, No Author

Clinton unveils plans to trim programs. 1994. *Chicago Tribune*, 19 December, 1.
 Give the title first if no author is named.

Newspaper Article, Discontinuous Pages

Chandler, Clay. 1994. Treasury analysis finds GOP "flat tax" too costly.
 Washington Post, 31 October, 8 and 12.

ERIC Microform Document

Hamner, Carole J. 1993. *Youth violence: Gangs on Main Street, USA*. A report from the
 Pew Partnership for Civil Change program, Philadelphia, PA. ERIC, ED 366 706.

Citation taken from a secondary source. If you read Hunter, who referred
to Wuthnow, your in-text reference would cite Wuthnow, with the explanation
that you found the material in Hunter. In the "Works Cited" list, you would handle the reference to Wuthnow as follows:

Wuthnow, Robert. 1988. *The restructuring of American religion: Society and faith
 since World War II*. Princeton, NJ: Princeton University Press. Quoted in James
 Davison Hunter, *Culture wars: The struggle to define America*. New York: Basic
 Books, 1991.

Electronic Media. When citing electronic sources such as CD-ROMs, databases, or Internet documents, include the same basic information that is needed for print
sources: author and title of the item; name and description of the source (i.e., whether
it is CD-ROM, an on-line database or journal, etc.); the name of the publisher or vendor (or both); the location of publication; the date of either publication or access (or
both); and some description of the pathway needed to access the source.

Here are two examples. The first is a reference to an **electronic journal
article**; the second is a reference to a **CD-ROM**:

Caporael, Linda. 1995. Sociality: Coordinating bodies, minds and groups.
 Psycoloquy 6 (January). On-line journal. Available from
 ftp://princeton.edu/pub/harnad/Psycoloquy/1995.volume.6

Oxford English Dictionary. 1992. 2d ed. S.v. "anomie." CD-ROM. Oxford: Oxford
 University Press.

TURABIAN NOTE AND BIBLIOGRAPHY (TNB) STYLE

"Turabian" is the name given to a brief form of the Chicago style of documentation. It is named after Kate Turabian, who first issued a short manual to help writers use this style. The Turabian style offers a choice of using either author-date

parenthetical references or notes (either footnotes or endnotes). For convenience, the Turabian note and bibliography style will be called "TNB" style. (The parenthetical style with reference list will be called "TRL" for "Turabian Reference List" style; it is explained in the preceding section.)

When following Turabian note and bibliography style (TNB), you should use either footnotes or endnotes to cite sources that you borrow from in your paper, whether they are quoted, summarized, or paraphrased. You designate both footnotes and endnotes with Arabic numerals placed slightly above the baseline of text, and usually after the period of the sentence where your borrowed material ends. In some cases, you might place numbers in the middle of a sentence when you are combining ideas from several sources and want to show which author deserves credit for each idea. Or you might use note numbers within sentences to distinguish between a borrowed idea in the first part of the sentence and your ideas in the second part.

GENERAL FORMAT FOR FOOTNOTES AND ENDNOTES

Footnotes should appear at the bottom of the page on which they are referred to. Endnotes appear as a numbered list at the end of a paper, right after the last page of text and before the bibliography and any appendixes. Both footnotes and endnotes should follow the guidelines below:

- Indent the first line of the note five spaces.
- Make all other lines flush with the left margin.
- Single-space within each note.
- Double-space between notes.

The information required for both footnotes and endnotes is the same. The following general guidelines address what you need to include to cite the most common types of works:

Book. The first note referring to a book should include the following information in this order:

1. Name of author(s)
2. Title (and subtitle, if any)
3. Editor, compiler, or translator, if any
4. Author of preface, introduction, or foreword, if different from author of book
5. Number or name of edition, if not the first
6. Name of series, if any, with volume or number

7. Facts of publication (place, publisher, year) in parentheses

8. Page number(s) specifically cited

Chapter in an Edited Book. The first note referring to a chapter in an edited book should include the following information, in this order:

1. Name of author(s)

2. Title of chapter

3. Title of book, preceded by the word "in"

4. Editor(s) of book, preceded by "ed." or "eds."

5. Facts of publication (place, publisher, year) in parentheses

6. Page number(s) specifically cited

Periodicals. The first note referring to an article in a journal, magazine, or newspaper should include the following information, in this order:

1. Name of author(s), if any

2. Title of article

3. Name of periodical

4. Volume or issue number

5. Publication date, if any, in parentheses

6. Page number(s)

Subsequent References. If you cite the same page of the same source two or more times in succession, in all references immediately after the first, you may simply use the word *Ibid.* If the subsequent reference refers to the same work, but different page numbers, use *Ibid.* with the new page numbers (e.g., "Ibid., 98.").

If a subsequent reference to a work does not immediately follow the first reference, you may shorten the subsequent reference by giving the author's surname and the page numbers (e.g., "Calloway, 34.").

USING NOTES TO DOCUMENT QUOTATIONS, PARAPHRASES, AND SUMMARIES

Suppose you wanted to cite the following passage from pages 187–188 in Jared Diamond's book *The Third Chimpanzee: The Evolution and Future of the Human Animal*, published by HarperPerennial (New York) in 1992:

> Besides malnutrition, starvation, and epidemic diseases, farming brought another curse to humanity: class divisions. Hunter-gatherers have little or no stored food, and no concentrated food sources like orchards or herds of cows. Instead,

they live off the wild plants and animals that they obtain each day. Everybody except for infants, the sick, and the old join in the search for food. Thus there can be no kings, no full-time professionals, no class of social parasites who grow fat on food seized from others.

You could summarize, paraphrase, or quote part or all of this passage in your paper. Following are examples of how you would document such borrowings with notes. In each case the line indicates that the note is at the foot of the page on which the borrowed text appears.

Documenting a Summarized Source. Regardless of whether you give the author's name in the text or not, you should give the author's name in the note:

Some archeologists suggest that our race's shift from hunting and gathering to farming for food may have given rise to class divisions.[1]

---

[1] Jared Diamond, *The Third Chimpanzee: The Evolution and Future of the Human Animal* (New York: HarperPerennial, 1992), 187–88.

Documenting a Paraphrased or Partially Quoted Source. Following is how you would cite a passage that is paraphrased, with a partial quote included:

Diamond notes that farming may have caused the rise of class divisions. He argues that, before we as a race started farming, our hunter-gatherer predecessors each had to contribute more or less equally to the ongoing search for food and therefore didn't live off the efforts of others. Unlike an agriculturally based society, in a hunter-gatherer society "there can be no kings, no full time professionals, no class of social parasites who grow fat on food seized from others."[1]

---

[1] Jared Diamond, *The Third Chimpanzee: The Evolution and Future of the Human Animal* (New York: HarperPerennial, 1992), 187–88.

Note that the page numbers are included in every note, regardless of whether you have quoted, paraphrased, or summarized. When you paraphrase material, it's important to somehow signal where your own thoughts end and where borrowed ideas begin. One effective way to do this is to give the author's name at the beginning of the paraphrase, as in the example above.

Documenting Quoted Material. Brief quotations such as the one cited above within the paraphrase can be included as running text in the paper:

One of the most socially attractive aspects of hunter-gatherer societies is that they are egalitarian, for "there can be no kings, no full-time professionals, no class of social parasites who grow fat on food seized from others."[1]

[1] Jared Diamond, *The Third Chimpanzee: The Evolution and Future of the Human Animal* (New York: HarperPerennial, 1992), 188.

Be sure to give the page number the quoted material came from, and even when you give the author's name to introduce the quotation, you should still give it in the note.

In TNB style long quotations are put in *indented blocks*. The Turabian style manual defines a long quotation as anything two or more sentences long which runs to four or more lines of text. These block quotations are single-spaced and are indented four spaces (about one-half inch) from the left margin (eight spaces when a new paragraph begins within the quotation). Do not use quotation marks. Double-space between the rest of the text and the block quotation. The following is an example of a block quotation in TNB style:

> Diamond argues that the rise of agriculture may not have been entirely beneficial for human society:

> Besides malnutrition, starvation, and epidemic diseases, farming brought another curse to humanity: class divisions. Hunter-gatherers have little or no stored food, and no concentrated food sources like orchards or herds of cows. Instead, they live off the wild plants and animals that they obtain each day. Everybody except for infants, the sick, and the old join in the search for food. Thus there can be no kings, no full-time professionals, no class of social parasites who grow fat on food seized from others.[1]

[1] Jared Diamond, *The Third Chimpanzee: The Evolution and Future of the Human Animal* (New York: HarperPerennial, 1992), 187–88.

GENERAL GUIDELINES FOR THE BIBLIOGRAPHY

In TNB style, the complete citations of all the works used in a paper are listed in alphabetical order by author's last name at the end of the paper. The following guidelines will help you write the entries for this list correctly.

General Format

- Entitle this section "Selected Bibliography," "Works Cited," or "Sources Consulted," and place the title at the top, centered.
- Arrange references alphabetically, by author's surname. Write the first line flush with the margin and indent all subsequent lines.
- Single-space each reference. Double-space between references.

Format for Authors' Names for Books and Periodicals

1. Give full names of all authors.

2. For works with one author, invert the author's name, giving the surname first, followed by the first and middle names. Separate the surname from the rest of the name with a comma.

3. For works with multiple authors, invert *only* the first author's name. Separate authors' names with commas, and precede the last name with "and."

4. End this element with a period.

Title

Books

1. Capitalize the title like a headline.

2. Italicize the title.

3. Place a period after the title.

Article Titles

1. Capitalize the title like a headline.

2. Place the title within quotation marks.

3. Place a period after the title, *before* the final quotation mark.

Names of Periodicals

1. Give the full name of the periodical.

2. Capitalize the name like a headline.

3. Italicize the name of the periodical.

4. If the periodical is a magazine, place a comma after the title.

Publication Information

Books

1. Give the city where the work was published and, if the city is not well known, the state or country. You may abbreviate names of states. Put a comma between the city and the state or country. Put a colon after this information.

2. Give the full name of the publisher, followed by a comma.

3. Give the year of publication, followed by a period.

Journals

1. Give the volume number after the title.
2. In parentheses, give the date of the journal issue. Follow the last parenthesis with a colon.
3. Give the page numbers of the article.
4. Put a period after the page numbers.

Magazines

1. After the name of the magazine, give the date in this order: day, month, year. Do not put commas between the elements of the date. Do not put the date in parentheses.
2. Put a comma after the year, then give the page numbers of the article.
3. Put a period after the page numbers.

EXAMPLES OF TNB STYLE

If your specific question is not addressed in the examples below, check the lists of general formatting information above for more specific guidelines, or consult the Turabian manual itself. Note that in the examples below, the first example, labeled with "N," shows you how to write the note; the second example, labeled with "B," shows you how to write the bibliographic entry.

Books and Related Works

Book by a Single Author

N   [1] Yves Bizien, *Population and Economic Development* (New York: Praeger, 1979), 55.

B   Bizien, Yves. *Population and Economic Development.* New York: Praeger, 1979.

Two Books by the Same Author in the Bibliography

B   Williams, Robin M. *American Society: A Sociological Interpretation.* New York: Knopf, 1960.

B   _____. *Sociology and Social Change in the United States.* St. Louis: Social Science Institute, Washington University, 1969.

The author's name need not be repeated; it should be replaced by an eight-space line. Arrange the author's works either alphabetically by title or chronologically by date of publication.

T
N
B

Book by Two or More Authors

N   [2] Nancy Ewald Jackson, Halbert B. Robinson, and Philip S. Dale, *Cognitive Development in Young Children* (Monterey, CA: Brooks/Cole, 1977), 88.

B   Jackson, Nancy Ewald, Halbert B. Robinson, and Philip S. Dale. *Cognitive Development in Young Children.* Monterey, CA: Brooks/Cole, 1977.

Give the full names of all authors and invert only the first author's name in the bibliography. Separate the names by commas and use "and" before the last author's name.

Book Authored by a Corporation, Institution, or Organization

N   [3] New York City Youth Board, *Reaching the Fighting Gang* (New York: New York City Youth Board, 1960), 32.

B   New York City Youth Board. *Reaching the Fighting Gang.* New York: New York City Youth Board, 1960.

Use the corporation or institution name as the author. If the organization is also the publisher, use the organization name as the publisher.

An Edition

N   [4] Nelson A. Barr, *The Economics of the Welfare State*, 2nd ed. (Stanford, CA: Stanford University Press, 1993), 114.

B   Barr, Nelson A. *The Economics of the Welfare State.* 2nd ed. Stanford, CA: Stanford University Press, 1993.

Book With an Editor or Compiler

N   [5] Emanuel E. Garcia, ed., *Understanding Freud: The Man and His Ideas* (New York: New York University Press, 1992), 55.

B   Garcia, Emanuel E., ed. *Understanding Freud: The Man and His Ideas.* New York: New York University Press, 1992.

Use the editor's name as the author, followed by a comma and "ed." (or "eds." for more than one).

Article or Chapter in an Edited Book

N   [6] Jack B. Gabbert, "The Mexican Chief Executive," in *Chief Executives: National Political Leadership in the United States, Mexico, Great Britain, Germany, and Japan*, eds. Taketsugu Tsurutani and Jack B. Gabbert (Pullman, WA: Washington University Press, 1992), 79.

B   Gabbert, Jack B. "The Mexican Chief Executive." In *Chief Executives:*
     National Political Leadership in the United States, Mexico, Great Britain,
     Germany, and Japan, eds. Taketsugu Tsurutani and Jack B. Gabbert,
     61–110. Pullman, WA: Washington University Press, 1992.

Anthology or Compilation

N   [7] Daniel E. Williams, ed., *Pillars of Salt: An Anthology of Early American*
     Criminal Narratives (Madison, WI: Madison House, 1993), 89.

B   Williams, Daniel E., ed. *Pillars of Salt: An Anthology of Early American*
     Criminal Narratives. Madison, WI: Madison House, 1993.

Multivolume Work

N   [8] Paul H. Barret and R.B. Freeman, eds., *The Works of Charles Darwin,*
     (London: W. Pickering, 1986), 17: 224.

B   Barret, Paul H. and R.B. Freeman, eds. *The Works of Charles Darwin.* Vol. 17.
     London: W. Pickering, 1986.

Book in a Series

N   [9] William Dudley, ed., *Crime and Criminals: Opposing Viewpoints,*
     Opposing Viewpoints Series (San Diego, CA: Greenhaven Press, 1989), 43.

B   Dudley, William, ed. *Crime and Criminals: Opposing Viewpoints.* Opposing
     Viewpoints Series. San Diego, CA: Greenhaven Press, 1989.

Translation

N   [10] J. Alonso Salazar, *Born to Die in Medellin*, trans. Nick Caistor (London:
     Latin America Bureau, 1992), 111.

B   Salazar, J. Alonso. *Born to Die in Medellin.* Translated by Nick Caistor.
     London: Latin America Bureau, 1992.

Government Publication

N   [11] Congress, Senate, Committee on Labor and Human Resources,
     Homelessness Prevention and Community Revitalization Act of 1990 Report
     (Washington, DC: GPO, 1990), 78.

B   U.S. Congress. Senate. Committee on Labor and Human Resources.
     Homelessness Prevention and Community Revitalization Act of 1990 Report.
     Washington, DC: GPO, 1990.

Use the name of the government agency as the author if no other name is given.
You can refer to the publisher in any one of the following styles as long as you
use the same style consistently throughout the paper:

Washington, DC: U.S. Government Printing Office, 1990.
Washington, DC: Government Printing Office, 1990.
Washington, DC: GPO, 1990.
Washington, 1990.

Pamphlet

N   [12] U.S. Congress of Industrial Organizations, Department of Education and Research, *Keep Our Nation Prosperous* (Washington DC: U.S. Congress of Industrial Organizations, Dept. of Education and Research, 1952), 4.

B   U.S. Congress of Industrial Organizations, Department of Education and Research. *Keep Our Nation Prosperous.* Washington, DC: U.S. Congress of Industrial Organizations, Dept. of Education and Research, 1952.

Unpublished Dissertation or Thesis

N   [13] Ray Brown, "The United States Humanitarian Aid to Third World Children: The Case of Bolivia" (Ph.D. diss., Boise State University, 1976), 21.

B   Brown, Ray. "The United States Humanitarian Aid to Third World Children: The Case of Bolivia." Ph.D. diss., Boise State University, 1976.

Periodicals

Journal Article, One Author

N   [14] James R. Lasley, "Age, Social Context, and Street Gang Membership: Are 'Youth' Gangs Becoming 'Adult' Gangs?" *Youth and Society* 23 (June 1992): 435.

B   Lasley, James R. "Age, Social Context, and Street Gang Membership: Are 'Youth' Gangs Becoming 'Adult' Gangs?" *Youth and Society* 23 (June 1992): 434–51.

Journal Article, Two Authors

N   [15] Susan Moore Johnson and Niall C. W. Nelson, "Teaching Reform in an Active Voice," *Phi Delta Kappan* 68 (April 1987): 595.

B   Johnson, Susan Moore, and Niall C. W. Nelson. "Teaching Reform in an Active Voice." *Phi Delta Kappan* 68 (April 1987): 591–8.

Journal Article, More Than Two Authors

N   [16] Geoffrey Hunt, Stephanie Riegel, and Tomas Morales, "Changes in Prison Culture: Prison Gangs and the Case of the 'Pepsi generation,'" *Social Problems* 40 (August 1993): 403.

B   Hunt, Geoffrey, Stephanie Riegel, and Tomas Morales. "Changes in Prison Culture: Prison Gangs and the Case of the 'Pepsi Generation.'" *Social Problems* 40 (August 1993): 398–409.

List all authors' names, inverting only the first one. Separate the names with commas; use "and" before the last name.

Journal Article, Paginated by Issue

N   [17] Paula Tortora, "Fashion Magazines Mirror the Changing Role of Women," *Journal of Home Economics* 65, no. 3 (1973): 20.

B   Tortora, Paula. "Fashion Magazines Mirror the Changing role of Women." *Journal of Home Economics* 65, no. 3 (1973): 19–23.

Include the issue number immediately following the volume number.

Magazine Article, Monthly

N   [18] Mary-Lou Weisman, "When Parents Are Not in the Best Interests of the Child," *The Atlantic Monthly*, July 1994, 43.

B   Weisman, Mary-Lou. "When Parents Are Not in the Best Interests of the Child." *The Atlantic Monthly*, July 1994, 42–63.

Magazine Article, Weekly

N   [19] Tom Masland, "Voted into the History Books," *Newsweek*, 2 May 1994, 51.

B   Masland, Tom. "Voted into the History Books." *Newsweek*, 2 May 1994, 51.

Newspaper Article, No Author

N   [20] "Clinton Unveils Plans to Trim Programs," *Chicago Tribune*, 19 Dec. 1994, A1.

B   "Clinton Unveils Plans to Trim Programs." *Chicago Tribune*, 19 Dec. 1994, A1.

Newspaper Article, Discontinuous Pages

N   [21] Clay Chandler, "Treasury Analysis Finds GOP 'Flat Tax' Too Costly," *Washington Post*, 31 Oct. 1994, 8 and 12 (E).

B   Chandler, Clay. "Treasury Analysis Finds GOP 'Flat Tax' Too Costly." *Washington Post*, 31 Oct. 1994, 8 and 12 (E).

ERIC Microform Document

N   [22] Carole J. Hamner, *Youth Violence: Gangs on Main Street, USA*, Report from the Pew Partnership for Civil Change program, Philadelphia, PA, 1993, ERIC, ED 366 706.

B   Hamner, Carole J. *Youth Violence: Gangs on Main Street, USA.* Report from the Pew Partnership for Civil Change program, Philadelphia, PA, 1993. ERIC, ED 366 706.

Personal Communication. Communication such as personal letters and interviews are not recoverable and therefore need not be cited in the bibliography. However, you should cite the source in note form when you refer to it in your paper. Give the full name of the person from whom you obtained the information (unless it appears nearby in the text), then a description of the kind of communication, and finally the date:

[23] Stan Getz, telephone interview, October 6, 1995.
[24] Cecilia Terry, letter to the author, September 10, 1996.

Citation Taken From a Secondary Source. If you read Hunter, who referred to Wuthnow, your note and bibliography citations would cite Wuthnow, with the explanation that you found the material in Hunter. Handle the note and bibliography references as follows:

N   [25] Robert Wuthnow, *The Restructuring of American Religion: Society and Faith Since World War II.* (Princeton, NJ: Princeton University Press, 1988), 86, cited in James Davison Hunter, *Culture Wars: The Struggle to Define America* (New York: Basic Books, 1991), 87.

B   Wuthnow, Robert. *The Restructuring of American Religion: Society and Faith Since World War II.* Princeton, NJ: Princeton University Press, 1988. Cited in James Davison Hunter. *Culture Wars: The Struggle to Define America.* New York: Basic Books, 1991.

Electronic Media. When citing electronic sources such as CD-ROMs, databases, or Internet documents, include the same basic information that is needed for print sources: author and title of the item; name and description of the source (i.e., whether it is CD-ROM, an on-line database or journal, etc.); the name of the publisher or vendor (or both); the location of publication; the date of either publication or access (or both); and some description of the pathway needed to access the source.

Here are two examples. The first is a reference to an **electronic journal article**; the second is a reference to a **CD-ROM**.

N   [26] Linda Caporael, "Sociality: Coordinating Bodies, Minds and Groups," *Psycoloquy* 6, January 1995 [on-line journal]; available from ftp://princeton.edu/pub/harnad/Psycoloquy/1995.volume.6

B   Caporael, Linda. "Sociality: Coordinating Bodies, Minds and Groups," *Psycoloquy* 6 (January 1995). On-line journal. Available from ftp://princeton.edu/pub/harnad/Psycoloquy/1995.volume.6

N   [27] *Oxford English Dictionary*, 2nd ed., s.v. "anomie." [CD-ROM] (Oxford: Oxford University Press, 1992).

B   *Oxford English Dictionary*. 2nd ed. S.v. "anomie." CD-ROM. Oxford: Oxford University Press, 1992.

REFERENCES

American Psychological Association. 1994. *Publication manual*. 4th ed. Washington, DC: American Psychological Association.

Turabian, Kate. 1996. *A manual for writers of term papers, theses, and dissertations*. 6th ed. Chicago: University of Chicago Press.

INDEX